W9-CGX-699

Fly Fishing Digest

by Bill Wallace

Follett Publishing Company / Chicago

T-0325

THE COVERS

Rod and reel shown on the front cover furnished by Martin Reel Co. who also provided the flies pictured on the back cover.

Copyright© MCMLXXIII by Digest Books, Inc., 540 Frontage Rd., Northfield, Illinois 60093. All rights reserved. Printed in the United States of America. No part of this publication may be reproduced without the prior written permission of the publisher. Printed in U.S.A.

The views and opinions of the authors expressed herein are not necessarily those of the editor or publisher, and no responsibility for such views will be assumed.

ISBN 0-695-80325-5   Library of Congress Catalog Card #71-165451

Author
Bill Wallace

Associate Editors
Charles Most
John Spehn

Assistant Editor
Patricia Wallace

Table of Contents

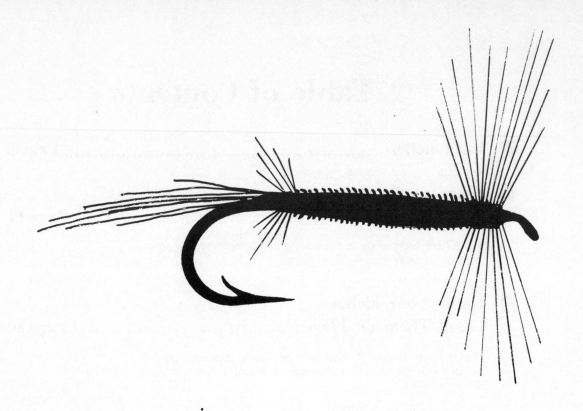

Introduction

This book was written for several reasons, but the main was to give accurate, up-to-date information and simple, easy to understand instructions about all aspects of what I consider to be the highest form of the angling arts — fly fishing.

Strangely, the idea for a book on fly fishing that would tell it like it is, started with a moose hunt I experienced some 15 years ago.

During the years preceding this hunt I had read many stories in the outdoor magazines where the author had been confronted by a charging, snorting antlered, bull moose which, judging from the painting, looked to be about 20 feet high with a rack at least 12 feet wide. The bull was described as charging toward the author at freight train speed while absorbing shot after shot from a magnum caliber rifle, but didn't fall until it was only 1/8 of an inch from the famous author's nose. The writer always made an estimate of the moose at somewhere between 1600 and 1800 pounds.

Somehow, though, there were never any decent photos, if any, of the carcass which would give a fair idea of the size by showing some other object of known dimensions.

Armed with this and much other misinformation, I ventured into northwestern Ontario one fall in quest of one of these giants.

Five days after arriving at camp on Big Canon Lake, 25 miles up the Wabigoon River, the best my Ojibway guide and I had managed, was to find a few tracks, made mostly by cow moose. We had hunted the river by canoe, starting out every day at 4 a.m. in total darkness and combed the bays and inlets until we were sure the moose had bedded down for the day.

On the 6th day we saw a bull with a fair rack on shore. He wasn't snorting in a rage, but he was charging—straight away from us as fast as he could go and quickly disappeared in the dense Canadian forest and thick, tangled underbrush.

The next day we decided to hunt for deer for a change, on foot and about 4 in the afternoon we came across the fresh track of a sizeable bull moose. I had a 30-30 with me for deer instead of the .338 Winchester Magnum I had brought for moose, but the guide said it would be OK as we would probably get a close shot.

He was right.

Twenty minutes later after a short run through the brush, I had a broadside shot at a bull trotting only 35 yds. away. I hit him behind the shoulder with a 150 gr. handloaded flat nose slug and he stumbled on for another 60 yds. and dropped dead. No charge, no rage, no snorting. He turned his head and looked at me a few seconds before I pulled the trigger, but just kept on going until he fell.

The guide estimated his weight at about 1,000 lbs. Actually I wound up with about 390 lbs. of meat which would indicate his true live weight to be closer to 800 lbs. than 1,000.

Curious about the vast differences between what I had read about moose hunting, and the real experience, I asked the guide why neither bulls had charged us as both been in rut.

His reply was simple.

He said, "I guess they were afraid and they didn't want to be shot," and also stated, "I have never been charged and I have never seen one charge a hunter. They all run away."

I asked him if this particular moose was a small one and he assured me that it was somewhat above average, that the biggest one he'd ever seen had been about 1300 lbs. with a 53" antler spread. The one I had just killed had a spread of 48".

My purpose in telling this story is related to my fly fishing experiences—what I read in books, more often than not, didn't bear any resemblance to what I found when actually fishing streams, rivers and lakes, and this fact and others made me decide to write this book.

I have been fly fishing for about 14 years. The last 2 years of my experience has been extensive, because I have had the opportunity to fish almost on a daily basis as I live in Montana and own part of a beautiful trout and whitefish river high in the Rockies. I have also been exploring the waters of most of the blue ribbon streams of the west and the high alpine lakes that are major producers for fly fishermen.

I was fortunate when I first decided to try fly fishing. I bought my first rod, reel and line from the owner of a sporting goods store in Chicago. He was a highly knowledgeable man and saw to it that I got a rod and line that were perfectly matched and balanced. The brands he chose were a Shakespeare rod, Pflueger reel and a Cortland line, all quality products in durability and performance. I still have and use this same outfit frequently.

When I first started fly casting on a Canadian stream a few weeks later I was grateful and amazed to find that after about 5 minutes of practice I could cast 20 to 25 feet. In 10 minutes I managed to hang my backcast in a tree for the first time. From then on I began learning by doing and while I did fairly well on the actual techniques of fly casting, I didn't score on catches. I went up rivers, down canyons, fished smaller lakes and ponds, but the total take for 2 weeks was only 3 small brook trout, the biggest running all of 10 inches. Actually I hooked 4, but a seagull swooped down and grabbed one before I could get it to shore.

Before making my next trip to Canada, the following year, I read many books on fly fishing and bought 50 or 60 fly patterns in different sizes.

I was ready this time. I would watch for rises. Cast to the feeding fish and above all I was prepared to MATCH the HATCH and brother, that should get them every time.

When I actually got back into action on a north-of-the-border lake I couldn't even find a hatch let alone match it, so I tied on a yellow bodied, rubber legged popper and caught about 15 nice smallmouths in a half hour. This was in 15 feet of water 250 yards from shore.

The next evening I went back to the same little lake which was at the end of a short portage and tried the edges of weed beds with dry black gnats and mosquitos on number 10 hooks. These worked great, but strangely there were no gnats or mosquitos flying around as this was late July and these pesky bugs for some reason I've never found out, disappear at the end of June and don't return until the following year.

At this point I was starting to learn that much of what I had read could be discounted.

Match the hatch?

Sounds clever but fish can be caught on flies that don't match anything and actually there are very few artificial flies that look even close to the insect or larvae they are supposed to imitate. About the only ones that do are the May fly patterns, but there's **no** real fly that has a hook curving out of its tail.

Over the years I have come to prefer fly fishing over all other techniques for many reasons. It is not difficult. It produces excellent catches. Seldom do you lose a fish because the flexibility of the gear allows for sudden runs, darts, changes in direction without danger of tackle breaking.

I have caught large and smallmouth bass up to 6 pounds, northerns to 15 pounds, 4 and 5 pound walleyes, rainbows, browns, brookies, cutthroat up to 6 pounds and out of about 300 total have only lost 3 fish.

These simply got off the hook, they didn't break the tackle. Another advantage of fly fishing, seldom if ever mentioned, is the fact that you can make as many casts as you want without having to retrieve your line by winding it back onto the reel as is necessary with spinning, spin-casting or casting with spool type reels.

Even though fly casting is my favorite, I have not become a "purist." I like dry fly fishing best, but if I chose to label myself I would say I was an "All-ist." That is I enjoy fishing streamers, wets, nymphs and have even been known to slip on a red worm to get a few browns when the water is high and roily in the spring.

Because I believe in catching fish not only for the sport, but also to eat I cannot go along with the "ultra-purist" who uses barbless hooks and returns the fish unharmed (he says) to the stream.

First, if the waters fished are so lacking in fish that those caught must be returned to maintain the population, they should be closed completely.

Second, if a lake has ample numbers, keeping the fish will provide a healthy balance between food and fish...throwing them back will eventually overpopulate and create schools of vicious runts. I have seen lakes where a 5 inch rock bass will strike an artificial lure intended to take large northerns.

Third, I have doubts as to the motivation of the ultra-purist, but that is an area best left to psychologists and those schooled in studies of human behaviorism...I'm not.

Fly fishing is just now coming into its own, although it is perhaps one of the oldest forms of fishing known. There has hardly been a time in the past 2 years that some spin fisherman hasn't approached me, while fishing in western streams with the statement, "I would like to learn to fly cast someday."

My answer is, "why not right now "—"here, take my rod and I'll show you how in 15 minutes, and in a half an hour you'll be capable enough to catch fish." They did. I did.

You can, too.

Learn to Fly Cast in

30 Minutes -

Here's How!

Over the years a myth has persisted about the difficulties of fly casting until it has become a legend.

The perpetuation of this myth is due, to a large degree, to the so-called experts who would have you believe that only a select few have the necessary ability and skills to be capable fly casters.

Fly casting WAS a difficult form years ago. However the problem was in the poorly designed and constructed tackle, not the average would-be fly fisherman. 30 years ago and more, fly rods were made mostly of split bamboo, all hand crafted. They were of fine quality and their design in regard to weight and balance were excellent.

But the fly lines of the day were something else. Made of braided silk they left much to be desired in uniformity of shape and weight and without a constant application of dressing would sink like a log after a few minutes use.

There was little uniformity from line to line and even the lines themselves varied greatly from one end to the other. This made it almost impossible to properly match a rod to the line and the only practical type line was the level design.

Both rods and lines were extremely expensive and only a few well heeled fishermen could afford them, mostly the wealthy landowners and aristocracy of England and Europe.

Leaders were also a problem. In order to have a tapered leader that would roll and straighten out presenting the fly without a big splash it was necessary for the fly fisherman to construct one using various strength leader material and tying them with knots. These actually were not tapered leaders, they were stepped leaders as the changes in sizes of the strands were abrupt. The first few feet would be 30 pounds test, then 20 pounds, then a few feet of 12 pounds, followed by 8 pounds and finally the tippet or end would be anywhere from 2 to 6 pounds.

This type of leader worked reasonably well, but certainly did not give the smooth performance of today's knotless, one-piece true taper leaders.

The same is a fact about all modern fly fishing tackle. Today's manufacturers have done a fine job of producing quality rods, lines, reels and leaders and offering them at reasonable prices.

Rods are now made of hollow tubular glass to exacting specifications that give them uniformity of thickness and taper and assure proper flexibility and correct weight-for-length dimensions.

Lines are also better than ever. They are now manufactured to standard specifications established by the American Fishing Tackle Manufacturer's Association. This means that if a rod is made for use with a WF7F or DT7F line, any line so designated will fit and match the rod no matter what company produces the lines.

The excellence of modern fly fishing equipment is why it is easy to learn to cast well enough to catch fish in such a short time, (30 minutes or less). Acquiring a matched rod and line is a must and the first step on the way to becoming a capable fly fisherman.

To pick a rod that is right for you, try several. You can usually tell which one is for you by the way it feels. If the handle is comfortable

and the rod itself is of a weight that you can easily swing back and forth and obtain a reasonable flex, it will probably be suitable. Rod lengths for a beginner can be 7-1/2, 8 or 8-1/2 feet, just as long as the line weight matches correctly. Although any line type will do, a weight forward, floating line would be best as it is easiest to get long casts with at the beginning.

There are two basic types of fly reels, single action and automatic. A single action model would be the best choice to start with. Reels serve mostly to store lines and also as a pendulum balance on your rod. Many models today also have drag devices to slow down a fast running fish.

The best place to get your equipment is from your local sporting goods store. A knowledgeable salesman will be of real help, but remember you can be sure of getting quality tackle if you choose name brands. Fine rods are offered by Berkley, Fenwick, Garcia, Martin, Shakespeare, Browning, South Bend and others.

Quality reel brands are Garcia, Martin, Feurer Bros., Shakespeare, Pflueger and South Bend to name a few. Well known line makers are Cortland, Gudebrod, Garcia, Shakespeare, and Gladding. All of these companies make fly lines in level, double taper, and weight forward or torpedo tapers in both floating and sinking models. Modern materials used in the construction of these lines makes it unnecessary to grease them or to use dressings. If you fish roiled or silt carrying waters it might be a good idea to use a line cleaner occasionally. Otherwise if you fish clean water all that would be needed is to wipe off your line with a damp cloth before storing for the winter.

Basically the following items are all that are needed to start you off on

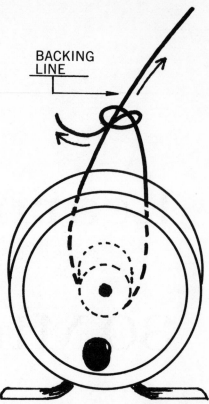

Use about 50 yds. of 20 lb. test braided nylon backing line. Attach to axle of reel with a slip knot. This is simply a common overhand or "A" knot tied around the line and pulled tight on the axle. Wind backing line on spool slowly and evenly from side to side.

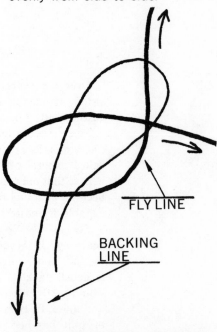

The "Bowline" knot is effective in tying the backing line to the fly line. The backing line goes up through the loop, around the fly line and then back down through the same loop. Pull tight to test holding.

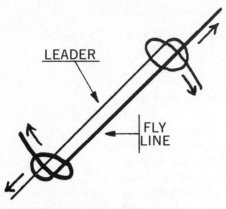

LEADER

FLY LINE

To attach leader to fly line, first tie an overhand knot around the fly line with the leader, and then tie another overhand knot around the leader with the fly line. Pull leader and fly line in opposite directions and the two knots will meet and hold.

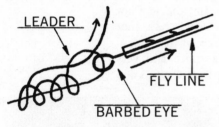

LEADER

FLY LINE

BARBED EYE

This method of attaching a leader to the fly line uses a barbed eye made of steel. The barbed shaft is inserted into the hollow tip of the line by working the line slowly over the shaft. If it does not go on easily at first, cut off about six inches of the fly line and place the whole line in the refrigerator for about 15 minutes. After the barb is installed, use regular jam knot through eye to attach leader.

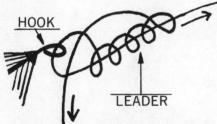

HOOK

LEADER

The simple, easy-to-tie jam knot is the best for attaching the hook to the leader. To get the loops around the leader, hold leader and leader end between thumb and index finger and twist the fly about five turns, then loop the free leader end back through the open loop in front of hook eye.

a beginning of many years' enjoyment of fly fishing:

1. Rod- 7-1/2, 8 or 8-1/2 feet long weighing 3-1/2 to 4-1/2 ounces.
2. Matching line-weight forward. No. 6, 7, or 8 according to recommendations on rod. Preferably a floater.
3. Single action reel with adjustable drag.
4. 7 and 9 foot tapered, knotless, sinking leaders (2 or 3 of each).
5. 100 yards of braided dacron backing line, 20 lb. test.
6. A few strands of inch-long red, yellow or white yarn.
7. Barbed shaft with round eye for attaching leader to line.

First, tie the backing line to the axle of your reel and wind on slowly making sure to wind it evenly, cranking the reel with your right hand and winding the line on from the bottom. When you reach the end, tie on the fly line. There's usually a small tag showing which end to start with. A double simple overhand knot will do to connect the two lines.

Wind line on, holding it between 2 fingers under some tension and shift the line back and forth from side to side in order to wind it on as level as possible.

When the fly line is on, push the barbed shaft into the end which is hollow. Check to see that the end of the line is also the end of the taper. Some lines come with 2 or 3 feet of small diameter level line at the end. If your line has this it will have to be cut off at the point where the taper ends. If you have trouble inserting the barbed shaft even after cutting the excess line, try placing the entire line in the refrigerator for about 15 minutes, then work the eyes shaft into the hollow slowly, being careful not to let it cut through the side.

Now use a standard clinch knot to attach the leader to the eyelet. If the leader has a loop on the heavy end it would be better to cut the loop off and use the clinch knot anyway. It makes a smoother connection, causes less wind resistance and makes casting easier.

Tie 2 or 3 strands of yarn to the end of your leader with a clinch knot which is the same as you'll be using for tying on an actual fly, and you are ready to start practicing.

The yarn serves 3 purposes: 1. It enables you to see where your line is going. 2. It makes your line perform as though it had a real fly attached. 3. It prevents you from accidentally hooking yourself or other objects on your back cast.

In order to get the feel of the rod strip about 10 feet of line off your reel and wave the rod back and forth through the air until the line passes out through the guides. When this is done you'll have about 17 feet out, 7 feet of leader and 10 feet of line.

Wave this short section back and forth several times, but don't let the leader of the line touch the ground. This practice can be done anywhere you have enough room in front and in back of you.

Do this for several days, a 1/2 hour per day. The reason for the advance practice is to strengthen the muscles you'll be using in actual casting. Casting on water for 2 or 3 hours at a time requires strength of muscles not ordinarily used in every day activity. This pre-practice, though not absolutely necessary, will be of great help when you start casting on water.

And a word of caution here. When you start practicing and begin to learn how to strip off more line and get longer casts, be sure you do it over some kind of water, a pond, lake, river, park lagoon or even a swimming pool. Do NOT practice in the grass, a field, on asphalt, cement or wooden floor.

You won't get the feel of water and in many cases you'll damage your

New Leader-line Connection Device

A boon to fly fishermen, a new Leader-Link has been developed by the Wright & McGill Company of Denver, Colo.

Made of high impact nylon, the device permits fishermen to connect the butt end of the leader to the line in seconds without old-fashioned splicing or "nail" knotting. Also, one size handles the popular size tapered lines, and another the level lines.

The new Eagle Claw link is smaller in diameter than most splices, permitting it to pass easily through the smallest tip-top and snake guides—with or without tension on the leader.

Its size and weight also enables the Leader-Link to float with a floating line, sink with a sinking line and wind onto the reel better than most splices.

Another major feature of the unique Eagle Claw connector is that it holds the line and leader in fixed axial alignment for perfect follow through turnover of the leader at presentation without a long stiff section.

It also eliminates the possibility of collapse at the juncture of the line and leader, a common fault when some knots are used with a looped leader or when the line finish fractures next to a splice.

In addition, the tiny Eagle Claw link presents less wind resistance than either a splice or nail knot, weighs less than a splice and very little more, if any, than a nail knot.

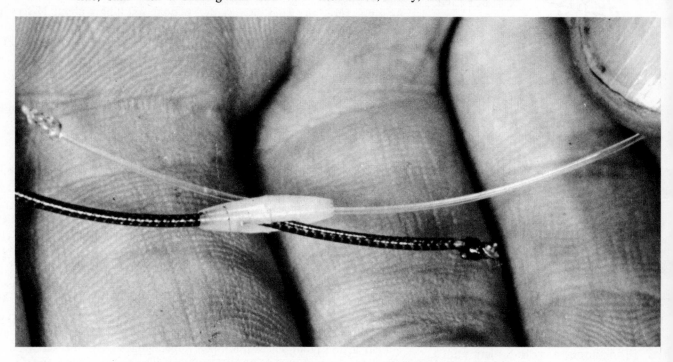

Insert line through end of link and out side slot. Tie overhand knot. Insert butt of leader through other end of Link and out opposite side slot. Tie clinch knot. Pull knots tight using pliers. Cut tag ends close. Press knots into slot and pull hard on line and leader to test.

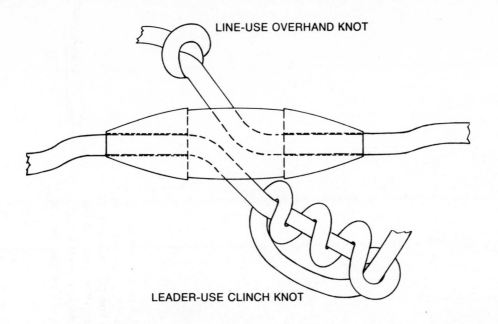

LINE-USE OVERHAND KNOT

LEADER-USE CLINCH KNOT

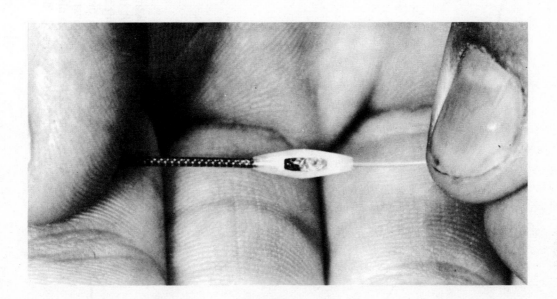

The simplicity of assembling the Eagle Claw Leader-Link is seen in above photo. The regular clinch knot is made in the leader after inserting it through the Link. An overhand knot is then tied in the line and the Leader-Link is ready.

line badly. Stand close to the edge of the water and whip out about 15 feet of line plus your leader and let it fall to the surface in front of you.

You are now ready to progress through the cycle of a complete cast:

1. Pick most of your line up off the water by lifting the tip of your rod. You don't have

to get the entire line and leader off the water but enough of it so that there is only a minimum of capillary resistance to overcome as you apply the power to your backcast. Now pull your line slightly upward and whip it out behind you. Turn your head and watch

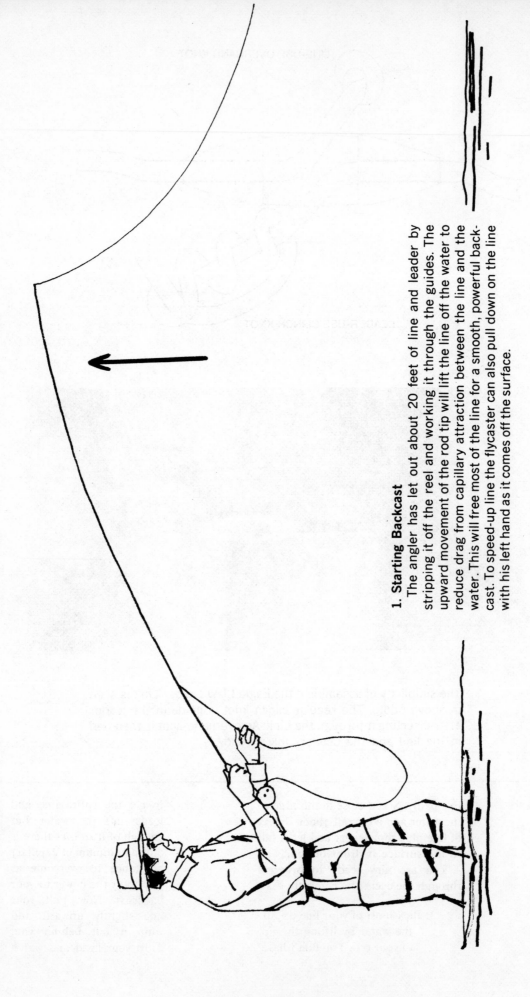

1. Starting Backcast

The angler has let out about 20 feet of line and leader by stripping it off the reel and working it through the guides. The upward movement of the rod tip will lift the line off the water to reduce drag from capillary attraction between the line and the water. This will free most of the line for a smooth, powerful backcast. To speed-up line the flycaster can also pull down on the line with his left hand as it comes off the surface.

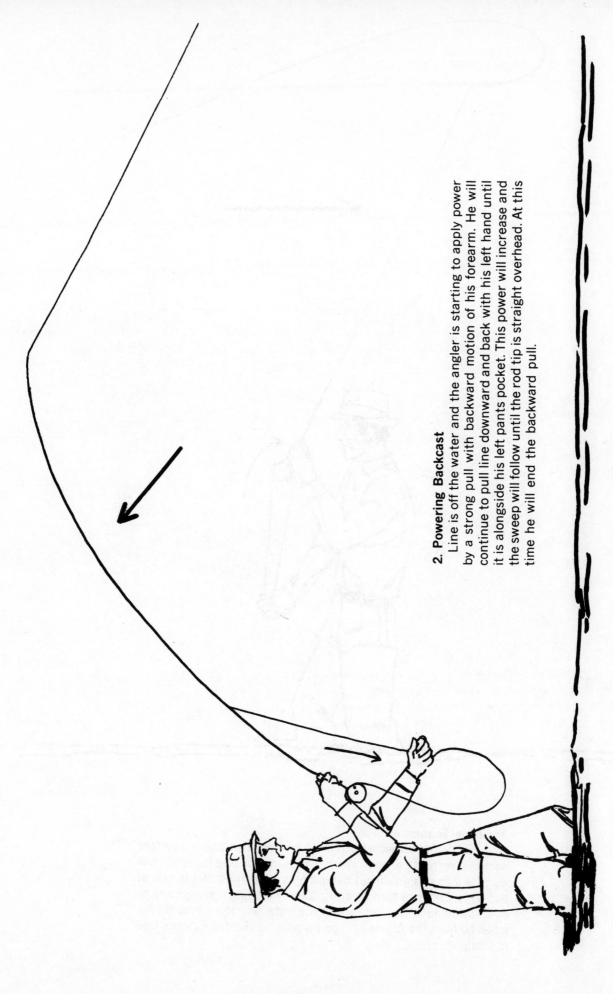

2. Powering Backcast

Line is off the water and the angler is starting to apply power by a strong pull with backward motion of his forearm. He will continue to pull line downward and back with his left hand until it is alongside his left pants pocket. This power will increase and the sweep will follow until the rod tip is straight overhead. At this time he will end the backward pull.

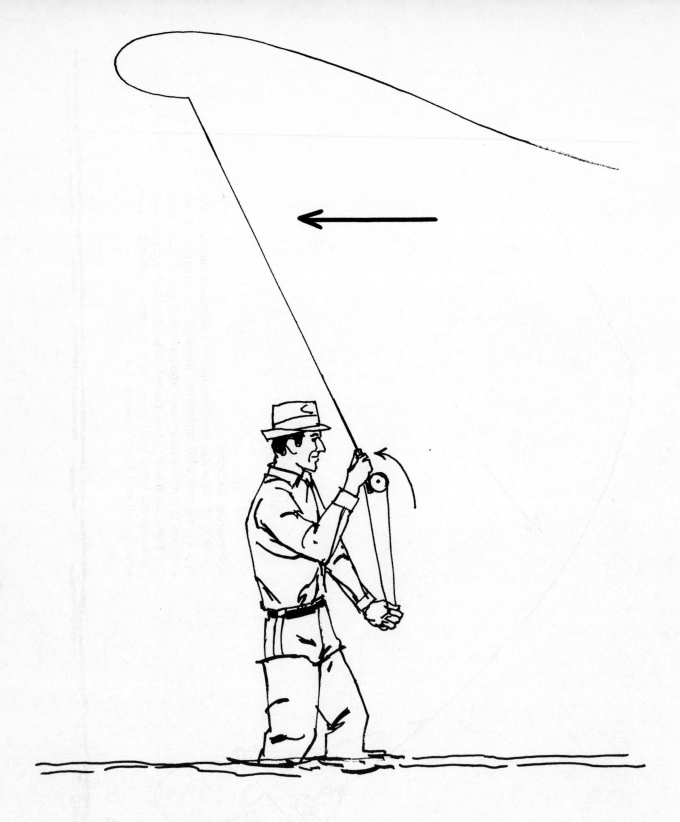

3. Timing Sequence

At this point the flycaster has let his rod drift about two feet back of a vertical position. The line is in motion and he must now wait for it to straighten out behind him. He can do this in one of two ways. Either by turning around and watching it straighten, or by counting one, two, three and then starting the forward cast when he feels the tug on his rod tip which indicates that the line is straight.

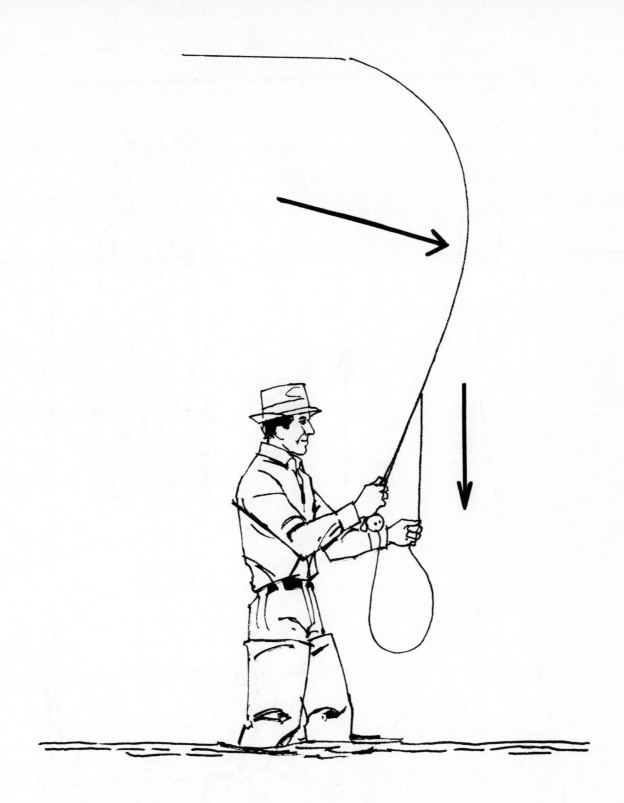

4. Starting the Forward Cast

To increase speed on the forward cast this angler is hauling downward on the line with his left hand. He will also use his entire arm and wrist to get more power into the cast in order to shoot out more line. When he has 50 or 60 feet of line out he can also use his shoulder and turn his upper body to get maximum power for distance casting.

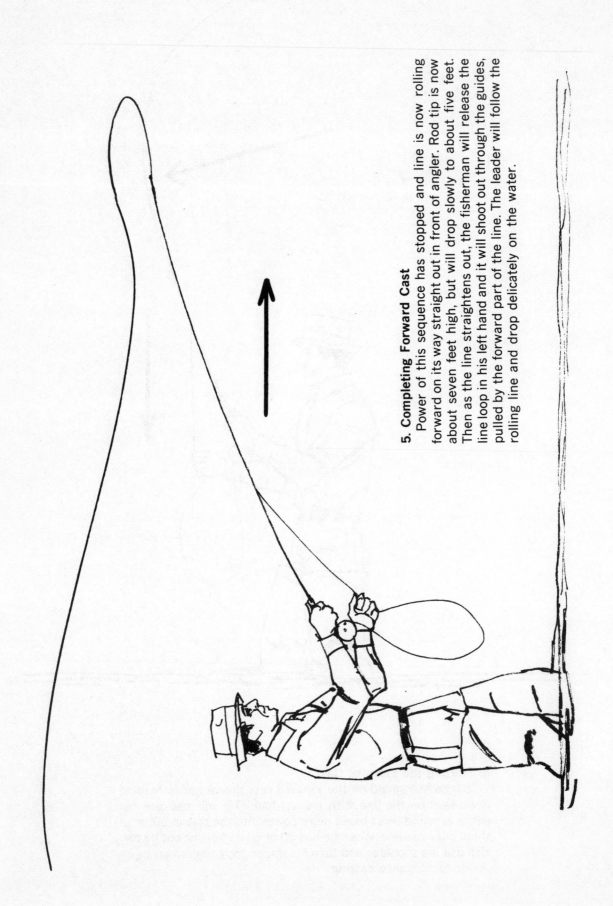

5. Completing Forward Cast

Power of this sequence has stopped and line is now rolling forward on its way straight out in front of angler. Rod tip is now about seven feet high, but will drop slowly to about five feet. Then as the line straightens out, the fisherman will release the line loop in his left hand and it will shoot out through the guides, pulled by the forward part of the line. The leader will follow the rolling line and drop delicately on the water.

it as it straightens out behind you. At the moment it is straight, start your forward cast.

2. Let your line fall to the water again and then repeat several times casting through each time with easy swings or whips. Watch the timing on your forward cast. If you have previously learned to spin cast or cast with a spool type reel you may have a tendency to snap your forward cast too fast and this could break off the yarn or fly or cause your line to drop on your head or at your feet.

3. After a forward cast and your line is laying on the water strip off about 2-3 foot loops of line and hold them in your left hand. Now pick up your line, power it backward, start your forward cast and as your rod begins to straighten in front of you, release one of the loops with your left hand. You'll see the loop shoot through the guides and the length of your cast increase. The leader will follow the line and roll out straight in front of the line tip.

4. Up to this point you have been mostly using your wrist and part of your arm, but as you begin to lengthen your casts you will have to put your whole arm into them.

If you can now cast 20 or 30 feet you can catch fish in just about any kind of water, rivers or lakes, but to increase the area you can cover from one spot you should keep practicing until you can cast 35 to 45 feet.

Many casters put a lot of stock in false casting to get distance, but it isn't necessary and cuts down on the possibility of getting fish. A false cast is simply not letting your line fall to the water on your forward cast and starting your backcast while it is still in the air in front of you. On each forward cast you let another loop or 2 shoot out in front.

However you can't catch fish unless your line is in or on the water so it is better to make only 1 or possibly 2 false casts, but after your line is out as far as 20 feet let your fly fall to the surface. You may pick up fish on this short cast.

If you are trying for distance simply feed out line on each forward cast, but go through the full cycle. On longer casts you will have to wait longer for your backcast to straighten out behind you. If you don't want to turn around and watch your line you can count 3 seconds out loud—1, 2, 3—and then start your forward cast.

To Correct Faulty Casting

The foregoing describes what is called the standard overhead cast and most of the other casts, side, horizontal or skycast, are simply a variation of this basic type.

To correct any fault it is only necessary to check the swing of your rod through the casting arc. Especially critical is your backcast. If this is not good, your forward cast will not be either.

To determine the extreme positions of your rod tip in the casting sequence, first point it straight above your head, then move the tip to a point about 2 feet behind your head. Your rod should go no further back than this on your backcast. In order to achieve this you should slow up your cast when your rod is directly overhead and hold it firm when it reaches a spot 2 feet back of vertical.

On the forward cast your rod tip should be completely stopped by the time it reaches a position level with your eyes or about 5 to 5-1/2 feet above water. At this point the rod will be slanted slightly upward. This is an efficient angle for shooting out line. Practice will enable you to determine how much power to apply, and where to accelerate throughout the casting arc.

Naturally you will need more power as your casts lengthen and for extremely long casts you will have to put your whole wrist, arm, shoulder and body into the rod as the distances approach 70 and 80 feet. There won't be many times you'll find it necessary to make casts this long, but it is reassuring to know that you can if it would be an advantage to do so.

Remember though, that the casting arc should remain about the same no matter how long the cast. You might have to straighten out the rod in front of you more on the forward cast, but only about another 6 inches.

In most instances the overhead cast of various distances will be all you'll need to catch limits, but it would also be wise to learn 2 or 3 other variations to help you in places where the overhead cast is not practical or impossible.

These types would be the roll cast, the side cast and the sky or tower cast. These would be used in cases where you are casting in brushy areas or want to flick a fly under an overhanging bush or tree. The side cast is the one most suitable for these situations. Frequently you'll find yourself in a position on the bank of a stream or lake with trees or high shrubs at your back where your backswing would certainly snag in the branches.

The Roll Cast

This is a simple cast used to change the position of the line after it is already in the water or to straighten it out in front of you when the current has carried it downstream. It can also be used to cover other waters higher upstream without going through the complete casting cycle again. It is also a valuable cast to get under branches and around and over rocks to keep your fly flowing naturally with the current.

To execute the roll cast you first pick your line partly off the water and hold the rod above you and a little to one side, to the right if you are right handed and then twist your wrist as you apply power in a downward direction. Your line will roll out of the water and the tip, leader and fly will follow it out. This is a full roll cast. With the full roll cast you can also let line shoot out for greater distance using the same method of stripping off loops with your left hand and releasing them when the line goes forward, as you do in the overhead cast.

To accomplish a partial roll cast for getting your line over a riffle or rock and beyond, into quiet water, hold your rod straight out in front of you about 3 feet over the water and start the line rolling by swinging your rod in a fast arc from right to left or vice versa, with the top of the arc-circle being about 4 feet high at the top. Your line will roll out like a snake and reposition itself in a straight line extending from the rod tip.

The Side Cast

The side cast is used when you can't step into the water and make an overhead cast parallel to the river or bank. It is essentially the same as the overhead cast, but the rod is powered through a horizontal arc only a few feet above the water. You would use this cast to get up or downstream, under overhanding obstacles in a situation where the backcast of a standard cast would be obstructed. It is a valuable cast to perfect for fishing the smaller feeder streams for brook trout or for rainbows at higher altitudes. Because of the shortness of the arc permitted by the side cast it is not possible to get a very long line going, but it usually isn't necessary if you are cautiously quiet and are careful not to let the line splash but rather lay it delicately on the water.

The Sky Cast

This is a very useful cast, but not an easy one to perform at first. Even after much practice it is not possible to get much distance, but it is one worth knowing. The main use for it is when you have your back up against trees, a canyon wall or any other situation where you cannot make a free backcast.

To start, you strip off about 10 to 15 feet of line and shake it out through the guides and let it lie on the water, then pick up the line and thrust your rod straight up using your forearm only. Stop your cast abruptly at a position about a foot in front of a vertical position. When the line is almost vertical start your downward cast and when the line starts to curve out in front feed another 5 feet or so by letting the weight peel off a loop into the guides.

This will give you about 20 feet plus your leader and should be enough to get fish if they are there.

The conditions that determine the use of side, roll and sky casts are about the same. First, use them if you cannot make an obstruction free backcast. Then, only if you cannot wade out into the water because of it being too deep or too fast. If you can wade it is better to make a regular overhead cast either up or downstream.

Casting and Wind

Sooner or later every fly fisherman is faced with the problem of casting on a windy day that makes casting difficult to say the least, but if the breezes are average, say 15 to 25 miles per hour, it is still possible to do a fair job of putting out your line. If you know how.

When the wind hits 30 mph and over I would suggest trolling if you are in a boat or simply feeding out line and letting the current take your fly downstream if you're fishing a river.

If, however, you do want to cast, consider these points:

1. Casting into a headwind is the least difficult of all because your forward cast is naturally lower than your back cast and keeping your line low is the secret of casting either in a tail or headwind. Your backcast should be somewhat higher for a headwind cast because it will be blown lower as it stops just before you start applying the forward power.

Apply the power in your forward stroke progressively, putting the greatest amount of pressure into the last 2 or 3 feet of your forward-downward push. Here's where one of the greatest benefits of using a weight forward tapered line shows up. A double taper line will do well too, but you'd have trouble with a level line. Strangely enough you'll be able to cast the small, lightweight dry flies into a headwind easier than you would the heavier streamers, marabous and bass bugs. The reason is that the larger flies and lures offer more wind resistance and upset the balance of the line weight. Actually, in most cases the line carries the fly instead of the lure carrying the line as in regular bait casting. Sometime though you'll want to try the ultra-light, tiny spoons, spinners and miniatures of the standard artificials and then you'll find that both the line and the lure weight will be utilized in the actual cast and will contribute to getting the leader and line out.

2. **Casting with a Tailwind.**
Casting with the wind

blowing from behind you presents a problem on the backcast and it can be overcome in either of two ways. One, keep your backcast low by putting more power into it and letting your rod drop slightly lower behind you.

If this is too difficult at first, then simply turn around and make a forward cast away from the water and into the wind. You can, with ease, turn around slightly while your line is in the air and cast another forward cast toward the water. In effect you are eliminating the backcast into the wind by making two forward casts, one into the wind and one with the wind without the necessity of making a high backcast.

3. Casting with a Crosswind.

There will be times when you'll be faced with casting when the wind is blowing sharply from your left or your right side and it will cause some difficulty.

If you are a right handed caster, simply using a modified sidecast will prevail against a wind coming from the left. In this cast though, remember to make an exceptionally strong forward cast. If the wind is coming from the right side you can try two different methods. One, is to cast a half "X" cast, i.e. to cast more to the right and quarter into the wind on both the forward and back casts. The wind coming from the right will tend to straighten them both out. If this is not suitable or the wind is exceptionally strong, hold your rod across the front of your body to the left and make a modified sidecast on your left

side. A modified sidecast is one which travels an arc about halfway between vertical and horizontal.

4. Changing Direction.

There are at least 2 ways to change the direction of your cast in order to cover more water area and thereby increase the chances of catching fish. The easiest way is to change the direction of your backcast. If you want to cast more to your left, instead of casting directly behind you on your back cast, pull your line to the right on your backcast and then cast to your left in a direct line on your forward cast. If you decide an area to your right is likely looking water, cast to your left on the back sweep and then a direct line to the front.

A second way to change direction is while the line is in the air. This is somewhat more difficult, but with practice it becomes fairly simple.

You make your backcast as usual, but after your backcast is complete and you start your front cast you tilt your wrist and arm in the direction you wish to cast (to the left or right) and wind up with your rod pointing to the spot you want your fly to drop in. Be careful not to change the direction before the backcast has completely straightened out behind and you are a foot or so into the front cast. Also it is more effective if you have 30 to 40 feet of line out. Again, it is easier to change direction if you are using a weight forward line.

The major factor involved in fly fishing, like all forms, is line control and that is what most of the

The fisherman above is wearing sun glasses, as he should, to protect his eyes from water glare and he is holding his rod and line in a perfect position to start his backcast. The line is coming up, off the water and he is hauling it in and downward with his left hand to give it more speed for a long, low backcast.

preceding chapter is concerned with. You will find with experience that line control in fly fishing includes the use of both hands. The right hand to handle the rod and the left hand to control the line. The exception is when fishing for the larger species such as steelhead or salmon.

With these two and other salt water fishes you play them with the reel more than with the hand and your equipment is better designed for this type, being heavier and of larger capacity. Reels handle more line of higher test and the rods are longer and stiffer.

For all fresh water species that are suitable for taking with fly tackle, you'll be using your left hand for pulling the fish in and a combination of your rod and line hand for playing the bigger fighters.

Your left hand also plays a very important part in getting longer casts, and in improving the accuracy of your casts. In starting your back cast for example, if you pull down and back on the line as you lift your rod tip up, your line will come off the

water faster and give much more speed to your back cast with less effort of your rod hand. Then as you start your forward cast another pull on the line downward and back toward your left pocket will also increase line speed and lengthen your forward cast.

Remember though, more important than length of cast is the accuracy and control you develop. This takes practice, but as time goes by and you exercise those particular muscles needed for precise casting you will be amazed to find that you can lay out a beautiful, graceful, curving arc on both your back and forward casts and drop a tiny dry fly onto a tumbling riffle of white water, or into a quiet little pool next to the far bank without disturbing the water with anything more than a small blip.

When this happens and you begin to tie into some scrapping brookies, and a few rugged browns and feel the excitement through that delicate leader and highly sensitive rod...you may become a fly fisherman, exclusively.

This angler has about completed action on his forward cast and is aiming at a point across the river on the edge of some weedbeds. The line is just beginning to roll out, and when it reaches a straight out position he will let out a loop from his left hand to get a little more distance. He is using a fairly light rod and line.

Flycaster shown above has a nice roll going forward. It is somewhat high, but from the looks of the water and the smooth curves in the line, there is little or no wind to bother it. This cast will go out about thirty-five feet. His success in getting fish is attested to by the deep crease of his creel strap across his back indicating weight in the basket.

This shows an example of perfect timing at the end of the forward cast. This line is pulling forward and the angler's left hand has completely released a loop or two of line that will shoot through the guides to lengthen the cast. Note that he also wears sun glasses to protect his eyes from water surface glare.

Here's the end-reward of correct flycasting. This fisherman is pulling a steelhead toward his net which is held motionless, waiting to scoop up fish. He has been playing fish by pulling line in with his left hand and clamping loops to the rod with his right hand.

Know Your Fishes - Catch Them on Flies

Almost every fish known that can be caught on baited hook and line can be caught by fly fishing. However, there are relatively few that are really suitable for taking on fly equipment. These species are covered in this chapter.

It is certainly a great help to learn, through the written word, all you can about the habits and habitats of fish you'd like to catch, but there's no guarantee you'll fill your creel or stringer because you have this knowledge.

However, coupling this information with actual experience on a river or lake known to be a fairly good producer of fish catches should, over a period of time, increase your ability to bring home your limits and decrease your chances of being skunked.

Each river, each lake, any body of fish-containing water has its own special characteristics in regard to purity, temperature, currents, type of bottom, fish food, prevailing winds and, unfortunately pollution. All these factors determine the actions, size and migrations of the fish populations.

Therefore it is almost impossible to establish any specific rules for catching them in any or all waters. The best that can be done is to explain as many general rules as possible and to point out methods or procedures for exploring and discovering the specific nature of any one individual lake, stream or river. This would also include the general nature of the fish sought by the fly fisherman.

First of all, most fish that feed from the surface of the water at one time or another, will take a dry fly during some season of the year or at some time of the day.

All fish that feed from the surface of the water also feed under water. Then there are varieties that feed only under water and can never be caught with surface lures. The underwater feeders can be taken fairly easily and frequently on wet flies, streamers, bucktails, nymphs and muddler type flies.

Most of the trout, char and salmon species can be enticed to take a dry fly readily and they will take the underwater fly lures with equal enthusiasm when the time is right.

Largemouth and smallmouth bass and the panfish sized sunfishes will all take dry and wet flies of the proper sizes. The bass, however, seem to prefer the floating popper type lures and will come up from as deep as 15 feet to strike hard and get a light colored (yellow or white) rubber legged bass bug.

All fish strike at a lure for 1 of 3 reasons. Most often they are seeking food, but they will also strike in a reflex action when surprised by a lure dropped suddenly and close, they will also hit a lure as a protective measure. A typical example of this is seen in the male bass patrolling an area where spawn is planted. He will strike hard at any object that seems to present a threat to the eggs.

Generally speaking, though, fish strike flies and other lures in their quest for food about 99 percent of the time.

Brown Trout

I have chosen this species for the first fish to be discussed because I consider the brown to be the most important to fly fishermen, both from the standpoint of catching and eating.

The brown is probably the most available of all the trout because of his widespread domain and because of his prolific breeding and ability to exist in warmer and more polluted waters, than other trout.

The territory of the brown lies clear across the northern half of the United States and extends into many southern states east of the Mississippi River. There are also a few in California, New Mexico and Arizona.

They are found in lakes, rivers and medium sized streams but not in the tiny feeder creeks that brookies like. They can subsist in warmer and more polluted waters than any other trout, but if given a choice they prefer the fairly cold waters of a flowing river. Browns also adapt very well to large cold water lakes where they grow to substantial sizes. 5 to 12 pounders are frequently caught in the big waters.

In rivers in the more northern territories they run somewhat smaller. Over a 5 mile stretch in a medium sized river, most browns will average 10 to 14 inches, but if there are suitable deep holes and an abundance of food many will reach 4, 5 and 6 pounds.

This is the ideal fish for the fly fisherman as the brown loves to surface feed, is also an avid underwater feeder and will take nymphs readily because he feeds well on the bottom, too.

Though the brownie has many virtues, not the least of them is his unpredictableness. I've heard it said that the brown is the most timid of all trout and that a fleeting shadow or the splash of a small pebble will scare him a block away in a flash. This is not always true. It is not true most of the time. Just sometimes. On many occasions I have cast a streamer into a small pool about 4 or 5 feet deep and had a brown follow it out on the retrieve and come up as close as 10 feet. Even when the fish saw me he did not dart away, but turned lazily and swam slowly back into the pool.

This has happened more than once, but always at the same time of the day . . . about an hour before dusk and the fish involved have always been of good size, 2 pounds and up.

Since browns are mainly nocturnal feeders it is possible that these fish were in the process of becoming active from a semi-dormant daytime state and had not fully come alert, explaining why they were not frightened and why they weren't interested enough to take the streamer.

During the daytime hours it is not easy to catch browns and they do scare somewhat easier. Also the fish caught are mostly in the 10 to 14 inch range. They can be caught on a variety of flies and many of the patterns that are producers on other kinds of trout also take browns. However, the browns seem to prefer lighter shades such as white, yellow,

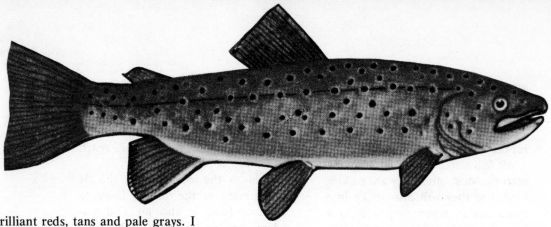

brilliant reds, tans and pale grays. I purposely used the word "shades" in the preceding sentence because I don't believe fish can distinguish color.

I do believe they can tell the difference in shadings between the range of black and white. This is the reason they prefer one fly over another. They either like darker flies, medium tones or bright, light gradations.

Dry flies that have been most successful for browns have been the Royal Coachman, Red Ibis, Yellow Ibis, Yellow Wooly Worm, Light Cahill and the Ginger Quill.

Exceptionally good wet flies for browns are the Parmachene Belle, Yellow Sally, Silver Doctor, Queen of Waters, and the Professor. Streamers that were very suitable especially just before and after dark are the Supervisor, Black Nosed Dace, Black Ghost, Light Edson Tiger and the Mickey Finn.

Some of the more effective nymphs for browns are the Caddis, Light Cahill, Breadcrust Nymph, Hellgramite, Stone Fly and Dark Hendrickson.

Dry flies are effective from just after dawn to just before dark and should be fished in fairly long casts that reach close to the far shore of a stream or river. Cast across and upstream and let your dry float down within 1-5 feet of the opposite bank. Let the fly swirl around rocks, stumps or points as freely as possible, but when your cast is as far downstream as it can go, give it a couple of short jerks with your line hand. Then "mend" your line by lifting the tip of your rod about 6 or 7 feet high and pull your line

BROWN TROUT

Widely distributed from the Atlantic to the Pacific in the northern half of the U.S. and southern Canada. Feeds mostly at night.

sharply off the water and swing your rod in an upstream direction. When it is more nearly out in front of you pick up the line and start another cast. To get it upstream again you'll have to change direction on the forward cast.

Repeat your casting once or twice more in the same spot and if there are no rises or strikes, change position . . . move either up or downstream and try the banks again.

The best fishing time of the day for browns is from about 2 hours before dark through midnight, but dry flies will only be effective until late dusk. In the evening, though the browns will move out from their daytime hideouts to feed in shallower, more open waters.

Insects will become more active too, which accounts for the browns feeding. Now the best places to cast to will be any juncture between fast and still water. Wherever a flow of the main stream goes past a small bay or inlet the brown will station himself at the point where the 2 meet, facing upstream. In the poor light it doesn't matter too much whether you fish up, across or downstream, but you should give your fly time to float with the current in a free, natural way before it reaches the likely spot where a brown could be waiting.

Keep just a minimum of slack in your line and be ready to set your hook with both your line hand and your rod. If you would get the really large browns your chances are better if you fish a couple of hours from dusk in total darkness. In this case you must change over to wet flies or preferably streamers. Be sure you know the river well if you do any wading at all. If you stay on the banks you can probably do as well casting into the dark and letting your streamer sink below the surface. This way you'll have to be very alert because the only way you'll be able to detect a strike is by feel. This shouldn't be too hard because the chances are you'll get larger fish and any brown from 1-1/2 pounds up can be detected easily when he strikes and starts to run with your fly. Browns are active through most of the warm months of the year, but they are the hardest to catch during the spring when the water is high and roily. This is the time when large, bright streamers, the weighted types are best, will get them if worked in the right spots. Nymphs will also produce some brownies, but they don't do as well as streamers and must be fished differently than when fishing in clear waters.

Fall is probably the best time of all for brown trout. They spawn in the fall anytime from the middle of September and in early winter until February. During the warm days of September, especially in an Indian Summer period they will take dries, wets, or streamers with relish.

In many streams the browns do a fine job of breeding and adapt themselves to the extent that stocking is not necessary. In effect they become "natives." In some areas the brown has a reputation of being hard to catch, but this is another facet of the un-predictableness of this species. Sometimes a stream loaded with browns will send anglers home empty handed for weeks at a time. Then it seems there are times when anyone

can catch them on just about any type fly or lure offered.

Browns are not too difficult to identify. In over-all appearance they might be called brown, but the actual brown part is on top of the fish and it lightens up to a rather golden color toward the sides and bottom. There are numerous dark brown or black round spots on the back and upper sides and on the gill covers.

Intermingled with the black spots on the sides along the lateral line is a series of bright red round spots with a thin ring of a bluish white color around them. They have a slightly forked tail when young, but with age it becomes squared off and sometimes has a very small outward curve at the rear center.

In some parts of the west there is another trout or at least the westerners say it is a different kind, called a loch leven. This fish came from Scotland and resembles a brown very closely, but fish biologists say that now there is no pure strain of loch leven, having interbred with the brown for so long that the species has been wiped out. The charac-teristic that identified the loch was the lack of red spots. Occasionally a trout bearing the general markings of the loch leven, minus the red spots is caught in the Yellowstone and feeder rivers in Montana.

The meat of the brown is often a very pale pink, sometimes ivory and is mild tasting. Fine eating in any size, the smaller ones up to 2 pounds are excellent broiled in butter, but over 2 pounds it is better to bake them. They are a real delicacy smoked. Use any fruitwood such as apple or cherry or the time honored hickory chunks soaked in water.

The Rainbow Trout
Probably the best known of all the trout family. It originated on the west coast and ranged from California to Alaska. It is a great

fighting fish and reaches sizes that would test any fisherman's ability and strength. Because of extensive plantings it is now well established all across the northern half of the U.S. down as far as Kentucky and Tennessee. Most of the Canadian drainages from Newfoundland all the way to the Pacific coast of British Columbia boast of heavy rainbow populations.

Though planted rainbows breed and produce in large numbers it is lakes where they are much harder to take by fly fishing.

A planter that isn't caught the same year he is stocked will move downstream to larger waters before the end of the season. This may be a migration of 5 to 10 miles to an area where the same river is wider. Then the next year he will move further down into a larger river if there is one, or a lake. When mature they will swim back up the same river to spawn.

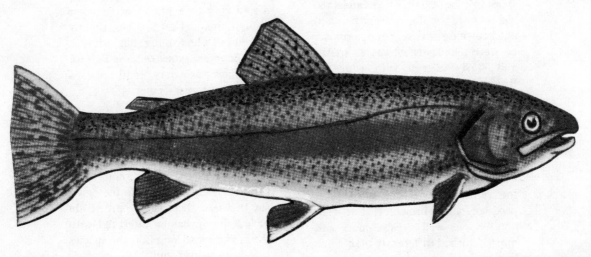

RAINBOW TROUT

hard to keep suitable populations of them in smaller rivers. Most states, for this reason, have a put and take program. That is they stock several thousand catchable sized fish each spring. These are about 10 inchers. Most of these are caught during the season, but some survive to an age where they can breed.

What happens from the time of egg laying and fertilization is that brown trout eat many of the eggs, then after the ones left hatch out they become prey to browns again, birds, and snakes. Only 3 or 4 fish out of many thousands hatched live to spawning age or to a size where they are really good catches.

There is another form of attrition inasmuch as many of the planters and natives have a tendency to migrate into the large rivers and

Found in waters over most of the U.S. and Canada to Alaska in rivers and lakes. An excellent fighter, leaps high out of water and battles every inch of the way to the net.

Strangely, though, not all planters will move down river. Many, if they find good food and fast, clear water, will become permanent residents of a 1 or 2 mile stretch of prime water.

Rainbows will take many different types of dry flies, but are also caught readily on wets, streamers and nymphs. They will take most bright patterns, but to be really effective it is a good idea to use 2 flies on your leader when fishing the fast water that rainbows like so well. The way to rig your leader is to tie 1 fly at the end and then about 36 inches above the first fly, tie on a dropper about 6 to 8 inches long and then another fly of a different pattern on the dropper.

The dropper is simply a piece of monofilament line or leader material. It is a good idea to first tie a knot in your leader at the point you want your dropper to hold. Tie your dropper above the knot so it won't slip toward the first fly.

Cast these 2 flies above fast riffles, even shallow ones no deeper than 10 or 12 inches and let both flies float free across the white water. In most cases you won't be able to see the 'bow when he takes the fly, but you'll know it when he starts running. If he's any size at all, 15 inches up, you'll see a lot of him as he clears the water in spectacular leaps and tail walking acrobatics. A 2 or 3 pounder can easily strip your line, including the backing, down to the bare spool in one of his speed runs, so be ready to give him line directly off the reel.

This is one of the reasons it is a good idea to use a single action reel with an adjustable drag on it. Most models would be adequate to slow a rushing rainbow with the drag resistance set at a medium graduation.

Though rainbows, like other trout, can be caught more easily in the early morning and evening hours, they are much easier to catch during the daytime hours than other fish.

Many fish will not take a lure of any kind during the spawning season, but this is not true of the rainbow. It is not known exactly why, but the rainbow will slash quickly at flies or bright lures dropped within striking distance when getting ready to spawn or just after dropping their eggs. Since observation at this time doesn't seem to indicate that they are feeding it is more likely that the strike is a protection reflex against an object that threatens safety.

Rainbows found in small lakes will seldom take flies during the day with any constancy unless there is a small ripple on the water. They will take flies very well as evening nears and on still waters, especially when there are many live insects dimpling the surface. During some hatches of insects they feed extremely well and will take an artificial fly of the same size as the hatching bugs.

In larger rivers, though the average size of the rainbow increases, they become harder to catch, especially on flies. In fast deep water, dry flies are practically useless and it is here that the large streamers and bucktails prove their worth. It is necessary also to use sinking fly line of the weight forward taper and cast sharply up and across the river.

When you do hook into a large river rainbow you've got a terrific battle on your hands because these fish are not only bigger, but very much stronger from fighting the massive fast water. You fight not only the fish but the pull of the rushing water, too. It's worth the battle when you finally ease a big one toward your landing net and scoop him out of the water with a quick thrust.

Here is a point to remember about landing trout. Never push your landing net toward the fish as it has a tendency to scare him and gives him a good chance to get off the hook. Always put your net into the water slightly in front of you and ease the fish toward the net. Scoop him out fast only after he is safely above the mouth of the net. Keep your rod tip high with a line tight enough to keep the fish's head up while you bring him to the net.

Effective dry flies for rainbows are: Brown and yellow bivisibles, Dark Hendrickson, Adams, March Brown, Cahill, Irresistable.

Wet: Gray Hackle, Badger and Brown Bivisible, Grey Wulff. regular and yellow Wooly Worms, McGinty, March Brown and Grizzly King. Streamers that are fine producers of rainbows are: The famous Muddler

Minnow, Dark Tiger, Nine Three, Green and Gray Ghosts and Bucktails.

Though these are great fly patterns, have taken their share of all kinds of trout and will continue to do so, other patterns will also do very well.

One of the most important aspects of the suitability of any fly is the part each fly puts on or into the water. For example, a dry fly that has a lot of above-water appendages doesn't necessarily produce well. In a dry fly, the number of hackles or hairs or points of whatever material, that protrude into the water and make dimples or in some way change the surface characteristics, is the factor that makes it a good or bad fly. The more dimples it makes the better. Whatever is above the water is simply window dressing for the fisherman.

The best colors are the various shades of browns, grays, off-whites, pale blues and pinks. Two fine solid tones are yellow and white, though white is actually not a color, but rather an absence of color.

Hair winged flies with wooly or chenille bodies are excellent because they are very fuzzy, look like food and can be used in almost any situation. They don't resemble any particular insect, but have a general resemblance to many mature stage insects.

It is not hard to identify a native rainbow. They are a darkish green on the back around the dorsal fin, but this green mostly fades as it gives way to the pinkish band that runs along the lateral line from the gill covers to the tail. From the pink band to the underside, the rainbow is a bright silvery white. Above the pink band there are dark spots, rather large in size, that become fewer and smaller along the pink band and almost disappear below it.

Hatchery raised trout that are kept captive in ponds don't have the pink band and seldom ever develop it. Those that are stocked in a natural flowing rivers eventually develop the band and become as bright colored as natives.

The meat of rainbows caught in fast clear, cold waters of natural rivers and streams, is generally white although you will occasionally find one that has a pink tinge to it. The flavor of rainbow meat is fine, though many times it is stronger than that of the brown. It tastes good broiled, baked or smoked. In the smaller lakes the rainbow is a bottom feeder most of the time though he can be taken on floating flies or on streamers trolled only a few feet below the surface. The meat of these fish is not quite up to the quality of the river caught 'bows. Good eating nevertheless.

The Sea Run Steelhead

Wherever rainbows are not landlocked and can get to the sea

STEELHEAD

A sea run rainbow caught mainly on its return to river spawning grounds. They run large and special heavy tackle and different fly patterns are required to take them.

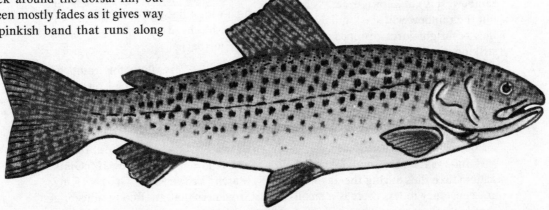

they will migrate in large numbers and spend 2 or 3 years in the ocean or large lakes. This is especially so on the west coast of the United States, where there is a heavy run into the Pacific Ocean from the rivers of California, Oregon, Washington, and British Columbia and Alaska.

When a rainbow goes to sea it becomes a steelhead and loses the coloration of a fresh water inhabitant. At the end of 2 or 3 years, the steelhead returns to the fresh water river it was born or planted in, regains the rainbow color, and spawns. Unlike the salmon varieties that return to the rivers to spawn and die, the steelhead lives and goes back to the ocean after spawning and will return 2 or 3 times during its life to the river to deposit eggs.

The steelhead is a fighting fool, a big brawny, tackle busting bruiser and you need heavy rugged tackle to get him. As a rainbow, he might have reached a weight of 4 to 6 pounds and sometimes, though rarely, have gotten to 10 or 12 pounds. When he goes to sea as a steelhead, he really grows and when he returns to the rivers each spring or fall he'll go from 5 to 40 pounds and will average 10 to 15 pounds.

To get him with flies you'll need a 9 foot special steelhead rod, usually a No. WF11S size line which is a heavy sinking type, and an extra big reel with large line capacity. Ordinary flies won't do either, you must use special steelhead flies in large sizes.

Standard steelhead flies vary in size from number 2 to number 8 and are usually tied sparsely so they'll sink easily, because most steelheads are taken by letting the fly drift on the bottom of the river. Fly colors range from very gaudy to rather conservative. In many areas you'll find hand tied flies offered by local fishermen and it pays to get a few of these as the residents usually know what types do a better job of getting the steelies.

Steelheads run in groups and where you find one you'll find others, but, since they are constantly moving, you might only catch 2 or 3 before they've gone past the place you're fishing. But simply wait awhile and another run will come by. If you catch one from a certain pool or riffle or run, it's quite possible that the same area will produce another if you wait awhile. Steelhead, like salmon, seem to follow the same paths through the rivers and loaf in the same pools year after year, therefore if you can read the waters correctly you'll fill your stringer in no time.

Though they are rough and tumble fighters, steelhead take the lure very delicately, making it somewhat difficult to distinguish their bite from a snag or from the hook dragging bottom or bumping a rock. Once the steelie takes it though, it is not hard to set the hook. The safe procedure, therefore is to go through the motions of setting the hook every time you feel the slightest tug or pull on your line.

Steelhead are not found in the Atlantic Ocean, but there are considerable numbers in the Great Lakes and they run up the rivers in Michigan, Wisconsin, Minnesota and into Ontario in Canada.

Steelhead flies are of the modified streamer design and good producers tied on size 2 to 8 hooks are: Jock Scott, Thunder and Lightning, Lady Godiva, Gray Hackle, Black Gordon, Coles Comet, Burlap, Silver Demon, Skunk, Boss, Improved Governor and Royal Coachman.

For some of the best steelhead fishing to be found anywhere the rivers of Oregon and Washington can't be beat. Besides the natural born steelies these states have stocked the rivers at different times of the year and since steelhead make their runs at specific ages they now run to a greater or lesser degree every month in the year.

The Brook Trout

The conservationists and ecologists should love this fish because he is the best indicator of clean (or polluted) water to be found anywhere. This fish is rapidly diminishing in numbers because he cannot exist in any, but the purest of waters. Although many large brookies are found in some of the larger fast water rivers of northern United States and Canada, most of them are small in size and like the

flourished in very many areas. In the west it is found in the very small high mountain streams and some lakes from 5 to 8 thousand feet in altitude, but not in great numbers or size.

In the small streams it is extremely timid and difficult to catch on flies though live bait seems to produce good catches. Once established in the small streams of 3 to 10 feet in width they seem to be content to spend a lifetime there. They spawn

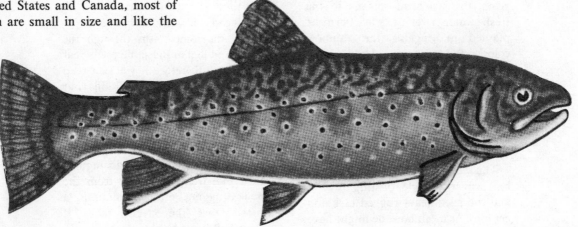

BROOK TROUT

Also known as speckled trout. A beautiful fish that provides much action and good eating. Needs cold, fast, uncontaminated water for survival. Ranges across northern U.S. and Canada.

tiny, fast water feeder creeks. These little streams are often not more than 3 or 4 feet wide and 8 to 10 inches deep though there may be some holes of 15 inches to 3 feet deep.

The sizes of the brook trout in these small waters run from 8 to 15 inches with an average being close to 9 or 10 inches. A 15 incher is a giant.

The original geographic distribution of this fish was the east coast of the U.S. from Maine to Alabama and Georgia, and from Saskatchewan to Labrador through Canada. Names for this species are eastern brook trout, brookie, speckled trout, salters, and spotted sea trout.

It has been widely transplanted and stocked throughout the U.S. and Canada, in those lakes, rivers and streams where temperatures are not much over 60 degrees in the summertime. The species has not

October through December in most areas and sometimes will then move downstream a short way to slightly larger waters, but for the most part they seem to stay near to their own birth place.

Where they exist in larger lakes and rivers they travel up the smaller stream to lay their eggs then return to the larger waters. Though they do prefer fast moving rivers to lakes, when they are in lakes they seem to like the deeper water when they get larger. They are always deep in the hot days of summer, but the smaller ones will feed near shore just before dark, taking fly hatches and mosquitoes.

In the larger waters and rivers they can be taken quite well on flies. Dries will get them in pools, but they can be caught in the very fastest of white water on streamers and bucktails. When brook trout are taken from these cold, very fast waters they are extremely strong fighters and though they don't come out of the water, they will let you know you've battled a real game fish.

Those brook trout (really a char if it makes any difference) taken from the clear, Canadian waters are unbelievably colorful and sleek. Their back from the top of the head to the tail is usually a dark metallic green interspersed with irregular chip-shaped patches of lighter colors. Then as this color lowers to the side, it blends into an irridescent purplish blue, then it fades to a light pink below the lateral line and in older spawning fish to a deep red on the belly.

All ages of brookies have orangish-red lower fins with a white leading edge and a thin black stripe just behind the white. There are many small yellow spots on the sides and a sprinkling of larger bright red spots circled with a light blue ring.

The redish color of the lower fins makes it easy to identify the brookie when you spot him in clear water. The coloration of this species varies widely from locality to locality and in areas where he has access to the sea.

In the far western waters where it has been transplanted, it is far less colorful than those in eastern waters. It has only a few yellow dots, many times no red dots and is more steel gray to silvery with many black spots. The lower fins, however, do retain their redness with the white and black stripes.

Color of the meat varies also. In some Canadian waters the brooks have a pink meat. These come mostly from water having a high iron content and are very fine eating. Those from lakes seem to run more white and sometimes a pale yellow. The western brookies are mostly white fleshed, but also very fine tasting.

When the brookies have access to the sea, mostly from the rivers of Maine and Canada they will migrate to the ocean where they become sea trout for a stay of about 2 years. While at sea they change colors like the rainbow trout and when they come back to a river they are darker on the back and more silvery on the sides. But after spending a week or so in fresh water their natural color returns. It doesn't seem to make much difference whether or not they return to the same river they were born in, and they frequently don't.

After spawning the sea run brookies are in fine condition physically as they return to the sea for another 2 years.

Brookies are heavy feeders and will gobble up almost anything that looks like food and that they can catch. They will eat chubs, minnows, other trout, small whitefish, hellgramites, nymphs, flies, crayfish, worms, grasshoppers, small rodents, baby birds and almost any other form of insect or animal life that is washed along by the river.

Therefore, it is not really too hard to catch them using the same techniques in fly casting you would use for most other varieties. They aren't known to be night feeders though. Mostly they will take dry flies during the warm summer months in the early morning daylight hours and in the early evening hours. During mid-day they can be taken in very rough, fast waters on big streamers and bucktails cast directly above the white water and allowed to be sucked into most turbulent part.

The brook trout is probably my favorite of all fish to catch with flies because it is the first species I ever caught on a fly rod many years ago.

I am saddened when I hear reports from across the U.S. and Canada that the natives are fast disap-

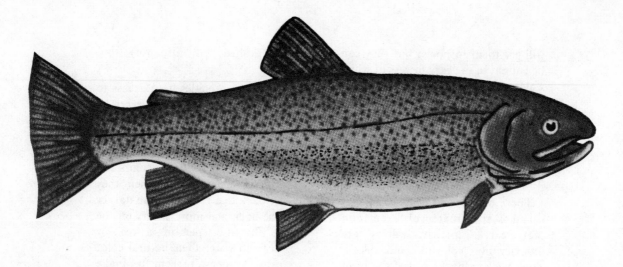

pearing, because like the magnificent grizzly bear, it cannot cope with the encroachment of civilization. Hatchery raised planters will probably continue to be available on a put and take basis for some time, but, to me at least, they don't come even close to measuring up to the exotically beautiful native.

The Cutthroat Trout

This trout, like the rainbow, is a true native of the west. In many states it is actually referred to by the residents as the "native." The name "cutthroat" is derived from the fact most of these fish have a red slash mark on their lower jaw, but there are so many sub species and interbred varieties and even pure specimens with different colorations, that in many cases they are very hard to identify. Even some of the pure species do NOT have the red slash on the lower jaw. Cuttroats and the sub species and hybrids are found over a vast range in the western states. Starting in the northwest you'll find them in the Yukon Territory of Canada, in southern Alaska, British Columbia, Washington, Oregon, northern California, Nevada, Utah, Idaho, Montana, Wyoming, Colorado and parts of New Mexico and Old Mexico and North and South Dakota.

Within this large area they will be found in all types of waters, in Alpine lakes high in the mountains, in mountain streams, in large rivers in

CUTTHROAT
Native to and found only in western and northern states, Canada and Alaska. Though sometimes hard to identify, most cutthroats have a crimson slash mark under lower jaw on both sides.

the valleys and in small and large lakes at all altitudes.

The cutthroat is a very attractive fish being light green on the back and having shades of pink along the lateral line changing to very light silvery green on the belly. They have dark spots on their body but not many of them. Their upper fins and tail are thick with dots however and there is an increase of spots toward the tail on the body.

Many times they will have a bright red coloring, especially in the spring that may cause the angler to mistake them for rainbows and sometimes a spawning brookie. He soon discovers though that it couldn't possibly be a brook trout because of the season.

Although in the inland waters the cutthroat averages about 2 to 3 pounds they will at times reach 30 pounds and over in the larger waters. Generally the sea run cuts average out bigger than the inland river inhabitants and it is not at all unusual to take specimens of 20 inches or over.

As time goes by, the numbers of pure strain cutthroat continues to diminish through assimilation into other breeds. Cutthroats are notorious interbreeders with rainbows and with other subspecies of their own and this interbreeding is not localized but is happening over the entire broad range of their territory.

When they continually interbreed with rainbows the eventual outcome is that the characteristics of the cutts disappear. A rainbow-cutthroat cross is not an undesirable fish in the least. They are terrific fighters and the meat, a pale orange is second to none.

Cutthroat are very fond of flies and will take floaters or wets with enthusiasm at the right times. They are an ideal fish for the backpacker who likes to camp on the high Alpine lakes because they can be easily caught from shore and from around the inlets of small creeks into the mountain lakes. They are not timid and don't seem to be frightened by man at all. But even though they don't spook at the sight of man or a fly cast close to them, they don't readily take lures of any kind under these circumstances. They are good morning feeders and will feed again late in the afternoon. Such dry patterns as the Ginger Quill, Spiders, Bivisibles and Wooly Worms take their share of cutthroats.

The Dolly Varden
The Dolly Varden trout is another misnamed fish because it too, is really a char. It is closely related to the arctic char and may be only a sub-species. It is known by many other names in the locales it inhabits, but probably the best known of its other names is bull trout.

This is a fine fish, a good rough fighter and it will take flies about like other chars or trout, but it is not too well known or sought after by the fly fisherman.

The Dolly is colorful being a dark greenish bronze on the back with light spots, then fading to a lighter bronze along the lateral line, sporting orange spots on the rest of its body with the exception of the head fins and tail.

In size it ranges from the small 8 to 12 inchers of the inland mountain lakes and streams in northern California, Wyoming, Montana, Idaho, Oregon, Washington, and British Columbia to the larger specimens in big waters. The sea run Dolly Vardens are generally larger, but many taken from Lake Pend Oreille, Idaho and the West Fork of the Flathead River and Flathead lake itself will go as big as 15 pounds.

Some time ago it is said the Dolly had a bad name among the commercial salmon fishery because they said it gobbled up salmon eggs and young salmon by the thousands. This seemed unjustified because a lot of other fish devour salmon and eggs by the tons. Even the salmon eat their own eggs and small fry.

Today the Dolly Varden enjoys a good reputation among sport fisherman who have tangled with it, but it is still overshadowed by the well known trout and chars. The smaller Dollys will take dry flies, but as they get bigger, streamers and bucktails fished deep and in the wider rivers are needed to connect.

The Golden Trout
The Golden trout is one that many trout fishermen would like to put in their creel and though the distribution of this fish is extremely limited, it is quite well known.

Once this fish was found only at altitudes above 9,000 feet in feeders of the south fork of the Kern River in California. Over the years it has been transplanted into the highest alpine lakes in the California Sierras, Wyoming, Montana and Washington where it has survived and bred fairly well. The largest Golden ever reported was one taken from a Wyoming lake that weighed 11 pounds, but others as big as 18 to 20 inches have been

DOLLY VARDEN

caught with some regularity out of the lakes. The brook caught specimens average only eight to ten inches.

There are several high country lakes in the Beartooth Primitive Area between Red Lodge and the northern boundary of Yellowstone Park in Montana that give up Goldens of two or three pounds to those who are rugged enough to get into these skyside lakes and persistent enough to fish them for several days at a stretch.

When they do start a feeding spree they'll take dry flies tied on number 12 or 14 hooks best of all.

It is a good eating fish, having firm pink flesh and their external coloring is fabulous. The back of a golden is a shaded green color that blends out to an overall color close to a golden green, then there is a pink band running the length of the lateral line. Over this pink band are about ten oval shaped spots, dark green in color and called parr marks. The dorsal fin and tail are olive green and are covered solidly with dark spots. The forward tip of the dorsal fin is white with a black stripe running under it. This trout is worth every bit of the difficulty it takes to get him. One of the hardest aspects of catching this fish that he is not often caught from shore and the angler who can get boats into the high lakes where he lives are few. The best idea is to take an inflatable raft type boat up with a pack horse. It is wise to bring at least a 2 man size because the wind can get pretty strong on

Native to western and northern states they range far into Canada and Alaska. They attain considerable size, 15 to 20 pounds and are also known as bull trout.

some of the upper country lakes.

Many of the fishermen who complain that the Goldens aren't biting simply cannot cover the area necessary to find them. Most of the lakes containing Goldens are surrounded in part by steep cliffs and large rocks and by some brush, and the angler who tries only 2 or 3 spots from shore isn't going to get much unless he's very lucky. With a rubber boat, however, you can cover almost the entire lake in one day and your chances of picking up 3 or 4 Goldens are very good. They seem to prefer white, yellow or red dry No. 12 flies cast into quiet pools. If you plan a trip to take some of these prize specimens be certain to include a camera and plenty of color film.

Lake Trout

Lake trout can be caught on wet flies and bucktails when the time is right. But the time isn't right very often. About 2 weeks in the springtime when they come into the shallow shoal water and about 2 weeks in the fall when they again come into shallow water to spawn.

In the spring it takes some techniques to get them and besides casting, trolling a streamer will often hook them. It is a good idea to use a steelhead type rod and line for lake trout because you can tie into some husky, heavy fish occasionally and the heavier tackle will be necessary to bring them up.

Lakers are not spectacular fighters, very seldom if ever do they jump out of the water. More often they will run to the bottom and just loaf, though at times some will give you an underwater battle. The easiest time of all to get them is in the fall when they are spawning. They'll take almost any bait cast to them.

One time just to see what they would take, I cast out a bare treble hook and within seconds after starting my retrieve, hooked into an eight pounder. So use any large streamer you may have on a 4 or 2 or larger hook.

Lake trout are spread throughout the northern border lakes of the U.S. and from Labrador to the west coast of Canada. They are a cold, deep water fish so they'll be found mostly in northern lakes, big waters where the depths are 70 to 2 or 3 hundred feet. When they go deep in the warm days of summer, fly fishing is out, but in the spring and fall they are worth trying for. Their meat is reasonably good tasting, but not tops in my book.

GOLDEN TROUT

Exist only in a few western states in lakes above 8,000 feet. Hard to catch, but will take flies as often as anything else. Originated in Alpine California lakes.

Smallmouth and Largemouth Bass

The smallmouth bass is second only to the trout on the list of favorite fish of the fly fishermen. Though not as much a target of the long rodders, the smallmouth combined with the largemouth are present in every state in the continental U.S., except Alaska. They are to be found in lakes of all sizes and depths and in rivers of every description. They are also plentiful in the rivers and lakes of southern Canada (the smallmouth more than the largemouth).

The most popular lure for both large and smallmouth is the floating, popping bug which is not a fly. The popping bug or "popper" is a small wooden or plastic lure with a dished out face, rubber legs, sometimes a hair tail and a single hook imbedded the length of the body, and protruding from the rear.

These come in many sizes and colors but the best for bass are the yellow or white ones on a number 6 or 4 hook, usually they have white rubber legs. They are excellent producers when the bass are surface feeding in the evening hours and they will take them even in deeper waters over rock beds.

A 20-30 foot cast in open waters or to the weed beds along shore is about as long as is needed. Many times when the smallmouth is on a feeding spree they will hit poppers 2 at a time a short way from your boat or from where you are standing if you are wading.

If you are casting from a boat you can get twice the number of chances

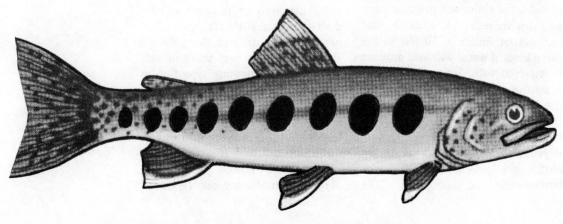

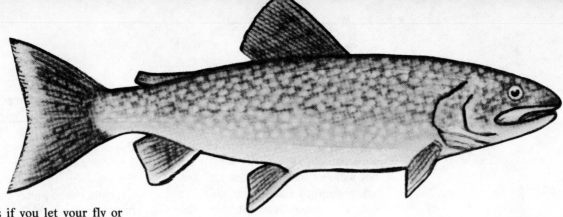

Taken from deep northern lakes in spring and fall. Only wet and streamer flies are suitable as they do not surface feed. Many 10 to 20 pounders are caught every year.

to hook a bass if you let your fly or popper drop into the water on both your back and forward cast.

When you play the bass from a boat, the easiest way is to pull him in with your left hand taking in the line and at the same time control him with the rod. Let the retrieved line fall to the bottom of the boat and each time you pull more line in, clamp it to the rod with your right hand until you reach for another pull with your left. Use a net to land him.

Both largemouth and smallmouth will take dry flies on either rivers or lakes, but you must give these insect imitators more action than for trout. It is OK to cast up and across the stream and let it drift down, but you must also twitch it and jerk it frequently if you want to score on bass.

Bass will also take wet and streamer flies, but it is more difficult to fish these in a lifelike manner and if you can't get fairly good action it will be hard to get them. You can get more variation into the movement of wet and streamer flies when fishing flowing rivers because the water does much of the work for you, but lake fishing is a different story. During a quiet summer evening after a warm day a large, hairy dry fly cast over some calm, but deep water, and jerked a few times will produce some nice bronzebacks. A streamer cast out and let sink 5 to 10 feet in the same kind of water will also produce if retrieved with darting spurts.

Best of all is the fine action you'll get from bass on a fly rod. The slender, sensitive shaft will give you the feel of every rush every leap and if you also fish bass with spinning outfits you'll see the vast difference immediately and have more of an

understanding of the appeal of fly rodding. A good size for a bass rod is a 7-1/2 footer with a number 6 weight forward line. You can get bass on a fly rod with poppers when nothing else, short of live bait, will take them. In identifying these bass the difficulty lies in telling the difference between the two, but it really isn't hard.

The biggest difference between the two is in the name itself. In the smallmouth the mouth opening never extends to the rear of a line drawn down from the back of the eye. In the largemouth the mouth opening extends back of the eye anywhere from 1/4 to 1 inch depending on the overall size of the bass. In many areas the smallmouth has red eyes. The main difference in coloring is that the smallmouth has a bronze green tone on its back. But the main way and easiest to tell the difference is in the size of the mouth.

Bluegills and Other Panfish

These little, but game fighters, that will fit into a frying pan are great fun to catch on flies and a fly rod. They are easy to catch and for their size good little scrappers. You need tiny flies to catch them though since they have a very small mouth. They will take floating type flies at times, but often they are found in water 10 to 15 feet deep and it is better to use a wet fly with a sinking leader that will allow the fly to go down about 3 to 5 feet.

Some of the midget poppers that are now available are also very good

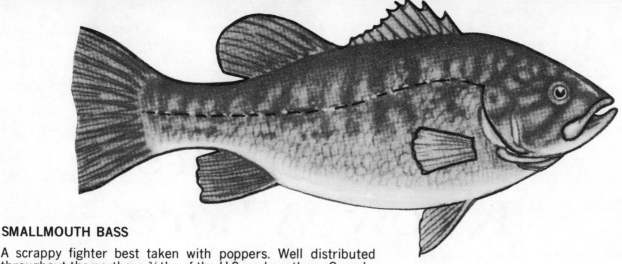

SMALLMOUTH BASS

A scrappy fighter best taken with poppers. Well distributed throughout the northern ¾ths of the U.S. and southern Canada. Good eating from colder waters.

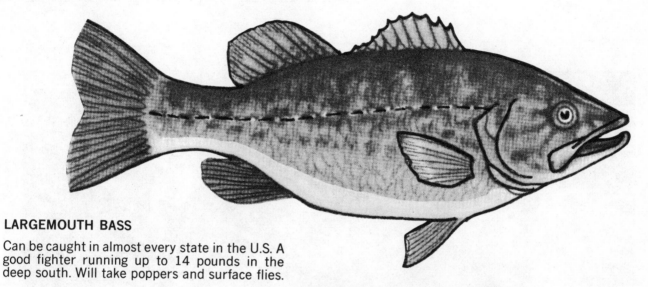

LARGEMOUTH BASS

Can be caught in almost every state in the U.S. A good fighter running up to 14 pounds in the deep south. Will take poppers and surface flies.

for taking pan fish. Sunfish, black crappie and white crappie can all be caught fly fishing. The sunfish can be taken in the same way as bluegills, but crappies and rock bass should be offered small bucktails or streamers fished on sinking leaders and given some action by a jerky retrieve.

BLUEGILL

Will take small flies fished a foot or two below the surface and sometimes a dry fly. Fun to catch on a light rod. Have amazing strength for their size. They bite hard.

Learn How to Read the Waters - Know Where the Fish Are.

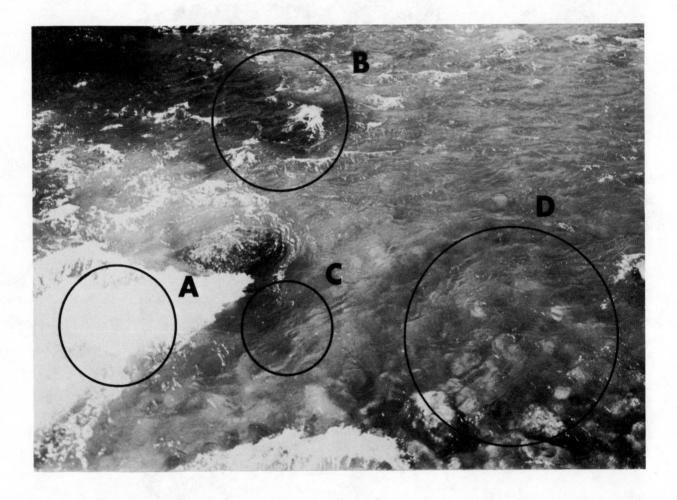

There are certain spots in a fast flowing river that are preferred by feeding fish. In the photo above area (A) would be ideal for brook trout and a streamer fly cast to the edge of the white water would likely take one. Area (B) is the edge of a hole and could produce a brown trout or two. Area (C) would be good for rainbow with a wet fly and area (D) could produce rainbows with dry flies. In each case you would cast across and above the areas circled.

Reading the waters will help you catch more fish,
but if you also know how to read the sky, the wind,
the temperature and the weather in general
you'll increase your chances even more.

Reading the waters is one of the most interesting, challenging and enjoyable aspects of fly fishing. It means learning the nature of rivers, creeks, and various types of lakes in regard to the fish populations found in them.

It is necessary to consider the main differences between lakes and rivers which are: size, depths, mineral and other chemical content, lateral and vertical movement of the water, temperatures and the kinds of food available for fish consumption.

Because of these differences, various bodies of water will support only certain species of fish that are particularly suited to the water conditions and that can survive on and adapt to the food therein.

Reading the water as a method of finding fish is effective, but not easy. The problem lies in the fact that most of the time we can only see the surface, but we need to know about what lies underneath.

You can discover much by examining the land immediately surrounding any body of water, whether a river, lake or pond, but it tells only a small part of the story of what lies beneath the water. If there are trees, brush, grass and weeds growing on the banks you can be sure that any fish present will have terrestrial insects as a food source.

I say "any fish present" because I have, on several occasions, examined out of the way lakes in the upper midwest and in the high country of the southwest and northwest and

have been very surprised at what I found.

Most of these lakes were surrounded by some type of vegetation that would produce insect life, and most also had water breeding type insects indicated by the presence of larvae and nymphs.

The waters were clear and unpolluted, were not silted, were sufficiently deep to provide varying degrees of temperature, had a source of fresh water such as springs or creek inlets and there was cover-brush or logs in the water.

Yet, there were no fish.

At one time, most of these lakes had contained fish, but over a period of years had lost the entire population due to severe winter kills. Some of the lakes never had any natural fish in them and were considered unsuitable for stocking because they were too unaccessable for the average fisherman.

An underfished lake will eventually become overstocked and produce only undersized runts.

Some years ago I visited a friend who lived on a small lake in Wisconsin. After fishing this lake for two days with no "luck," my friend offered to take me to a lake where "they would really bite anytime."

He took me on a short portage to one of the most beautiful midwestern lakes I have ever seen. It was perfect. Sunken logs along the shoreline. Heavily overhung with brush and trees. It had about a 15 foot drop-off 30 feet from shore. The

water was reasonably clear and I could see a patch of weed beds at the far end of the lake.

The woods and trees were alive with small animals and a great variety of birds, all excellent indicators of a healthy wildlife condition. This lake should be tops for bass.

I tied on a mosquito with a number 16 hook and began casting shoreward and then dropping the fly on the water on my backcast too. After about ten minutes I had hooked two bluegills and two sunfish, these were also favorable signs for good fishing as bluegills and sunfish are readily eaten by bigger bass.

It was around four o'clock, somewhat early for bass so I wasn't concerned that I didn't get any. Then about six o'clock the bass began to strike at every cast and hit viciously. I caught six on six casts and the largest one was 8 inches.

Runts.

I thought their appearance was strange because all of them had the blackish-green coloring all the way to their underside, but young bass usually have only a light green shading just a short way below the lateral line.

The answer was obvious. Although these fish were only six to eight inches long, they were several years old as indicated by the extent of the black markings. They were hungry and there were plenty of them and I knew why. This lake had been underfished for years and had not had a winterkill for some time, if at all.

My friend confirmed that it was only lightly fished in the years he had lived there and that he seldom saw another fisherman on the lake.

On another fishing trip up the Wabigoon River in Ontario, Canada, my Indian guide friend asked me if I would like to portage in to what he was sure was a virgin lake.

I thought this was a great idea and we started. This was only a short way, about one-half mile, but somewhat rough going as it was through deadfalls, blowdowns and heavy brush tangles. The thought of great fishing in a virgin lake made it seem worth the tough hiking, however.

When we got to the lake I was glad I'd come. It was a jewel, and my Indian buddy predicted it would be full of northerns. He was right. I hooked into a four-pounder on my first cast and before we were through for the day we had caught over 80 fish, BUT . . . the largest was only five pounds and the average was only two pounds. Many of these fish bore scars caused by tooth marks evidently made by other northern pike. These fish, although fun catching, were really very much undersized for their specie. Here was a lake that probably had not been fished at all and had also not been controlled by winter-kill, with very undesirable results.

The lesson to be learned from the characteristics of these lakes is that one good way to read waters is to read other fishermen. If you don't see other anglers or signs of them it doesn't necessarily mean that the fishing is good. It may mean an empty lake or waters containing only runts.

A good fishing lake with ample food and reasonably clean water is seldom overfished. The fishermen are controlled by nature as well as the fish. If word gets around that "they're biting" at a certain lake the number of fishermen increases and the number of fish decreases—word gets around that "they're NOT biting" anymore and the fishermen quit coming. The balance is preserved.

Reading Rivers and Creeks

Most of the rivers and creeks in the United States and Canada are of the rain and/or snow fed type. Even the small clear creeks that derive most of their waters from springs must, at times, carry water from rain or melted snow.

Rain and snow fed rivers have runoffs and flow at different velocities at different times of the year, but they are always flowing to some degree, except in years when an extreme drought might dry them out.

Rivers are usually highest throughout the spring season when the first waters drain into them from the melting snow. Then as the snow disappears and the weather warms, the springs rains come to keep the river waters high and fast flowing. In most years the flow, though lessened, will continue all summer long and be replenished occasionally by a July or August storm.

Fly fishing the rivers is not always easy, especially during the spring when the waters are very swift and roilly. Even the crystal clear streams of summer will become cloudy during the spring runoff. But they can be effectively fished at this time if you use the right flies and have the know-how.

Nymphs and bushy streamers and bucktails will take both rainbows and browns from high spring waters. The trick is to know where and how to fish any particular river.

In order to understand how to fish this condition it is necessary to know something about the actions of fish in a flowing river.

First of all, there has been a myth about the position a fish takes in a moving stream. This wrong information has been perpetuated long enough and it's time to dispel it.

Fish, trout or any other species, do NOT always face upstream. They do NOT even always face the current, and if you insist on continually casting upstream you will spook and miss about 50 per cent of your opportunities to get fine catches. The best cast is across and slightly upstream.

Many times trout will lie behind a rock, facing downstream and take feed from the water as it flows in a swirling eddy around the stone. In this situation it makes better sense to cast downstream.

About 50 per cent of the time brook trout will face the bank, broadside to the current, watching for food to be blown or fall into the stream from the shore.

To catch browns or rainbows in high spring water it is wise to use a weighted nymph or streamer and to cast into fast water just above a point where the stream flows past a quiet backwater or inlet. Trout will lie at the point where the fast water flows past the quiet area. In most cases you can actually see a line between the fast and slow currents. Even though the water may be murky, if your fly is under the surface, the trout can see it and grab it. Many times you'll get several fish from the same spot . . . both browns and rainbows and generally they will be larger fish. The famous muddler minnow is effective when weighted.

Another way to get trout in cloudy water is to locate a bank that borders a long trough or drop-off two or three feet deep and make a 50 or 60 ft. parallel downstream cast about one or two feet from shore and then work your streamer up river by pulling it toward you and then letting it sink into the flow and go downstream two or three feet. Trout like to lurk in these areas waiting for worms to be washed from the bank, but will take other food, too.

One of the great advantages for the fishermen in spring water is that the fish won't spook as easily because of poor visibility. However, there is a big disadvantage, too, because it is extremely dangerous to try and wade this very fast water. A misstep and even your waders wouldn't save you. You'd be carried under and downstream in seconds.

Clear Water

As summer approaches the streams and rivers will begin to clear, slow down and return to normal levels. You can usually be certain that a clear, fast flowing, cold water stream will have trout in it. Most states that have waters like this have stocked them and those that haven't been stocked probably have native trout populations.

Fishing a clearwater stream is a challenge and it's fun. As stated previously, the problem in reading a river or lake is that most of the time you can only see the surface, and it's necessary to see under the water to be able to tell where the fish might be.

Even in clear water your vision is limited if you are standing on the bank. If the sun is low you can see under the water only in one direction and not very far at that. If the sun is overhead you have a better chance of seeing the bottom for about 50 feet in all directions.

On a cloudy day the chances are the reflection of the sky will tend to produce a solid glare on the water that will completely block out your vision.

The best way to see into the water is to use polaroid glasses and to climb a high bank or tree, if you can, and to look into the water from a point 50 to 70 feet high. From a high position you can see the rocks, deeper holes, sunken logs, type of bottom and many times even spot fish.

Holes and deeper water appear as darker areas from above. If you note where they are located from above, you'll also be able to tell where they are when you are on a low bank or when you are wading.

From a high position you'll note that the holes are mostly located near banks where the water is faster and this is usually on the outside of a bend in the river. There will also be holes and undercut banks in straight stretches of water under willows, cottonwoods, and aspens and under grassy shorelines.

All these are good places to find fish and a bucktail or streamer cast above fast water that flows into a pool or undercut will very often produce a good size trout. The muddler minnow, black ghost, supervisor, warden's worry or hell cat streamers produce very well in this kind of water.

Note from your lofty view that large rocks or a large rock produces larger areas of white water with deeper swells in fast water, and creates swirls in slower moving water. These swirls or eddies that curl around a large rock usually flow in the opposite direction than the river and produce an ideal station for feeding fish. They position themselves facing downstream and wait for food to be floated to them in the curving flow.

This is an ideal situation to use a high floating dry fly. Cast it across the river, just a little way upstream from the rock and let it float naturally into the curving current around the rock.

You'll get rainbows or cutthroats this way and get them in the middle of the day when you least expect them.

Water flowing over shallow gravel bars or small, tightly packed rocks make small riffles on the surface and are favorite places for feeding rainbows. This water which varies from 8 to 12 inches deep will hold fish as big as 4 pounds and there will sometimes, in early spring, be six to ten fish in one 20 foot long riffle.

Two factors make them easier to catch in this situation. First, they ARE feeding and a feeding fish is not too concerned with the fisherman and will not scare as easily. Second, the ripple and riffle (white water) serve to partly obscure the fish's vision.

Here is where a dropper fly tied about 36 inches from the first fly on the end of your leader will really produce. Cast across stream above the riffles and let both flies (dry) drift across the ripples freely. The probabilities are about 99 per cent that you will hook your fish on the dropper fly. Using two flies on one leader is a good idea anywhere, but check the laws. Some places don't allow it.

Slow Rivers

Most slow moving rivers have characteristics that differ greatly from fast waters. They are usually located at low altitudes and have mud or sand bottoms rather than rocky beds. When mud or sand is washed into slow rivers by rains, they sink to the bottom instead of being washed downstream.

Slow rivers do not have white water or riffles which makes it difficult to locate sunken rocks and logs, or to find shallow sand bars.

Low velocity streams have more turns and curves and a strong tendency to meander through the lowest areas of the landscape on the way to the sea.

Temperatures of these rivers are generally higher than mountain streams and therefore will support not only trout, but also bass, walleyes and northern pike. When a river has a catfish population too, it is not usually suitable for trout.

Many lowland rivers have weedy bays along their course, which are ideal type waters for bass and northern pike.

The foregoing facts largely determine how to read and fish a slow river depending on the species of fish being sought.

Mud and sand bottoms will support weeds, minnows, crayfish and mussels. Trout, bass, walleyes and northerns all feed on minnows or crayfish or both. Therefore a wet fly or streamer will produce catches

(A) Sloping hill draining into river. This will wash food into water making the shoreline at (D) and (B) good places to fish during a rain. (C) A curve in the river usually has a deep trough or undercut and is a likely spot for feeding fish. (E) White water caused by rock. Cast to either side for best results.

of either. Mud and sand bottoms will also produce large numbers of insects and where there is an aquatic insect cycle, trout and bass will surface feed and take dry flies.

Northern pike will readily gulp down large, bushy streamers fished on or just below the surface in weedy areas.

If rocks or logs are not too far below the top, they will create a swirl on the surface of slow moving water. This swirl sometimes resembles an oil slick.

A wet fly such as a muddler minnow or wooly worm cast into one of these swirls and allowed to be

pulled under freely will often hook a good fish.

Sand bars or the drop-offs on their edges are very good fish producing areas.

They can be located by color. The water over a shallow bar appears to be a lighter green or tan in color. Drop-offs are dark green to black.

When fish are spawning in sand or gravel or feeding on minnows, in the same areas, they can be caught on dry flies or wet streamers cast directly over the bar.

Wet flies cast above drop-offs and allowed to sink deep, almost to the bottom of the drop, will consistently get bass or walleyes.

The fact that slow streams meander and create curves is a plus for fishermen. Sand bars are created on the inside of curves and deep

holes and undercuts are made on the outside.

Fish the deep holes with dry flies or the undercuts with wet flies and you'll fill your bag limit in a hurry. Fish from the sand bars on the inside curve.

A word of caution: while the slower water velocity practically eliminates being swept off your feet, the sand and mud bottoms can sometimes give way underfoot and pull you under. Also holes and drop-offs seem to be more abrupt in slow water and one step can put you in water over your head. A wading staff can prevent either of these from happening. Use one if you do much wading.

Lakes

Many of the rules for reading river

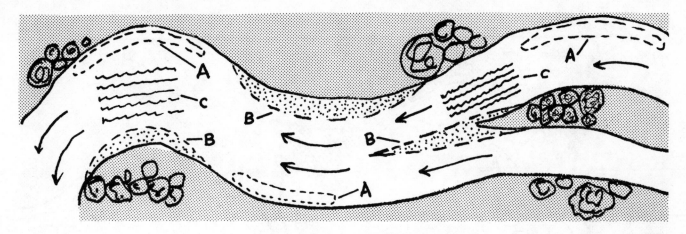

In a meandering, fairly fast flowing river, good spots to cast to are: (A) deep troughs located on outside of curves, (B) edge of sandbars especially when bar is located where two branches of river flow together, (C) riffles located over rocks as indicated by white water.

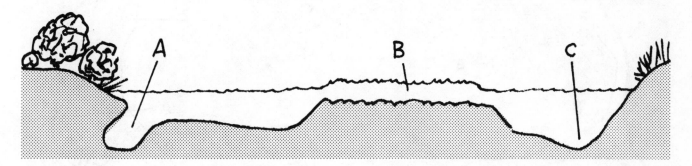

Cross section of river showing (A) undercut bank, a good hiding place for large trout or bass, (B) riffles, feeding area for trout throughout the daytime, (C) deep troughs usually holding several fish late in day.

waters also apply to lakes. The rules of fly fishing likewise apply.

Any live lake that has a healthy fish population must have a constant supply of fresh, moving water of some kind.

All lakes get this supply from one or more of three sources: river or creek inlets and outlets, underground springs, rain or melting snow and consequent runoffs.

Fish in lakes are attracted to the moving water of creek inlets or flowing springs and they can be found near these areas at about any time of day, but more often at morning or evening feeding times.

Generally, dry flies and popping bugs work best for fly fishermen on lakes. Shorelines of bays, rocks, logs, sand bars all offer good spots on lakes.

Many times bass will come up from ten to fifteen feet to take a floating fly or popper. These are usually smallmouth bass schooling over rock beds to feed in the evening from five o'clock to dark in the summer months.

Largemouth or smallmouth bass, or northerns can be taken on dry flies cast to the edge of weedbeds.

Rainbow trout are often caught in western lakes by trolling a wet fly from a boat in six to ten feet of water, a hundred yards or so, offshore.

Walleyes will take a bucktail streamer trolled slowly ten to twenty inches above the bottom of a lake.

Seasons

Fresh water fishing in most of the U.S. is best in the warmer months of spring, summer and fall. Fly fishing is good in all warmer seasons, but it is better in late spring when water levels become normal after flooding subsides. In many years, the early spring, the last two weeks of July and the first two weeks in August are the poorest for fly fishermen.

Best times are the last week in June, the first two weeks in July and from the third week in August until late October.

Rainbows, walleyes and smallmouth bass fishing is best in spring and early summer, largemouth bass in the warmer months, and brown trout in the fall months.

Seasons are also affected by cycles. Some years will be excellent for one or two species of fish. Some years will

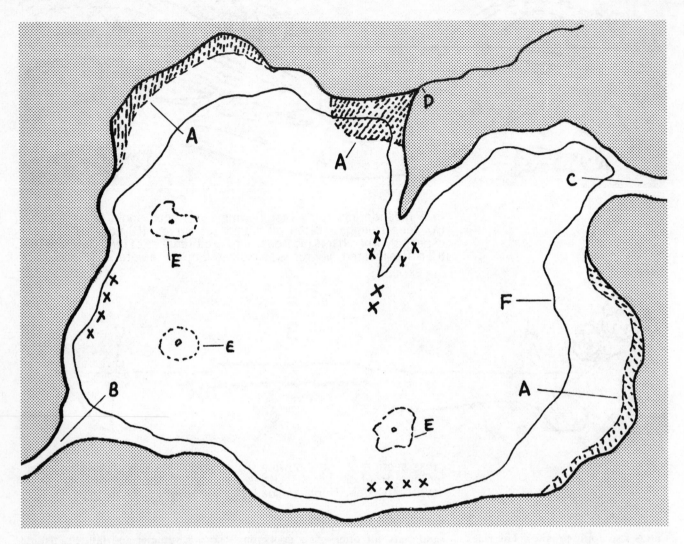

Best places to fly fish lakes are (A) weed beds, (C and B) inlets and outlets, (D) tiny creeks flowing into weed beds, (E) spring holes, either warm or cold, (F) drop-offs, (X) sandbars and sandy drop-offs.

be excellent for all fishing and some will be poor for all fishing. In many instances the cycles only affect certain lakes. That is, a lake which is poor fishing one year will be great the next and vice versa.

By fishing the same lake or river for a few years and noting the results, these cycles can often be determined.

Time of Day

Time of day is easily the most important factor to consider in successful fishing. It is also the easiest to determine.

For all fish the best time is from four p.m. to midnight.

The second best time is from an hour before sunrise to an hour after.

Some fish, however, will bite all day long. Rainbows, walleyes, panfish can be taken at any time of day, but of these, rainbows and walleyes will also bite better at night.

Weather

Much has been said about how weather affects fishing, but there's little been proved.

The only two aspects having much credence as far as my personal experience is concerned are:

1. Fish do feed frantically during a summer rain, and take just about any dry or wet fly no matter where or how it is cast in the water.

2. The period in the middle of a front produces best. The middle of a front is about halfway between the start of a rain period (cloudy-low front) and the end; or halfway between the start of fair (sunny-high front) weather and the end of fair weather.

Some say fish are hard to catch during a full moon and easiest on dark nights.

I have noted some better catches on dark nights and also some good takes on moonlight nights.

Take your choice.

Modern Fly Fishing Equipment

Fly fishing tackle offered for sale today by most companies is the best ever made.

Each year, over a period of 30 to 40 years fly tackle has been improved in design, construction and durability.

In the early days of fly fishing in America the split bamboo rod was considered to be the finest available and it was certainly the most expensive.

As more fishermen became interested in taking fish on flies, manufacturers started experimenting with other materials in the making of rods. They tried tubular steel, solid steel, solid glass but these proved to be too heavy and did not have the proper distribution of flexibility to give the necessary action.

Then the process of manufacturing a hollow fiberglass rod blank was developed and almost over night, it changed the entire industry.

The blanks are made basically by winding or fitting fine threads of glass around a mandrel or shaft and then bonding them with an application of super strength resin epoxy. When the epoxy has hardened the shaft is pulled out leaving a hollow tubular glass rod blank.

In order to provide the action needed for both bait and fly casting these hollow rods were tapered as were their predecessor steel and bamboo rods.

The fiberglass rods proved to be ideal as they are strong, can be tapered to give the exact action desired and can be made at a reasonable cost.

Glass fly rods have now been developed and refined to a degree where they are as good or better than the highly praised bamboo rods. AND most of them are lighter than the equivalent length bamboo which is, in my opinion, a definite advantage.

As far as cost is concerned there is no comparison. An excellent quality, beautifully designed, fine handling tubular glass rod can be bought for $30 to $45. A bamboo rod will run from $125 to $400.

This is not to discredit bamboo rods. It requires the skill and ability of many years to make a split bamboo rod. The finished rod is a masterpiece of craftsmanship. The bamboo rod used on the quiet chalk streams of England or some of the slow moving, pool forming rivers of the eastern U. S. is probably quite suitable.

For all around fly fishing though, over rough terrain and in rushing, rock bottomed rivers and lakes I prefer a tubular glass type. Many times while wading a rushing river I get into a deep hole or a rock gives way underfoot and I find I must really scramble to get to shallower water or to shore.

In situations like these I find it easier if I have my hands free and consequently I throw my rod and reel up on the bank. Sometimes the shore is grassy or brush lined, but often it is rock covered.

In slower waters I use my rod as a wading staff or I hook the reel over a small limb to pull myself out of the water.

All these actions are tough on a rod and reel and I judge tackle as to how it holds up under rugged usage because this is part of fishing.

Over the years it has been my experience that poorly made, usually the cheaper equipment, does not stand up as well as better quality tackle.

This is also true when rods or reels were used solely for fishing and catching fish - they performed better, for a longer period of use without need for repairs.

A good quality, tubular glass rod and reel made by a reputable company will stand up very well for many years even under rugged use and handling beyond just fishing.

How To Choose A Rod

The first consideration in choosing a rod is how well it "fits" the person who is going to be using it.

This can be determined almost by "feel" alone. If it feels comfortable to the hand, if the weight distribution feels balanced, if it doesn't feel awkward or clumsy, chances are it is "right".

Whipping a rod back and forth overhead will indicate something about the flexibility of a rod, but not much.

A better way is to let the handle lay in the open palm of the hand and let the tip rest on the floor.

Although this is not as effective as actually testing the rod with a reel and line, it will give some idea as to the type of action a rod will provide.

Note the curve in the rod. If only the first 1-1/2 feet of the tip bend, it is a strong or fast action, if the bend extends about half way down from the tip it is a medium action, if the bend runs from the tip the entire length to the butt and handle, it is a slow or weak action.

Many times when buying a fly rod for the first time, the purchaser will be asked "What kind of fishing will you be doing? Bass? Trout? Panfish?" It is not wise for a beginner to try to be a specialist, therefore the best rod to get is one suitable for all around fishing.

This would be a 7-1/2 or 8 foot rod with a medium fast action made to handle both a No. 6 sinking line or a No. 7 floating line. Weight should not go over 3-1/2 ounces.

Although rods are manufactured to handle certain weight lines and to provide a specified action, the feel and performance will vary from one manufacturer to another, even though the dimensions are the same.

Therefore it is best to try three or four rods made by different manufacturers before making a decision. Choose well known brands of medium priced rods to test. If price is not too important, it would be better to buy a more expensive model, but even here it is not necessary to spend more than $50. But if a $20 or $30 rod "feels" better you can't go wrong taking it in preference to the more costly rod.

Choice of Reels

The basic function of a fly reel is to hold or store the line. It is not used in the actual casting of the line and though it is sometimes used to retrieve line after hooking a small fish, it's not a wise policy to try and play a larger fish with it.

Three types of fly reels are currently offered: the single action which consists of a spool, frame and handle and one that has a 1 to 1 retrieve ratio, the multiple action type with a frame, handle and geared spool which permits a faster retrieve ratio of 3 or 4 to 1, and the automatic in which the spool rewinds the line with a spring powered gear assembly.

All but the cheapest reels have some type of drag device to slow down the run of a fish and to keep the line from unwinding during regular use.

Some drags are simply a click mechanism. Others provide a means of varying the degree of resistance.

A drag is many times a much needed feature because some larger fish, especially a trout in the 2 to 6 pound class and up, can make a run long enough to strip all the fly line plus the backing line and break off the leader, if not slowed by some type of brake on the reel.

The choice of a single action or multiple action is mostly determined by personal preference, but for a beginner, the single action type is probably best.

The single action is lightweight and easy to handle. An automatic saves work, but is somewhat heavier than a single action.

This is one item needed by fly casters where there would be a temptation to economize. The best advice is DON'T!

There might be some justification in buying a less expensive single action reel, but remember there will be some situations in fly fishing where you will need a strong, rugged reel that can take punishment without falling apart. Cheap reels can't.

In the case of automatics, a quality reel is a must. Besides rough handling the automatic must be able to withstand the winding and rewinding of the spool thousands of times during its useful life. it makes sense to buy a good one.

Multiple action reels are geared for faster retrieve and should also be a good quality. They are used mostly by fishermen who prefer single action handling, but who will be fishing under conditions where long casts will be the rule.

Various manufacturers offer fly reels with certain extra features to make operation easier or more versatile.

Single action reels are available with additional spools to permit changing lines without tools. This makes it possible to switch from a floating to a sinking line at streamside to lure fish found to be bottom feeding.

Spools on many single action reels can be set up for either right or left hand retrieve. Guides on the reel also accomodate either right or left handers.

Multiple action reels also come with interchangeable spools and ones that can be adapted to right or left hand use.

Spools on automatics can be easily changed to provide for different types of lines, but it is not necessary to provide left or right handers since the trigger mechanism can be used by either, just as they are.

As far as quality is concerned, most of the time price can be a reliable guide. Single action reels priced from $7 to $15, multiple actions from $10 to $20 and automatics from $12 to $25 could be depended on for satisfactory performance over a period of years.

It is also a wise idea to select well known brands whenever possible.

Presented on the following pages are descriptions of rods, reels, lines and accessories made by several different manufacturers. These are all quality products, but not the only brands available. These were chosen, described and illustrated to show a cross section of the various types and grades of fly tackle being made today. Names and addresses of other fly equipment makers are listed on pages 254 and 255.

Fly fisherman landing a brown from river in southern Montana. He is using a Martin Tuffy Model 3-016, 8 ft. tubular glass rod, rigged with a Martin single action Model 62 reel. The line is a level 7 weight floating with a 7½ ft. sinking 4X leader. Sinking leader is being used with a dry fly to make the leader invisible. It will not, however, take the fly under with it.

MARTIN REEL CO.

Typical of many pioneer tackle manufacturers, Martin was started because of a need for certain equipment. This need was for a reel and was discovered under actual fishing conditions. The Martin Story follows:

Back in the late 1800's, the sportsmen in the Mohawk Valley took their fishing pretty seriously. This was only natural because of their proximity to the Adirondack region with its many excellent streams and lakes. One of the group was Herman W. Martin, a watchmaker, who apparently preferred fishing to his watch repair business.

For several years this group of anglers had been holding an informal contest to determine who could catch the largest bass. One day in the summer of 1881 Martin hooked into a bass which he knew would place him well on top of the list, but things didn't go too well for Martin, and in playing the fish, his line got tangled up in his oar and around his feet. At this point the giant bass made a powerful lunge and threw the hook. Martin exploded!

He returned to his shop determined to develop some type of reel which would enable the fisherman to control his slack line at all times and thus prevent tangling . . . something his single action action fly reel did not do. Martin knew from experience that it was humanly impossible to hold a fly rod in one hand, play a fish with the other, and at the same time to keep all of the slack, or surplus, line stored safely on the reel by cranking. The only possible solution to his problem was to devise some mechanical means of controlling the line.

Martin's watchmaking experience proved to be a valuable asset in the development work which followed. With a collection of clock and watch parts plus a good deal of hard work, Martin provided his first automatic fishing reel. It was a large, crude affair which bolted to the butt of the rod, and weighed approximately three pounds.

It controlled slack line by means of tension which was produced by winding a gear on top of the reel which compressed a large clock spring. Once the reel was properly wound, the tension could be thrown on or off by means of a long reverse lever which was also located on top of the reel. The first reel, though very crude, actually worked, and the basic principle which Martin had evolved is still employed in the modern automatic reels of today. Martin was issued a series of patents on these basic designs during the 1890's.

When Martin actually took his first reel into the field his results were not too successful. He soon learned that his reel was far too heavy and clumsy for actual fishing. Nevertheless, this crude model did retrieve slack line, and prevented it from becoming entangled while playing the fish. Martin decided that the idea was right and believed that if he could improve the design and eliminate some of the dead-weight, he would have a reel that would increase the pleasure of thousands of fishermen.

Then Martin incorporated the results of his findings in the field in a new reel. This reel was much lighter in weight than the previous model, many of the projections on the reel which tended to snag the line were removed, and the product was strengthened throughout by the use of better design. A United States patent was granted on this reel.

Unfortunately, this original reel has had rather rough treatment. In 1936 the Martin factory experienced a rather disastrous fire. In spite of the fact that this reel was subjected to terrific heat — when recovered, the reel still operated and is still in operating condition today.

Still not satisfied by about 1890, Martin developed a third reel. This model was round, it fastened to the rod butt with a reel seat, as do the present-day reels, and it was equipped with two protruding handles for winding.

These handles were soon discarded as Martin learned to keep away from any projections on the reel and thereby eliminate the possibility of fouling or damaging the line. This final reel, after a few refinements in design, was the first automatic reel to be manufactured in quantity and was the first product to be offered to the public by the Martin Company.

When Martin first started to manufacture automatic reels, he was so long filling orders for the "new" reel that very little was done about changing the design for several years. When aluminum was introduced, Martin was quick to adopt it for use in his reel. This new material reduced the weight of the product, but unfortunately, the softness of pure aluminum limited its use.

During this period The Aluminum Company of America was making rapid strides in the development of aluminum alloys. One of these new alloys, Duraluminum, seemed to have all of the characteristics necessary to make it a "natural" for the manufacture of fishing reel parts; but the material had never been thoroughly tested to determine its reaction to forming under pressure, which is a necessity for use on the punch press machines which are used in the production of fishing reel parts.

The Martin Company agreed to make the necessary tests on their presses, and in cooperation with Alcoa engineers, made many test runs. During this period, weaknesses in the alloys were determined and eliminated. The Company is proud of the part it played in the development of a metal which not only helped them to solve their biggest production problem weight, but which has been of inestimable value in many phases of modern industry.

At the present time, Martin Reel Company manufactures the largest line of automatic reels in the world. The quality of its products is recognized throughout the world, and its many awards and honors include: a certificate of Excellence from The Sportsman's Research Institute at Van Nuys, California; The National Medal of Honor, and a place in the Fishing and Hunting Hall of Fame by the Sportsmen's Club of America.

Some of the modern models contain as many as 43 parts, some of which require up to 23 separate operations in their manufacture. Actual factory production of Martin Automatic Reels started in the early 90's at the Ilion Novelty Works, Ilion, New York. By 1908, business had expanded so rapidly that the company was re-organized and the name changed to the Martin Automatic Fishing Reel Company.

Later, in 1921, the company was incorporated and moved to Mohawk, New York, where it occupied a large mansion which had been built during the Civil War. The mansion was destroyed by fire in 1936, but because of its historical significance, the Martin people restored it to its original state and it now houses the main office of the company.

Continued expansion of the company has necessitated a number of additions to the factory which is one of the most modern and up-to-date fishing tackle factories in the country.

The watchword at Martin through over 86 years of existence has always been quality. Over a period of many years, Martin has endeavored to produce fishing reels, that provide the maximum in dependability and ease in use.

The Company now offers a complete selection of fishing tackle. It is especially proud of the fact that it offers to the fly fisherman more varieties of single action, multiple action and automatic fly reels than any other firm in the world.

This is the Martin Model 8363 "Portage" fly fishing set. It includes the Model 63 reel with extra spool, a 6 piece, 6½ ft. fast action fly rod, a fly safe fly box and a No. 6 weight level fly line. The case stows away easily in a small suitcase or back pack. It is only 15¾" long, 7¼" wide and 2¾" thick.

Above is an open view of the Martin Fly Safe Fly Box. It holds up to 72 flies, streamers or nymphs and keeps them in a position to prevent damage or loss. Suspends flies in hook sizes from 16 to 1/0 in an upright position and protects wings and hackles and prevents dulling of hooks.

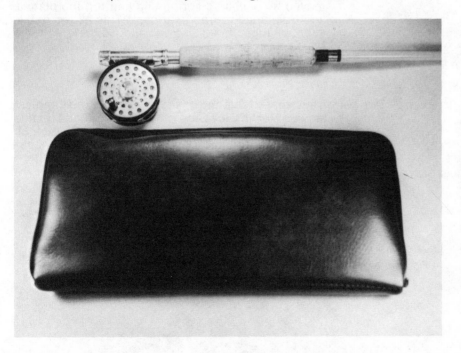

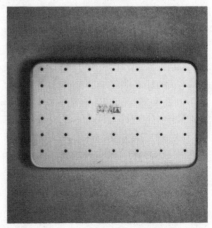

This view shows the Martin "Portage" travel fly fishing set as it looks closed. The case is quickly and completely closed with a zipper on three sides. The outside is made of tough, durable Naugahyde and the inside is lined with a silk grain wipe-clean fabric.

This is the Fly Safe box in closed position showing ventilating holes that dry flies fast. The case is made of anodized aluminum giving rigid strength and a non-glare surface. Size is a mere 6¼" long, 4" wide and 1⅛" thick when closed.

Besides manufacturing the largest line of automatic reels, Martin now offers rods, single and multiple action reels, lines, flies, fly boxes, fly tying vises, leaders, a complete line of imported spinning reels and several accessories.

The fly rods are offered in two grades, Blue Chip and Tuffy. Though the Blue Chip line is higher priced and considered tops by Martin, the Tuffy models, moderate in cost, are well constructed and give very satisfactory performance.

Both grades are somewhat deceptive. When handled and thrust back and forth without a line, neither models seem to have much action, but when rigged with reel, line and leader, the line control achieved is excellent. Both rods produce long distance casts with little effort, and handle a level line exceptionally well.

Blue Chip rods come in a 7-1/2 foot ultra light model for a No. 5 line, an 8-1/2 foot model using a No. 8 line, and a 9 foot heavy duty model that will handle a No. 9 or 10 line for coho, steelhead or salt water fish.

Tuffy grade models are produced in 8 and 8-1/2 foot lengths. All standard Martin rods are two-piece, tubular glass construction.

A third model in the Martin line is a unique six piece type designed for use by travelers who can pack it in an ordinary suit case. It is also ideal for back packers.

Each of the six sections is only 13-3/4″ long and they assemble into a 6-1/2 foot rod.

This rod is of Blue Chip quality and provides exceptionally fine action for a pack rod type. It is available in a set which includes either a single action or automatic reel, an extra spool, a line and a fly box, or the rod is sold separately. The set is

Above is the Martin Model 72 fast retrieve multiple action reel. The face plate on the handle side is removed by releasing spring clip and turning plate a short distance to free gear case. This allows quick spool change. It can also be changed to right or left hand retrieve.

Two Martin automatic reels shown mounted on fly rod handles. Top is the famous Martin Blue Chip which is guaranteed for five years because it is so well made. Bottom reel is the Model 39 Fly Wate silent wind automatic. Used with either a double taper or weight forward line up to No. 8 size. Has push-button tension release.

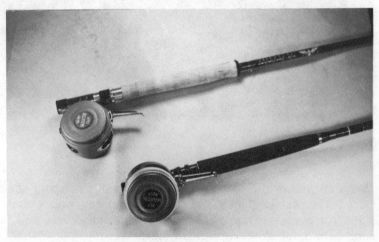

This unique fly tying vise is only 4½ inches high, yet is completely adequate for the average hobbyist tyer. It mounts on table or board with three screws and can be positioned in from edge of board. Model 100 equipped with knurled knob on rear of jaw shaft which controls opening that clamps hook.

New "See-Through" Fly Box

Martin Reel Co. has a new, patented fly box which should prove a great aid to fly fishermen.

The new "Sovereign" 660 has six individual compartments for storing small flies, midges etc. without risk or damage to hooks or hackles. The "see-through" lid of each compartment holds a sample of the pattern stored below.

The angler can tell at a glance what patterns lie below without having to open the box or compartment. In addition each lid is removable so that appropriate assortments can be made up before the fishing trip starts.

The new box is formed from durable ABS plastic which is impervious to lacquers, dopes, etc., measures 1¼" x 3¾" x 4¼", just right for slipping into pockets of a fly fishing vest and will float even when full of water.

Model 200 has same dimensions as Model 100, but has cam arm which locks hook in jaw opening. These vises are sturdily made of steel and are plenty strong enough to hold fly hook securely. They are guaranteed for one year against defects.

contained in a zippered soft cover case only 15″ long and 7″ wide.

Martin's line of fly reels provides a wide choice of both single action types and automatics.

There are two multiple action models which feature quick spool change and convert easily to right or left hand retrieve.

Eight single action reels come in a complete range of sizes based on line capacity, and all feature an interchangable reel system.

There are 12 automatic reels in the Martin line, also in a range of line capacities to fit all fly fishing conditions. All Martin automatics feature a slip clutch that lets line strip off freely even though the spring is fully wound.

Martin automatics come in all grades from the Blue Chip model, which is of such high quality that it is guaranteed for five years, to the Tuffy models which are ruggedly constructed, but moderately priced.

Between the Blue Chip and Tuffy lines are the Fly Wate models which have line capacities up to No. 8 double tapers, but are lighter weight than standard models. The Fly Wates are silent wind types and have push button tension control. Extra spools are available for the entire automatic line of reels.

Having established a policy to specialize in fly tackle, Martin now offers a complete selection of artificial flies including dry, wet, nymph and streamer types. All are hand tied in the U.S. or in Kenya, Africa.

They are tied in accurate, authentic patterns on quality, forged hooks. Materials used, such as hackles, wings, tinsel, floss, hair, thread, and cement are of top grade thus assuring long life and good catches even under the most rugged conditions.

All patterns have been field tested and have proven highly effective when used under the conditions they were designed for.

Two unique, well designed items in the Martin line of accessories are

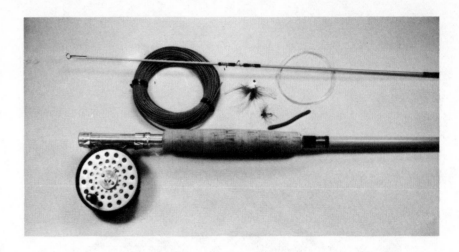

an aluminum fly box and a plastic "see through" fly box.

The aluminum "Fly Safe" model holds 72 flies in individual clips that accept hook sizes from 16 to 1/0. Clips are spaced to provide room for all size flies without crushing or breaking hackles or wings. Flies are held securely in upright position and can't fall or be blown out.

Clips of stainless steel don't contact hook points and thus protect them from breakage or becoming dull.

Box is ventilated to dry out flies when stored. Box size is 6-1/4″ x 4″ x 1-1/8″ and fits easily into jacket or fishing vest pocket.

The plastic model "see through" fly box has unique trap doors over each fly compartment. These hinged trap doors have a window and slot in the top that provides space for one fly. This fly is the same pattern as the one contained underneath, but it can be identified without opening the lid.

The box contains six compartments each holding three or four flies. Box size is only 3-3/4″ x 4-1/4″ x 1-1/4″ and fits into most any pocket.

Martin also offers fly lines in level, double taper and weight forward designs in floating types, and sinking types in double tapers and weight forward styles.

They also furnish knotless leaders in 0X to 6X tippets, 7-1/2 foot and 9 foot lengths.

Martin offers a combination package which includes every item for the beginner fly fisherman. It contains a Tuffy rod, a level fly line, tapered leader and three lures, popper, fly and plastic worm. Shown above is the 833 Combo with a Model 60 single action reel.

The three automatic reels above indicate the versatility of the Martin line. Top is the Model 81, a medium priced reel with capacity to handle double taper or weight forward lines. Middle reel is the Model 94, a light weight model for double taper No. 6 lines. Bottom reel is Model 35 heavy duty. It will take 150 yards of backing plus a weight forward No. 9 fly line.

FENWICK—

SEVENSTRAND

TACKLE

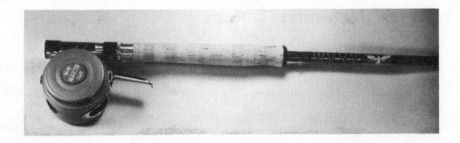

The standard model Fenwick rod above, has an ample cork handle comfortably shaped for hours of tireless casting. This rod features the Feralite self contained ferrule which produces a continuous curve and smooth action similar to a one-piece rod.

Sevenstrand Tackle Co. manufactures rods under the trade name of Fenwick.

Though this company also produces spinning and bait casting rods they have devoted much time and money to the development of fly rods. As a result Fenwick fly rods compare favorably with the best.

Sizes and types of Fenwick fly rods range all the way from a light six-foot, fresh water model to a heavy duty nine-foot, three inch salt water model.

Included in the Fenwick line is a complete selection of travel type rods known by the name Voyageur. These are multi-piece rods designed for convenience of carrying made possible by the short length of the sections. They are ideal for backpackers.

A special feature of the Fenwick rod is the Feralite self contained ferrule. This unique design is accomplished through the use of two separate rod blanks made for each rod.

Basically the Feralite design is simple. The butt piece of the rod is slightly tapered and fits directly into the hollow end of the tip section.

The tip end is also tapered and causes a wedging effect to lock the two sections together. There is no metal or other device involved. It provides a glass to glass connection.

This type of connection produces a full power, continuous, smooth curve which makes casting easier and more accurate.

Even the travel rods having three, four and five sections, are smooth

Fenwick makes a fine travel rod which is an excellent type for backpacking into high country. Models include fly rods and combination spinning and fly rods in three to five piece types breaking down to sections as short as 22 inches.

in casting performance because of this Feralite construction. It almost feels like a rod having a one or two piece shaft.

All models of Fenwick fly rods have actions that are slightly on the fast side, but they give top performance regardless of size.

Guides, wrappings and handles are all durably made and will with-

stand rugged use without breaking or failing.

The rods are lightweight for their length and yet extremely strong. When matched with the line weight recommended by the company, their performance leaves little to be desired. Prices are reasonable, well within the reach of a fly fisherman who wants a rod that will give years of service.

Fenwick Freshwater Fly Rods

Model	Length	Weight	Fly Line Spec.	
FF60	6'	2-5/8 oz.	5-6	Ultra light, medium action. For use with midge flies on small and/or brushy streams.
FF70	7'	3 oz.	5-6	Light, medium action dry fly rod. Ideal midge and other small dry fly fishing situations.
FF75	7-1/2'	3-1/4 oz.	5-6	A great choice for the all around dry fly action rod. This is the rod that fits in any place a trout does.
FF79	8'	3-1/2 oz.	6	A light regular action dry fly rod in 8' length. Designed for the dry fly fisherman who fishes the larger streams and brooks. Adequately handles a sinking line where one is needed.
FF80	8'	4 oz.	7-8	A medium fast action all-around 8 ft. fly rod. Extremely versatile, can be used fishing trout with dry flies, streamers or nymphs. This is a fine bass bug rod.
FF84	8-1/2'	4 oz.	5-6	A medium action slow taper 8-1/2 ft. fly rod. Handles beautifully a #5 line, and makes a wonderful dry fly rod for sensitive fishing situations.
FF85	8-1/2'	4-1/8 oz.	7-8	The truly all-around fly rod. Works well in fishing a dry fly. It handles a sinking fly line with superb ease.
FF86	8-1/2'	4-1/8 oz.	6	A light action regular taper 8-1/2 ft. fly rod designed to handle a 6 line. A truly beautiful trout rod.
FF90	9'	4-3/4 oz.	7-8	A medium light fast taper 9 ft. trout rod.

Fenwick Salmon & Steelhead Fly Rods

Model	Length	Weight	Fly Line Spec.	
FF107	9'	4-3/4 oz.	8-9	A rod nearly as versatile as the FF85, yet 9 ft. in length. A fine light action Steelhead and Atlantic Salmon fly rod. A fine rod for bassbugging.
FF108	9'	5-1/8 oz.	10	A medium heavy fast action rod, extremely useful in fishing big waters for big fish. Handles a shooting head with precision.
FF98	9'	4-3/4 oz.	10-11	A medium, heavy regular action powerful rod. Designed for use with heavy weight forward floating and sinking lines, sinking shooting heads and lead core lines. A rod designed for steelhead fishermen.
FF112	9'3"	5 oz.	9-10	A heavy action regular taper power rod based on the FF98 design yet 3" longer. The additional 3 in. give you that extra length that is needed in handling long and heavy lines while wading deep or while pushing a heavy wind resistant fly in a big wind. Also doubles as a salt water fly rod for the smaller in shore fish.
FF112S	9'3"	5 oz.	9-10	Same specifications as FF112, except has a 6" detachable fighting butt.

Fenwick Saltwater Fly Rods

Model	Length	Weight	Fly Line Spec.	
FF114	9'3"	5-3/4 oz.	10-11	A heavy duty regular action all-around salt water fly rod. Used to handle stripers, blue fish, albacore. A truly versatile rod for the salt water angler. Has permanently attached 2" fighting butt.

Fenwick Travel Fly Rods

Model	Length	Pack Length	Weight	Fly Line	
FF70-4	7'	22"	3-1/8 oz.	6	A four-piece medium light action fly rod for the small brush streams of the high back country. Breaks down to 22" sections. "TW" 14 oz.
FF75-4	7-1/2'	24"	3-1/2 oz.	6	A four-piece, truly versatile 7-1/2' pack rod with light action, regular taper. Designed for small bush streams, yet will lay out a long enough line for those back country lakes. Breaks down to 24" sections. "TW" 14 oz.
FF80-4	8'	25"	3-3/4 oz.	6	A four-piece medium regular action delicate trout rod. Designed for the big fish in big waters found in the back country. Breaks down to 25" sections. "TW" 15 oz.
FF85-3	8-1/2'	35-1/2"	3-7/8 oz.	6-7	A three-piece medium fast action fly rod that handles both sinking and floating lines. Makes dry fly fishing for small back country trout a real pleasure, yet has the power and action required to handle big fish. Breaks down to 35-1/2" sections. "TW" 16 oz.
FF85-5	8-1/2'	21-3/4"	4-1/8 oz.	8	A five-piece suitcase power action fly rod. Bassbugs, bonefish, stripers, and big trout water all fit into its qualifications. Breaks down to 21-3/4" sections. "TW" 16 oz.
FF107-5	8'10"	22-1/2"	4-3/4 oz.	9	A five-piece salmon and steelhead suitcase fly rod designed to reach out. Works well on small inshore salt water fish. Breaks down to 22-1/2" sections. "TW" 18 oz.
FF112-5	9'3"	23-5/8"	5-1/2 oz.	9-10	A five-piece salmon, steelhead and traveling salt water fly rod. The most powerful of the fly rod Voyageur series. Breaks down to 23-5/8" sections. "TW" 20 oz.

THE GARCIA CORP.

Garcia makes four different grades of fly rods in standard models, and two expensive models which were recently added.

All Garcia rods are made by a company called Garcia-Conolon. The name "Conolon" was included years ago when Garcia bought the Conolon company. Conolon had a reputation for building rods of fine quality, a reputation that has continued to this day.

Grades of Garcia-Conolon rods range from the top Deluxe models through the Brown, Avocado and Blue grades. The last three mentioned are moderate to lower priced models.

The two new lines offered are the Charles Ritz and the Lee Wulff models.

The Charles Ritz rods are described as long-flex, long-lift. Charles Ritz developed a technique of fly casting called High Speed - High Line and these rods are designed to perform these functions. The rod action gets the line off the water with little effort and the maximum flex and straightening power produces a higher than average back cast, which in turn develops a higher line speed. The total result of the foregoing is to produce longer casts, especially with heavier lines.

These rods featuring an internal ferrule come in lengths of 6-1/2', 7'1", 7'10", 8'2", 8'5", and salt water models in 8'5", and 8'10" lengths.

All length Charles Ritz rods are exceptionally strong and have fast actions, but are very easy to use, as timing of the cast is not as critical as in most rods. They are ruggedly built to stand hard use.

Another new fly rod in the Garcia line is the Lee Wulff model.

These are fine, high priced rods designed to give top performance in casting and in playing fish.

Lengths offered in this model are 6', 7', 7-1/2', 8', 8-1/2' and 9'. All have stainless steel guides and all are two-piece except the 7' model which is a four-piece backpacker model.

Light in weight, the Lee Wulff models are delicately balanced and comfortable to use. They are capable of producing line control second to none. Although seeming to be fragile, they can handle a tackle testing trout with ease.

Standard models in the Garcia stable of fly rods are of the expected high quality even in the lower priced lines.

Garcia also offers three models of fly reels, the Abu Delta 5, four standard single action reels, and the Mitchell Model 710 Automatic.

These are all top quality reels with the Abu Delta 5 being a superb single action, rugged, large capacity model that's a joy to use.

A complete range of fly lines are offered by Garcia, in floating and sinking types, in level, double taper and weight forward styles.

Long-Bellied Garcia Fly Lines

Fly fishing, like flying or gliding, is a thing of the air...strongly affected by air currents and wind. Just as a pilot learns to correct and allow for wind flow and gusts in bringing his plane to a perfect landing, so does the fly fisherman correct his casts as they make their final forward thrusts in order to place the fly perfectly.

In the same way, that a quick movement at one end of the rope will travel its length, and move the far end of the rope in response, a quick movement of the fly line, while the cast is unfolding, can move down its length and correct for wind displacement or other casting errors.

In actual fishing, few casts are perfect as made...most are corrected by shortening or extending the cast or changing the landing point to right or left. This can only be done when the heavy section of the line is still in the guides. Once the heavy section has left the guides, the lighter shooting line does not have enough weight to influence the "belly" while in its motion.

This is a great advantage for the skillful angler and one of the reasons many have clung to the old-style double-tapered lines. The main advantage of the double-tapered line for the expert fisherman, is that he has better control on long casts. The second is increased roll casting distance.

Garcia's long bellied-forward tapered fly line is identical in every respect with a double-tapered line, until the full belly and leader...about fifty feet...is extended beyong the guides. This covers most fishing casts.

Beyond this point, the Garcia long belly gives a greater length of cast, a casting length equivalent to that of the average forward taper.

Garcia lines not only are listed by number, but Garcia gives you the essential information necessary to make the proper selection: the diameter, the length of belly, the specific gravity.

ADVANTAGES

1. They still have the practical advantages of all forward taper lines in that:

a. They cast farther because they shoot line better than double tapered lines do. (The light line is easier to shoot through the guides behind a heavier head).

b. They take up less space on the reel than the double taper with its longer length of full diameter ...for the same total length.

2. They have the essential advantages of a double taper line in that:

a. They can be roll cast (for the full length of the belly).

b. They have the same longer front taper as the double taper for delicate fishing.

c. They offer cast correction control for longer casts ... which is extremely important for accuracy on long casts.

Above is the fine Garcia Abu-Delta 5 single action fly reel. It is not only unusual in appearance, but also in performance. It is made to take rugged use, however, it is light in weight giving a fine balance with any fresh water rod.

Charles Ritz and two battling size salmon taken on his Long Flex/Long Lift Garcia-Ritz fly rod using his high speed, high line casting technique. This new rod comes in longer, somewhat heavier models and it has great power incorporated into a fast action.

This gets the line off the water faster and contributes to a higher backcast. The action, plus the high backcast produce higher forward line speeds and thus accuracy.

It is an excellent choice rod for steelhead, Atlantic salmon and generally, larger fish in any waters.

The Garcia Mitchell 710 automatic fly reel is designed and engineered as a precision instrument. It has a built-in friction clutch that allows line to be stripped even when wound and a large capacity, open sided spool well. Tension is released quickly with turn of dial.

Garcia produces a wide choice of quality fly rods in all lengths to fit any kind of fly fishing situation. They are available at prices to fit any budget and in a broad range of actions to satisfy the personal likes of all fly fishermen. The high priced Lee Wulff and Charles Ritz models will delight the experienced fly man, while the Brown and Avocado models will suit the beginner or economy minded fly caster.

SHAKESPEARE

Shakespeare's rods are called "Wonderods". The company has made rods of all types for many years and their fly rods are among the best available.

A broad range of grades is offered from the top of the line Purist Series, to the moderate and lower priced Standard Series.

They also have a specialty line featuring ultra-light and heavy-duty salt water models designated as Ferrule-Free Wonderods. They come in a variety of lengths and actions from a fast taper to a universal action in lengths of 7'9", 8'6", 9', and 9'6".

Shakespeare Wonderods have a long time reputation for excellence in quality and performance and it has been earned on lakes, rivers and on saltwater by actual use.

The action of Shakespeare fly rods is very interesting in that it is hard to classify. It is an easy-to-cast action and seems to be the same for all lengths except the 9' and 9-1/2' heavy-duty models which are designed to handle larger fish.

Though Shakespeare rods are limber, the action is fairly fast, but not too stiff to prevent playing a fighting fish effectively.

Shakespeare offers a comprehensive selection of fly reels which includes three vertical automatic models, four horizontal automatics, three single action standard models, a heavy-duty single action type and three imported English single action reels.

Shakespeare fly lines include the Purist, Presidential and 7000 types. Purist lines are available along with Presidential lines in both floating and sinking styles.

The 7000 Model is a camouflage type only offered in a floater model.

All of these lines have proven to perform well under the conditions for which they were designed.

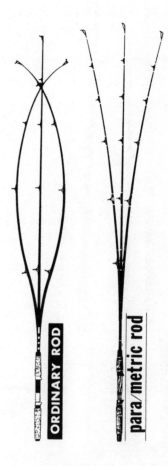

ORDINARY ROD   para/metric rod

This (below) is Shakespeare's heavy-duty fresh or salt water fly rod and reel. The reel is Model 1898 which will hold any fly line plus 200 yards of backing. The rod is Model FY940, a 9' long, Ferrule-Free type weighing 6-1/4 ozs.

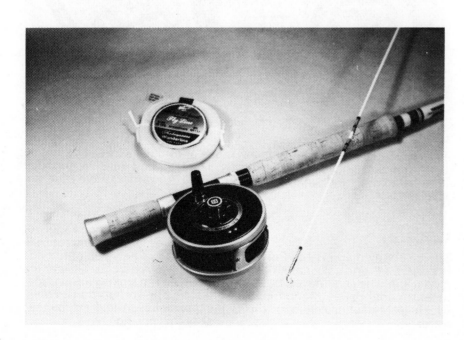

Berkley

Berkley Para/metric curved taper rods give high performance to any kind of fly casting. The action produced by this special taper gives extra power, sensitive, accurate casting with a minimum of vibration and whipping.

Fly rod models offered are the Custom Deluxe, Standard, Micro-Flex fast tip and the New Signature line.

All have the much desired curved taper action and are priced from moderately low to medium and are offered in popular lengths and in various actions from light to fast.

Line Manufacturers

Cortland

Cortland is one of the oldest fly line makers and have developed excellent lines of all types and sizes. Their Micro-Foam line is one of the finest floating lines available. The 333 line is moderately priced and the 444 line is the top of the line. Both come is floating and sinking types.

Garcia

The Garcia Corp. makes a complete range of fly lines. The Lee Wulff Long Belly line is the newest model offered. The standard lines are produced in both floating and sinking types in weight forward, Double taper and level models.

Shakespeare

The company markets the Purist, Presidential and a camouflage model line. They also have a translucent model called Mono-Blend which is almost invisible in the water.

Gudebrod

Gudebrod makes a wide variety of fishing lines and a complete selection of fly lines. Top of the line are the G-5 Nylon floater and the Sink-R Dacron sinking lines. Gudebrod has a fine reputation for making quality lines and the fly models justify this position.

BROWNING

Browning rods carry the name Sila-Flex a long time manufacturer of quality products. SilaFlex fly rods are probably the lightest of all and they feel like a feather when you pick one up. Nevertheless they are very strong and will project a line of any type with ease and accuracy. Browning offers eight fly rod models in 6', 7', 7½', 8', 8½', and 9' lengths and a 7' combination fly and spinning backpacker rod.

A

B

C

(A) This is a level line which is the same diameter its entire length. Can be used for all fly fishing conditions. (B) Double taper line has larger diameter center 20 to 25 yards long, and it tapers to a smaller diameter at both ends. Handles well in the wind and is used for dry, wet or nymph fishing. Provides longer casts than level type. (C) Weight forward taper line has larger diameter for 10 to 15 yards at the front end nearest the leader. Rear part of line is level. This line makes possible the longest casts with the greatest ease. It can be used for all types of fly fishing and handles well under all conditions, including wind.

Lines

Today's fly lines are a marvel of modern technology. Made of Nylon and other synthetic materials, they deliver excellent performance when properly matched to a well balanced rod.

Needing only a minimum of care they last for years in normal use.

Unlike the old silk lines, it is not necessary to dry them out after each days' fishing, and although cleaning them is recommended, this only needs to be done when fishing dirty or algae choked waters. In clean flowing rivers cleaning the line isn't needed at all.

When done fishing for the summer it is better to take the line off the reel, roll it into large loops and hang it on a hook for the winter.

Basically there are two types of fly lines, sinking and floating. There is another type, a combination that has a tip section of about 10 feet of line that sinks, but it is a highly specialized line and not in general use yet.

There are three basic fly line designs, level, double taper and weight forward or torpedo head.

Each of these designs are available in either sinking or floating types and in a choice of weights, usually from a No. 5 to No. 11.

Most popular and easy to use weights are 6, 7, and 8. Weights over or under call for very specialized and therefore limited use rods. Lines of 3, 4 and 5 weight require ultra light rods and are only suitable for small streams and pan sized fish. Lines in the 9, 10 and 11 weight class are for steelhead, atlantic salmon and larger ocean fish and are used on long, stiff rods 9, 9-1/2 and 10 feet in length.

No. 6, 7 and 8 lines are intended for general purpose, all around fresh water use. Equipped with the proper leader they are completely suitable for fish of 1 to 10 or 12 pounds that are taken with average length casts from fairly fast flowing streams or from reasonable depths in lakes.

Level lines are general purpose types for moderate distance casts in areas where wind is no problem. Double taper lines are good wind buckers and will allow longer casts than level types. Weight forward or torpedo heads handle well in high winds and can be cast longer distances than any other design.

Some suitable lines for deep water, either river or lake fishing would be a level, sinking type with a short, sinking monofilament leader; a sinking double taper with sinking leader for waters 5 to 10 feet deep when lake fishing for bottom feeding fish.

An adequate all around combination would be a floating, weight forward line with a sinking 7-1/2 foot leader for wet or dry flies or even streamers or bucktails.

Leaders

Early day leaders were made by tying together 2 or 3 foot pieces of monofilament of different weights to produce a proper rolling effect at the end of the line.

These leaders would have a piece of 12 pound test at the butt and then succeedingly less test pieces down to a tippet of 3 or 4 pound test.

Today leaders can be bought that achieve the same goal with one single-piece line of nylon or monofilament. They are tapered gradually from the butt to the tippet and make a delicate roll cast, gently and gracefully, and drop a fly onto the water without creating anything more than a dimple on the surface.

Leader lengths are mostly either 7-1/2 or 9 foot and tippet strength runs from 1 lb. test to 10 lb. test.

In clear shallow water it is best to use a 9 foot leader. For fast, translucent water a 7-1/2 foot one is suitable.

For fishing deep water with wet flies or streamers a shorter leader, 4 to 6 foot is best.

How to Tie

Your Own Flies

WHY TIE FLIES?

Only a few, more fortunate fly fishermen have the time and money to follow the sun in pursuit of fishing adventures. Most devotees of the long rod have to be content with an all too short season that is squeezed between the high water of early spring and storms of autumn.

For the majority of fly fishermen then, fly tying can be a way to extend their fishing fun through the winter months. It becomes a hobby within a hobby.

Also, fly tying is a way for advanced fly fishermen to carry out personal ideas on fly design and construction. Even when tying the standard patterns, quality is likely to be improved as a good amateur can spend time and personal effort to produce exactly the effect he seeks. There is no pressure to rush the job or use a fly that does not turn out just right.

"Store bought" flies are costly but economy is only a minor reason for taking up the art of creating flies from steel, feathers, fur and silk. This is the usual stated reason for tying flies for personal use but it doesn't hold true for those who have become hooked on the idea. The deeper a fisherman becomes absorbed in this most delightful pursuit, the more likely he is to invest in expensive tools and exotic materials to carry out his creative impulses.

Fly tying is one of the most fascinating facets of the fly fishing game. It's also one of the most productive—the results are likely to be reflected in a heavier creel at the end of a fishing day.

THE TOOLS FOR TYING

The right tools are vital for tying good flies. A vise to hold the hook during the tying operation, scissors to trim materials, hackle pliers for winding hackles, and a bodkin or dubbing needle are all the tools actually needed to turn out a good product but most tiers eventually add other items to make the job easier. These often include a bobbin to hold the thread, a whip finisher or half hitch tool to finish the fly head, a lance or razor blade for various cutting operations, winging pliers for attaching feather section wings, hackle guards, hook sharpening stone and other implements to simplify the tying of quality flies.

A pair of "vise-grip" pliers held down with a "C" clamp will hold most hooks but a good vise is infinitely better. Such an instrument will hold the hook securely while various materials are being attached, it will have smooth, tapered jaws to prevent snagging the tying thread and to allow more working room, it will hold the fly at the right height during tying operations, and it will quickly grasp or release most sizes of hooks.

Less expensive vises often have a knurled knob that is turned to tighten or loosen the jaws. More expensive models use a lever principle to clamp the jaws together. Pushing down on the lever closes the jaws on the hook; pushing up on the lever releases the hook. One type of vise has jaws that rotate—instead of winding materials around and around the hook, the jaws are rotated by turning a small wheel while materials are fed onto the hook shank.

Most professionals and top amateur tiers use the lever-operated, stationary-type vises.

Whichever type is chosen, the outside surfaces of the jaws must be smooth and the mechanism that opens and closes the jaws should work easily. Some vises are adjustable for hook size and this is a good feature if a variety of fly sizes are to be tied.

Scissors for fly tying should have sharp points. Special fly tying scissors are excellent but good embroidery scissors from the local sewing shop will do almost as well. Scissors developed for performing delicate surgery, such as eye operations, are the very best but they are quite expensive.

It is a good idea to have 2 pairs of scissors—small, fine pointed ones for close work and a heavier pair for cutting tinsel and other tough materials.

Hackle feathers, particularly those long, slick types that are best for dry flies, are normally wrapped around the hook with the help of a pair of hackle pliers. The so-called English type, made of round wire with flattened, tapered jaws, have long been the standard but they have to be carefully selected. Jaws must come together evenly to prevent cutting the hackle at the critical moment. Jaws that are scored too deeply will also cut hackle feathers. Some American made hackle pliers have rubber pads in the jaws to prevent hackle cutting. These are excellent but the jaws are somewhat too wide for tying very tiny hackles on size 16 or smaller hooks. Again, medical science fills the gap— arterial forceps from surgical supply houses have proven ideal for handling tiny hackles, although they too are expensive.

A bodkin, dubbing needle, or stiletto is really nothing more than a needle with a handle. The better ones are made specifically for fly tying but one can be easily made by pushing the eye of a large needle into a piece of wood dowel, plastic, or a large bottle cork. A magnetized point on the bodkin is handy for picking up small hooks but the home-made bodkin can be quite easily magnetized with any small magnet simply by stroking from handle to point on the bodkin. A bodkin is very useful for picking out hackles that become accidentally wrapped under, placing cement on the fly head after it is tied off, and for numerous other jobs around the fly tying bench.

Various methods are used to tie off the thread after a fly is finished. The best of these employ the so-called invisible knot to prevent the fly head from unraveling. The whip finisher is a rather complicated gadget for doing this but nothing seems to do the job as well.

Half hitch tools—tapered instruments with a hole or depression in the small end—also do a good job. One can be made from an old ball point pen if the tip doesn't taper too abruptly.

Some tiers simply throw a number of half hitches to finish off the fly head but this looks sloppy and is more likely to begin unravelling.

Even the very finest fly tying hooks are seldom as sharp as they should be to prevent missing strikes. A hook stone will solve this problem. Before a fly is tied, it's an easy matter to touch up the hook point with the right kind of stone. Regulation hook stones are sold by most sporting goods stores but they are usually a little too thick for sharpening the smaller hooks. A jeweler's file works on small hooks if a light touch is used. Best of all is a knife-edged Arkansas oil stone sold in most drafting supply stores. Such stones are white, about 3-1/2 inches long and thick on one long edge and beveled to a thin "blade" on the other long edge. The grit is very fine and the thin edge is narrow enough for honing the inside of the point on the tiniest hooks. Again, higher quality naturally costs more.

A single edge razor blade, a sharp lance or one of the X-acto-type knives with interchangeable blades is useful for cutting dangling threads, stray hair fibers, and for removing all materials from a hook when the tying effort has gone wrong. Some of the X-acto-type handles will hold injector-type razor blades and this

combination is nearly perfect for fly tying work.

One of the most difficult operations in tying flies is attaching wings made from sections of duck and other wing feathers. Such wings require the tier to "squeeze" the fibers together while preventing a natural tendency to curl or roll. Such wings are quite fragile as they tend to split apart after taking a fish or 2. Consequently, they are gradually being phased out of many a fly box. They should, however, be part of any good fly tier's "repertory." 2 instruments have been specifically designed to make this particular operation easier.

Winging pliers hold such feather sections absolutely flat while the tying thread compresses the fibers down onto the hook shank. Experienced fly tiers learn to use the thumb and index finger to hold the sections flat but the beginning fly tier might well consider winging pliers to do the job faster and neater.

Another gadget called the wing former also simplifies this operation. The wing former uses metal combs to squeeze the fibers together and form a series of wings from a feather. The narrow "waist" formed for each wing when the fibers are compressed is then coated with a special, clear cement to hold that shape. Wings are then cut from the feather as needed. Combs with teeth of varying widths are supplied to allow forming wings of different sizes.

FLY TYING MATERIALS

Practically anything and everything has or can be used in making flies. Some materials are common, everyday items that can be found around the house; others are strange sounding, exotic feathers or hair imported at considerable expense and effort from various parts of the world.

Small cork stoppers can be turned into bass-busting top water bugs,

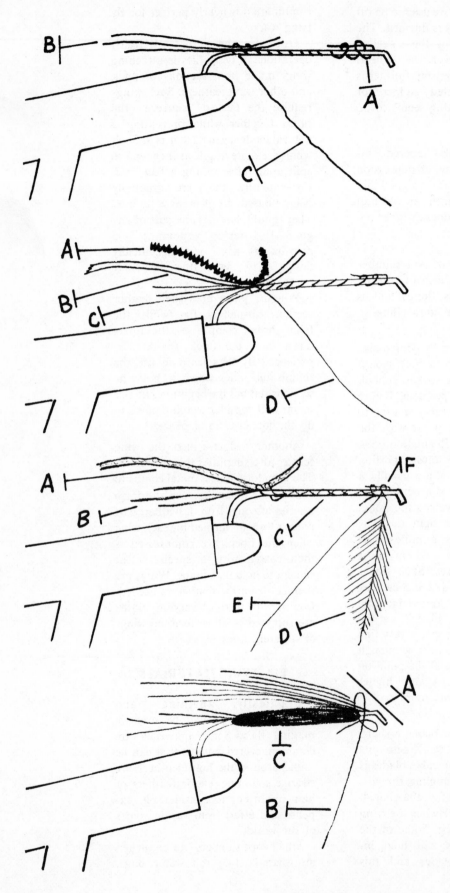

To start most flies, wax the tying thread, then tie or wrap end on shank of hook about 1/16th to 1/8th inch behind the eye (A). Wrap about ten turns around shank of hook to the bend at rear. At this point tie in tail hairs (B) or feathers. (C) Tying thread leading to bobbin or spool.

To tie in any material before wrapping on hook it is necessary to wrap tying thread around the entire length of the shank. Then Chenille (A) or tinsel (B) can be attached at rear with the tying thread. Either one or both tinsel and chenille can be attached. Thread is then wound to the front of the shank. Chenille and/or tinsel are then wound forward over the thread and tied off about 1/8th inch behind the eye.

If a hackle feather is to be used, it can be tied in at the front of the shank with thread and then wound around the shank at (F). The hackle is wound over itself. (A) Shows how wool can be tied in, the same as chenille or tinsel. Thread is wound over itself (C) and back to the front to tie hackle (D). (B) Tail. (E) Thread.

To tie in hair at front it is necessary to cut hair on a slant (A) from front to back. Hold hair between thumb and index finger, place drop of cement on hair, then tie with thread and hold with half-hitch until cement is dry. (C) Wool body. (B) Thread.

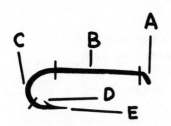

Parts of a hook: (A) Eye, (B) Shank, (C) Bend, (D) Barb, (E) Point.

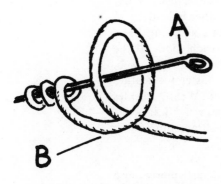

When it is necessary to anchor the thread at any point, use a half-hitch as shown as this allows thread to be used in a continuing procedure without cutting and retying.

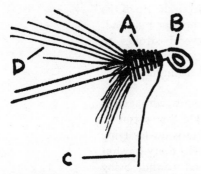

All heads are tied with thread and should be tapered (A). Thread is built up where hair or hackle (D) start and then tapered down to just behind eye (B) with progressively fewer turns of thread (C).

It is easy to place drop of cement accurately on any desired spot by using pointed wooden toothpick.

Fly Tyer's Glossary

Barb-Needle sharp projection facing opposite direction of hook point to keep fish from escaping.

Bend-Round part of hook curving from shank to barb and point.

Bobbin-Device that holds spool of tying thread controlling feed of thread through a narrow tube.

Body-This is the part of the fly tied on the shank of the hook. It is made of various materials such as floss, wool yarn, tinsel, chenille, fur, hair or combinations of two or more of these materials.

Butt-Made of wool or chenille tied on at end of shank just before the bend of the hook. Also called an egg sac by many tyers.

Cement-Usually thick, fast drying lacquer used to secure the tying thread, chenille, wool, tinsel and other materials to hook.

Chenille-Looks like a caterpillar without legs. It is made by weaving silk or rayon fibers between two threads. It comes in many colors and is used for the body on dry or wet flies or nymphs.

Egg Sac-Extra piece of wool or chenille tied on hook at the end of the shank just before the bend. Is of larger diameter than body. Also called the "Butt."

Eye-Round loop at the end of the hook used to attach leader or line.

Floss-A loosely woven thread having a high lustre. Furnished on small spools of two or four strands. Two or four strands unwind at the same time. Used mainly to build up fly body of all types of flies.

Fur-Used for fly bodies. Usually comes from small animals such as rabbits, moles, badgers, beavers, muskrat and others. Some animals like beavers and badgers provide both hair and fur, the fur coming from an area close to the skin.

Hackle-A small, but long and narrow feather from the neck area of domestic fowl or wild ducks, geese or upland birds. It is tied into a fly pattern just behind the eye of the hook. The tip is tied to the shank of the hook and then the rest of the feather is wound around it and secured with a halfhitch and cement. The hackle is also used on the body of a wooly worm being interwrapped with chenille along the entire length of the shank. Most flies, both wet and dry, have a hackle of some kind.

Hackle pliers-A small clamp type tool for holding hackles or thread in an out-of-the-way position while working on another part of the fly. Clothes pins will do the same job.

Half-hitch-A simple loop made with the tying thread to hold it in place without cutting the thread. It allows the tyer to continue wrapping the same thread to secure other parts of the fly.

Hair-Stiff bristly fibers from polar bears, deer, squirrels, moose, calves, badgers or skunks. Used mainly for wet flies or streamers.

Head-Area just behind the eye of the hook made with several wraps of the tying thread. It is either cemented or lacquered.

Lacquer-A fast drying, clear synthetic liquid having a high cellulose content. Used as cement when thick, as a paint when thinned and colored.

Legs-Made from thick bristles or rubber strips to imitate insect legs.

Ribbing-Usually made with tinsel. Is wrapped leaving spaces between turns. Applied to body of fly often over wool or chenille.

Shank-Straight part of hook between eye and bend.

Silk- Tying thread. Sometimes nylon thread is used.

Tag-Tied on rear end of hook at the start of the bend. Made of wool or tinsel.

Tail-Three or four hairs tied at rear of hook. Extends from one-half to one inch to the rear of shank.

Thread-Same as tying thread. Made of silk or nylon. Used to attach most parts of a fly pattern.

Tinsel-Flat metallic tape in gold or silver and other colors. Comes in various widths from 1/16th to 3/8ths of an inch.

Tip-Same as Tag.

Vise-Tool used to clamp hook in position at convenient working height.

Wax-Beeswax or paraffin wax. Used to coat the thread and make it adhere lightly to hook.

Wing-Part of fly made to imitate insect wings. Made from hair or from actual sections of wing feathers.

Wool-Yarn of the same kind used in knitting. Used to make fly bodies by wrapping around shank of hook.

and wool and thread from the little woman's sewing basket can be transformed into buggy looking nymphs that are deadly for trout.

On the other hand, bali duck, macaw or blue chatterer feathers as well as monkey hair, seal fur and other unique but often useful materials can be difficult if not downright impossible to get.

Fly tiers who hunt realize the value of the hair, fur and feathers worn by game they collect, but vast quantities of good fly tying materials are thrown away annually by other hunters. Non-hunting fly tiers should ask hunting friends to save certain materials useful for tying flies.

Various feathers probably constitute the majority of fly tying materials, and hackle feathers are among the most important of all. Hackles come from the neck and back of various kinds of birds but those found on domestic chickens bred for the purpose are the most useful.

Hackles form the "legs" on most wet flies and nymphs, while high floating dry flies have a collar of one or more turns of stiff hackle. Hackle feathers are also used for streamer fly wings, and hackle tips make excellent wings for dry and wet flies.

Neck hackles are most commonly used. These come from the area on a chicken's neck beginning just behind the head and extending well onto the back. Spade hackles, which are short and wide, are found on the back, while the long, narrow saddle hackles grow just forward of the tail.

Neck hackles are standard for wet and dry flies; spade hackles, which are seldom available from fly tying supply houses, are prized for making the wide hackled, spider-type dry flies; and saddle hackles will frequently work as dry fly hackle if narrow enough. They are practically standard as streamer wings, and the wider ones will sometimes serve for hackling spider flies.

Hackles also come from ringneck pheasants, grouse, guinea hens, and a few other birds, but these usually have specialized uses, such as legs on nymph flies.

Neck hackles from hens are usually softer, not so narrow for their length, and with more "web" than rooster hackle. Web is usually obvious when the feather is held up to the light. It appears as a dull band extending along each side of the feather shaft. The wider this web, which is soft, the faster the feather will soak up water. Webby hackles then are best for wet flies, while hackles with a small amount of web are better for drys.

Rooster hackles, particularly those from older, more weathered birds, are usually long and narrow. They have a definite sheen and are usually much less webby. Good rooster or dry fly hackles can be tested by stroking the fibers from the tip of the feather toward the heavier butt end. It should take several strokes to make the fibers stand out at right angles to the feather shaft.

The true test comes with actual use. Rarely, a hackle that seems to have all the characteristics for tying good dry flies will twist every way but the way it's supposed to while being wrapped on a hook. Such hackles will cause more frustration than they are worth.

Chicken hackles come in a variety of natural colors, and practically any dyed color. Natural colors include: reddish brown, often referred to as red in fly tying lingo; coachman brown, a flat, rich brown; ginger or tan; cream, an ivory or off white; blue dun, which is light gray; iron blue dun—dark gray; bronze blue dun or gray with a rusty red tinge; badger, a white or creamy tan feather with a dark center stripe; furnace, brown with a dark stripe down the center; grizzly, a black and white barred feather commonly referred to as gray; ginger grizzly, a light ginger with brown barring; red grizzly, a dark ginger with fiery brown bars; multicolored, a grizzly with tinges of rusty brown; and even one known as cochy-bondhu, a furnace with black edges.

Reds, yellows, greens, blues, etc., are dyed hackles. Black hackles of dry fly quality seldom occur naturally so good black hackles are almost always dyed. If the original quality was good, careful dyeing does not reduce the strength of the fibers or their ability to float a fly. However, dyed hackles are usually considered inferior to the natural ones because the natural hackles are thought to have more "life" or sparkle.

Neck hackles are usually available on the skin, which is then called a hackle neck, or in small packets of a dozen or so loose feathers. Necks provide a wider variety of hackle sizes and are likely to be less expensive in the long run.

Saddle hackles usually come in packets, but are sometimes available either bundled or strung on thread. If only a few are needed, the packets are good. When a lot of saddle hackles are to be used, bundled or strung feathers are more economical.

Some flys require herl or quill bodies. A herl is 1 fiber from a large feather, usually ostrich or peacock. Such fibers make lifelike, fuzzy bodies that are very effective, and they are sometimes used to form legs for nymph patterns. If the fluff is rubbed off of a herl, either with a soft eraser or by scraping with a blunt edge, it leaves a flexible strip called quill that produces buggy looking, segmented bodies when wrapped on a hook. Peacock quills

sometimes have a 2-color effect that is particularly good for fly bodies.

Peacock herls are a buggy, metallic green color, but ostrich herls are available in many dyed shades. Various colored ostrich herls are sometimes required for tying Atlantic salmon patterns.

The individual fibers from a ringneck pheasant tail feather also makes excellent fly bodies in the smaller sizes. Though quite fragile, such fibers produce a fuzzy silhouette that is particularly attractive on small nymphs and dry flies. Fibers from the flight feathers of the South American condor have long been used to make fly bodies. These natural gray fibers can be used in their fuzzy original state or stripped for excellent quill bodies. Almost any large bird—goose, swan, heron, etc.,—has large flight feathers that have fibers of use in making fly bodies. Most such birds are protected to varying degrees by State or Federal laws and fly tiers must rely on loose feathers picked up afield or birds that have been legally taken during hunting season.

The barred body feathers found on most wild ducks, as well as body feathers from many different birds, are useful for tying flies. The lemon-shaded flank feathers from wood duck drakes is prized by most fly tiers, and the rusty, barred flank feathers on mallard drakes, plus barred black and white breast feathers on mallard, teal, gadwall and various other ducks are also good. Such feathers are usually used to make wings on both wet and dry flies, and as buggy looking feelers on various nymph patterns.

Body plumage from grouse, partridge, and guineas have bars that make them suitable for nymph legs. The various pheasants also have body feathers that are required for

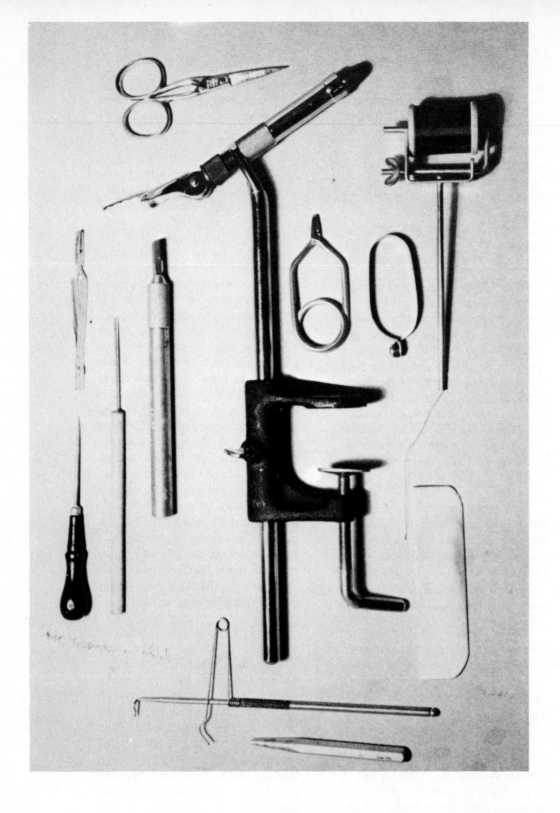

An assortment of fly tying tools. The vise is in the center; to the left are two bodkins, an interchangeable blade knife and a pair of winging pliers. Above the vise is a pair of sharp pointed fly tying scissors. Two different styles of hackle pliers are to the right of the vise, and a bobbin with a spool of black thread is right of the hackle pliers. The white object below the bobbin is a white Arkansas knife-edge stone used for sharpening hooks. Immediately below the vise is a whip finisher and below it is an aluminum half-hitch tool.

tying many standard fly patterns. Golden pheasant tippets—orange neck feathers with black bars—are used for making tails on many standard ties, as are the pure white, black barred tippets from the Lady Amherst pheasant. The brilliant yellow crest feathers from the golden pheasant is also used as a topping on many of the colorful Atlantic salmon flies.

Junglefowl, also known as jungle cock, have a unique feather that many fly tiers use. These so-called "nail" or eye feathers from the neck and back have a glossy, plastic-like spot that makes lifelike eyes on streamer and bucktail flies. These nail feathers also form the wing on the popular jassid-type flies.

The familiar ring-necked pheasant rooster has an abundance of colorful feathers that can be used in fly making. The bluish-green neck feathers are excellent for making beetle imitations, and the other body feathers make excellent nymph feelers, wet fly wings, and tails.

The fluffy plumes from the lower body and legs of Africa's carrion eating marabou stork is used to make about the fish-catchingest streamer flies known. These plumes are available in many different colors with the most popular being black, white and yellow. Marabou plumes are so light and fluffy they are difficult to work with and the resulting streamer would seem to scare more fish than it would catch. When these fibers get wet, however, it's a different story. The slinky action makes marabou streamers one of the most productive flies for several different kinds of fish.

Although wing and tail feathers were touched on lightly in the discussion of herls and quills, their primary usefullness in fly tying is in making wings for wet and dry flies. A section of these fibers are removed, being careful not to let them separate, and then matched with a section from the opposite, matching wing feather, and tied on with the use of winging pliers, or fingers if the tier is experienced. Although such wings are opaque, which reduces their imitative ability, and quite fragile under fishing conditions, they are the standard for many fly wings. In some cases, they are the only material that will come adequately close in color and shape.

Sections from wing and tail feathers are also used for making the tail on simple wet flies, and the individual fibers make excellent feelers for nymphs.

Many different kinds of hair also see considerable use in the making of fishing flies. In fact, hairwing flies that simulate minnows and other small fish are usually called bucktails, regardless of the type of hair used to make them. The original flies of this type were tied with the tail hair from buck white-tailed deer. Squirrel-tail flies are another bucktail-type fly named for the material used in their construction.

Deer body hair has long been used in making flies, particularly floating bugs for bass. Early American Indians used to make flies by wrapping soaked deer skin, with the hair left on, around a bone, wood or metal hook. Deer body hair is hollow, making it an excellent floating material. In recent years, dry flies with clipped deer hair bodies have become increasingly popular, particularly in the brawling western streams. Some deer body hair is used to make wings for dry and wet flies.

White-tailed deer usually have the best hair for fly tying purposes, although mule deer hair is also good. Some hides from certain Asiatic deer

NEW FLY TYING DESK

The fly tying desk is ideal for those only having limited work space and who don't want a permanent tying table. This new desk is a perfect size, being a compact 10'' x 15½''. The vise stand is detachable so that either side of the base can be used. One side is cork covered and the other is hard-surfaced for cutting. The vise stand is equipped with wires to hold flies while they dry. The desk was designed by and is available from Ed Sisty Angling Adventures, 3751 Inca St., Denver, Colorado. 80211.

are imported and the weird sounding Brazilian mouse deer has hair that makes excellent wet and dry fly wings.

Bucktails from white-tailed deer are white on the underside and grayish-brown on top. The white hair takes dyes readily and is available from fly tying supply houses in a number of colors. Tail hair is not hollow so it readily sinks and it is long with fairly fine texture—characteristics that make it ideal for many bucktail fly patterns.

Caribou have body hair of a finer texture than white-tailed or mule deer hair and it is better for spinning hair bodies, particularly in the smaller sizes. Pronghorn hair is courser than deer hair, but it is fairly easy to work and makes fine bass bugs.

Calf tail, also known as kip or impali, is available in a variety of dyed and natural colors. It has a crinkled texture, a natural sheen and is easy to use. The longer hair is excellent for making bucktails, and the shorter hair is outstanding for winging hairwing dry flies and wet flies. Calf tails in white, black, red, yellow, brown, and gray should be in every fly tiers kit. Single color, bi-color, and tri-colored bucktail wings are easy to tie with inexpensive but highly useful material.

Various kinds of squirrel tails are also used in tying flies. The common gray squirrel and the fox squirrel are most widely available, but major fly tying material suppliers import other squirrel tails, several with pretty weird names. The diminutive little pine squirrel, colorwise a junior edition of the fox squirrel, has good fly tying hair. All squirrel tails are very good for bucktail wings, salmon fly wings, and for winging the larger wet and dry flies. Squirrel tail has a fish catching sheen and action but the hair is not easy to tie on so it will stay. Squirrel tail hair is very hard and will not compress the way some other hairs will. It's hardly un-common for squirrel tail wings to pull loose all at once. Throwing an extra loop or 2 of tying thread just around the half seems to help hold it on but even this doesn't always do the trick.

Polar bear, black bear, and grizzly bear hair are all good for fly tying purposes, with polar bear hair being the most useful. It has a natural translucence that produces a look-alive appearance in the water. Polar bear hair comes in the natural off-white shade, and dyed black, red, yellow, blue, green and almost any shade in-between. It is primarily used in making bucktails and steelhead flies. The under-fur from polar bear is also used as dubbing material for fly bodies. Hair from other bears is usually fine-textured and crinkled, making it also effective for bucktails when the color is appropriate.

Although difficult to acquire, some types of monkey hair make excellent fly wings. Orange baboon, silver monkey, black monkey and black and white monkey are the most useful. Some of this hair is long and soft, producing excellent bucktail wings. Other is of firmer texture, often with a beautifully speckled appearance, that is ideal for wet and dry fly wings and tails.

Badger, skunk, fox, and just about any hair of the right length and texture can be used for tying flies. Even moose mane has a role in the fly tying game. 1 black and 1 white hair from the back of a moose's neck can be wrapped on the hook shank in alternating bands to produce an attractive, mosquito-like body. Moose mane is also useful as feelers for nymphs.

The shorter, finer textured fur found on a number of common animals produces highly effective fly bodies when spun on the tying thread and then wrapped around the hook shank. Depending on the kind of fur used, such bodies have good floating qualities. Certain other furs soak up water a little faster and these are excellent for wet flies and nymphs.

Fur bodied flies seem to be particularly translucent and lifelike in the water. The indistinct outline, tiny bubbles caught in the fur fibers, and the crawly movement of the longer fibers seem to suggest food to most species of fish.

Fur for fly tying is available on the skin, or already spun into strands and then wound on cards. The spun fur is the easiest to use by beginning tiers but it is limited in texture and resistance to water. Most spun fur is made from rabbits. It usually consists of 3 strands so it can be wound as is for heavier bodies, or separated and wound for smaller bodies. Spun fur is easy to work with and it produces effective bodies but the more experience a fly tier gains, the more he is likely to turn to spinning his own "dubbing" from fur that comes right off the skin.

Fur bearing animals that live in or near the water produce the best fur for fly tying, particularly dry flies. Muskrat fur is one of the best. This beautiful, water resistant fur is generally a flue-gray color fading to light, almost white next to the skin. The tip of most of the fibers is a soft brown. Long, glassy guard hairs are scattered through the fur and these make excellent tails for dry flies. Muskrat fur dubbing is called for in a number of standard fly patterns.

Other water oriented animals such as beaver, mink and otter also have fur that is excellent for making dry fly bodies.

Seal fur is considered the best of all the dubbing furs. This soft, silky and translucent fur is extremely easy to spin, it's available in natural plus a number of dyed colors, and simply has that extra something that brings on the strikes. Seal fur is rarely found on the skin; most of it is sold in loose packets after being clipped from the hide.

Red fox skins have a soft underfur in varying shades that produces fine fly bodies and some patterns require cream fox belly fur. Fur from moles, squirrels, rabbits, lynx, Australian possum, badger and many other animals can also be spun for fly bodies.

Wool yarn, which is actually an animal's "fur", was one of the first materials to be used for making flies. Wool that is specially spun for fly tying is best. Regular knitting yarn is often too thick for smaller flies but crewel yarn is excellent. Wool yarn comes in just about every color under the sun, but it does soak up water which makes it more suitable for use in making wet flies and nymphs.

Grass is even used to make fly bodies. A material known as raffia, which comes from a tough grass found in Africa, is excellent for making segmented fly bodies similar to those wrapped with quill. Raffia is available in various colors but it is somewhat fragile. It is wrapped on the hook shank the same way quill is applied.

There are a number of synthetic or man-made materials that have been developed or adapted for fly tying. Fly tying chenille is one of the most useful. Chenille supposedly comes from the French word for caterpillar. It consists of fibers spun onto a central core to produce a fuzzy, rope-like strand. Chenille is available in different sizes and practically all the fly tying colors. Chenille bodies are particularly effective on streamers and wet flies. This is the standard body for the famous wooly worm pattern.

Floss is a smooth material, either of silk or nylon, that forms nicely tapered bodies on smaller flies. It is unusually effective when ribbed with shiny tinsel. Silk floss is usually available in truer colors but it will not last as long and it is more difficult to work. The fine fibers catch on the slightest roughness, such as chapped hands or rough fingernails. Nylon floss is tougher, will stretch somewhat and therefore make smoother bodies, and it will not rot. Another type of floss, usually of rayon, can be wrapped on the hook, then dipped into acetone to melt it together for an unusual and practically indestructible fly body.

Various reflective materials, usually of metal but lately of plastic, are frequently used in making flies. Most of these tinsels are made so they will not tarnish. Tinsel can be flat and in varying widths, oval—narrow flat tinsel wrapped around a thread core—thin wire, embossed to increase its reflective qualities, and all tinsel chenille.

Tinsel, especially the embossed kind, is available in a variety of colors but gold and silver should be chosen unless some special application is foreseen.

Several kinds of wire have entered into the fly tying picture. Brass, copper or silver wire is frequently used to wrap bodies on the colorful flies designed for steelhead fishing. The extra weight helps to sink the fly to fishing levels in the fast moving western steelhead rivers, and the additional flash just adds to the attraction for these sea-going rainbows.

Lead wire in various diameters is frequently used to weight flies. Weighted nymphs and bucktails often produce when unweighted patterns fail, especially in fast water or deep, mountain lakes. The lead can either be wrapped around the hook shank before the body is applied, a method that builds up weight very fast, or 1, perhaps 2, pieces of lead wire the length of the hook shank can be wrapped to the shank with tying thread. Lead wire must always be coated with cement before the fly body is wrapped as the lead will discolor most other materials.

A plastic floss is available from several fly material supply sources. This material is a small tube of plastic, sometimes in different colors, that can be wrapped onto the hook for a tough and lifelike fly body.

There are also certain plastics that can be molded on the hook to form fly bodies. Such flies often look good to fishermen but they seem to lack appeal for the fish! They are fun to work with and some interesting results can be obtained, especially when combined with other, more natural materials.

Sponge rubber bodies make effective flies. This material is usually available as closed cell—meaning it has closed air spaces and therefore floats indefinitely—and as open cell which absorbs water to sink. Deadly panfish flies can be constructed by trimming a piece of open cell sponge rubber to shape, glueing it on the hook, and then adding rubber band legs by pulling them through with a needle. The "crawly" action of the rubber legs combined with the soft, "squishy" body is particularly good for bluegills.

Plastic foam, balsa wood, and cork are all used to make hard bodied bugs for panfish and bass. In larger sizes, they are also used for salt water fish such as snook. These materials

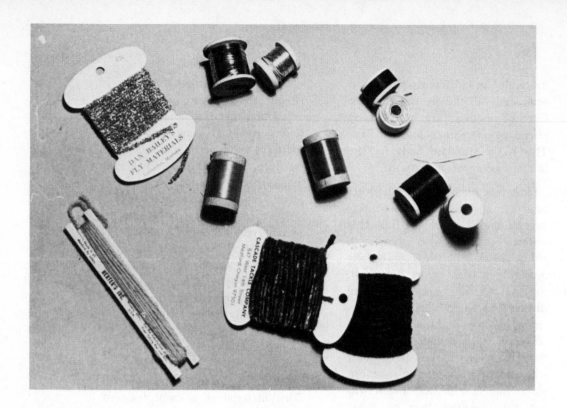

Ready made fly tying body materials include: chenille shown in the lower right; wool on lower left; tinsel chenille in upper left; flat and oval tinsels at top; button hole twist silk in upper right; floss on right and copper and brass wire on spools in center.

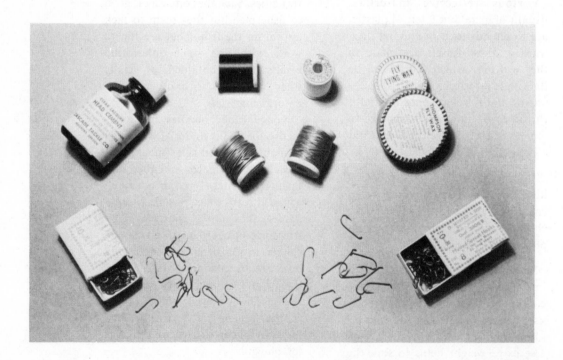

Fly tying hooks, head cement, black and white threads, and fly tying wax are vital for fly tying. The two sizes of lead wire shown in center are useful for weighting flies.

are trimmed to rough shape with a razor blade or sharp knife, sanded smooth, glued on the hook and then painted.

Most of the fly tying materials discussed have to be attached to the hook with tying thread. Threads come in a number of different sizes, several colors, round or flat, and silk or nylon. Thread size is determined by the size of the fly and the materials being used. The sizes best suited to fly tying are usually designated by numbers—2-0, 4-0, 6-0 and 8-0. There are in between numbers but these 4 sizes will handle just about any fly tying job. The 2-0 is the heaviest. The 8-0 size is quite fragile and should be used on only the smallest flies, and then only after considerable experience.

Black is the most common color for tying flies but white is a close second and should be used on the lighter colored flies. Other colors, such as red, yellow, brown, green and gray, have specialized application as in tying nymphs.

Anytime 2 fly tiers get together, they are liable to begin arguing the relative merits of silk thread over nylon, or vice versa. Silk has long been the standard and is still preferred by most professional fly tiers. It is strong, easy to work, and does not stretch. It does rot over a period of time but many silk-tied flies have been in service for years.

Nylon is usually stronger than silk of the same diameter, it tends to be wiry in the larger sizes, it will not rot but it does have some stretch. Nylon thread is not as expensive as silk and is perfectly suitable for most fly tying work. A new type of nylon, called Monocord, recently became available to fly tiers. Monocord is a flat, single strand thread that is available in several colors. It is somewhat wiry but does an excellent job in most situations.

There are other types of flat nylon threads on the market and these are particularly good for making nymph flies. Silk buttonhole twist, available on small spools from most sewing shops, is fairly large, available in numerous colors, and makes excellent ribbing material for flies.

Size 4-0 nylon thread in both black and white colors is a good choice for beginning tiers. With some experience, 6-0 in nylon or silk should be added for tying the average size trout flies.

Fly tying hooks are practically a study in themselves. Nearly every size, length, shape and weight has some application in making fishing flies.

For example, hook eyes are sometimes formed from wire that is the same diameter as the shank, which makes it a ball eye, or it might be formed from a tapered end of the wire, hence becoming a tapered eye. Hooks that have tapered eyes are preferred for making dry flies as the weight is less, however slight the reduction might be. Ball eye hooks are best for wet flies, nymphs and other flies designed to sink.

Hook eyes are sometimes straight out (ringed eyes), or kinked up or down. Turned up eyes (TUE) are often used for dry flies on the theory that they aid pickup of the fly. The idea is that turned down eyes (TDE) might scoop or dig into the water. In fishing, no advantage seems too small!

Turned down eye hooks are a bit easier for beginning fly tiers to use as the thread is usually pulled vertically during final tying operations and it tends to slip off up-eyed hooks. It takes considerable experience at tying flies before learning to leave enough space behind the eye for

Many and varied are the types of hair used for fly tying. The few shown here include: moose mane on the left; polar bear hair above the moose mane; deer body hair, badger hair, and caribou hair in that order to the right of the polar bear hair. The two long white tails at the bottom are calf tails, often called kip or impalla; and across the center are a fox and a gray squirrel tail.

Various furs, especially from aquatic animals, are among the best materials for making fly bodies. These include spun furs shown on cards at top of photo, muskrat to the right, black seal fur, white dyed beaver, bluish-gray mole, and chinchilla.

finishing off the head. Once this has been learned however, it makes little difference to the tying process whether the eye is turned up, down or ringed.

Hook bends are quite varied. The old sneck bend looked as though it had been bent around a box. It was formed of 2—90 degree kinks. Perfectly round bends have been used along with a number of other shapes. Most fly tiers today are concerned with only 3 shapes or bends. These are: the *round bend,* which seldom has a bend that is perfectly round as it usually begins somewhat gradually at the shank and tightens just slightly behind the barb (variously called round bend, Model Perfect, Viking, etc.); the *sproat* which has a slightly sharper bend behind the barb; and the *limerick* which varies, according to manufacturer, from a near sproat to a shape having a definite kink at the lower end of the bend just back of the barb.

A somewhat standardized system for measuring hook size is generally accepted but there is likely to be some variation among manufacturers. Size is usually designated by a number with the larger hooks carrying a smaller number designation. Even numbers from size 2 to 24 are most common in America. In England and certain other countries, odd numbers such as 5, 7, etc., are sometimes used. For hooks larger than size 2, the designation drops to 1, then to 1-0, 2-0, etc. Sizes such as 2-0 and 3-0 are sometimes used for tying salt water flies but most flies are tied on hooks ranging from 4 to 16. Very tiny midge flies require hook sizes 18, 20, 22, and 24. The smallest hook generally available is a gold colored size 28.

Hook length is expressed as 1X, 2X and so on up to perhaps 8X long,

or from 1X down to about 7X short. What this means is that the shank length of the hook is the same as that of a hook 1, 2, 3 or however many sizes larger or smaller. For example, a hook that is size 10, 3X long would have a shank length comparable to a regular length size 4 because size 4 is 3 sizes larger than size 10. Conversely, a size 10, 3X short would have a shank length comparable to a regular length size 16 as a size 16 is 3 sizes smaller than a size 10.

A similar system is used to indicate the relative weight or diameter of wire used to make the hook. A hook designated as 1X fine is made from wire that would be standard for a hook one size smaller. A hook marked 3X stout has wire of a comparable weight of a hook 3 sizes larger. The 1, 2 and even 3X fine hooks are ideal for tying dry flies as the lighter wire is easier to float. Conversely, steelhead flies which must sink deep into fast water might have wire hooks as heavy as 5X stout.

So, in buying fly tying hooks, the box might well be marked: 12, TUE, Ex. Long, 2X Fine. This means a size 12 hook (a good trout size), turned up eye, a shank the same length as that of a size 10 (one size longer), and made from wire the same diameter or weight as that used in making a standard size 16 (2 sizes finer). Such a hook would be an excellent dry fly hook.

A hook designated as: 6, TDE, 2X Short, 4X Stout, would be a size 6 with turned down eye, a shank the length of a size 10 (2 sizes shorter), and made from wire that is normally used in making a standard size 1-0 hook. This would indicate a specialized hook primarily useful for making steelhead flies.

The bend of the hook and whether or not the eye is tapered, ball, etc., is

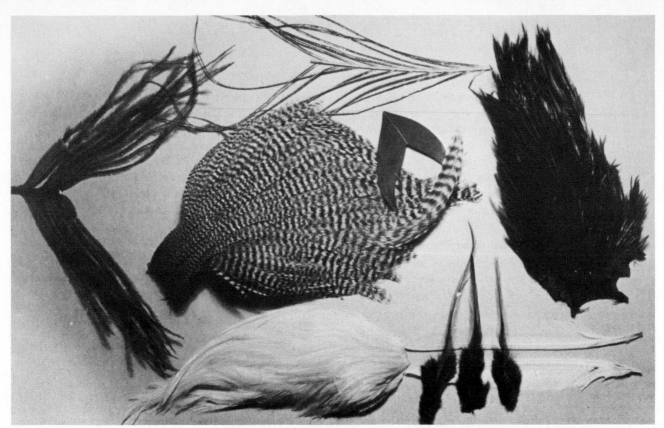

Many feather materials are used in tying quality flies. Shown in the lower right are two quill or wing feathers from a duck; dark saddle hackles are shown on top of the quill feathers; a cream hackle neck is at the bottom: ostrich plume is on the left; peacock herl across the top; a dark hackle neck is on the right and a grizzly hackle neck is in the center. The piece of feather partially on top of the grizzly hackle neck is condor quill.

Body feathers from ducks, grouse and other birds are used to make wings for wet and dry flies, and legs for nymph patterns. Moving clockwise from the top, this photo shows a gadwall duck body feather, a grouse body feather, two wood duck flank feathers, a mallard breast feather, guinea, and a mallard flank feather.

also normally spelled out on the label.

Some hooks have what is known as an offset point. This means that the point of the hook does not parallel the shank but rather is twisted or bent out to one side. Avoid such hooks for making flies. The offset feature will cause the fly to spin in the water and it reduces the hooking ability somewhat.

A specially concocted wax has many uses in tying flies. The primary purpose is for making the tying thread tacky when using dubbing furs. Special cement for fly tying is advised. So-called model airplane dope and various other glues tend to become thicker as they dry out. Fly tying cement usually comes in bottles, it can be thinned with lacquer thinner, and it does a better job. If hard bodied bass bugs are planned, various colored lacquers will add the finishing touch. Any lacquer or cement should be tested on foam plastic before the body is shaped. Some of these chemicals will dissolve plastic foam.

THE TECHNIQUE OF TYING

The very best way to learn how to tie flies is to watch a good tier in action; the second best way is to read how it's done. Actually, tying presentable flies is not difficult with the proper tools and an assortment of suitable materials. Here is how to tie a standard wet fly pattern—the Professor.

Set up the fly tying vise so the jaws face to the right and clamp a size 10, regular shank, TDE Sproat hook in place. The jaws should cover most of the hook below the bend but not necessarily the entire point. Covering too much reduces working room although there is some danger of

cutting the thread on the exposed hook point. Hone the inside of the hook point (that part facing the shank) until the point is sharp to the touch.

Now, take the bobbin and insert a spool of black 4-0 thread. There is a trick to threading a bobbin—insert the thread into the bottom of the tube (making sure there is enough slack) and then suck the thread through the tube. If no bobbin is available, break off about 16 inches of thread.

To attach the thread to the hook, hold one end just below the hook and stretch the thread upwards so it is touching the hook shank on the near side about 1/8 inch back of the eye. With the right hand, wrap the thread over the hook, under and up, then to the left to go over the short end of the thread and to wrap it down. Make 2 additional wraps over this short end and let the weight of the bobbin (hackle pliers if no bobbin) hang free to hold the thread in place. This step should be practiced several times because it is a little difficult to master but is basic to all fly tying operations.

With the thread securely attached to the hook shank, wrap it around and around the shank to a point just short of where the bend of the hook begins. These wraps should not overlap each other but they should be touching. If the thread is held back at a very slight angle from the direction it is being wrapped, each turn will "click" into place.

With the thread now at the beginning of the hook bend, the next step is to learn the half hitch. This is a basic and simple knot that should be tied following each operation to prevent the preceeding work from coming loose. To throw the half hitch, lay the first 2 fingers of the right hand, well spread, on top of the thread which should be stretched tight, use the left hand to bring the

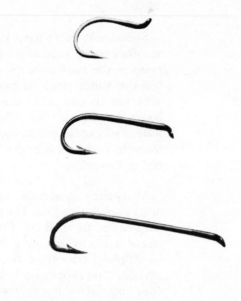

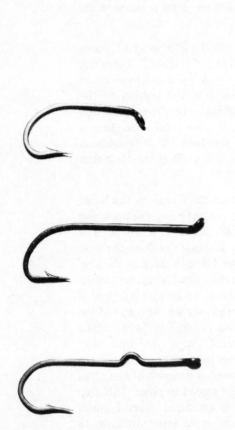

Shank length for fly tying hooks can vary greatly. At the top is a turned up eye, 5X short shank hook. The middle hook is a turned down eye, 1X long shank hook. The hook on the bottom, best suited for tying streamers and bucktails, is a turned down, loop eye, 6X long shank.

Specialized fly tying hooks. At top is a short shank, ball eye, heavy wire hook best suited for steelhead flies. In the center is a black finished, turned up, loop eye salmon hook traditionally used in tying atlantic salmon patterns. At the bottom is a ringed eye, long, humped-shank hook made especially for building bass bugs. The hump prevents the bug body from twisting on the hook shank.

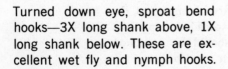

Turned down eye, sproat bend hooks—3X long shank above, 1X long shank below. These are excellent wet fly and nymph hooks.

Turned down, ball eye, sproat bend hook is shown on the left. On the right is a turned up, tapered eye, model perfect. The left hook is usually preferred for wet flies and the right hook for dries.

thread up and over the two fingers and down to the left of the thread where it is stretched between the fingers and the hook. Now take this loop, not changing its original alignment, slip it over the eye of the hook, slide it back to where the thread wraps ended on the hook shank, slip out the fingers and pull the thread tight. This half hitch should be practiced until it becomes practically second nature.

The next step is to take half a dozen or so red hackle fibers, kip tail fibers, or a section of red dyed goose feather containing about four of these heavier fibers and hold it on top of the hook with the small ends extending out over the hook bend to the left. This will be the tail of the fly and it should be about as long as the shank of the hook. Hold these tail fibers in place with the left hand and make three or four wraps of the thread over the fibers to bind them in place. If the first wrap is too tight, the tail fibers are likely to roll away from the thread around the far side of the hook. Make the first wrap fairly loose until it is well over the fibers and then pull the thread directly down to lock the fibers in place. After making several close wraps, make a half hitch and cut off the excess or butt ends of the tail fibers with the scissors.

It's a good idea to place a small amount of fly head cement on these tail wraps to insure the tail will not pull out.

Now to build the fly body. Take about a 3 to 4 inch piece of narrow gold tinsel, hold one end down on top of the tail wraps with the longer part extending out over the bend of the hook to the left, make two wraps over the end of the tinsel leaving about 1/8 inch extending out from under the wraps. Fold this short stub over the first 2 wraps and make 2 or 3 more wraps, half hitch, and cut off the excess stub. This system of folding the tinsel over and making

additional wraps, locks it in place so it will not pull loose. The long part of the tinsel extending out to the left will be used for ribbing the body of the fly.

The body itself is made of yellow floss. Using either silk or nylon floss of a bright yellow shade, cut off a piece almost 4 inches long, lay it on the previous tail and tinsel wraps with the long part extending out to the left. Wind over about 1/8 inch of the floss end, cut off the excess, half hitch, then spiral the thread forward to where it was first attached to the hook near the eye. Half hitch again, and extend the thread out to the right by laying the bobbin down on the table or attach the hackle pliers and lay them several inches out to the right of the vise. This is to get the thread out of the way while the body is wrapped.

If the floss is single strand, simply wrap it around and around the hook shank to form a smooth, nicely tapered body. If multi-strand floss is used, separate the strands and wind them on one at a time to keep the body smooth. After the floss body is built up and wrapped to near the eye of the hook, make several wraps over it with the thread, half hitch, and cut off the excess floss.

Now take the piece of tinsel that has been extending out to the left of the fly, attach the hackle pliers to the end, and spiral the tinsel forward in 3 to 5 evenly spaced wraps and bind it down the same way it was tied on at first. Remove the excess tinsel and the fly body is complete.

The next step is tying in the hackle which is brown. This particular pattern calls for beard hackle which consists of a few strands of hen hackle fibers tied in under the hook shank at the head of the fly, not wrapped completely around the hook

Elements of an Effective Fly Pattern

Two factors would seem to be most important in the making of a highly effective fly pattern... visibility and movement. A dry fly must depend more on visibility than movement. It should create visibility in two areas. First, it must reflect light to a high degree. Second, it should make a change in the surface of the water by dimpling it with hackles, hair or chenille. Both the reflected light and dimples are readily seen by fish and serve as attractors.

The movement of a dry fly depends on flowing water or working the rod tip when fishing still water. A dry fly that rides high, as it should, will also be moved by the wind.

Characteristics of a streamer fly that give best results are mainly those that attract through movement, therefore the materials used in tying should be limp when wet and should react to the water currents. Bright colors are most effective, though grays and browns are also good as indicated by the success of those tied with deer and squirrel hair. These streamers are fished at mid-depths; or sometimes close to the bottom, depending on the flow of the water.

Nymphs are usually best in dark colors with furry bodies and only a few short legs, Small in size, mostly tied on No. 10 or smaller hooks, they should be heavy enough to ride on, or just above, the bottom in moving water. They are good fish producers in murky streams.

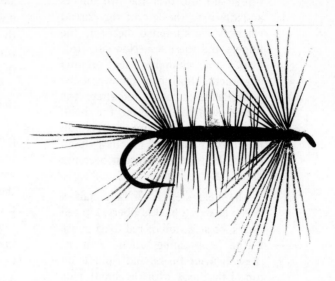

This would be an excellent dry fly pattern. It is a combination of a wooly worm body with hackles at both the head and tail. It would reflect above water light and also dimple the surface water. Flotation would be acceptably high.

This streamer has a floss body and chenille arms. Chenille is an excellent material for wet streamers as it is limp to give top action in the water and it comes in a wide variety of colors.

The best material for a nymph body is either thick chenille, wool or fur in dull dark colors. Legs can be made from short pieces of rubber or peacock herl. For fast moving waters it is a good idea to weight nymphs with lead wire tied around the shank of the hook before tying on the chenille, or wool yarn.

as in most dry flies and a number of wet fly patterns. The hackle fibers are tied in the same way the tail was attached. The length should be so the tips just reach the point of the hook. To make the hackle fibers stand away from the hook at the right angle, hold the tips of the fibers out from the hook while making a few wraps of thread under and just behind the hackle. As always, half hitch after each operation.

The wing on the Professor is made from a black and white barred side feather from a mallard drake. Strip the fluffy fibers away from the base of the feather until good firm feather fibers are reached. Cut 2 equal sections about 1/4 inch wide from each side of this feather. These sections will have a natural curve so position them between the thumb and forefinger of the left hand with the concave sides together and the tips of the sections pointing toward the palm. Holding these feather sections firmly, place them on top of the hook with the tips about even with the bend of the hook. Take the thread up between the thumb and the feather sections, relaxing the grip slightly to do so, then bring the thread down between the finger and the sections. Holding the feathers so they will not roll, pull the thread straight down to "squeeze" the fibers down on the hook. Repeat this maneuver, then move the fingers back to hold the wing steady while making several more wraps. Half hitch the thread 2 times, then trim off the excess wing material that is protruding over the eye of the hook.

The final step is tying off the fly head. Make a number of tight wraps with the thread to make a smoothly tapering head and half hitch again. If a whip finisher or half hitch tool is to be used, follow the directions and illustrations that came with the tool to show how it works. If neither of these tools is available, make a number of half hitches, cut the thread off closely, and coat the fly head liberally with fly head cement. Before the cement becomes completely dry, push the point of the bodkin into the eye of the hook several times to prevent the hook eye being cemented shut.

Tying the Nymph

Nymph patterns are supposed to imitate some form of underwater creature, usually the immature stage of mayflies, stoneflies, or caddis flies. Nymphs are not difficult to fish, they are very effective during almost any time of the day, and they are among the easiest flies to tie well.

The best nymphs have rough, shaggy bodies to produce an indistinct shape when viewed by fish. Spun or dubbed fur, wool yarn, or herl bodies have proven most effective for nymphs. These materials can be used singly to form the complete body, or mixed with others to give a 2-color, 2-texture effect. Woven hair or nylon monofilament bodies have also been very successful in nymphs. These bodies are constructed by either wrapping the hair or monofilament around the hook shank while at the same time, weaving a piece of floss around each pass of the primary body material to create a contrasting stripe down the belly, or by weaving 2 colors of material together in such a fashion that the belly of the fly will be lighter than the back.

Here is how to tie a simple but effective general purpose nymph for trout fishing. Clamp a No. 10, 2X Long, TDE, Sproat hook in the fly tying vise. Sharpen the hook, then attach the fly tying thread, brown if available, just behind the eye and wrap closely to the bend of the hook. Half hitch the thread. Take 4 to 6 mottled brown feather fibers such as found on the flanks of a mallard drake or the partridge hackle sold in fly tying supply shops, and tie them in so the tips point to the left. The length of these tail fibers should correspond to about half the length of the hook.

Next, attach a 2 inch piece of brown buttonhole twist silk or heavy thread with the ong end extending out to the left. Then tie in a 2 inch piece of tan or light brown crewel yarn, wrap the tying thread forward to about the mid point on the hook shank and half hitch it. Wrap the yarn forward to the same point, tie it down, half hitch, and cut off the excess. Take the buttonhole twist or heavy thread tied in earlier and spiral it forward as a rib to where the yarn was tied off. Half hitch and cut off the excess ribbing.

Now take 4 1-1/2 inch pieces of dark brown or black floss and tie them in on top of the hook so the long ends point back toward the tail of the fly. This floss should be tied in just where the ribbing was tied off. Half hitch and cut off the short stubs of the floss. Attach a 2 inch piece of brown yarn, about the same shade as the ribbing, spiral the tying thread forward to about 1/8 inch back of the hook eye and half hitch. Build up a fat hump of the brown yard, beginning where the tan yarn and ribbing were tied off and extending forward to where the tying thread is half hitched. Care should be taken not to let the brown floss strands become wrapped under as they will be needed next. They should still be well out of the way to the left. The yarn hump should cover up any thread wraps used to tie in the yarn, floss and ribbing. Take 2 wraps of the tying thread over the brown yarn and half hitch.

Then grasp the tips of the floss pieces and pull them forward over the brown yarn hump and gather them just ahead of this hump. Take

2 wraps of the tying thread over the floss, half hitch and cut off the excess. The band of floss tied in over the yarn hump is to simulate the wing case that mayfly and stonefly nymphs develop prior to hatching or emerging as adult insects. Next, take 6 or 8 of the same fibers used in making the tail and hold them crossways on top of the hook just ahead of the yarn hump. Criss-cross the thread around the hook and in front of and behind these fibers so they will stand out at right angles to the hook shank. Wrap a smooth head and whip finish. Now clip the fibers just tied in so they extend out to the sides not more than 1/4 inch. With thumb and forefinger, "pinch" these fibers in toward the hook so they will kink and form lifelike legs. Coat the fly head with cement and the nymph is finished.

Although yarn makes good nymphs, dubbed fur is by far the best body material for nymphs. Some tiers dub the fur onto a separate piece of thread by coating the thread with wax and rolling it over the clipped fur. In this way, they build up a strand of fur yarn which is tied in just like other materials and then wrapped on the hook. However, there is a much better way to do this. Simply wax the tying thread with a tacky wax, pull or clip small amounts of fur from the skin, and roll it on the thread between the thumb and forefinger. The thread should be attached to the hook and at the stage where the body material will be wrapped on next. Stretching it tight then makes it easy to spin the fur directly on the tying thread.

Other effective nymph bodies are made with peacock herl, chenille, quill and even embroidery cotton. Peacock herl is easy to work with and the metallic green fibers have great fish appeal. Many tiers use this material in such a way that the fly

FLY PATTERNS

Various published reports estimate the number of standard fly patterns to be 2,000 to 4,000. Even the 4,000 figure would seem to be reasonable considering the vast number of combinations possible, but it is more likely that, if by "standard" it is meant a pattern currently being manufactured, the number would be closer to 200.

Though there are formulas and specifications to guide in the tying of each specific pattern, there are variations due to different colors of materials used and to the necessary lack of exact dimensions.

Most patterns, though, do look enough alike as to be readily identified by anyone familiar with the particular design. On the following pages you will find illustrations and descriptions of 100 popular standard patterns and several originals. They are all proven fish catchers, but you'll find that some are better than others for the fishing areas you cover.

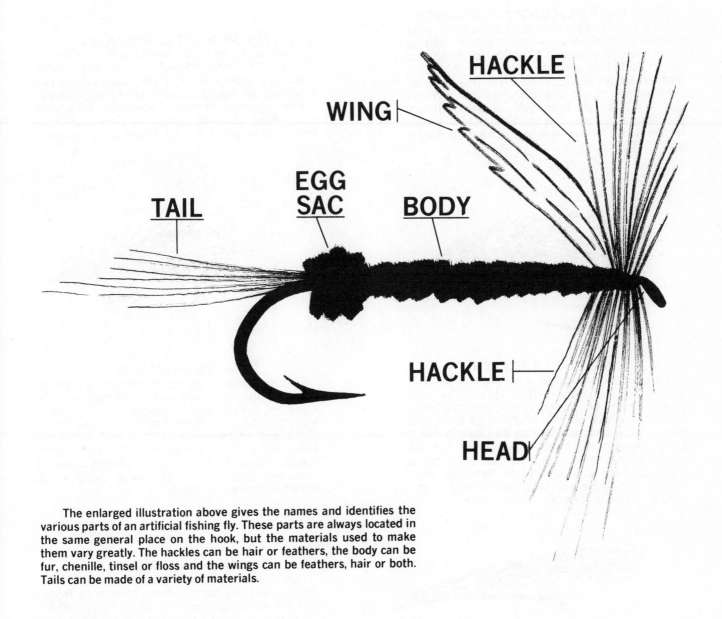

The enlarged illustration above gives the names and identifies the various parts of an artificial fishing fly. These parts are always located in the same general place on the hook, but the materials used to make them vary greatly. The hackles can be hair or feathers, the body can be fur, chenille, tinsel or floss and the wings can be feathers, hair or both. Tails can be made of a variety of materials.

Streamers and Bucktails

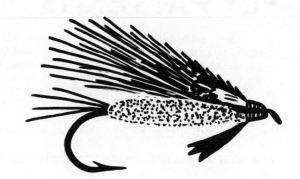

CAIN'S RIVER SILVER DOCTOR STREAMER

(The Cain's River series of streamers were originally designed for Atlantic salmon fishing. They have also proved effective for trout and bass.) **Tail:** Two sections of barred wood duck feather. **Body:** Medium flat silver tinsel. **Wing:** Two medium brown saddle hackles with a grizzly saddle hackle on each side. **Cheeks:** Jungle cock. **Collar:** A few turns of a French blue saddle hackle with a few turns of a grizzly saddle hackle ahead of this.

EDSON DARK TIGER BUCKTAIL

(Excellent trout and landlocked salmon fly. Also good for bass.) **Head:** Yellow. **Tag:** Three turns of narrow flat gold tinsel. **Tail:** Tips of two small yellow neck hackles, back to back. **Body:** Yellow chenille. **Throat:** Two small red hackle tips. **Wing:** A small bunch of brown bucktail extending to bend of hook. **Cheeks:** Jungle cock.

NINE-THREE STREAMER

(Originally designed as a smelt imitation for landlocked salmon, the Nine-Three—the first salmon caught on it weighed nine pounds, three ounces—has also proven effective for trout and bass. A variation has Mylar strips on each side.) **Body:** Medium flat silver tinsel. **Wing:** A small bunch of white bucktail topped with three medium green saddle hackles tied flat, over which are two black saddle hackles tied in the regular manner. **Cheeks:** Jungle cock.

MUDDLER MINNOW

(Designed for large brook trout. Effective on brown trout, rainbows, and river smallmouth. Excellent grasshopper imitation.) **Tail:** Turkey wing quill section. **Body:** Flat gold tinsel. **Wing:** Black and white mixed calf tail hair with matched sections of turkey quill on each side. **Hackle:** Bunch of deer body hair placed on top of hook and tied so it flares widely. **Head:** Trim flared deer hair to shape.

RED AND WHITE BUCKTAIL

(Excellent smallmouth bass and pickerel fly. Also a good standard bucktail for trout.) **Body:** Flat silver tinsel with oval silver tinsel. **Wing:** Small bunch of red bucktail or calf tail fibers tied over a small bunch of white bucktail or calf tail fibers.

will not last long under fishing conditions. They simply attach the tip end of a herl to the hook with tying thread and wind the herl around and around the shank. Should this piece of herl break on the sharp tooth of a fish, the entire fly is likely to be ruined. To make herl bodies, tie in 3 or 4 herl strands, half hitch the thread and draw it straight up vertically above the hook. Grasp the herls and twist them around and around the tying thread, then wrap them all around the hook together— herls and thread at the same time. The thread and the herls themselves reinforce the fibers and prevent easy unraveling of the fly body.

Most of the natural nymphs found in trout streams are compressed or flattened laterally because they live around and under rocks and sometimes in relatively fast currents Some tiers, in order to achieve this flattened appearance, soak wool yarn or embroidery cotton fly bodies in cement, allow to partially dry, and then squeeze them flat with a pair of pliers. This method however, does away with the fuzzy outline considered so important for successful nymph patterns.

A better method of obtaining this flat shape while retaining the desirable indistinct outline is to tie in a piece of nylon monofilament about as long as the hook shank on each side of the hook, wrap closely with thread, and then coat this underbody with cement before tying the fly in the normal manner. The monofilament strands extend the body out on each side to give the flattened effect. If the nymph is to be fished in deeper pools, substitute the appropriate size lead wire for the monofilament. These materials,

especially the monofilament, are quite slippery and tend to slip around the hook shank. A little practice will overcome this problem.

An effective imitation of the fresh water shrimp, an important trout food in many waters, can be tied on a No. 10, 4X *Short*, TUE, Sproat hook. Attach the thread behind the eye, then take a piece of lead wire long enough to extend part way around the hook bend, hold the wire under the shank and wrap it in place with the tying thread. The soft wire will conform to hook bend as the thread is wrapped. Now half hitch the tying thread and tie in a few mottled tail fibers of a subdued shade—mallard side for a brown fly, wood duck for tan or yellow, and guinea for gray or black—as a tail. This tail should point nearly straight down as it will be tied in part way around the hook bend.

Next, attach a short piece of buttonhole twist so it lays out to the left to be used later as a rib. Half hitch the tying thread and spin a dubbed fur strand of muskrat, beaver or other fur after first coating the tying thread with a tacky wax for the length needed for wrapping the body. Wrap this fur strand to a point about 1/8 inch behind the eye, half hitch the tying thread, and spiral the ribbing forward. Tie off the ribbing and add a beard hackle of the same material used to construct the tail. This beard should extend downward at least to the point of the hook to imitate the shrimp legs. Wrap a smooth head, whip finish, and coat the head with cement.

The result is a fly with the characteristic "curved" shrimp form and lightly weighted for fishing near the bottom or around weed beds

Streamers and Bucktails

WARDEN'S WORRY
(Brook trout and landlocked salmon pattern.) **Tag:** Three turns of narrow flat gold tinsel. **Tail:** Narrow section of red duck or goose quill feather. **Body:** Orange-yellow wool or chenille, rather full. **Ribbing:** Narrow oval gold tinsel. **Throat:** Yellow hackle, tied beard style or as a collar and gathered down. **Wing:** Small bunch of light brown bucktail.

NITE OWL
(Developed as a steelhead fly. Also good for bass.) **Tag:** Flat silver tinsel. **Tail:** Section of yellow goose quill as long as hook. **Butt:** Scarlet wool, fur or ostrich herl. **Body:** Yellow floss ribbed with oval silver tinsel. **Wing:** Wide white hackles with narrower scarlet hackles on each side. Scarlet hackles should be half the length of the white hackles.

BLACK GHOST STREAMER
(One of the landlocked salmon and brook trout patterns that originated in Maine. Has reached nationwide popularity as a trout and bass streamer. It is particularly good on crappie.) **Tag:** Flat silver tinsel. **Tail:** Small bunch of lemon yellow hackle fibers. **Body:** Black floss ribbed with flat silver tinsel. **Wing:** Four white saddle hackles. **Cheeks:** Jungle cock. **Hackle:** Lemon yellow, tied on before wing.

GOLDEN WITCH STREAMER
(One of the earliest landlocked salmon and trout streamers from Maine.) **Tag:** Four turns of narrow silver tinsel. **Body:** Orange floss, tied rather thinly. **Ribbing:** Narrow flat silver tinsel. **Throat:** Small bunch of white bucktail under which is a small bunch of grizzly hackle fibers. Tied rather long, beyond point of hook. **Wing:** Four strands of peacock herl topped with four grizzly saddle hackles. **Shoulders:** Golden pheasant tippets, one-third length of wing. **Cheeks:** Jungle cock.

YELLOW BUTCHER STREAMER
(Excellent trout streamer and also good for smallmouth bass.) **Body:** Medium oval silver tinsel. **Wing:** Tips of two yellow maribou plumes tied back to back extending one-half inch past hook bend, topped with a bunch of brown maribou fibers stripped from plume. **Sides:** Three peacock herl strands tied in on each side to extend length of wing. **Cheeks:** Jungle cock. **Throat:** Small bunch of red hackle fibers.

ALASKA MARY ANN
(Developed from a primitive eskimo fly called the Kobuk hook. Used primarily for steelhead but is also good for regular trout fishing.) **Tail:** Red hackle fibers. **Body:** White or cream yarn, ribbed with wide silver tinsel. **Wing:** White polar bear hair. **Cheek:** Jungle cock.

where fresh water shrimp usually are found.

The fabulously successful wooly worm pattern is essentially a nymph although it more closely resembles a caterpillar. This was originally a bass fly from the Ozark Mountain region but is now more famous as a trout fly, particularly in big western rivers.

To tie the wooly worm, take a No. 4, 2X Long TDE, round bend hook and clamp it in the vise. Sharpen the hook and attach the tying thread about 1/8 inch back of the hook eye. Wrap the tying thread back to the bend of the hook and half hitch. Many wooly worms have a tufted red tail and if this is desired, tie in a large piece of wool yarn, loop it short, and tie down the other end. Now tie in the tip of a long saddle hackle and half hitch the thread. This feather should project out to the left so it will be out of the way during the earlier tying steps. Next, attach a 3-inch piece of narrow tinsel as described in tying the Professor fly, folding the end over and wrapping again to lock it in place. Half hitch again. This tinsel should also extend to the left with the saddle hackle. Take a piece of medium to heavy chenille about 4 inches long and scrape the fibers away on one end until the thread core is exposed for about 1/4 inch. Bind this thread down at the bend of the hook so the chenille also extends out to the left, half hitch the tying thread and spiral forward to about 1/4 inch from the eye. Stripping fibers off the chenille to expose the thread core allows the chenille to be attached without unnecessary bulk.

Grasp the end of the chenille strand with the hackle pliers and wind it evenly along the hook shank to where the tying thread was half hitched. Wrap the chenille down with the tying thread and half hitch again. Cut off the excess chenille,

disengage the hackle pliers and attach them to the end of the tinsel. Spiral the tinsel evenly forward to rib the body, tie it off and half hitch the thread. Cut off the excess tinsel, disengage the hackle pliers again and grasp the butt of the saddle hackle. Extend this hackle above the hook to face any natural curvature towards the eye of the hook and wind it "sideways" around the hook, following the same path as the tinsel. Hold this hackle in place at the front of the fly while making 3 wraps of the tying thread over it, then half hitch the thread and snip off the excess hackle. Use the bodkin to pick out any hackle fibers that may have been wrapped under. Wrap a smooth head with the tying thread, half hitch it, whip finish and cut the thread loose. Coat the fly head with cement and the wooly worm is complete.

Wooly worms are effective in almost any color but certain combinations have become more or less standard. A green body with grizzly hackle, black body with grizzly, black with yellow, brown with ginger, gray with black, and orange with black are among the most popular. Darker patterns are usually ribbed with silver tinsel and lighter ones with gold. Wooly worms are particularly effective when weighted. A piece of lead wire wrapped under the hook shank adds just about the right amount of weight for successful fishing and ease of casting. Tying in the tinsel is a step that can be avoided with the use of chenille that has a tinsel core.

A No. 4, 1X Long, TDE, Sproat hook is about right for these particular flies. Clamp the hook into the vise and sharpen it. Attach black or gray fly tying thread behind the hook eye and wrap it evenly back to the bend of the hook. Make *two* half hitches. Take the thread down around the fingers of the left hand and back to the hook, make two

Streamers and Bucktails

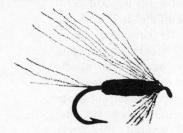

JIM'S GEM STREAMER
(This is a popular West Coast steelhead fly.)
Tag: Flat silver tinsel. **Tail:** Bunch of yellow hackle fibers. **Body:** Heavy black chenille ribbed with flat silver tinsel. **Wing:** White bucktail. **Hackle:** Badger collar tied over wing.

SKYKOMISH SUNRISE BUCKTAIL
(One of the most colorful and effective West Coast steelhead patterns.) **Tag:** Three turns of narrow, flat, silver tinsel. **Tail:** Small bunch of red hackle fibers, topped with a bunch of yellow hackle fibers, rather long and not mixed. **Body:** Heavy red chenille ribbed with narrow, flat silver tinsel. **Wing:** Small bunch of white polar bear hair. **Hackle:** Red hackle and orange hackle feathers would mixed as a collar over the wing.

CAIN'S RIVER
BLACK DEMON STREAMER
(Although the Cain's River series of streamers began as Atlantic salmon flies, some of the newer arrivals were developed for other types of fish. The Black Demon is primarily a West Coast steelhead fly.) **Tail:** Two sections of barred wood duck feather. **Body:** Medium flat gold tinsel. **Wing:** Four black saddle hackles. **Cheeks:** Jungle cock. **Hackle:** Orange saddle hackle tied as a collar.

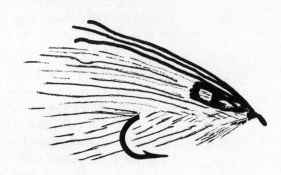

WHITE MARABOU STREAMER
(An outstanding pattern for trout fishing. Also effective for bass.) **Tag:** Flat silver tinsel. **Tail:** Small bunch of red hackle fibers. **Body:** Flat silver tinsel ribbed with oval silver tinsel. **Wing:** The tips of two white marabou plumes tied back to back. Additional fibers are then stripped from the remaining plumes and tied in on top. These marabou fibers are then topped with four to six strands of peacock herl. **Cheeks:** Jungle cock. **Hackle:** Bunch of red hackle fibers tied in beard style.

BLACK NOSED DACE BUCKTAIL
(Excellent bucktail for trout fishing, especially good for brown trout.) **Tail:** Red wool, very short. **Body:** Medium flat silver tinsel, ribbed with oval silver tinsel. **Wing:** A very small bunch of white bucktail or calf tail fibers, over which is tied a small bunch of black bucktail or calf tail fibers, over which is tied a small bunch of brown bucktail or calf tail fibers. The black hair is slightly shorter than the white and brown fibers. It is easy to overdress this fly so very small bunches of hair are necessary.

wraps, half hitch two more times and spiral the thread forward to about 1/4 inch back of the hook eye. The idea is to form a loop of tying thread about four inches long.

Insert a pair of scissors or some other tool into the loop to keep it from twisting shut and then clip out three bunches of muskrat fur. Each of these bunches should be about the amount that can be easily held between thumb and forefinger and must include the long guard hairs as well as the underfur. Lay these three bunches where they can be easily reached, open up the thread loop and rub it liberally with tacky fly tying wax. Place two fingers of the left hand in this loop and pull it straight up above the hook. Insert one bunch of muskrat fur in the loop and slide it down until it almost touches the hook shank. Position fur bunch number two about one to one-and-a-half inches above the first bunch. Insert bunch number three with about the same spacing. Slip the fingers carefully out of the loop and grasp the end of the loop with hackle pliers and pull it tight.

The next step is to spread the 3 bunches of fur through the loop until the fur is evenly distributed from hook shank to about 3 inches out in the loop. Now begin twisting the hackle pliers. Twisting the loop 10 to 20 times will form a chenille strand of shaggy fur. Wrap this strand around the hook shank, using the bodkin to pick out guard hairs that have been wrapped under, and continue wrapping to where the tying thread is half hitched. Take several wraps over the end of the loop to hold the fur strand in place, half hitch the tying thread again and cut off the excess thread from the loop.

The Fledermouse is finished by placing a short bunch of gray squirrel tail fibers on top of the hook just behind the eye and making a half dozen wraps to hold it in place. The several wraps are taken just around this wing to pull it up at about a 45 degree angle to the hook shank. Cut off the butts of the squirrel tail hair, wrap a smooth head whip finish and coat with cement. One caution—squirrel tail hair is hard and wrapping a very tight head after the hair butts have been cut will sometimes force the hair out from under the wraps. Firm wraps that are not overly tight will do the trick.

The Gray Nymph differs from the Fledermouse in having a tail of badger fibers and a grizzly hackle collar.

Tiny, worm-like nymphs that imitate the midge pupa, immature aquatic forms of small insects known variously as gnats, punkies, no-see-ums, and $?&&$!0$, are often effective for catching highly selective trout. Although tied on ultra small hooks that complicate the tying, the actual fly is simplicity itself. On a size 18 or 20 hook, attach red, green, brown, or black tying thread and wrap back to the bend and then forward again to make a smoothly tapered body. At a point about 1/3 the shank length back of the eye, attach a tiny hackle of matching color, or an ostrich herl that is fairly close in color and make just one turn. The idea is to have a wisp of fiber to simulate gills on the tiny midge larva. Tie off the hackle or herl, half hitch and then build a smooth head with a few more wraps of tying thread. Whip finish, cut off the excess tying thread and coat the head with cement.

Working with flies that are this small requires some tying experience but midge nymphs are a good way to work into the construction of small flies.

Nymphs

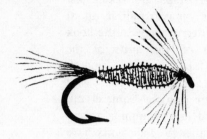

GRAY NYMPH
(This is an excellent trout and panfish nymph. In larger sizes does well on river smallmouths.) **Tail:** A few strands of badger hair with white tips. **Body:** Muskrat dubbing, rather full, with guard hairs left in. **Hackle:** One to two turns of soft grizzly hackle.

BEAVER NYMPH
(An impressionistic nymph for brown and rainbow trout.) **Tail:** Short wood duck flank feather fibers. **Body:** Natural beaver fur, tied full and then ribbed with fine gold wire. **Hackle:** Gray partridge, tied beard style. **Head:** Brown lacquer.

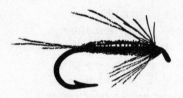

HENDRICKSON NYMPH
(An outstanding eastern trout nymph that is also proving effective on western trout streams.) **Tail:** Wood duck flank feather fibers. **Body:** Blend of dubbed tan, gray and claret fur ribbed with olive thread. **Wing Cases:** Section of blue wing quill tied over front third, or thorax of body. **Hackle:** Brown partridge.

IRON BLUE NYMPH
(Trout nymph of primary importance on eastern streams, but effective everywhere.) **Tail:** Cream or gray hackle fibers. **Abdomen:** Bluish muskrat fur ribbed with gold wire. **Thorax:** Bluish muskrat fur, tied rather full with no rib. **Hackle:** Grayish cream.

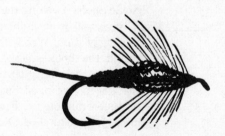

HORNER SHRIMP
(Originally designed as a steelhead fly for fishing near river mouths, this fly also takes Pacific salmon and several salt water species such as bonefish.) **Tail:** Extension of wing. **Body:** Flat silver tinsel over padding. **Hackle:** Medium brown. **Wing:** Brown bucktail tied over hackle, then brought to rear and tied down at rear end of body to form a "shell" back and a tail.

MONTANA NYMPH
(Trout stream nymph that is particularly effective in the northern Rockies.) **Tail:** Short black crow feather fibers. **Abdomen:** Black chenille. **Thorax:** Yellow chenille ribbed with soft black hackle. **Wing:** The wing case is formed by tying two short strands of black chenille over hackle and thorax.

There are few truly standardized nymph patterns so tying these imitations of aquatic insects and crustaceans can really unleash an imaginative fly tier's creative instincts, possibly to the detriment of the local fish population.

Bucktails and Streamers

There is a story that the first fly to effectively imitate minnows and small fish was actually a standard wet fly on which one end of the hackle had come loose. Whether or not this story is true, it is a fact that elongated flies to imitate small fish have been around for some time and that they are effective on most species of game fish.

Generally speaking, streamer flies are supposed to have feather wings and bucktails are supposed to have hair wings. It's not all that simple. One of the first such flies to be tied, this prior to 1915, had wings of both hair and feather material. Also, such famous streamer-bucktail patterns as the Nine-Three and the Supervisor have wings containing both hair and feathers. If the fly wing is predominately hair, it will probably be called a bucktail; if it is predominately feather, it is usually called a streamer.

Bucktail and streamer bodies can be constructed in a number of ways. Since the small fish these flies are designed to imitate are usually rather flashy, tinsel is often used in tying such flies. Flies with all tinsel bodies and those with considerable tinsel ribbing each carry out this theme. All tinsel bodies for bucktails and streamers can be made in several ways. The most common is simply to wrap the hook shank with wide, flat tinsel.

Here is the accepted method for doing this.

Attach the tying thread to the hook, usually a 4X to 6X Long Limerick, and wrap the thread back to the bend of the hook. Without half hitching the tying thread, start wrapping it right back over itself in a second layer all the way back to where it was originally attached. Half hitch the thread. Now cut off a 6 - 8 inch piece of tinsel (experience will soon dictate how long for what length hook) and attach one end just behind the eye of the hook. It frequently helps with wide tinsel to clip the end off diagonally to hold bulk to a minimum. Remember to bend a short ear over and wrap that under too to lock the tinsel on. Half hitch the tying thread and move the bobbin or tying thread held by hackle pliers well to the right of the vise to provide plenty of working room.

Next, coat the thread wrapped hook shank with cement. Without waiting for the cement to dry, begin wrapping the flat tinsel toward the bend of the hook, squeezing the wet cement out between the wraps. These tinsel wraps can usually be felt "clicking" into place off of the preceeding turn. When the tinsel wrapping reaches the bend of the hook, start wrapping it back over itself, all the way back to where it started, being careful to keep the wraps tightly together. Such a double wrap of tinsel covers any inadvertent gaps in the tinsel wraps, and the cement that was squeezed out between the wraps in the first layer helps cement the second layer of tinsel in place. Once the tinsel is tied off, using the lock wrap again, clip off the excess and then coat the tinsel wraps with cement to bind them firmly into place and to prevent tarnishing.

Tinsel is pretty slippery stuff and hackle pliers might be needed to hold it during the wrapping operation.

Nymphs

ZUG BUG
(An eastern trout stream nymph that has proven effective also in the mid-west and west.) **Tail:** Three strands of green peacock sword herl. **Body:** Heavy peacock herl ribbed with silver tinsel. **Wing:** Mallard flank feather, cut short and extending over forward one-fourth of body. **Hackle:** Soft brown, rather long.

LIGHT CAHILL NYMPH
(Excellent for brown and rainbow trout throughout the country.) **Tail:** Three lemon colored wood duck feather fibers. **Body:** Tannish-cream fur dubbing with small amount of yellow added. **Wings:** Pale gray mallard flank feather fibers. **Hackle:** Pale ginger.

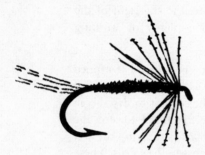

GRAY FOX NYMPH
(This is an eastern nymph pattern that has proven effective for trout throughout the country.) **Tail:** Gray partridge fibers. **Body:** Gray muskrat fur dubbing ribbed with fine gold wire. **Hackle:** Gray partridge. **Wings:** Tips of two small grizzly hackles tied flat over back.

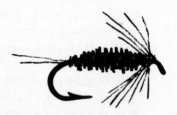

LEADWINGED COACHMAN NYMPH
(Excellent general purpose trout nymph.) **Tail:** Dark brown hackle fibers. **Body:** Bronze peacock herl ribbed with fine black silk. **Wings:** Small black duck wing feather clipped to shape. **Hackle:** Dark rusty brown.

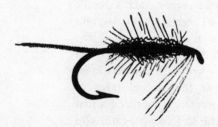

ATHERTON'S MEDIUM NYMPH
(Though developed in the east, the Atherton series has proven very effective for trout throughout the country.) **Tail:** Three short strands from a ring-necked pheasant tail feather. **Abdomen:** Hare's ear dubbing ribbed with narrow oval gold tinsel. **Thorax:** Hare's ear dubbing, rather full. **Wings:** Bright blue floss or section from bright blue mallard wing feather. **Hackle:** Brown partridge.

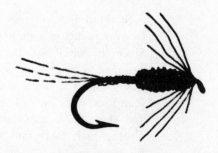

MICHIGAN NYMPH
(Though primarily a midwestern brown trout pattern, the Michigan nymph is an excellent trout pattern throughout the country.) **Tail:** Speckled gray mallard flank feather fibers. **Abdomen:** Center quill from stripped grizzly hackle feather. **Thorax:** Bluish-gray rabbit fur dubbing. **Wings:** Orange silk floss tied over thorax. **Hackle:** Reddish-brown.

The prerequisite to smooth tinsel bodies is a smooth underbody. If a tail or other embellishments are tied in, the tying thread must be built up over the rest of the shank to keep the body smooth and even. It sometimes helps to use rather long fibers for such tails, leaving the butts long enough to wrap over all the way back to just behind the eye. This will help to keep the underbody smooth.

If additional flash seems warranted, a tinsel ribbing can be added to an all tinsel body. When the first layer of thread reaches the bend of the hook, half hitch it and tie in about 3 inches of oval tinsel. Oval tinsel is flat tinsel that has been wrapped over a thread core. To tie it in, unwrap a few turns of the oval tinsel from its thread core and tie the core to the hook. This helps to reduce bulk at a critical place. Half hitch the thread again and wrap it tightly back to the eye of the hook. Wrap the main flat tinsel body just as before, all the way to the bend of the hook and then back over itself to the eye. Tie it off and half hitch the thread. Now take the oval tinsel that has been hanging from the bend of the hook and spiral it forward, keeping it in the cracks between the last tinsel layer wraps. Tie off the oval tinsel and coat the entire body with cement.

The flashiest tinsel bodies of all are made with an all tinsel chenille. This "chenille" has a tinsel core and each of the fibers projecting from this core is a narrow piece of tinsel. This material makes an extremely effective fly body, particularly for streamers tied with marabou feathers. Tinsel chenille is wrapped on the hook just like any other chenille.

Brass, copper and silver wire bodies have become quite popular for steelhead bucktails. These wires are not tied down like tinsel. Rather they are simply wrapped around the hook shank over a base of tying thread. The rough ends are filed smooth with a jewelers file, being careful not to cut into the thread base, and then wrappings of thread are built up even with the wire at boths ends. The entire body is coated with clear cement to prevent tarnishing.

Floss, wool and chenille bodies are all effective on bucktails and streamers. Floss and wool bodies seem unfinished without a tinsel ribbing but chenille bodies are good both with or without a rib. Chenille and wool produce fat, "juicy" bodies for large flies that are particularly attractive to bass. Peacock herl is a standard body for at least 2 patterns of these longer flies. Such bodies should consist of 4 herl strands twisted around the tying thread as mentioned earlier.

Many streamers and bucktails have tails, usually consisting of a colorful section of fibers from a flight feather, or several hair or hackle fibers. Red seems the most popular color.

Some streamers and bucktails have a collar of hackle, either under or over the wing. Most patterns, however, call for a short beard hackle or none whatsoever. Shoulders of duck body feathers, various exotic toppings over the wings, and jungle cock "nails" tied in to simulate eyes are all used to embellish these colorful fish imitations. Much of this is superfluous. Simple patterns seem to be just as effective at taking fish and they are so much easier to construct.

The famous Royal Coachman pattern, familiar to practically all fly fishermen, can be tied in both streamer and bucktail versions. The streamer is more popular in the eastern United States and Canada

Nymphs

QUILL GORDON NYMPH
(Outstanding nymph for trout fishing.) **Tail:** Two or three wood duck flank feather strands length of hook. **Body:** Rough tied tannish-gray muskrat fur. **Wings:** Trimmed gary mallard flank feather tied over front third of body. **Hackle:** Honey dun clipped on top.

BLUE QUILL NYMPH
(Effective nymph pattern, particularly for trout in eastern streams.) **Tail:** Blue dun hackle fibers. **Abdomen:** Light peacock quill. **Thorax:** Dubbed blue-gray muskrat fur. **Hackle:** Several turns of soft blue dun hackle.

BROWN NYMPH
(Excellent brown and rainbow trout nymph.) **Tail:** Short bronze mallard fibers. **Abdomen:** Dark brown dubbing ribbed with bronze or gold wire. **Thorax:** Tan fur dubbing, tied rather full. **Wings:** Section from brown turkey feather tied over thorax. **Hackle:** Brown hackle fibers tied crosswise to project out on each side. **Feelers:** Two fibers from wing case material left projecting over head.

HARE'S EAR NYMPH
(Effective trout nymph throughout the country.) **Tail:** Brown hackle fibers. **Abdomen:** Rough dubbing from fur on European hare's ear, ribbed with oval gold tinsel. **Thorax:** Hare's ear dubbing tied rather full. **Wings:** Gray goose or duck feather section tied over thorax. **Hackle:** Thorax dubbing picked out along bottom and sides.

while the bucktail version sees wide use in the West.

The body is essentially the same for either version. Here is how to tie it.

Clamp a No. 6, 6X Long, TDE, Limerick hook in the vise and sharpen the point. Attach the tying thread about 1/8 inch behind the hook eye and wrap it tightly to just short of the hook bend, then half hitch it. If a weighted fly is preferred, lay a small diameter piece of lead wire underneath the hook shank and cover it with this first wrap layer. If lead is used, coat the wrap with cement to prevent discoloring the body materials. Tie in a piece of narrow, flat gold tinsel, wrap it about 1/8 inch down on the hook bend, then back over itself and tie off. This forms what is known as a tag. Tie in a bunch of about six golden pleasant tippet fibers for the tail. This tail should extend a distance corresponding to about half the shank length of the hook. Half hitch the tying thread and tie in a 3 inch strand of red floss and 3 of the longest available peacock herls. Half hitch again.

Now extend the thread above the hook and twist the herls around it. Wrap this herl and thread strand forward for about 3/16 of an inch, right over the floss which should be pulled toward the eye of the hook so it is flat against the hook shank. When the herl and thread strand is wrapped the 3/16 of an inch, untwist the remaining herls from the thread and make 2 half hitches. Now pull the floss out of the way toward the bend of the hook and wrap the thread forward over the herls which should be held flat against the hook shank. Stop wrapping about 3/8 of an inch back of the hook eye, half hitch and push the bobbin (or hackle pliers holding the thread) well to the right of the vise. The herls should be pointing to the right, out over the eye of the hook. Take the floss and wrap it forward over the herls where they

were wrapped under with the tying thread, stopping where the tying thread is half hitched. Tie off the floss, half hitch the tying thread, and cut away the excess floss. Extend the tying thread vertically, twist the herls around the thread again, and wrap a shoulder of peacock herl, the same width as the butt of peacock herl tied in earlier. This should leave about 3/16 of an inch of hook shank between the shoulder and the hook eye.

Some tiers prefer a hackle collar on the Royal Coachman but a beard hackle serves just as well. If the hackle collar is preferred, select a brown hen hackle about 5/8 of an inch wide. Strip away the fluff at the base of the feather, separate the fibers a short distance back from the tip and tie in this tip so the natural curvature of the feather is toward the bend of the hook. Half hitch the tying thread and cut off the tip of the feather that extends out from under the wraps. Now grasp the butt of the hackle feather with the hackle pliers, hold the hackle out from the hook and stroke the fibers so those on both sides of the feather shaft point toward the bend of the hook. Fibers on one side of the feather shaft should be at about a 90 degree angle to those on the other side. Use the right hand to wind this hackle around the hook shank just forward of the shoulder, stroking the fibers with the fingers of the left hand to keep them aligned toward the bend of the hook. After 2 complete wraps, take the tying thread over the hackle, make 2 wraps and half hitch. Cut off the excess hackle.

A beard hackle is constructed by tying soft, brown hen hackle fibers under the hook so they project toward the hook point. These fibers should extend about 1/2 inch.

With the fly body complete, the next step is to attach the wings. For

Wet Flies

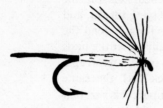

PROFESSOR
(A standard eastern wet fly for trout.) **Tail:** Scarlet hackle fibers. **Body:** Yellow floss ribbed with narrow gold tinsel. **Hackle:** Ginger. **Wings:** Speckled gray mallard breast feather sections.

SILVER PRINCE
(An attractor type wet fly good for brook trout and rainbows.) **Tail:** Three short strands of peacock herl. **Body:** Flat silver tinsel ribbed with oval silver tinsel. **Hackle:** Black. **Wing:** Bronze mallard feather sections.

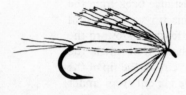

LIGHT HENDRICKSON
(An outstanding fly in both wet and dry forms. Particularly good for brown trout.) **Tail:** Lemon wood duck flank feather fibers. **Body:** Fawn colored fox fur dubbing. **Hackle:** Blue dun. **Wings:** Lemon wood duck flank feather sections.

GORDON
(An eastern trout wet fly pattern.) **Tail:** Lemon wood duck flank feather fibers. **Body:** Antique gold floss ribbed with narrow gold tinsel. **Hackle:** Cream badger. **Wing:** Lemon wood duck flank feather sections.

COWDUNG
(An outstanding general purpose trout wet fly.) **Tag:** Flat gold tinsel. **Body:** Olive wool or fur dubbing. **Hackle:** Dark ginger. **Wing:** Gray duck quill sections.

BLACK GNAT
(An excellent brook trout pattern in Canada and the eastern United States.) **Body:** Black chenille. **Hackle:** Black. **Wing:** Gray duck quill feather sections.

the Streamer version, select 4 white neck or saddle hackles about 1/3 longer than the hook. With the longer saddle hackles, part of the butts will have to be cut away to leave the correct length. With the scissors, clip off the fibers from the butt end of the feathers for a distance of about 1/4 inch, leaving short bristles to help lock the feather on during the tying operation.

Most feathers show a definite gloss or curvature that determines which side of the feather was "outside" when the bird was wearing it. These feathers must now be arranged so the shiny, "outside," or convex side of 2 of them will face one way while the outside surface of the other 2 will face the opposite direction. In other words, all 4 feathers should have the "dull" side facing in, 2 to a side. Hold the feathers tightly in the left hand so the trimmed butts project out from between the thumb and forefinger. Place these butts down on top of the hook just behind the eye and make several wraps with the tying thread while keeping a firm grip on the feathers. After making the wraps, release the feathers to see if the wings are on straight. They should be aligned on top of the hook in a perpendicular plane. If not, unwrap the thread and try again. Some tiers find it easier to tie in 2 feathers at a time until they develop more expertise at this. Once the wings are properly aligned, clip off the excess feather butts, wrap a smooth head, whip finish, and cut the thread. A coat of cement provides the finishing touch.

To make the bucktail wing, clip a small bunch of white bucktail, polar bear or calf tail about 1/3 longer than the hook. It should not be more than 1/8 inch in diameter. In fact, most bucktail wings are much too thick, having about as much action and appeal as a paint brush. Hold this bunch of hair by the tips and comb the bases several times with the bodkin. This will usually remove the soft, downlike fluff that grows near the skin. Hold this hair with the butts over the eye of the hook, not touching the hook, and make one turn of thread just around the hair and only the hair. Now lower the hair to the hook shank, pull the thread tight and make several more wraps. Making the first wrap just around the hair gathers it into one compact bundle and prevents it from rolling around the hook. Half hitch the thread, grasp the wing fibers lightly by the tips, lift up, and pass the tying thread around the wing only in sort of a figure eight to cock it up at the proper angle. Make two more wraps around hair and hook and half hitch the thread. Clip off the excess hair butts, wrap a smooth head, whip finish and coat the head liberally with cement. A second coat of cement is often helpful in binding the hair firmly into place.

Many tiers like to use the jungle cock feather "nails" as eyes on bucktails and streamers. These unique feathers are tied in on each side of the fly's head after the wing is attached but before the final hair wraps are made. Jungle cock eyes are expensive and it's questionable if they really add that much attraction to the fly. If eyes are wanted, coat the fly head with enough coats of cement to form a smooth, glossy head and let this thoroughly dry. Now take a nail with a head diameter of not more than 1/8 inch and with a definite bulge or convex head. Some of the smaller upholstery nails are ideal. Touch this nail head lightly to the surface of a contrasting lacquer and then touch it lightly to the side of the fly's head. If correctly done, this will leave a perfectly round spot of paint. If the fly head is black, which is the usual case, white lacquer makes a good eye. After the eye has thoroughly dried, touch the head of a straight

Wet Flies

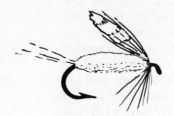

RUBE WOOD
(Primarlily an eastern trout fly.) **Tag:** Scarlet floss. **Tail:** Teal flank feather fibers. **Body:** White chenille. **Hackle:** Brown. **Wing:** Speckled mallard body feather sections.

ROYAL COACHMAN
(An attractor pattern that is probably the best known fly. Good for general trout fishing, and in larger patterns, for steelhead.) **Tail:** Golden pheasant tippet fibers. **Body:** One-third peacock herl at base of tail, one-third waist of red floss, and forward third of peacock herl. **Hackle:** Red-brown. **Wing:** White duck quill sections.

ORANGE FISH HAWK
(An attractor pattern useful primarily for eastern trout fishing.) **Tag:** Narrow gold tinsel. **Body:** Orange floss ribbed with narrow gold tinsel. **Hackle:** Light cream badger.

LEADWINGED COACHMAN
(An excellent general purpose trout fly, effective throughout the country.) **Tag:** Flat gold tinsel **Body:** Peacock herl. **Hackle:** Dark red-brown. **Wing:** Dark gray mallard wing quill sections.

PICKET PIN
(The Picket Pin is primarily a western fly for rainbow, cutthroat, and brown trout.) **Tail:** Brown hackle fibers. **Body:** Peacock herl. **Hackle:** Palmer tied brown hackle. **Wing:** Gray squirrel tail fibers with distinct white tip. **Head:** Peacock herl.

WESTERN BEE
(An effective western trout pattern, especially for lake fishing.) **Tag:** Flat gold tinsel. **Body:** Alternating bands of black and yellow chenille. **Hackle:** Ginger. **Wing:** Gray mallard wing quill sections.

pin to the surface of some black lacquer and then touch it to the center of the eye. This produces a pupil for the eye and the total effect is quite attractive, at least to fishermen.

Marabou streamers are among the deadliest of the streamer-bucktail family. The hypnotic, breathing action of marabou fibers has proven the downfall of many a fine trout or bass, but to be most effective, marabou wings should be constructed in a specific manner.

Many tiers use marabou by just stripping fibers off one side of a marabou plume and binding the butts to the hook. Most commercial marabou streamers are made this way. A more pronounced breathing action, however, is produced by tying in the tips of the plumes. To do this, measure the correct wing length down from the tip and cut the feather shaft at this point. Do this to a second plume and tie in the butts of each on opposite sides of the fly so the tips will fan out from the fly body. Once these short plumes are securely bound and straight, strip additional fibers from the butts of the plumes from which the tips were taken and bind these on the hook over the butts of the plume tips to add some bulk. Snip off the excess feather fibers, wrap a smooth head, whip finish and cement. Some marabou patterns call for a topping of peacock or ostrich herl. 4 herls the length of the marabou wing are usually tied in by the butts on top of the marabou. Sometimes herls are tied in on each side to create a lateral strips.

Wet Flies, Simple and Otherwise

Most wet fly patterns were designed to imitate drowned insects. Although many in number, methods for tying most of the standard patterns are quite similar. Some of the techniques have already been covered.

Hackle flies, including the gray hackle peacock, gray hackle yellow, and gray hackle red, along with brown hackle flies tied with peacock, yellow and red bodies, are simple to tie and effective on fish. The gray hackle peacock is tied with a sparse red tail, peacock herl body (tied again by twisting the herls around the tying thread and then wrapping the whole thing on the hook), and a soft grizzly hackle feather. The gray hackle yellow substitutes a yellow body, either of chenille or spun fur, and the gray hackle red has a red body. The brown hackle patterns use these same bodies but with a soft, brown hackle.

Many wet fly patterns call for wings made from sections of body feathers while many others use wings made from sections of flight feathers. Of the 2 types, those made from flight feather sections are the most difficult to tie and usually are no more effective at catching fish. Making such wings, generally called quill wings because they are cut from quills or wing feathers of a bird, requires considerable practice to do correctly.

Select a matched pair of duck wing quills. Matched means the identical feather from opposite wings and these feathers are usually sold this way. At the same approximate point on each of these quills, cut a narrow section of fibers, being careful not to let the fibers separate. Sections about 3/8 of an inch wide are about right for a No. 10 hook. Finish the fly body and have the tying thread half hitched about 1/8 of an inch behind the hook eye.

Grasp the 2 quill sections between the thumb and forefinger of the left hand with the heavy or butt end of

Wet Flies

MARCH BROWN SPIDER
(A good simulator wet fly for trout and panfish.) **Tail:** Speckled brown partridge tail fibers. **Body:** Hare's ear fur dubbing ribbed with gold tinsel. **Hackle:** Brown partridge, rather long.

FEMALE BEAVERKILL
(This is primarily an eastern trout pattern developed in the Catskill Mountain region of New York.) **Tail:** Gray speckled mallard flank feather fibers. **Butt:** One turn of yellow chenille to simulate egg sac. **Body:** Muskrat fur dubbing. **Hackle:** Medium red-brown. **Wing:** Gray mallard wing quill sections.

DARK CAHILL
(An excellent trout fly in both the wet and dry styles. Effective throughout the United States.) **Tail:** Lemon wood duck flank feather fibers. **Body:** Blue gray muskrat fur dubbing. **Hackle:** Medium red-brown. **Wing:** Lemon wood duck flank feather sections.

MC GINTY
(Similar to the Western Bee and effective under approximately the same conditions.) **Tail:** Red hackle and barred teal flank feather fibers. **Body:** Alternate bands of black and yellow chenille. **Hackle:** Medium red-brown. **Wing:** White-tipped mallard wing sections or white-tipped turkey sections.

GOLD RIBBED HARE'S EAR
(One of the most famous and most successful trout patterns for both eastern and western waters.) **Tail:** Brown hackle fibers. **Body:** Hare's ear fur dubbing ribbed with gold tinsel. **Hackle:** Body dubbing picked out at throat. **Wing:** Light gray duck wing quill sections.

SCARLET IBIS
(Primarily a brook trout pattern popular in eastern Canada and the northeastern United States.) **Tail:** Small strip from red dyed duck wing quill. **Body:** Scarlet silk floss ribbed with oval gold tinsel. **Hackle:** Scarlet. **Wing:** Scarlet duck wing quill sections.

the sections projecting slightly out from the ends of the thumb and finger. The natural curvature of the sections can either be flared out or in, a matter of personal choice. Most professionals flare them out. The tip or small end of the sections should sweep up from the hook shank, rather than curving down. Place the thumb and forefinger holding the sections down on the hook shank with the section butts over the eye of the hook. Relaxing the grip on the sections only slightly, bring the tying thread up between the thumb and the sections, leave a little slack in the thread, and then bring it down between the forefinger and the section it is touching. Pinch rather hard against the sections and then pull the tying thread directly down toward the tying bench. The idea is to compress these sections without allowing them to roll or fold over. Without releasing the pressure any more than necessary to pull the thread up and over the sections again, repeat the wrap and pull tight. Now release the grip to see if the sections are evenly balanced without being folded or rolled. When they are straight, make several more wraps, snip off the butts of the sections and wrap a smooth head. Whip finish and cement.

The wings made from body feather sections are tied as described earlier in making the Professor fly.

Hair wings for wet flies are tied quite similar to those for bucktails. This type of wing is becoming increasingly popular and has even invaded that last stronghold of tradition, the Atlantic salmon fly. Hair wings are rugged, easy to tie and they have fish appeal.

Wet flies are not as popular for trout fishing these days as they were a few years ago. The more "glamorous" and easier to fish dry fly has moved into the limelight but the wet fly can still play an important role in the angler's kit.

Tying the Dry

Fly Fishing was a well established sporting pursuit before an Englishman named Frederic M. Halford began expounding the virtues of flies that floated on the water like an adult mayfly. Despite some resistance from traditional-minded Englishmen, Halford, for all practical purposes, succeeded in making the dry fly the only socially acceptable method of taking trout from England's famous chalk streams.

Then, in 1890, America's Theodore Gordon received an assortment of Halford's dry flies and the new method spread to the Western Hemisphere. Dry fly fishing became the sporting thing to do and many anglers who fly fish for trout have only in recent years began using other methods to round out their fly fishing bag of tricks.

It's little wonder that dry fly fishing proved so popular. The flies are delicate, marvelously balanced creations and the rise of a hefty trout to a high floating artificial is one of angling's greatest thrills.

Dry flies look as though they would be extremely difficult to tie. Of course they are of more complex construction, but tying them is not too tough for anyone with a measure of patience and some degree of manual dexterity. The keys to tying high quality dry flies lie in developing a sense of proportion and using quality materials.

Developing a good sense of proportion for dry fly components comes from seeing and handling well tied artificials, but finding quality dry fly materials is just a matter of knowing what to look for and where

Wet Flies

COACHMAN
(An excellent trout pattern through the United States; and highly effective as a panfish fly.) **Tag:** Flat gold tinsel. **Body:** Peacock herl. **Hackle:** Red-brown. **Wing:** White duck wing quill sections.

QUEEN OF WATERS
(A very effective eastern trout pattern.) **Tail:** Speckled gray mallard body feather fibers. **Body:** Orange floss ribbed with gold tinsel. **Hackle:** Ginger tied palmer. **Wing:** Speckled gray mallard body feather sections.

WOOLY WORM
(The wooly worm originated as a bass fly for smallmouth fishing. It has become one of the most effective trout flys in the West. A number of color variations are also very effective.) **Tail:** Red quill feather section or none. **Body:** Black chenille ribbed with silver tinsel. **Hackle:** Grizzly tied palmer.

BLUE DUN
(The Blue Dun has been a popular trout pattern since the days of Izaak Walton. Outstanding pattern throughout the United States, especially for brown trout.) **Tail:** Blue dun hackle fibers. **Body:** Muskrat fur dubbing. **Hackle:** Blue dun. **Wing:** Gray duck wing quill sections.

RIO GRANDE QUEEN
(Developed as a trout fly in the southern Rocky Mountain area, this pattern has proved highly effective throughout the West.) **Tag:** Red floss. **Tail:** Yellow hackle fibers. **Body:** Black chenille. **Hackle:** Black. **Wing:** White duck wing quill sections.

MARCH BROWN
(This English pattern is also an effective trout fly throughout the United States.) **Tail:** Speckled partridge tail fibers. **Body:** Hare's ear fur dubbing ribbed with primrose yellow thread. **Hackle:** Speckled brown partridge. **Wing:** Hen pheasant wing quill sections.

to get it. The stiffest, most springy neck hackles in a variety of sizes and colors, naturally water resistant materials such as fur from water dwelling animals and waterfowl body feathers, teamed with light wire hooks and fine tying thread provide the right combination.

Dry flies come in several different styles and incorporate a number of different methods of construction. Wings made from feather sections, hackle tips and hair are all utilized. Some patterns have no wings. Bodies range from none whatsoever to heavy, clipped deer hair for extra durability and floatation. Some drys have nothing but hackle, others have 2 bands of hackle. There are patterns with the hackle wound laterally instead of vertically as in the parachute fly, and there is a series of new patterns tied without hackle.

The Light Cahill is a good example of the conventional dry fly. It is an effective trout fly, both east and west, and it is fairly easy to tie.

Select a fine wire hook, about size 12, and clamp it in the vise. Sharpen the hook and attach 6/0 tying thread, preferably white, just behind the hook eye. Wrap this thread to the mid-point on the hook shank and half hitch it. The sequence of tying on various dry fly components varies from tier to tier but the most commonly used method calls for tying the wings on first. This allows plenty of working room during the most complex stage and the butts of the winging material can be hidden under body and hackle materials.

The Light Cahill has wings of wood duck flank feather fibers. Take one of these feathers, the lemon colored ones without the black and white barred tip, and separate the fibers on both sides of the feather shaft by stroking the fluffy fibers back toward the feather butt. Now lay this feather on top of the hook with the "waist" positioned over the half hitched tying thread and the feather tips projecting over the eye of the hook. Make 2 wraps of tying thread over the waist and let the weight of the bobbin hold tension on the thread. Grasp the feather butt with the left hand and pull it toward the bend of the hook, being careful not to let the thread wraps slide on the hook shank. Pull the feather until the tips project from the winds a distance equal to the length of the hook shank. Make several more wraps over the feather, then lift the tips and make several wraps in front of the tip against the feather shaft.

Make enough wraps so the feather fibers stand vertically from the hook. Half hitch the tying thread and snip off the butt of the feather, including all the fluffy fibers.

Now take the bodkin, and sighting down the hook shank from the eye, separate the feather fibers into two equal bunches. Make a wrap of thread between these bunches and continue with figure 8 wraps until the 2 wings are cocked evenly. Some gentle pulling to position one or the other wing while making these wraps may be necessary to get the right balance and separation. When these wings are properly set, wind the thread behind the wings and half hitch. It's a good idea at this point to place a drop of cement on the base of the wings to lock them in position. Wrap the tying thread back to the bend of the hook and half hitch.

The next step is to tie in a tail of stiff ginger hackle fibers or hair from a fox squirrel tail. A dozen fibers is about right and they should project a hook shank length from where they are tied in. Make several wraps over these tail fibers, half hitch, and cut off the tail fiber butts well forward, just behind the wings, to prevent causing a bulge in the fly body. Now

Wet Flies

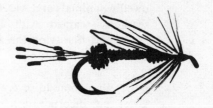

RIO GRANDE KING
(An effective trout fly throughout the West, particularly in the southern Rocky Mountains.) **Tail:** Yellow hackle fibers. **Tip:** Gold tinsel. **Body:** Black chenille. **Hackle:** Yellow. **Wing:** White duck wing quill sections.

CALIFORNIA COACHMAN
(A variation of the Royal Coachman trout fly that is popular on the West Coast.) **Tail:** Golden pheasant tippet fibers. **Body:** In three equal sections beginning with a peacock herl butt, followed by a narrow waist of yellow floss, and then a peacock herl shoulder. **Hackle:** Pale yellow. **Wing:** White duck wing quill sections.

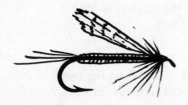

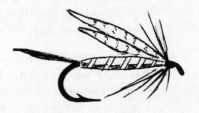

CAMPBELL'S FANCY
(An attractor trout pattern, particularly useful in the northeastern United States.) **Tail:** Short golden pheasant crest fibers. **Body:** Flat gold tinsel ribbed with fine gold wire. **Hackle:** Light furnace. **Wing:** Darkly barred teal flank feather sections.

GRIZZLY KING
(An effective trout pattern for both eastern and western waters. Also an excellent panfish pattern.) **Tail:** Narrow section of red duck wing quill. **Body:** Green silk floss ribbed with narrow flat gold tinsel. **Hackle:** Badger. **Wing:** Speckled gray mallard flank feather sections.

STONEFLY
(A rather subdued trout pattern that produces throughout the United States, particularly with brown trout.) **Tail:** Three strands of speckled partridge or bronze mallard fibers. **Body:** Light gray fur dubbing ribbed with primrose yellow thread. **Hackle:** Dark grizzly. **Wing:** Hen pheasant wing quill sections.

wax the tying thread heavily and spin a 1-1/2 inch strand of cream dyed beaver or fox belly fur. Wrap this body material forward to the wings and half hitch the tying thread.

Hackling of dry flies can be frustrating for beginning tiers, especially if the hackles are not of first rate quality. Select a dry fly quality, ginger hackle feather of the right size by bending the hackle shaft over the hook just ahead of the wings. The hackle should reach almost but not quite to the wing tips. Hackle gauges are available to help determine hackle size but experience will soon prove just as reliable. Snip the hackle feather shaft where the fluffy fibers end and the smooth, glossy hackle fibers begin. Now clip these stiff fibers on each side of the shaft for a distance of about 3/16 of an inch. These short barbules will help anchor the hackle when it is tied in. Now stroke the hackle to make the fibers stand out at right angles.

Hackle feathers are normally curved somewhat from tip to butt and also from the tips of the fibers on one side of the shaft to the tips on the opposite side. Dry fly hackles should always be wrapped so this natural curvature "cups" toward the front of the fly. Lay the trimmed hackle butt on top of the hook shank, immediately in front of the wings so the natural curvature is back and up and then tie it in this position. Once the hackle butt is securely wrapped down and the tying thread half hitched, grasp the hackle feather tip with the hackle pliers, lift the feather tip to nearly vertical, then wrap the hackle sideways, over and under the hook, then up and *behind* the wings. Make at least one turn of hackle behind the wings, two if possible. Now bring the hackle forward and wrap in front of the wings. If there is not enough feather to make two

wraps behind the wings and three in front, tie the hackle tip down, half hitch, clip excess or askew fibers away, and tie in another hackle with which to finish the job. Once the fly hackle has been completed, wrap a smooth head, whip finish, and cement.

A more recent dry fly development has been the use of hair wings. Rugged and highly functional, hair winged dry flies have supplanted many of the more traditional ties in the kits of both eastern and western fly fishermen. The Wulff series of dry flies is an outstanding example of this development.

Hair wings, usually of deer hair, squirrel tail or calf tail fibers, are tied in the same way the feather wings were on the Light Cahill. The hair is stiffer and therefore more difficult to work with but the tying technique is similar. Before tying the small bunch of hair fibers on the hook, try to get the hair tips even. This can be done by placing the hair, tip down, in a 35mm photo film can, a plastic prescription tablet container, or a similar short tube with a flat bottom. Tapping the bottom of the container while holding it at about a 45 degree angle will even the tips. The hair should be tied in so the tips project forward, just as with the feather fiber wing. Then wrap in front of the hair to make it stand vertically, separate the fibers into two equal bunches with the bodkin and then wrap in between with the figure eight wrap. Care should be exercised in cutting off the hair wing butts. This can relax tension on the wings, permitting them to twist.

One of the most effective dry fly wings is made of hackle feather tips. The Adams, one of the finest, all around dry flies known, has this type of wing. The Adams starts out like the Cahill, using black thread this

Dry Flies

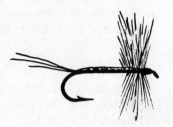

LEADWINGED COACHMAN
(An excellent general trout fly, especially popular on eastern waters.) **Tail:** Medium blue dun hackle fibers. **Body:** Peacock herl. **Wings:** Dark gray duck wing quill sections. **Hackle:** Red-brown.

QUILL GORDON
(Probably the first true American dry fly. Developed on eastern streams but has since proved an excellent choice on almost all trout waters.) **Tail:** Medium blue dun hackle fibers. **Body:** Stripped peacock quill. **Wings:** Lemon wood duck flank feather sections. **Hackle:** Blue dun.

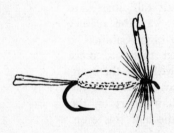

RAT FACED MC DOUGAL
(An excellent rough-water trout fly. Also useful for river smallmouths.) **Tail:** Ginger hackle fibers. **Body:** Clipped tannish-gray deer hair. **Wings:** Pale grizzly hackle tips. **Hackle:** Ginger.

MARCH BROWN (FLICK)
(An excellent trout dry fly for matching many of the brown shaded mayfly hatches.) **Tail:** Dark ginger hackle fibers. **Body:** Sandy tan fur dubbing. **Wings:** Lemon wood duck flank feather sections. **Hackle:** Reddish-brown with a grizzly hackle wound in front.

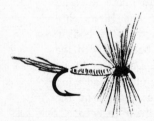

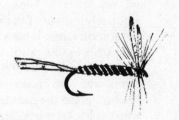

GRAY WULFF
(This was the first of a series of dry flies that have proven highly successful for rough water trout fishing and, in larger sizes, for Atlantic salmon.) **Tail:** Dark brown bucktail. **Body:** Gray fur dubbing. **Wings:** Dark brown bucktail. **Hackle:** Medium blue dun.

MOSQUITO
(This delicate creation is an excellent trout fly, especially on flat, slow moving stretches and on lakes.) **Tail:** Grizzly hackle fibers. **Body:** White floss ribbed with black thread, stripped peacock herl, or a white and a black moose mane fiber wound together. **Wings:** Grizzly hackle tips. **Hackle:** Grizzly.

time, by wrapping back to hook shank mid-point. Half hitch. Now select two grizzly neck hackles having similar curvature and barring. Cut off the tips of these hackle feathers to a length about half again longer than the hook shank. Snip off the hackle barbules from the butt of the feather tips to a point where the unclipped portion equals hook shank length.

Now hold these hackle tips on top of the hook shank so they flare out on each side of the hook eye. Hold them firmly in this position while making several wraps over the clipped butts, then grasp the feathers, pull them up vertically and make several wraps immediately in front to hold them that way. The Adams is normally tied spent wing fashion, which means the wings extend more out to the side of the hook. Using the figure 8 wrap again, force the wings apart. It sometimes helps to make figure 8 wraps *under* the shank to pull the wings down into the spent wing position. Correct positioning and balance of hackle tip wings is critical. The stiffer center rib in the wing will cause an unbalanced fly to spin during casting, weakening the leader.

Once the hackle tip wings are cocked correctly, wind the thread back to the bend of the hook and half hitch it. Now take a half dozen or so dark brown saddle hackle fibers and a like number of grizzly saddle hackle fibers, combine them so they are well mixed and tie these in for the tail.

The Adams body is made of dubbed muskrat fur.

The secret of this fly's success is probably the unique hackle. It carries out the mixed effect introduced in the tail by combining a brown hackle with a grizzly one. The two hackles can be wound separately but mixing them together in this fashion results in wrapping under too many fibers. If the hackles are cut to exactly the same length, they can be tied in together and wound at the same time. It might be necessary while doing this to change the grip of the hackle pliers to keep tension even on both feathers. Once the two hackles are tied in and wrapped, whip finish the head and cement.

The well known Bivisible dry fly gets its name from the two colors of hackle used—one supposedly more visible to the fish and the other more visible to the fisherman. This is nothing more than a fly that has nothing but hackles, starting at the bend and extending continuously all the way to the eye of the hook. Brown, black, dun, ginger or grizzly are all commonly used for the main hackle color, with a white hackle collar of one, no more than two, turns at the front. Using neck hackles, it sometimes becomes necessary to tie in several as the wrapping progresses because neck hackles are seldom long enough for the complete job. Long, narrow saddle hackles are a better choice for the main hackle in bivisibles.

Fore and aft hackle dry flies have proven effective. They are particularly popular in the West. These flies are tied with one, usually slightly undersized, hackle at the bend of the hook, a body, and another, usually different colored hackle, of the correct size tied in the normal position behind the hook eye. The Renegade, which has brown hackle at the aft or tail position, peacock herl body, and white hackle behind the head, is a good example of this type of fly.

Clipped deer hair bodies are popular on some dry flies. The Irresistible is the best known example. Clipped deer hair bodies

Dry Flies

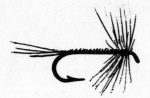

GINGER QUILL
(An English pattern that has proven an effective trout fly on north central and eastern United States trout waters.) **Tail:** Ginger hackle fibers. **Body:** Stripped peacock quill. **Hackle:** Ginger. **Wing:** Light gray duck wing quill sections.

LIGHT CAHILL
(A particularly effective trout pattern in both wet and dry versions. Good throughout the United States.) **Tail:** Lemon wood duck flank feather fibers. **Body:** Cream fur dubbing. **Hackle:** Pale ginger. **Wing:** Lemon wood duck flank feather sections.

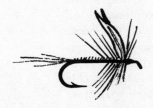

WICKHAMS FANCY
(Predominately an eastern trout pattern, especially good for brook trout.) **Tail:** Ginger hackle fibers. **Body:** Flat gold tinsel ribbed with oval gold tinsel. **Hackle:** Ginger tied palmer. **Wing:** Gray duck wing quill sections.

GRAY HACKLE
(The Gray Hackle, which is also tied with a yellow body, is one of the most effective trout flies, both east and west.) **Tail:** Narrow section of red duck wing quill. **Body:** Peacock herl. **Hackle:** Soft grizzly. Fish wet or dry.

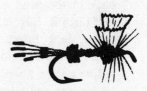

IRON BLUE DUN
(Ancient fly pattern effective for trout fishing in both the eastern and western United States.) **Tail:** Small bunch of Coch-y-bondhu hackle fibers. **Tag:** Red floss tied in over base of tail. **Body:** Dubbed mole fur. **Hackle:** Coch-y-bondhu. **Wing:** Dark gray duck wing quill sections.

FANWING ROYAL COACHMAN
(This fragile but fancy dry trout fly is often favored for late evenings.) **Tail:** Brown hackle fibers. **Body:** Rear third peacock herl, waist of red floss, and forward third of peacock herl. **Wings:** Matched white duck breast feathers. **Hackle:** Red-brown.

will be discussed later in detail under clipped deer hair bass bugs.

A different type of deer hair body is used on the Humpy, a popular western dry fly pattern. The tying thread in the Humpy is wrapped all the way to the hook bend, with no wings being attached on the way. A deer hair tail is tied in and then a longer bunch of deer hair, 1-1/2 to 2 times the hook shank length, is tied in on top of the tail with the fibers pointing the same way. A spun fur body is wrapped, then the longer bunch of deer hair pulled forward over the body, tied in, then wrapped so the remaining tips of the hair stand up in 2 clumps as wings. Dry fly hackles are tied in and wrapped, then the head is whip finished and cememted.

Spiders and variants are dry flies with oversize hackles, the spiders usually tied without wings and variants usually with wings. The usual spiders have long, thin tails but a variation known as skater is tailless. All these flies should be tied as sparsely as possible to achieve an ethereal, delicate effect on the water. Unfortunately, the spade hackles that are so ideal for tying these flies are extremely hard to find. Saddle hackles will work but not as well.

Most dry flies are designed to imitate mayflies, caddis flies and other aquatic insects. Terrestrials are dry flies designed to imitate land insects that frequently fall into the water. Grasshoppers, crickets, ants, beetles and leaf hoppers are among the insects most frequently copied. The Grasshopper and cricket imitations are usually made with deer hair tied on the hook shank, butts forward, with the butts then being clipped to form a head. Underwings, tied in before the deer hair, are usually quill feather sections of the proper size and color.

Dubbing fur is the thing for ant imitations and seal fur is the best choice. Clamp a size 16 or 18 hook in the vise and sharpen the point. Attach the tying thread just behind mid-point on the hook shank, wrap back to the bend and half hitch. Wax the thread and spin 1/2 inch strand of black seal fur. Wrap this strand to form the gaster, that enlarged part of an ant's body back of the waist. Half hitch the thread and tie in a small, black dry fly hackle. Make one turn of this hackle, tie off and cut the excess away. Wax the thread again and spin and even shorter strand of black fur to build a thorax or forebody, then skip about a hair's width of hook shank and wrap a head. Whip finish and cement the head. Ants can also be tied with red fur or with 2 color bodies.

Beetles and leaf hoppers are tied nearly alike except for the "wing." Wrap the hook shank with hackle as in a bivisible. Clip the hackles off on top and bottom of the hook to leave fibers sticking out only at the sides. Take 2 of the bluish-green feathers from the neck of a ring-necked pheasant rooster and clip fibers along both sides of the feather butts until the remaining feather fibers from an oval silhouette when viewed against the light. Lay one of these feathers over the other, dip the bodkin in fly head cement and coat the feathers. Allow the cement to dry and then tie the feathers in so they will lay flat over the hackle. The feather butts are overwrapped to form a head while the feather forms the beetle body. The hackles projecting on each side simulate the beetle's legs.

Leaf hopper imitations, tiny flies called jassids, are tied in the same fashion but a jungle cock nail is substituted for the two ring-necked pheasant feathers.

Dry Flies

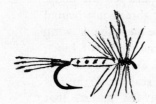

PINK LADY
(Primarily a trout fly for eastern streams.) **Tail:** Ginger hackle fibers. **Body:** Pink floss ribbed with flat gold tinsel. **Wings:** Light gray duck wing quill sections. **Hackle:** Ginger.

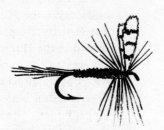

ADAMS
(Considered by most experts to be the best producing dry fly. Designed for Michigan waters but has now spread to trout streams throughout the world.) **Tail:** Mixed bunch of red-brown and grizzly hackle fibers. **Body:** Gray fur dubbing. **Wings:** Grizzly hackle tips tied spent fashion. **Hackle:** One red-brown hackle and one grizzly hackle wound together.

BADGER SPIDER
(Spiders in various colors are tied with extra large hackles or small hooks, or both, to produce a light, dancing effect on the water. A highly effective trout fly, especially for brown trout.) **Tail:** Badger hackle fibers. **Body:** Flat gold tinsel. **Hackle:** Extra long badger hackle.

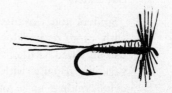

CROSS SPECIAL
(Although designed as an eastern trout fly, the Cross Special is a good imitation of pale mayflies of western rivers.) **Tail:** Light blue dun hackle fibers. **Body:** Grayish-white fox fur dubbing. **Wings:** Lemon wood duck flank feather sections. **Hackle:** Light blue dun.

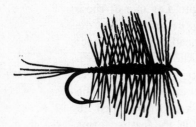

BROWN BIVISIBLE
(Bivisible dry flies, which are available in a variety of colors, are good floaters which makes them excellent for fast, bouncy water. Particularly good for rainbow trout.) **Tail:** Tip of long brown hackle. No wings or body. **Hackle:** Brown, tied palmer rather closely. A white hackle is wound on at the front, just behind the hook eye.

CONOVER
(Excellent flat water fly for brown trout fishing, both in the eastern and western United States.) **Tail:** Cream badger hackle fibers. **Body:** Dubbed fur of mixed blue-gray, red, and cream to produce a mixed creamy gray color with red tones. **Hackle:** Cream badger slightly longer than normal.

Hard-bodied Bass Bugs

Bass bugs of cork, balsa wood and plastic are excellent fish catchers and fun to construct. The basic rules apply: such bugs should have a "face" that slants up and forward over the hook eye; wings and other appendages that make bugs hard to cast should be kept to a minimum; and the body should not extend much below the hook shank to permit maximum possible hook gape.

Simple bass bugs can be constructed with bottle corks or corks specially shaped for making bugs. Cork and balsa bodies from scratch are first cut to rough shape with a razor blade and then finished by sanding with an emery board. A cupped face is little better than a flat one and much harder to shape. After the body is shaped, use a short piece of hacksaw blade or one of the saw blades made to fit the X-acto-type knife handle, to saw a shallow groove in the bug body from front to rear.

Special hooks are available for making hard bodied bugs. These have special humps or kinks in the shank to prevent their turning in the bug body. The long shanked type will usually hook more fish.

Place one of these hooks in the vise, attach 2-0 tying thread about 1/8 inch behind the eye and wrap back around any kinks or humps in the shank to where it straightens out again and half hitch. Clip a bunch of squirrel tail, bucktail, or calf tail fibers, somewhat heavier than would be used to make a bucktail fly wing, and tie this bunch of fibers on the hook shank a short distance back of the hump. Cut off the excess hair and coat the wrap with cement.

Now take the cork body and cut away enough material around the rear of the sawed out slot so the body will fit snugly over the hook, with the hump pressed into the cork and the butts of the hair, or bug tail, being hidden by the body. Coat the wrapped hook shank with cement, including a second coat on the hair butts and press the body securely into place. The hook eye should project far enough from the front of the bug body to expose a short distance of hook shank behind the eye.

After the cement has dried to lock the bug body onto the hook shank, open a small bottle of lacquer and dip the body to where the tail comes out. Hang the bug up to dry. Cork has pits and several coats may be needed to produce a good finish. A cork sealer is available and should be added to the tying kit if many hard bodied bugs are planned. Once enough coats have been added and the body is completely dry, usually overnight, scrape away the excess lacquer that has dried around and in the hook eye, including the short bit of shank behind the eye.

The final step, for added embellishment, is to paint eyes on the bug in the manner suggested for bucktails and streamers. Such a bug is pretty easy to cast and has good action on the water.

Frog imitations are tied very similarly but the hair "tail" is divided with the tying thread into 2 separate bunches that fork like the legs of a frog. Green bucktail and a green body with black spots makes an effective frog imitation. If bulging eyes are preferred, stick rounded-headed map tacks of the appropriate size into the bug body before dipping. Map tacks do add some weight. Another method is to insert small sections of a wooden match into holes dug in the body, leaving enough matchstick projecting to form the eye bulge.

The so-called crippled minnow bug, which is very effective around

Dry Flies

PALE EVENING DUN
(An important eastern trout fly.) **Tail:** Pale blue dun hackle fibers. **Body:** Yellow floss ribbed with narrow gold tinsel. **Wings:** Light gray duck wing quill sections. **Hackle:** Pale blue dun.

WHIRLING BLUE DUN
(An old standard for trout, especially in the east. An excellent brown trout pattern.) **Tail:** Blue dun hackle fibers. **Body:** Blue-gray muskrat fur dubbing ribbed with narrow gold tinsel. **Wings:** Gray duck wing feather sections. **Hackle:** Light blue dun.

DUN VARIANT (FLICK)
(An excellent brown trout pattern throughout the country. Particularly effective on flat water where delicate cast is necessary. The wide hackle practically prevents a sloppy presentation.) **Tail:** Blue dun hackle fibers. **Body:** Stripped dark brown hackle quill. If quill is too brittle, soak in water before wrapping. **Wings:** None. **Hackle:** Extra long blue dun.

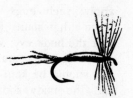

RED QUILL (FLICK)
(Primary an eastern pattern for brown trout. It has proved effective on midwestern and western trout waters.) **Tail:** Dark blue dun hackle fibers. **Body:** Stripped dark brown hackle quill. If quill is too brittle, soak in water before wrapping. **Wings:** Lemon wood duck flank feather sections. **Hackle:** Dark blue dun.

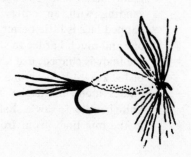

COFFIN FLY
(Excellent floater that is effective on trout, especially in heavy water. Also good for Atlantic salmon and smallmouth bass.) **Tail:** Black hair or hackle fibers. **Body:** White deer hair spun on hook and clipped to shape. **Wings:** Black hackle tips. **Hackle:** Badger.

IRRESISTIBLE
(This is another, possible the original, clipped deer hair bodied fly. It is excellent for trout in heavier water and works well for Atlantic salmon and smallmouth bass.) **Tail:** Dark bucktail or body hair from white-tailed deer. **Body:** Gray deer hair spun on hook and clipped to shape. **Wings:** Dark bucktail or body hair from white-tailed deer. **Hackle:** Dark rusty blue dun.

lily pads because of its more streamlined shape, is made with a bullet-shaped cork with the pointed end to the front. Hackle feathers tied so they flare on each side of the hook bend and a hackle collar over the feather butts will add length and motion.

Bug bodies of plastic foam are lighter than cork but not quite as tough. Foam plastic bug bodies are constructed the same way cork bodies are but before painting, touch a spot of paint to the underside of the body as a test. Some plastics dissolve when in contact with various chemicals and the particular paint or lacquer being used might not be compatible with the plastic.

Deer Hair Bodied Bugs and Flies

Some of the most effective bass bug and dry fly bodies are made by spinning deer body hair on the hook shank, compacting it tightly, and then trimming to shape. Bass bugs made with such bodies are lighter and easier to cast than those having cork or plastic bodies. The tying of such bodies is quite complex but practice will soon overcome most of the problems.

Deer body hair, as well as hair from bighorn sheep, pronghorn, and caribou, is hollow and when tied on a hook shank, tends to flare out in all directions. Deer body hair is the standard, pronghorn hair is coarser, but still spins well, and caribou hair is the softest which makes it particularly suitable for smaller flies.

Heavier thread is necessary for spinning hollow hair bodies. A size designated as "C" is about right. Attach this thread to the hook near the bend as hollow hair will resist spinning on a thread-wrapped shank. Tie in any tail of hair or feathers that might be needed. Now take a bunch of deer body hair, snipped off close to the skin, and comb out the loose fluff from the butts of the hair. The right size bunch for any particular tier is a matter of experience but one slightly less than the diameter of an ordinary pencil is good for starters.

Lay this hair parallel on the hook shank with the mid-point just where the thread is half hitched. Holding the hair firmly with the left hand, take two wraps of tying thread around the hair and the hook. Now as the thread is pulled tight, carefully relax the grip on the hair. It should spin around the hook shank to form a collar of hair not too dissimilar from a dry fly hackle. Once the hair flares and spins around the hook properly, bring the thread through the fibers and half hitch it immediately in front of them.

The hair has to be compacted as the tying operation continues. To do this, push the hair tightly to the rear with the fingers. Better yet, use a piece of plastic, like a tooth brush handle, with a smooth edged hole bored through it. Stick the hook eye through the hold and slide the plastic back on the hook shank to where it can be used to push against the hair. When the first bunch of hair is tied in and compacted, tie in a second bunch the same way and push it back hard against the first bunch. Keep repeating this until the space on the hook shank to be occupied by the body is completely covered.

All these comments and suggestions have only scratched the surface of the fly tier's art. Various fly tying "dictionaries" list literally thousands of patterns just waiting to be tied.

Fly tying is great fun, it is an excellent pastime for those long winter evenings, and it is guaranteed to improve the fly fisherman's days astream. It's the kind of hobby that can "hook" the fisherman just as surely as it does the fish that slams into that personal creation of fur, feathers and steel.

Dry Flies

BLUE QUILL
(A standard trout fly, especially for brown trout.) **Tail:** Medium blue dun hackle fibers. **Body:** Stripped peacock quill. **Wings:** Medium blue-gray duck wing quill sections. **Hackle:** Medium blue dun.

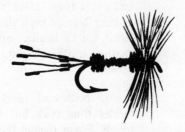

ROYAL COACHMAN HAIRWING
(A modern variation of an old pattern. One of the truly outstanding dry flys for all species of trout. Especially popular in the West.) **Tail:** Brown hackle fibers or golden pheasant tippet strands. **Body:** Standard royal coachman body of one-third peacock herl butt, one-third scarlet floss waist, and one third peacock herl shoulder. **Wings:** White calf tail evenly divided into two distinct bunches. **Hackle:** Natural red-brown.

TUPS INDISPENSABLE
(One of the oldest fly patterns. A trout fly that is popular in England and the eastern United States.) **Tag:** Yellow floss. **Tail:** Honey dun hackle fibers. **Body:** Mixed scarlet and cream dubbing, either lamb's wool or dyed fur. **Hackle:** Natural honey dun.

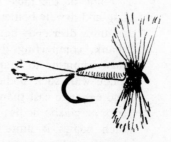

WHITE WULFF
(An excellent trout and Atlantic salmon fly, particularly when fishing heavy water or in poor light.) **Tail:** White calf tail or bucktail fibers. **Body:** White wool or fur dubbing. **Wings:** White calf tail or bucktail. **Hackle:** White or light cream badger.

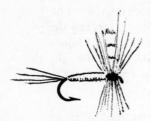

GRAY FOX
(Primarily an eastern brown trout pattern, the gray fox is an excellent general purpose dry fly throughout the United States.) **Tail:** Ginger hackle fibers. **Body:** Fawn colored red fox fur dubbing. **Wings:** Gray barred mallard flank feather sections. **Hackle:** One grizzly and one light ginger hackle feather wound together.

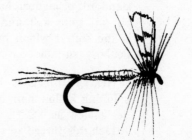

DARK HENDRICKSON
(An eastern developed brown trout pattern. It has proved excellent for trout in midwestern and western waters.) **Tail:** Dark rusty blue dun hackle fibers. **Body:** Grayish brown red fox dubbing. **Wings:** Lemon wood duck flank feather sections. **Hackle:** Dark rusty blue dun.

Dry Flies

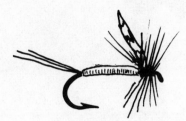

WOODRUFF
(An effective flat water trout pattern) **Tail:** Ginger hackle fibers. **Body:** Chartreuse (yellowish) green wool dubbing. **Wings:** Grizzly hackle tips tied spent. **Hackle:** Medium ginger.

PINK LADY BIVISIBLE
(A good floating trout fly for bouncy water. Also good for Atlantic salmon.) **Tail:** Light ginger hackle fibers. **Body:** Pink floss ribbed with gold tinsel. **Wings:** None. **Hackle:** Light ginger tied palmer over body, followed by a golden olive hackle behind eye of hook.

MALE BEAVERKILL
(A high floating eastern pattern, particularly for brown trout.) **Tail:** Ginger hackle fibers. **Body:** White floss. **Wings:** Light gray duck wing quill sections. **Hackle:** One dark brown hackle tied palmer over body, followed by dark brown hackle at shoulder.

GOLD RIBBED HARE'S EAR
(Differs from the wet fly version through the addition of stiff hackles and the more upright tie. An excellent trout fly for all waters.) **Tail:** Furnace hackle fibers. **Body:** European hare's ear dubbing ribbed with narrow gold tinsel. **Wings:** Light gray duck wing quill sections. **Hackle:** Furnace or Coch-y-bondhu.

BEAVERKILL RED FOX
(A good general purpose dry fly that is effective on trout, especially brown trout, throughout the United States.) **Tail:** Ginger hackle fibers. **Body:** Blue-gray muskrat fur dubbing ribbed with narrow gold tinsel. **Wings:** None. **Hackle:** Ginger immediately ahead of body, followed by a medium blue dun hackle.

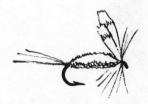

SPIRIT OF PITTSFORD MILL
(A Vermont-originated impressionistic trout pattern that has proved excellent for trout almost everywhere they are found. Particularly effective on brown trout.) **Tail:** Ginger hackle fibers. **Body:** Grayish-white duck down dubbing ribbed with clipped ginger hackle. **Wings:** Grizzly hackle tips. **Hackle:** Ginger.

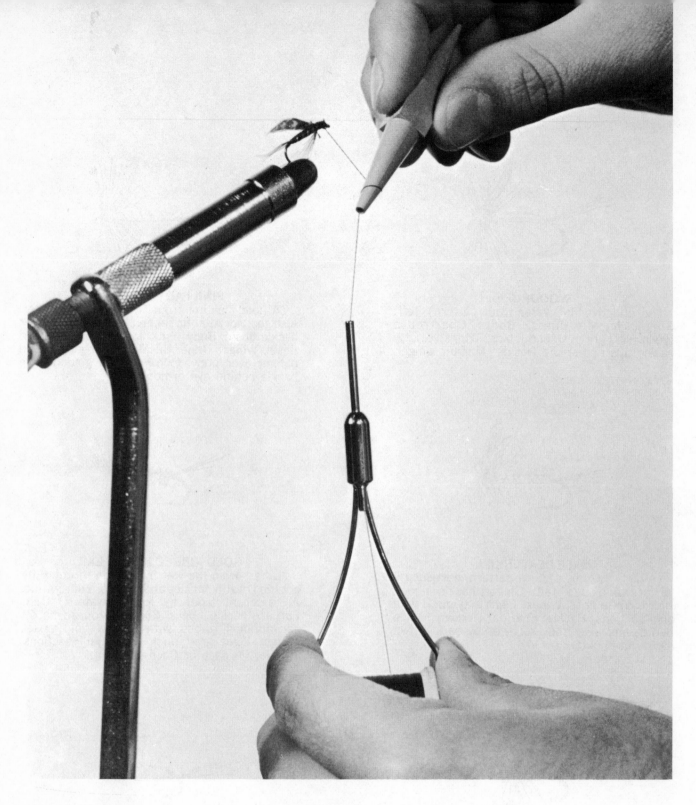

New Half-Hitch Tyer

On the stream or at home, fly tying enthusiasts can easily apply a tight, secure half-hitch knot to a finished fly by using a new Half-Hitch Tyer.

The handy, inexpensive tool (Shown on these two pages) is made from high impact Cycolac plastic to insure a smooth finish and long wear. Tapered portions of the tool are glass smooth to provide easy transfer of thread to the finished fly without danger

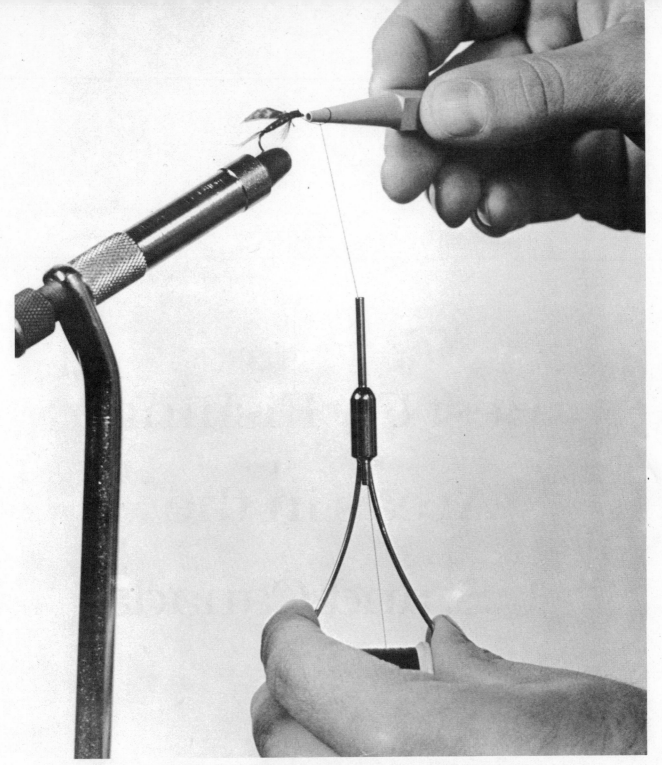

of damage to a fine thread with a low tensile strength. The sturdy Half-Hitch Tyer can be dropped without fear of damage to the thin walls at either of the tying ends.

A ⅛ inch diameter hole in the center of the lightweight tool allows it to be tied to a fishing vest or placed on a hook or nail at the tiers bench for easy storage. The center of the Half-Hitch Tyer is square to prevent rolling when placed on the table or work area.

The Half-Hitch Tyer can be used on hooks ranging in size from 8 through 22, the favorite sizes for most artificial flies.

This new Half-Hitch Tyer is made by Spectrum Enterprises, Box 224, Bainbridge, Pa. 17502.

Best Fly Fishing Areas in the U.S. and Canada

Alabama

Fly fisherman using lightweight rod and automatic reel is about to bring in a nice rainbow from an Alaskan river. Stream is in ideal stage for dry flies.

Sport fishing in Alabama is popular and productive, and the season is long and enjoyable due to its mild temperatures, which also provide a long growing season for the fish. Black bass and bream are the most commonly sought after fish, but fly-fishing is very effective in taking bluegills along the deep ledges and weedy banks during the spring, summer and fall. Verified catches of ten and eleven pound black bass on fly rods are available.

The Tennessee River with it's four large reservoirs - Guntersville, Wheeler, Wilson and Pickwick - provide some of the most excellent fishing in the state. Largemouth and smallmouth bass abound and most are good sized - six to eight pounds. The Chattahoochee, Tallapoosa, Coosa, Black Warrior, Tombigbee and Alabama Rivers, with their systems of locks and dams, create backwaters which teem with bass of various kinds, walleyes and a variety of other species.

State owned public fishing lakes which have been constructed by the state in areas which were not naturally supplied with fishing waters, have been stocked with bluegills, red ear sunfish and largemouth bass. In addition there are numerous artificial ponds and small lakes in Alabama which are open to the public for a small daily fee.

Alaska

Somewhere in Alaska it's open season on something - but there's often a "best time" for taking many species: King Salmon - In May and June the real lunkers are running. Silver Salmon - Autumn is coho time; August, September and October. Sheefish - The Inconnu run mainly in August and September. Steelhead - November and May are the best times. Grayling - All summer, from breakup to freezup. Cutthroat, Dolly Varden, rainbow, pike and other species are nearly always available, though sea-run fish of the first two species add to the excitement at certain times. Alaska has the finest fresh water fishing anywhere - but these are the worlds best: *Grayling* - Tikchik and Ugashik (Bristol Bay); Delta-Clearwater. *Rainbows* - Wood River System; Kvichak and Nakmek Rivers; Katmai National Monument. Fishing Licenses range from $5 for a visitor's 10-day fishing license to $20 for a combination hunting-fishing license.

Summer-time temperatures range from 50 degrees to 95 degrees, and May days are sunny days in Alaska. You'll escape from the heat, but it's still warm enough even for swimming in some areas.

The "Panhandle" - the long strip of land that runs from the Kenai Peninsula along the edge of British Columbia is rich in islands and canals and beckons the lover of true wilderness. The lakes and streams are rich in cutthroat and rainbow trout, and salmon and steelhead as well, in their seasons.

The Kenai Peninsula has an abundance of salmon, steelhead and rainbow trout in its rivers - chiefly the Kenai River, but don't neglect the Ninilchik, the Russian, the Anchor or the Moose Rivers - and it's lakes such as the Siklak, Kenai, Russian, Hidden and Jean.

Give thought to western Alaska, also, which includes the Brooks River (rainbow, grayling, lake trout, Dolly Varden, Northern pike, sockeye and coho salmon). Here are also excellent lakes - Iliamna and Tikchik to name just two.

The service of guides is recommended, as many of these rivers and lakes are cold, swift and treacherous and could be dangerous to boat on without the know-how of one experienced in their vagaries.

Since sporting goods stores are rare, try to remember extra tackle. Be sure to include a heavier fly rod and large line capacity reel, and your dry flies - Black Gnat, Mosquito, Royal Coachman, Yellow May and Parmachene Belle. You will also be using nymphs, large streamers and most of the common wet flies.

Mosquito repellant and sun protective lotion plus a pair of light gloves are your final "musts".

CAMPGROUNDS

Campgrounds in Alaska are maintained by the State of Alaska, Division of Lands, the U.S. Bureau of Land Management, the U.S. Forest Service, the U.S. Fish & Wildlife Service, and the U.S. National Parks Service.

Since many of the finest Alaskan waters are remote and far from motel and eating facilities, camping is almost a necessity. Here's a list of campgrounds near good fishing.

State of Alaska
Division of Lands Campgrounds
(For further information write: Division of Lands, Juneau, Alaska 99801).

1. **BEDROCK CREEK CAMPGROUND**—127 miles north of Fairbanks on the Steese Highway, within 33 miles of Circle City on the Yukon River. 2 camping units.

2. **KETCHEM CREEK CAMPGROUND**—Situated 2 miles west of Circle Hot Springs at Mile 146 of the Steese Highway. 1 camping unit.

3. **TOLOVANA RIVER CAMPGROUND**—Located at Mile 56 on the Elliot Highway (grayling fishing in the river and wildlife for the amateur photographer). 3 camping units.

4. **CHATANIKA RIVER CAMPGROUND**—Chatanika Campground, at Mile 39 on the Steese Highway. Large gold dredges have uprooted the land for miles. The gold panner can find "colors" in the streams, and there is fishing and hunting in the area. 18 camping units.

5. **SALCHA RIVER CAMPGROUND**—Situated on the river at Mile 323 on the Richardson Highway. Fishing and boating. 8 camping units.

6. **CLEARWATER-ALCAN CAMPGROUND**—At mile 1415 on the Alaska Highway, a side road takes you 8 miles northeast to the Clearwater Campground. Fishing and boating. 11 camping units.

7. **CHENA RIVER CAMPGROUND**—Located three miles west of Fairbanks just off Airport Road on the Chena River. 11 camping units.

8. **DONNELLY CREEK CAMPGROUND**—In the foothills of the Alaska Range, at Mile 238 on the Richardson Highway. A beaver dam in the middle of the campground gives the visitor an opportunity to photograph the animals at work. Grayling fishing upstream. 11 camping units.

9. **MOON LAKE CAMPGROUND**—17 miles west of Tok Junction at Mile 1332 on the Alaska Highway. Boat launching ramps. Fishing is "spotty" due to an abundance of natural fish food. 8 camping units.

10. **AMERICAN CREEK CAMPGROUND**—Located at Mile 154 on the Taylor Highway. Wildlife photography, gold panning and grayling fishing interest travelers. 6 camping units.

11. **LIBERTY CREEK CAMPGROUND**—Located at Mile 136 on the Taylor Highway. Gold panning produces a few flakes or an occasional nugget. Grayling fishing and moose, caribou and bear in area. 6 camping units.

12. **TOK RIVER CAMPGROUND**—Located 9 miles east of the American Customs Station on the Tok River, at Mile 1309 of the Alaska Highway. Water is not available, and visitors should bring a water bag for that morning cup of coffee. 10 camping units.

13. **CLEARWATER-SLANA CAMPGROUND**—Located 15 miles south of Tok Junction at Mile 109.5 on the Slana-Tok Highway. A clear stream flows through the area and hunting and fishing is found close by. Here the visitor can photograph wildlife. A rainshelter will be found in this camping area. 10 camping units.

14. **LAKEVIEW CAMPGROUND**—Situated at Mile 1257 on the Alaska Highway. Fishing for those with a boat in tow. A good camera location. 6 camping units.

15. **DEADMAN LAKE CAMPGROUND**—Scenic camping site located at Mile 1249 of the Alaska

Here's proof that Lake Michigan is starting to produce some fine large browns along with the chinook and coho salmon. These four fine specimens were taken in the lake off the western Michigan shore. It is possible to get them by wading offshore and using streamers on fly rods.

Highway with access to the lake for boat launching. 5 camping units.

16. **GARDINER CREEK CAMP-GROUND**—On Alaska Highway at Mile 1247, 80 miles from Tok Junction. 6 camping units.

17. **AHTELL CREEK CAMP-GROUND**—60 miles north of Glennallen on the Slana-Tok highway. 6 camping units.

18. **BRUSHKANA CREEK CAMPGROUND**—Located 109 miles west of Paxson on the Denali Highway (Mt. McKinley Road), in the midst of one of Alaska's greatest game areas. Many lakes and streams afford excellent grayling fishing. Brushkana Campground is equipped with a rainshelter. 8 camping units.

19. **CLEARWATER-DENALI CAMPGROUND**—Situated 60 miles west of Paxson on the Denali Highway. Fishing and hunting are good. Possible wildlife photos. 4 camping units.

20. **TANGLE LAKES CAMP-GROUND**—Located 18 miles from Paxson on the Denali Highway. A camera is a must. 3 camping units.

21. **TANGLE RIVER CAMP-GROUND**—At Mile 22 on the Denali Highway. 5 camping units.

22. **PAXSON LAKE CAMP-GROUND**—A small site 6 miles south of the Richardson-Denali Highway Junction. Boats can be launched. 3 camping units.

23. **SOURDOUGH CAMP-GROUND**—At Mile 147 on the Richardson Highway 18 miles north of Gulkana. 6 camping units.

24. **DRY CREEK CAMP-GROUND**—Dry Creek Campground, 5 miles north of Glennallen on the Richardson Highway. 12 camping units.

25. **LAKE LOUISE CAMP-GROUND**—Located 20 miles northwest of Mile 159 on the Glenn Highway. Has a boat launching area. Lake Louise is warm enough for swimming, water skiing and fishing. 3 camping units.

26. **TOLSONA RIVER CAMP-GROUND**—Situated at Mile 172 on the Glenn Highway. 6 camping units.

27. **SQUIRREL CREEK CAMP-GROUND**—Squirrel Creek is situated 79 miles north of Valdez on the Richardson Highway. 7 camping units.

28. **LIBERTY FALLS CAMP-GROUND**—Located 10 miles north of Chitina. 6 camping units.

29. **LITTLE TONSINA CAMP-GROUND**—Located at Mile 64 on the Richardson Highway. 6 camping units.

30. **WORTHINGTON GLACIER CAMPGROUND**—Located 28 miles north of Valdez on the Richardson Highway. 6 camping units.

31. **BLUEBERRY LAKE CAMP-GROUND**—This site is situated 22 miles north of Valdez on the Richardson Highway. A rainshelter has been erected in this campground. 6 camping units.

32. **VALDEZ GLACIER ROAD CAMPGROUND**—Located 2 miles northeast of Valdez. This site is close to fresh and salt water fishing, boating, glaciers, historic sites, and the many interesting events sponsored by the citizens of Valdez. 24 camping units.

33. **LITTLE NELCHINA CAMP-GROUND**—At Mile 149 on the Glenn Highway. The Little Nelchina River is silty and not suitable for drinking. 6 camping units.

34. **MATANUSKA GLACIER CAMPGROUND**—Situated at Mile 100 on the Glenn Highway. 6 camping units.

35. **BONNIE LAKE CAMP-GROUND**—On the Glenn Highway between Palmer and Glennallen.

36. **LONG LAKE CAMP-GROUND**—86 miles north of Anchorage on the Glenn Highway. Access to the lake from the campground. 5 camping units.

37. **MATANUSKA RIVER CAMPGROUND**—Located at Mile 70 on the Glenn Highway. A rainshelter provides a warm, dry area for camper's use. A small spring supplies adequate water through May, June, and July. 9 camping units.

38. **ONE MILE LAKE CAMP-GROUND**—Situated at Mile 1 on the Edgerton Highway. 3 camping units.

39. **FIELDING LAKE CAMP-GROUND**—Located at Mile 201 on the Richardson Highway. 5 camping units.

40. **MOOSE CREEK CAMP-GROUND**—5 miles north of Palmer on the Glenn Highway. 13 camping units.

41. **WILLOW CREEK CAMP-GROUNDS**—Located 1.5 miles northeast of Willow on Deception Creek. 15 camping units.

42. **ROCKY LAKE CAMP-GROUND**—Situated 2 miles from Big Lake, 28 miles west of Palmer via Wasilla. 10 camping units.

43. & 44. **BIG LAKE #1 & #2 CAMPGROUNDS**—Approximately 80 miles from Anchorage via Palmer and Wasilla. Many varied recreational activities such as swimming, water skiing, fishing, boating, flying, and hunting. #1—15 camping units. #2—6 picnic units, 6 camping units.

45. **PETERS CREEK CAMP-GROUND**—22 miles north of Anchorage on the Glenn Highway. 32 camping units.

46. **EAGLE RIVER CAMP-GROUND**—14 miles north of Anchorage on the Glenn Highway. This area receives the greatest use of any area in Alaska. The river water is not suitable for drinking. There is an artesian well about 1/4 mile upstream from the camping area. 34 camping units. 12 picnic units.

47. **BIRD CREEK CAMP-GROUND**—Located 26 miles south of Anchorage on the Seward High-

Much of the fly fishing in Alaska is done from banks. It is no drawback however because many shorelines have sparse vegetation making casting easy.

way. A rainshelter has been erected here. 6 picnic units, 20 camping units.

48. BERNICE LAKE CAMP-GROUND—Located 10 miles north of Kenai on the North Kenai Road. 9 camping units.

49. JOHNSON LAKE CAMP-GROUND—16 miles south of Soldotna on the Sterling Highway. 13 camping units.

50. NINILCHIK CAMPGROUND—At Mile 138 on the Sterling Highway. No water is available at this site. 13 camping units.

51. DRY CREEK—Near Ninilchik.

52. STARISKI CAMPGROUND—Located at Mile 154 on the Sterling Highway, 22 miles north of Homer. 8 camping units.

53. ANCHOR RIVER CAMP-GROUND—8 miles north of Homer on the new Anchor Point Bypass. 3

camping units.

54. HOMER SPIT CAMP-GROUND—Located 6 miles southeast of Homer. There is no drinkable water in the immediate vicinity. High tides of 22 feet flood Homer Spit twice a year. Check for availability as this area sunk after the earthquake and may be closed. 10 camping sites.

55. MOSQUITO LAKE CAMP-GROUND—Situated 27 miles north of Haines and 35 miles from the ferry terminal and on the Mosquito Lake Road. 6 camping units.

56. PORTAGE COVE CAMP-GROUND—Located 1 mile south of Haines and four miles from the ferry terminal. 6 camping units.

57. PAT'S CREEK CAMP-GROUND—Near Wrangell.

U.S. Fish and Wildlife Campgrounds

(For further information write: Fish and Wildlife Service, Juneau, Alaska 99801).

58. RUSSIAN RIVER—Mile 56, Sterling Highway.

59. HIDDEN LAKE—Mile 64, Old Sterling Highway.

60. LOWER OHMER LAKE—Mile 69, Old Sterling Highway.

61. ENGINEER LAKE—Mile 70, Old Sterling Highway.

62. UPPER SKILAK LAKE—Mile 69, Old Sterling Highway.

The South Fork of the Flathead River in northern Montana produces some fine rainbow and Dolly Varden fishing. Although the fisherman in the above photo is using a spinning rig, this is one of the best fly fishing rivers in the west. The rainbows go big and the Dolly's up to 18 and 20 inches.

63. **JEAN LAKE**—Mile 64, Sterling Highway.

64. **UPPER JEAN LAKE**—Mile 65, Sterling Highway.

65. **KELLY LAKE**—Mile 71, Sterling Highway.

66. **PETERSON LAKE**—Mile 71, Sterling Highway.

67. **WATSON LAKE**—Mile 73, Sterling Highway.

68. **BOTTINENTNIN LAKE**—Mile 79, Old Sterling Highway.

69. **LOWER SKILAK LAKE**—Mile 74, Old Sterling Highway.

Chugach
National Forest Campgrounds

(For further information write: U.S. Dept. of Agriculture, Forest Service, Juneau, Alaska 99801).

70. **BERTHA CREEK**—Mile 59, Seward Highway, 13 miles southwest of Portage. 8 camping units.

71. **BLACK BEAR**—4 miles east of Portage on Portage Glacier Highway, 10 camping units.

72. **BEAVER POND**—5 miles east of Portage on Portage Glacier Highway. 7 camping units.

73. **WILLIWAW**—5.5 miles east of Portage on Portage Glacier Highway. 38 camping units.

74. **GRANITE CREEK**—Mile 63, Seward Highway, 17 miles wouthwest of Portage. 24 camping units.

75. **PTARMIGAN CREEK**—Mile 23, Seward Highway, 16 camping units.

76. **PRIMROSE LANDING**—Mile 18, Seward Highway. 6 camping units.

77. **QUARTZ CREEK**—Kenai Lake, near Mile 46, Sterling Highway. 15 camping units.

78. **CRESCENT CREEK**—2-1/2 miles east of Kenai Lake, Mile 46, Sterling Highway. 9 camping units.

79. **COOPER CREEK**—2 miles west of Coopers Landing, Sterling Highway. 16 camping units.

80. **MUD LAKE**—6-1/2 miles east of Kenai Lake on Sterling Highway. 15 camping units.

Tongass
National Forest Campgrounds

(For further information write: U.S. Dept. of Agriculture, Forest Service, Juneau, Alaska 99801).

81. **MENDENHALL LAKE CAMPGROUND**—14 miles north of Juneau, Loop Highway, 35 camping units and 9 trailers.

82. **SAWMILL CREEK**—6 miles south of Sitka, 5 camping units.

83. **3 C's**—7 miles north of Ketchikan. 4 trailers.

84. **SETTLER'S COVER**—15 miles north of Ketchikan. 9 trailers.

Mount McKinley
National Park

(For further information write: Superintendent, Mount McKinley National Park, McKinley Park, Alaska).

85. **SAVAGE RIVER CAMPGROUND**—Located 11.5 miles west of McKinley Park Hotel on the park highway.

86. **TEKLANIKA RIVER CAMPGROUND**—28 miles west of McKinley Park Hotel on park highway.

87. **TOKLAT CAMPGROUND**—Located 52.5 miles west of McKinley Park Hotel.

88. **WONDER LAKE CAMPGROUND**—Located 83.7 miles west of McKinley Park Hotel on park highway.

U.S. Department of Interior, Bureau of Land Management Campgrounds.

(For further information write: Bureau of Land Management, 555 Cordova Street, Anchorage, Alaska 99501).

89. **FINGER LAKE CAMPGROUND**—This site is six miles northwest of Palmer and consists of a seven-family unit campground.

90. **BIG DELTA CAMPGROUND**—This site is on the northern outskirts of Big Delta. It consists of a seven-family unit campground.

91. **EAGLE CAMPGROUND**—This old historic site is on the Yukon River at Eagle. The five-family unit campground was constructed in 1963.

92. **EKLUTNA RECREATION AREA**—The Eklutna Basin is located 20 miles (airline) northeast of Anchorage. A total of thirty family units (camping) were scheduled for 1964.

Methods of travel in Alaska - By road to Fairbanks, Anchorage, the Yukon River, the Kenai Peninsula, Mt. McKinley National Park, and between and beyond.

By Rail between Seward, Anchorage, and Fairbanks; or stop off at Mt. McKinley and other intermediate points.

By Ferry to all the main towns of Southeast Alaska, and between Valdez and Cordova and to Kodiak from Kenai Peninsula Points and Anchorage.

By Air: Scheduled flights serve most towns and villages in Alaska.

By Charter Boat or Plane: to anywhere! Since most of the area of the 49th State which covers 586,000 square miles is wilderness, and much of its excellent fishing waters will be found far from the main cities, many sportsmen enlist the services of the bush-pilot, or chartered plane.

These knowledgeable and dependable carriers may be found in any of the larger cities such as Anchorage, Juneau or Fairbanks. They are equipped and ready to fly you and your equipment to some of the most world-famous and breathtaking areas for fishing anywhere, most of which are accessible only by air.

Out on the Alaskan Peninsula, for instance, Dollies, Sockeye and Coho salmon are to be found in wild and beautiful country, practically untouched by man. No roads or trails exist - they can be reached only by plane. The Kuskokwim watershed is completely roadless, and offers the fly-fisherman's pride, the Arctic grayling, whose spectacular performance of rising to the dry-fly, then arching completely out of the water before its awesome dive thru the water is worth almost anything to see.

Or try the Alaska Ferry System - Inside Passage Route. You can take one of Alaska's large ferries through the beautiful "Inside Passage" from Prince Rupert, B.C. to Skagway, Alaska, a 450 mile route, and drive off at either end to continue your trip by land. You can stop off at Alaskan ports, such as salmon-famous Ketchikan, the scenic towns of Wrangell and Petersburg, the capital city of Juneau, the Gold Rush town of Skagway, and Haines, where the highway leads to the state's interior. In the summer, the ferries call at these ports six days a week. The ferries stop at historic Sitka, capital when Russia owned Alaska. You'll enjoy exploring these cities, taking side trips to fjords and glaciers, or just fishing in a land that's a sportsman's paradise.

The U.S. Fish and Wildlife Service maintains a total of 18 wildlife refuges in the state. These range from well known areas such as the Kodiak Bear Refuge, the Pribilof Islands Fur Seal Refuge and the Kenai Moose Range to a number of lesser know bird, sea-life, and wildlife preserves.

For motor travel - the best time of the year for a trip? The Alaska Highway Interior Route is kept open all year. Although heavy snowfall is sometimes encountered on the summits during the winter months, it is immediately cleared for traffic. Extreme cold may be encountered by the traveler during the period November 15 to March 1. Winter temperatures of 30 or 40 degrees below zero are not uncommon in some areas. During late March and April the spring thaws can create poor driving conditions on sections of unpaved roads. Slush and mud may make some of these roads temporarily impassable. Summer and fall months are usually recommended for ease of travel.

Alaska Highway
Type and Condition.

The Alaska Highway is rated as the world's best major gravel road and is built to support the weight of heavy freight trucks. All major bridges are modern steel construction. The 1,221 miles of the highway in Canada is owned and maintained by the Canadian government, and is paved only on the first 100 miles. The entire length of the highway in Alaska is paved.

Rates: Hotel and Motel rates are about the same as elsewhere in the United States from about $7.00 per day to Royalty Suite prices. Single-with-bath averages around $9-$10, double-with-bath about $12-$13. Meals and food prices vary considerably; Burger-and-shake will be about $1.50-$2. while a dinner may range from a cafeteria's $2.50 to an equal-to-the-best-anywhere for well under $10. A quart of milk or a loaf of bread will cost 35 to 50 cents.

Arizona

This is one state in which fishing is practically year round. There is no closed season on any fish species in Arizona except sturgeon. Although some of the lakes freeze up during the colder parts of the year, the bulk of the state's fishing waters are open twelve months of the year. Fishing may be done at any time of the day or night.

Bag limits are on only a few species, and they are generous. A limit of 10 per day or in possession has been placed on both largemouth and smallmouth bass. The Salmonid family have an aggregate limit per day or in possession of 10 and this includes trout, grayling and salmon. The Colorado River has a minimum of sixteen inches for striped bass. Northern pike limit is three of any size. That's it - on all other fish species there is no bag limit.

Both largemouth and smallmouth bass are found in quantity in most of the streams and lakes, with smallmouth predominating in the major streams of the Verde River watershed and in Roosevelt Lake. Bluegills, crappies and sunfish abound in the warm water lakes, and in some waters may be found white bass, walleye pike, silver salmon and yellow perch.

Fishing Areas. There are two major areas - the Salt and Colorado River lakes and four individual lakes: Lakes Pleasant, San Carlos, Bartlett and Horseshoe. The Salt River chain of lakes in east-central Arizona is formed by a series of dams on the Salt River - by name Saguaro, Canyon, Apache and Roosevelt. Boats and camping facilities are available at all of them.

The Colorado River lakes begin at Glen Canyon Dam, which forms Lake Powell. This new lake is a fine fishery for bass and crappies as well as trout, and the Lee's Ferry Area below the dam provides good trout fishing. At the lower end the Grand Canyon, Lake Mead is formed by Hoover (Boulder) Dam at Boulder City. Silver salmon and striped bass have been stocked at Lake Mead.

Next is Lake Mohave, stocked with both bass and trout. This lake has yielded some huge rainbows, and towards the lower end where the water is not so cold, offers some very good fishing for bass.

Between this lake and Lake Havasu is sort of a swampy area

Here's one of the finest trout rivers to be found anywhere, the Selway. It is filled with cutthroat, rainbows and browns. This location is above the end of the road campground and is one of the take-off points into the beautiful Selway-Bitterroot Wilderness area in Montana and Idaho.

which provides some very interesting angling.

Then Lake Havasu itself - crappies and bass and most warm water species.

In these areas numerous boat landings are scattered along the rivers and lakes, and fishermen can usually find a boat to rent and a place to camp at most of the more popular spots. Some cabins are also available at the areas where there is a greater concentration of activity.

The Colorado River itself provides good fishing along its entire length from Lake Mead south to the Mexican border.

Only one species of trout is native to Arizona, the yellow-bellied Arizona native trout, which resembes the golden trout of the California Sierras and the gila trout of New Mexico. But man has taken over where nature has skimped, and the planting of trout, of creel size, plus some fry and fingerlings, is very successful, since the food supply for them is adequate. The hatcheries raise mainly rainbows, although some browns, cutthroats, grayling and silver salmon have been stocked in recent years.

The trout areas are mostly in the timbered section of the state - the White Mountain country, including the Fort Apache Indian Reservation, and the Mogollon Rim Area around Payson are the two sections best for stream trout fishing, with Oak Creek also very heavily fished.

Although trout can be taken on flies almost year long in one part of the state or other, generally speaking the best months would be April through September or early October. The standard well known dry flies are those most used - Coachman, Black Gnat, Ginger Quill, Hendrickson, etc.

Arkansas

This state, while adequately supplied with natural streams and lakes both in the flat areas and the mountainous and hilly portions, has been fortunate to reap the benefits of technological water improvements as well, such as the construction of a number of hydroelectric dams which, when they cease operations, drop the water level drastically and make for excellent fly fishing for big trout.

Inhabitants of Arkansas have long been addicted to warm water fishing in the bayous, streams and rivers, but the creation of artificial impoundments has improved both the quality and quantity of fishing to such an extent that this state has now raised to among the best in the nation.

Man-made reservoirs and public fishing lakes, side effects of flood-control and power developments, have created fishing areas which are a heaven for a huge influx of out-of-state and non-resident anglers.

As an example, the construction of the Nimrod Reservoir resulted in a fishing area which abounds in crappie, bream, largemouth bass and other varieties of pan fish. Norfolk Reservoir, Blue Mountain Reservoir and Lake Greeson, all constructed by the U.S. Corps of Engineers to aid in water control have had the beneficial effect for the sportsmen, setting up large areas whose potentials are only being realized as a source of prolific fishing fun.

The Arkansas Game and Fish Commission has conducted an aggressive program of constructing and furnishing fishing waters - by not only making the areas available but by keeping them stocked, properly drained and maintained so that they are constantly filled with desirable bream, bass and crappie.

They are plentifully supplied with other facilities for the angler - commercial boat rental facilities and boat docks, suppliers for bait, tackle and launching areas, and the restrictions placed on the use of these lakes for speed-boating and water-skiing benefit fishermen.

Overflow bottomland lakes which are the result of river and bayou topping out make for good natural fishing spots for those whose tastes lean that way. While a bit more skill and knowledge of the proper depth and flowage conditions is required for this type of sport, the results in fish catch and personal satisfaction make it most enriching.

The employment of local guides opens a rich area in some of the smaller and more obscure lakes and along the levees. Travel is either by gravel roads or by using small boats on the rivers and adjacent lakes.

Float-fishing is a unique experience which enables the nimrod to concentrate on the natural beauties of the rivers, net a bountiful harvest of fish, and be freed of the irksome details of supply and transport by transferring their responsibilities to the knowledgeable local owners of the floats.

As for trout, their natural food supply ranges largely from May flies and Caddis flies to helgrammites and sowbugs. This will clue you as to your choice of flies to use in attracting them. There are records of rainbows and browns caught which exceeded 15 pounds so be prepared. The water have been plentifully stocked by the Game and Fish Commission, after treatment to eliminate rough fish, and are kept re-stocked as a result of constant and careful scrutiny of fish populations.

Do give attention to the White River which long has been known as one of the "Firsts" for fishing. It is famous now for rainbow and brown

Flyman looks over selection of streamers and bucktails in order to choose one suitable for the fast rough water in background. Flies are stored in a special book type container.

trout whose fine firm flesh is due to the icy water surrounding the dams, Bull Shoals and Norfolk. Artificial lures only may be used in November, December, January and February. There are good camping areas along the river and plentiful commercial establishments to supply fishing needs and accessories as well as to arrange and conduct the popular "Float-Trips".

California

Seven species of trout are now present in California. In the list below, the official common names are shown in black type, while the corresponding scientific names in regular type identify genus and species in that order.

Brown trout - Salmo trutto, **cutthroat trout** - Salmo clarkii, **Rainbow trout** - Salmo gairdnerii, **Golden trout** - Salmo aguabonita, **Eastern brook trout** - Salvelinus fontinalis, **Dolly Varden trout** - Salvelinus malma, **Lake trout** - Salvelinus namaycush.

Of these seven, the cutthroat, rainbow, golden and Dolly Varden are natives, while the brown, eastern brook and lakers have been introduced into the state.

The cutthroat, rainbow and golden are generally considered to consist of two or more subspecies, although ichthyologists who

Here are five nice brook trout ranging in size from about eight inches to 15 inches. These are fine tasting either broiled or pan fried. Brook trout meat is flaky and mild and varies in color from white to pink.

specialize in the classification of trout are not in full agreement with respect to the validity of some of them. Those presently officially recognized in California are the following:

Coast cutthroat trout - Salmo clarkii clarkii, Lahontan cutthroat trout - Salmo clarkii henshawi, Piute cutthroat trout - Salmo clarkii seleniris, Steelhead rainbow trout - Salmo gairdnerii gairdnerii, Kamloops rainbow trout - Salmo gairdnerii kamloops, Shasta rainbow trout - Salmo gairdnerii stonei, Kern River rainbow trout - Salmo gairdnerii gilberti, Eagle Lake rainbow trout - Salmo gairdnerii aquilarum, Royal silver rainbow trout - Salmo gairdnerii regalis, South Fork of Kern golden trout - Salmo aguabonita aguabonita, Little Kern golden trout - Salmo aguabonita whitei.

The rainbow trout is widely scattered over California. It orginally occured in a large part of the trout streams of the state and in a few lakes. Since this is the fish most commonly raised in the trout hatcheries of California, it has been planted in nearly every lake and stream which is suitable for trout. Therefore, it is by far the most widely distributed trout in California.

In many coastal streams this species is represented by the migratory steelhead in the lower portions and by resident fish in the headwaters. In some streams the ranges of the two will overlap. Rainbows of one subspecies will hybridize with other subspecies and with cutthroat trout when their ranges are not separated by some barrier.

Resident rainbows rarely attain a large size in California. Steelhead rainbow grow much larger because they migrate to the ocean and spend one or more years under conditions much favorable to rapid growth than are found in fresh water. However, in a few of the larger reservoirs and lakes in California rainbows do grow rapidly and one weighing 18 pounds was recorded from Lake Almanor, in northeast California.

Steelhead rainbows - bright, silvery fish with relatively few spots along the back and on the dorsal and caudal fins. They may be found in most of the streams flowing into the ocean, from San Luis Obispo County north. In the far north streams, mainly the Klamath River, steelhead is king. The icy mountain streams which form this river are responsible for well-nigh perfect habitat, as is the Eel River (noted for the large size of the steelhead taken). The Mad and Salmon Rivers, in northwest California, have fine runs of steelheads.

This trout is famous for its quality as a game fish. Anyone who has taken a fresh-run steelhead on a fly and light tackle will never forget the experience. A good many young future steelhead are caught in fresh water before they have migrated downstream to the sea. These fish are commonly less than 8 inches long and, of course, are not able to put up much of a battle. They usually enter the ocean when they are 1 or 2 years old and then spend from 1 to 3 years at sea. When they come back to spawn they nearly always return to the same stream in which they were hatched. At that time they may weigh from 2 to 12 pounds or more. During the winter or early spring the spawning fish reach suitable gravel riffles in the upper sections of streams and dig their nests.

Kamloops rainbow trout - "The typical silver fish of large lakes is bluish above, with light silvery sides and belly. The spots are comparatively small and x-shaped, and are located chiefly above the lateral line, although there are a few below the line in front, but more posteriorly on the caudal peduncle. There are also a few rounded spots on the top of the head and below the eye. The dorsal and caudal fins are spotted; the anal usually has a few spots at the base and the pectoral on the anterior ray; the ventral is usually without spots. Except for the spots, the fins are white or faintly clouded. The chin and lower jaw are usually quite black." The preceding description is given by J. R. Dymond for Kamloops of large lakes in their homeland of British Columbia. The Kamloops rainbow was introduced into California in June, 1950 when 1,000 yearlings were released in Shasta lake, Shasta County. Since that time, other plantings have been made, but their distribution is still limited. They were brought from British Columbia by the sportsmen of Redding, Shasta County, on the strength of the reputation which they had gained in Idaho and British Columbia. A number of individuals weighing over 30 pounds have been caught by anglers in Lake Pend Orielle, Idaho. The record fish weighed 37 pounds.

The smaller Kamloops will take a fly very readily and put up a spectacular battle. In British Columbia they are regarded as equal to fresh-run steelhead in their fighting ability.

Golden trout. Typical golden trout is a highly colored fish with distinctive shades of yellow and red on the lower sides and belly. The cheeks and opercle often are red, as are the pectoral, ventral and anal fins. The dorsal and anal fins usually have distinct white tops, sometimes bordered with black. The spotting is distinctive, there being a relatively few round black spots well defined against a clear background. The spots on the dorsal and caudral fins also are distinct.

The parr marks are sharp, usually not only on the young fish but on the adults as well. This is usually a reliable distinguishing characteristic.

Although typical golden trout are easy to distinguish from other trout, there is a great deal of variation in their coloring and spotting. Some golden trout will be found to have many more spots than others, and sometimes the spots are confined to the caudal peduncle and tail.

Distribution: Originally golden trout were limited to a few streams in the upper Kern River drainage, at elevations of from about 6,300 feet to 10,500 feet. Beginning at an early date, man has extended their distribution, by transplanting wild fish or stocking hatchery-reared fish. Golden trout are now present in California in a number of streams and lakes of the Sierra Nevada from Alpine and El Dorado counties to the north to Inyo and Tulare counties to the south, mostly at elevations over 8,000 feet. In recent years they have also been introduced into waters in Siskiyou and Trinity counties.

The extremely beautiful coloration of the golden trout has resulted in their being named the state fish. Moreover, these fish are usually found in streams and lakes of great beauty.

Coast cutthroat - usually dark olive green - sides much lighter and belly is silvery white. Found in the lower courses of most coastal streams from the Eel River northward. Sometimes called the "redwood trout" because most of the California streams in which it lives are shaded by these giant trees.

Lahontan Cutthroat trout. Usually a dark yellowish olive color from back to belly. The side has a broad, pinkish stripe. The sides of the head are often scarlet. Found in the Truckee, Walker and Carson drainages and does not occur naturally in waters draining into the Pacific Ocean. This fish has been known as the Tahoe trout, because prior to 1940 it was very abundant in this lake. It became nearly extinct in this lake following the introduction of the lake and rainbow trouts, although insurmountable irrigation dams on the Truckee River and the market fishery may well have been contributing factors.

Brown trout. The coloration is quite variable; usually they are dark brown or olive brown on the back, shading to golden brown on the sides and white or yellow on the belly.

There are dark spots on the head, body and dorsal fin. These spots are relatively large and distinct.

There are red spots on the lower side, each surrounded by a light halo. There is a great deal of variation in the number and size of the dark and the red spots on the brown trout of California, but this is the only trout with both black and red spots on its body.

The brown trout is widely scattered throughout California. However, the waters in which it is abundant are relatively few. In past years this species was planted in all of the trout waters of the state, but in recent years only a few selected lakes and streams have been stocked with browns. A few browns, progency of earlier plants, can still be found in many lakes, reservoirs and streams in California, and in a good many streams along both sides of the Sierra the "brownie" spawns quite successfully.

A characteristic of the brown trout is it's wariness, and those who can catch the brownie rate him as a "fisherman's fish". The strain of brown trout brought to California many years ago never lost it's canny Scotch disposition, but another strain imported from Massachusetts in 1954 apparantly had some of it's wariness bred out through the years and is much easier for the average angler to catch.

Because of his disposition, the brownie escapes his enemies and often lives to a ripe old age. He also grows to a considerable size and record trout caught from time to time usually are browns.

Fishing in California has not been left to chance. Although blessed by an abundance of natural lakes and streams, they have all been carefully surveyed and studied, especially in the mountains, and man-made impoundements are found in some part of practically every body of water. While flood-control may have been the primary though in mind, the idea of preservation of natural endowments and catering to the state's golden crop—tourism—has always been fostered.

Although the logging industry did a great deal of harm by indiscriminate harvesting and unsupervised dumping and clogging of streams, most of these bad effects are slowly being corrected. At the present time anti-pollution agencies as well as the Fish and Game Commission are doing a remarkable job in keeping the state's natural resources in tip-top condition, and builders and industrialists are being made well aware of their responsibilities and debts to the fisherman and outdoorsman, both native and transient.

California has some of the most outstanding examples of lakes for fishing in all of the United States. One that most usually is cited is Lake Tahoe, with its waters of almost legendary clarity, permitting easy vision of tiny pebbles in the depths of its crystalline body, but Clear Lake and Shasta Lake offer just about every variety of freshwater fish available, and many more smaller lakes dot the state, offering good yields with the advantage of proximity.

Colorado

The Colorado Division of Game, Fish and Parks stocks fish in some 11,300 miles of streams and the majority of Colorado's 2,400 lakes. Most of these waters are open to public fishing and are located in

This scene is of a flyman on a lake in a state famous for its fly fishing waters, Maine. The fish shown here is a landlocked salmon from Sebago Lake. The landlocked salmon is a close relation to the Atlantic salmon and is also an excellent fighter when taken on a fly rod.

some of America's most spectacular scenery.

Among Colorado's most widely known trout streams are the Gunnison, now partly obliterated by Blue Mesa Reservoir; The Rio Grande, through the San Luis Valley and above it; the Arkansas, from below Leadville to Pueblo; the entire stretch of the Colorado, White, Yampa, North Platte and that portion of the South Platte above Waterton, south of Denver.

Some of the more popular trout lakes are Grand Lake at the town of Grand Lake; Granby and Shadow Mountain reservoirs near Granby; Green Mountain Reservoir near Dillon; Trappers Twin Lakes near Leadville; Monument Lake near Trinidad; Vallecito Reservoir near Durango; lakes of the Grand Mesa near Grand Junction.

Other popular trout lakes are Delaney Butte Lakes and Lake John near Walden; the Red Feather lakes northwest of Fort Collins; Eleven Mile and Antero reservoirs in South Park; Taylor Reservoir near Gunnison; Williams Creek Reservoir near Parshall; and Lon Hagler Reservoir near Loveland.

The relatively new waters of Dillon Reservoir at Dillon; Vega Reservoir near Collbran; Navajo Reservoir southwest of Pagosa Springs; and North Michigan Lake near Waldon all promise to be highly popular trout waters as should be the Blue Mesa Reservoir near Gunnison.

Some trout have been planted in plains lakes to offer additional sport to warm water fishermen, but the fish normally found in most of these waters are walleye, bass, perch, catfish and drum.

Top warm water fishing lakes are North Sterling Reservoir near Sterling; Jumbo Reservoir near Julesberg; Lonetree, Horseshoe and Boyd Lakes near Loveland; Adobe Creek Reservoir near Las Animas; Queens Reservoir near Eads. In

addition, stretches of the Arkansas and Purgatoire rivers on the Eastern Slope and stretches of the Dolores, Colorado, White, Green and Yampa rivers on the Western Slope offer fair warm water fishing.

Efforts to maintain and improve sport fishing for Colorado's growing multitude of resident and visiting fishermen, have resulted in an intensive fish rearing program. The Colorado Game, Fish and Parks Department maintains 21 fish propagation units. Each one is dedicated to producing as many fish as possible each year for the benefit of the fisherman.

Approximately 1,300,000 pounds of fish are produced yearly by these units. This means that 6 million catchable size (8 to 10 inches) fish are being planted in public waters every year. In addition 12 million fingerlings and 15 million smaller fish are also being planted to insure the future success of the fisherman.

The cost of fish propagation as well as fish management, research, law enforcement and administrative overhead is financed through the sale of fishing licenses. No tax funds are used for this purpose, only the fisherman's volunteer dollar pays the bill. And the sport fish program is expensive. Capital investment in property and buildings exceeds 5 million dollars. Maintenance and operating expenses of the unit average about one million dollars yearly.

Pollution, deforestation, reclamation, unwise drainage, channel clearing and other man-made factors have done much to reduce the habitat required to support good fish populations. Low water levels due to heavy irrigation use and frequent drought conditions often cause severe fish losses. Then in many waters the fish are unable to reproduce themselves successfully. All these conditions result in the need for replacement stocks of fish.

If the replacement stocks were not available, sport fishing in Colorado would be a thing of the past.

There are 7,100 miles of accessable streams open to public fishing in Colorado. An attempt is made to plant these streams with as many fish of the right size and species as possible to provide each fisherman with the highest success. Catchable size fish are normally planted at three week intervals from May through August each year in the streams. Severe winter losses prevent stream plants being made on a year round basis.

About 2,800 lakes and reservoirs comprise a total surface acreage of 130,000. Many small lakes and reservoirs near heavy population centers are planted with catchable size fish on a put and take basis. Fingerling size (2 to 4 inches) are reserved for planting in the large lakes and reservoirs where they have a good chance to attain natural growth. Smaller fish (less than 2 inches) are utilized for stocking high lakes, those waters above 10,000 feet in elevation. Exact stocking dates are scheduled each year. The dates will vary, due to water conditions and other factors.

Extensive automation of hatchery operations has more than offset the normal increase of fish production costs. The use of fixed winged airplanes and helicopters for planting fish has increased efficiency and served to lower stocking expenditures. New insulated tank trucks are able to travel farther with larger loads of fish, and as a result more fish can be planted at more frequent intervals than ever before. Loads in airplanes and trucks range from 1/2 to 2 pounds of fish per gallon of water. During clear weather periods, airplanes, helicopters and trucks are busy hauling fish from the fish farms to the public waters. Fish transportation vehicles travel over a million miles each year.

Water like this is a fly fisherman's dream. Fast current at bottom of both falls should produce good catches.

In recent years the advent of good, reasonable complete dry foods for trout and catfish has added to the progress of the fish cultural program. Ingredient mixtures such as a combination of liver, fish, wheat, soybean and malt meals that are fortified with yeast, fish solubles, minerals and vitamins are now used in fish formulas. The vitamin fortification provides the fish with the ability to resist diseases. Yet if some type of disease gets started, various medications can be added to the feed, or used on the fish directly for control or elimination.

Like other things of the space age, fish farms have become highly specialized. Some units function primarily as hatcheries where eggs are received for incubation and hatching into small fish. Small fish may be planted directly from these units, but the bulk of them are transferred to rearing units. Rearing facilities do just that, rear fish, usually for a 13 month period prior to planting. A fish in natural waters requires 2 to 3 years of growth to reach catchable size. But under an intensive rearing program, the fish reach an 8 to 10 inch length within 13 months. A number of fish farms are self-contained units, having both hatcheries and rearing facilities

These two fly fishermen are boating the famous Au Sable River in Michigan and the one in front is about to net a small steelhead. This river gives up some fine steelhead which are rainbows that have migrated into Lake Michigan and returned to the river to spawn. Many of these lake run rainbows will weigh ten pounds and over at spawning time.

available. These units may plant fish of all sizes.

One unit specializes in the incubation and hatching of salmon. Another unit serves both as a trout and pond-cultural facility. Then another unit operates primarily as a warm water fish hatchery and rearing unit. In addition, one unit acts in the capacity of a live fish warehouse, storing and transferring fish throughout the State.

Fifty million fish eggs are incubated and hatched each year in Colorado. Rainbow trout make up 44 percent of all eggs received, walleye 24 percent, salmon 20 percent and a miscellany of 12 percent made up of brook, brown, cutthroat and mackinaw trout, grayling, northern pike and channel catfish eggs. About 10 million other eggs are exchanged with other states and commercial vendors.

Movement of eggs in and out of the hatchery units occurs every month of the year. Trout eggs are incubated from mid-September through July, walleye and northern pike eggs during the period extending from mid-March through May. Channel catfish eggs are incubated during the months of June and July. Salmon eggs become available in November and are handled through February.

Normally when the eggs are received by the hatcheries they are eyed. This means that the fish embryo is in an advanced stage. The incubation period varies depending upon water temperatures. In 50 degree (F.) water, rainbow eggs will hatch within 30 days and 45 days for brook trout eggs. Channel catfish eggs would rot before hatching in 50 degree water; they require 78 degree water in order to develop satisfactorily.

When fish hatch from eggs, they are known as yolk or sac fry. This is because of the yolk sac that is attached to their bodies. The sac is a built-in food supply, which the small fish use until they are strong enough to search for natural foods. Once the yolk sac is absorbed and the fish begins to feed, the small fish are known as advanced fry. Survival rate from egg to fry vary among species. An 80 to 90 percent hatch can be expected from trout or salmon, and a 10 to 40 percent survival is expected from warm water fish species. The rate of survival to a catchable size fish may be around 80 percent for coldwater fish and about 10 percent for warm water species.

When you consider the amount of waters encompassed in this state—7,100 miles of stream open to public fishing; 3,100 miles of which are stocked with catchable fish and 4,000 miles considered as wild trout waters; 1,905 natural lakes in the elevation range of 8,500 to 13,500 feet which are open to public use, plus 300 reservoirs which are open to public fishing, it becomes immediately apparent that methods such as the foregoing are necessary for a smoothly-functioning operation. Fishing is Big Business in Colorado!

Connecticut

This state is a prime example of a densely populated and heavily industrialized area, near enough to a major metropolis for an annual influx of summer visitors of about 50,000—either situation which could pose a unique challenge to a game commission to provide adequate fishing. However, the Connecticut Board of Fisheries and Game has responded marvelously well to those challenges, and through a system of high development of existing waters, has managed not only to keep the fishing areas well stocked on a put and take basis, but to construct public launching and recreational facilities as well.

Probably the best fly-fishing in Connecticut is in the Housatonic River which runs along the western part of the state near Salisbury and Cornwall; the Salmon River, both the main tributary and the east branch, and the Natchang River. These are stocked mainly with brown trout in the 9 to 12 inch size class—these sometimes last the complete season and become wily enough to provide fun for even the experienced angler. In streams which are fortunate enough to contain a proportion of land-locked alewives, and some in which this desirable forage fish has been artificially introduced, the brown trout population becomes larger and occasionally lasts from year to year.

Besides the planted browns, brookies and rainbows are also available—and in some of the coastal streams sea run brown trout are available running 9 to 12 pounds. These are scarce but provide interesting fishing.

Ponds and lakes in the state have been reclaimed and managed and many provide a rich source of rainbows and lake trout—and also have the advantages of adequate and readily available commercial liveries and boat launching facilities. Crystal Lake, Gardner Lake, Wononscopomuk Lake and East Twin Lake are examples.

The best fishing months are May and June except that fly fishing in the Farmington River continues to be good throughout July, August, September and October. The best artificial fly patterns are those which imitate May flies, caddis flies and stone flies.

Florida

Although fly fishing is not the predominant method of taking fish in Florida, it is catching on, and since it can't be beat for thrills and action will doubtless continue to grow in popularity—for this is a state where fishing is an ever present and accepted way of life, and any variation of it is bound to have its adherants.

Black bass belonging to the sunfish family are the prime target for thousands of freshwater fishermen in Florida. They are the largest freshwater game fish in the state, and at times, the wariest. Bass not only are a popular sport fish but also a choice delicacy for the table.

There are 2 groups of black bass in Florida. The true largemouth group which includes northern largemouth and Florida largemouth is in one.

The other group includes Suwannee bass, spotted bass (sometimes called southern smallmouth), redeye bass, and possibly other species. The 5 species named above are the only ones currently recognized by fishery biologists.

The northern largemouth bass (Micropterus salmoides salmoides) is found in the extreme northern part of Florida and the Florida Panhandle and generally does not grow as large as the Florida largemouth bass.

The Florida largemouth bass (Micropterus salmoides floridanus) is the larger of the largemouth group found throughout Florida.

The Suwannee bass (Micropterus notius) is a small slender bass with a somewhat smaller mouth than the bass in the largemouth group. The Suwannee bass seldom if ever exceeds 12 inches in length and is found only in the Suwannee River system.

The spotted bass (Micropterus punctulatus punctulatus) is a slender bass with spots on the back. The top weight is around 4 pounds. It is found from the Apalachicola River westward.

The redeye bass (Micropterus coosae) is the best fighter of the Florida basses, pound for pound.

Almost all of them jump one or more times when they are hooked, and a large percent of them throw the fisherman's lure from their mouth. They are generally bronze colored on the side, grading into an olive background on the back. They are found in the Chipola River and the Apalachicola River.

Black bass spawning in Florida varies according to weather conditions and the location, but the major spawning period occurs in the spring and when the water temperature rises to approximately 70 degrees (F.). This usually occurs in March and April. However, young bass have been observed spawning at Winter Haven Fish Hatchery as early as December.

In the wild, usually a large percentage of the eggs hatch, but the number of young that survive is directly related to the condition of the body of water. Many factors control the hatching and rearing of fishes. Water temperature, silt deposits, predators and many other circumstances are involved.

The black bass eat other fish, mice, crabs, crayfish, frogs, birds, snakes, eels, turtles, shrimp, snails and other animals.

Growth rate varies in different states, but in Florida which has a 12 month growing season, under normal conditions a Florida largemouth will reach a length of 10 to 12 inches and weigh 12 to 14 ounces at the age of one year. At the end of the second year, the same bass should be 15 or 16 inches in length and weigh 2 to 3 pounds.

In rare cases, where the waters are very fertile and conditions of fish populations, etc., are favorable, bass will grow much faster. Some of the phosphate pits in Polk County produce 4 to 6 pound bass in 2 years. On the other hand, if the waters are out of balance and food conditions

are poor, the 2 year old bass may weigh less than 1 pound.

The largest black bass caught on rod and reel was 22-1/2 pounds, taken in Montgomery Lake, Georgia, in 1932.

Fly tackle, spin cast, spinning and bait casting tackle are all used. If the water is free of logs, weeds and other obstructions, lighter tackle can be used.

A fine choice would be an 8-1/2 foot dry fly action rod with a good weight forward line for bass bugging and weighted streamers. A heavy rod and a sturdy tippet help to get a good bass to head up and to the surface fast when in heavy weeds where he could get tangled and break off.

For bream, a light trout rod and small line for delicacy and feel with a dry fly is best for these sporty little gamesters.

Productivity on flies is good year around, with late summer and spring probably edging other times only slightly. Popping bugs, deer hair bugs, and wooly worms do well on bream and small bass. Streamer flies in mylar flash patterns score on chain pickerel and larger bass. Fishing in and around the emergent weeds and lily pads is the way that most fishermen in Florida fish for all species.

To go after a trophy bass on a fly rod, one would troll (by rowing) along the grass edge or over a drop off in deeper water. Using a sinking or sinking tip line, a tippet of 8 to 12 pounds test and a home tied mylar body, muddler minnow streamer or a brook silverside imitation on a #2 hook. The start and stop action of rowing would give the streamer action.

A brown or black over yellow pattern wooly worm fly behind a #1 Indiana spinner blade rig is deadly for jumbo shellcrackers and bluegill. Most fly fishing in the state is done from a boat with electric trolling

This is a beautiful trout stream and one providing ideal conditions for a good fish population. This type of water supplies ample fish food of all kinds. It contains the usual water born larva and nymphs which will hatch into food flies and the surrounding terrain is the kind that will produce several types of terrestial insects that trout love. It is the Buffalo River in Idaho.

motor or by wading where possible.

Some excellent lakes are in Polk County. The following are examples of reclaimed areas in Florida's phosphate lakes. Saddle Creek Park was donated to Polk County by the American Cyanamid Company in 1961. It has 740 acres, of which 500 acres are lakes.

This area has been developed by the county for public recreation and is open the year round. Facilities include picnic tables, swimming area, bridle path and fishing, which is managed by the Florida Game and Fresh Water Fish Commission.

This is 3 miles east of Lakeland on U.S. 92. Lake Crago Park, which is a 58 acre lake, one of 10 man made lakes formed when a 1,300 acre area north of Lake Parker in Lakeland was mined. Prior to mining, Lake Crago was nothing more than a swamp.

The land is still owned by the company, but open to the public. It can be reached by driving north on Florida 33, near Lakeland. Great for bass. Christina Park, comprised of 1,100 acres which is leased to the state for $1 a year by the Mobil Chemical Company, offers good fishing in any of the 250 acres of fresh water lakes. It is immediately south of Lakeland City limits off Florida 37. One of the largest areas available to the public for fishing is the Pleasant Grove Fish Management Area.

This popular spot has 505 acres of fishing in rehabilitated phospate pits. The area mined by Arico Chemical Company, a subsidiary of Continental Oil, is leased to the Florida Game and Fresh Water Fish Commission. The most advanced fishing techniques are being used here to manage the pools and produce quality fishing. It can be reached by driving east from Tampa on Florida 60, about 15 miles.

One of the first public parks to be created from mined out phosphate areas was the Peace River Park, on the Peace River in Bartow. This 110 acre area was donated by the Virginia-Carolina Corp., a predecessor of Mobil Chemical. The park is operated by the county and has picnic and playground facilities, as well as excellent fishing.

It can be reached by driving east of Bartow on Florida 60, about 2 miles. While you are in this area, be sure to fish Lakes Hatchinena, Kissimmee, Rosalie and Crooked Lake—fish every day of the year, no closed season, no size limits.

Georgia

The greater part of Georgia trout water is not what you would call ideal for fly-rod fishing. Trout streams in the mountains are generally narrow and bushy. However, some of the larger rivers are wide enough for enjoyable fly fishing. The following 4 rivers are perhaps the best bets for fly rod fishing in north Georgia:

The northern section of the Chattahoochee River is heavily stocked with rainbows. The town of Helen is right on the river and has motels and restaurants. That section inside the management area is also good fishing, but there aren't many sections slow enough for top notch dry fly fishing.

The Soque River is a fairly large stream. Most of the land is privately owned with the marked area around the bridge open to the public.

The main channel of the Chatooga has a good wild brown population, with a large number of stocked rainbows. This is one of Georgia's most fascinating streams. It is very primitive and is good for the experienced wilderness hiker.

The lower section of the Chattahoochee is the tailrace below Buford Dam. This is Georgia's largest trout stream and it has some of the largest trout. The water level varies according to the electrical generation of the dam. The schedule varies weekly, and it is best to call the U.S. Corps of Engineers for information. Fly rodding is best when there is no generation.

These streams are a fair representation of the open streams which are good for fly casting. They are for the most part large streams, so caution should be exercised while wading.

Fly fishing for the warm-water species is not overwhelmingly popular in this state. Most bass, bream, etc. fishing is done with spinning and spin cast equipment. Most of the bodies of water suitable for fly-rod fishing for bass and bream are privately owned, but there are spots on the large public reservoirs where it could be done effectively. In the northwestern part of the state there are several rivers which offer good fishing for smallmouth bass and could be excellent fly-rod streams.

The best fishing months are mid-March through June, and September and October for all species.

As for best flies, Georgia trout, southern trout, are not so noticeably selective as their northern counterparts, due to the smaller and less frequent insect hatches they seem more grateful for anything that comes along. Favored Georgia dry flies include:

Quill Gordon 16-18, Dark Hendrickson 14-16, Adams (male and female) 14-16, Light Cahill 14-20.

Wet Flies: March Brown 12-14, G. R. Hare's Ear 12-14, Light Cahill 12-14.

Nymphs: Tellico Nymph 12-14, Stonefly nymphs 10-12, March Brown 12-14.

For bream—small poppers and "rubber bugs". For bass—large poppers and in rivers streamers imitating the sculpin (muddler minnow) and the black-nosed dace.

As most fly fishing in Georgia is for trout, the majority of fishermen wade. Fly casters after bream and bass often use canoes and john boats on the small ponds they fish.

Truly the trout is a glamorous fish. Exactly why the thought of battling a leaping rainbow in a crystal clear mountain stream drives fishermen to distraction has yet to be determined. Even though most Georgia trout are relatively small, fishermen have been known to drive for hundreds of miles in the frail hope of outsmarting one. This usually is easier said than done, despite confused and hungry trout fresh from the hatchery who sometimes aren't above taking a kernal of corn, ball of cheese, cigarette filter, or even a bare hook.

The real problem with trout fishing is that there aren't enough trout streams to go around for all the trout fishermen, especially since the latter are increasing every year while the former are declining, due to "scenic highway" construction, etc. While Georgia has more than 700 miles of trout fishing, the latest census estimated that it has at least 381,681 fishermen who go after trout at least once a year. That comes to 546 fishermen per mile, if they all go fishing on the same day.

Since clear trout streams are relatively infertile from the standpoint of natural food production, Mother Nature can't feed enough trout fast enough for such a ravenous horde. Mud and silt have impaired the ability of trout eggs to hatch in some of the best mountain streams, and, as a result, such streams are merely cold water "bathtubs," suitable only for hatchery trout soon to be caught.

This is the Chattooga River in Georgia. It is a fine trout river and there should be some fine browns and rainbows come out of these rocky areas and riffles.

This flycaster shows excellent form as he brings a rainbow to net. He is not holding the line with his hand because he is using an automatic reel and has actuated it to take up all the slack and the line is held tight by the reel until stripped off.

Fly fishing attracts the younger ones too. Here an excited little boy hefts a stocky bream out with a fly rod while his partner sculls the John boat.

In order to make the number and the size of trout compatable with the number and the size of trout fishermen, the State Game and Fish Commission began raising keeper size trout for stocking in 1928, and hasn't slowed down since. Production still doesn't meet the demand, but the Commission does manage to stock, on the average, 2 fish per fisherman per trip in open trout streams in 11 northeast Georgia mountain counties from Elijay to Clayton. There are 138 streams in these counties which are open every day of the trout season, usually from early April to early October. The 2 most popular open streams are Cooper's Creek, north of Dahlonega, and the Talluhah River west of Clayton.

But the best fishing and the fewest fishermen are found on 23 streams in game management areas where the commission charges a dollar a day per fisherman. Trout are stocked in these streams twice as heavily as in outside streams, averaging 4 fish per fisherman per trip. Of course, a good early bird fisherman may catch his limit of 8 on Saturday morning to balance your zero score on Sunday afternoon. Managed streams are open 2 or 4 days a week on scheduled days each month, either Wednesdays and Thursdays or Saturdays and Sundays.

In addition to the mountain streams, trout are also stocked by the commission in the Chattahoochee River below Buford Dam on Lake Lanier (an 11-1/2 pound rainbow

was caught there in 1970) and the Savannah River below Lake Hartwell and Clark Hill. Trout also have been stocked above the dams in all 3 reservoirs, and have thrived in Lake Lanier. In addition, several streams in northwest Georgia have been stocked experimentally with trout with promising results.

While most trout streams are closed during the winter, designated stream sections containing some trout are open throughout the entire year. The best of these is the rugged Chattooga River between Georgia and South Carolina. Many trout streams are located on public lands in the Chattahoochee National Forest, only streams located on private land are not open to the public. United States Forest Service campgrounds are numerous in the area, but are crowded on weekends during the summer, as are several state parks in the northeast section.

If you don't mind hiking for several days and sleeping on the ground, there still are small remote native trout streams in north Georgia's rugged mountains that you can fish without fear of seeing another human being. If you're not willing to go that far, try a managed stream limited to artificial lures, like Jones Creek above Dahlonega or Waters Creek. Better still, fish for fun in Noontooley, a catch and release stream.

The scenic Blue Ridge Mountains of north Georgia hold a pleasant surprise for the angler who thinks top notch trout fishing is only found in the northern states. In the clear, fast water of the mountain streams a fisherman can take his pick of 3 species of trout, and the type of fishing which strikes his fancy.

In the remote headwater and feeder streams live wild brook trout which have never heard a hatchery truck. The small brooks they inhabit are far off the beaten track, and are made to order for the backpacker who enjoys the wilderness as much as the fishing.

Rainbow trout, famous for its jumping fight, is found in almost all the trout water in the state, but prefers the large, fast flowing rivers and streams. Most of these streams are easily accessible to fishermen and are heavily stocked to supplement the natural population.

The ever-wary brown trout is often found in slower and warmer waters than the other trout species, and consequently is more wide-spread in the state. Because the brown is so cautious he stands up well to angling pressure, and often attains trophy size.

There are more than 1,000 miles of stream officially designated "Trout Water" in North Georgia. Some of

these are tumbling mountain brooks and rivers where the high elevation keeps the water cool enough for trout. Farther south, the tailrace waters of some of the large reservoirs have been found cold enough and stocked with trout, creating "artificial" trout streams.

Most of Georgia's trout streams are located on the Chattahoochee National Forest making public access no problem. Motels and restaurants are available in many of the small towns in the area, and the Forest Service maintains many excellent camping areas along the more popular trout streams.

The rivers and streams of middle and south Georgia support some of the finest warm water fishing in the nation. These rivers include the Flint, Alapaha, Satilla, Suwanee, Ocmulgee, Altamaha, Canoochee, and Ogeechee.

Georgia's rivers abound with many varieties of sport fish and a mixed stringer of bass, pickerel and bream is possible for an adept angler. The largemouth bass is the primary game fish of the rivers, but the smaller panfish such as the bluegill, redbreast sunfish and the warmouth have quite a following.

The best fishing times are in the fall when the river is low and the fish are concentrated in pools, and in the spring. At other times the wise fisherman will probe the undercut banks around brush piles, and fish the shoal areas. Local fishermen often wade, but since these rivers have many abrupt dropoffs and swift currents, this practice can be treacherous until one is completely familiar with the area.

Boats used for floating these streams are generally of the flat bottom skiff type as there are many shallow stretches on most of the

rivers. Motors are a handy asset for the fisherman and because of the shallow water, a supply of spare shear pins is recommended. There are fish camps on most of the major rivers which provide bait and boats.

In addition to the freshwater fish mentioned, striped bass and American shad make spawning runs up the Altamaha, Canoochee, Ogeechee, Satilla, and St. Mary's rivers. These saltwater species are great fighters and provide good action for fishermen on these rivers.

Nestled in the Georgia mountains, the TVA lakes, Blue Ridge, Nottely, and Chatuge, and the Georgia Power lakes, Burton, Rabun, and Seed offer the angler some unique fishing opportunities. Smallmouth bass fishing is good in Blue Ridge and Chatuge, and walleye are found in Blue Ridge and Burton. Largemouth bass and crappie are present, and big trout are found in the deeper lakes. These impoundments are most productive in the late spring and early fall months.

Just south of the mountains, Lakes Allatoona, Lanier and Hartwell support good fishing near metropolitan Atlanta. The fish populations of these large impoundments are primarily made up of the warm water species, with largemouth bass, white bass, and crappie being the main attractions for fishermen.

White bass and crappie are taken during late March, April and May, and largemouth fishing is prime in April, May and early June. Lanier and Hartwell also offer trout fishing in the deep water near the dams and in the main channels in early and late summer.

The northern lakes have good public access, including public launching ramps, picnic areas, and camping areas. Most of the lakes also have commercial fishing camps which provide boat rental, bait and

The young man here is carefully working the large brown trout toward his net under the watchful eye of the older expert. This photo was taken on a northern Michigan River where browns are increasing in great numbers.

tackle, and in some cases, overnight facilities.

Middle Georgia Reservoirs—the heart of Georgia fishing. The principle game fish of this area are bass and crappie, with catfish and bream taken seasonally.

The main impoundments in this area include Bartlett's Ferry, Goat Rock and Lake Oliver, share with Alabama on the west; Lakes Jackson and Sinclair in the central part of the state, and Clark Hill on the South Carolina border.

Lakes Sinclair, Clark Hill, and Jackson support fine largemouth bass, white bass and crappie fishing. Crappie start hitting in late March and continue through April when largemouth and white bass take over. The white bass fishing is particularly popular during the spring spawning run up the tributary streams.

Crappie fishing at night holds up well throughout the summer and hits a peak again in the fall. Night fishing with a gas lantern during this period is especially popular.

Bass fishing usually peaks during April and May, and again during the fall months. Largemouth bass are the main game fish for these lakes, and average sizes run around 2-3 pounds. These lakes are not very heavily fished and fishing facilities are good.

Striped bass have been introduced into Sinclair and Jackson and seem to be doing well. Stripers are normally found in salt water, but live very well landlocked in freshwater lakes. They are great game fish and commonly attain weights of 30 pounds or more. If a population of stripers is successfully established, these middle Georgia lakes will take on a new look in the state's fishing picture.

Bartlett's Ferry, Goat Rock, and Lake Oliver usually provide fair fishing. Bass, crappie and white bass are the species most frequently taken.

South Georgia Reservoirs—For a true "Deep South" fishing trip

This is a great combination for fly fishing ... quiet water, a small canoe and a long, light rod and small tippet on the leader. He's landing a Georgia Bream.

complete with Spanish moss and cypress trees look to the lakes in extreme south Georgia. Lakes Blackshear, Worth, Walter F. George and Seminole are located in the southwestern portion of the state, and provide good fishing year-round.

The shallow water of these impoundments brings a slight shift in important game species. Largemouth bass is the king of the area's fishing, but bluegill and redear sunfish probably rank second in importance.

Lake Seminole, in the extreme southwest corner of the state, is probably the "Largemouth bass capital of Georgia," and commonly produces lunkers of 15 pounds and over. February, March and October are the top brass months, but the fishing is good all year. Seminole is full of standing dead timber and cypress trees, so heavier tackle comes in handy for landing big bass.

Walter F. George is a young reservoir now at its peak of productivity. Largemouth bass is the primary species, with crappie and white bass taking a close second. Bream, bluegill and redbreast fishing is also very good.

Lakes Blackshear and Worth produce largemouth, white bass, crappie and bream. According to numbers of fish caught, bluegill are most important, but white bass cause quite a stir when they school up to feed on shad. Fishermen take them by casting into or trolling through the schooling fish. Largemouth bass also rank high on the stringer, particularly during the spring and fall when they are most active.

These southern lakes have excellent fishing facilities and good public access to fishing areas.

Idaho

This is a state on which nature lavished her choicest blessings in order to provide a wide variety of fishing waters—high mountain lakes, wandering creeks, deep, clear streams and turbulent, tossing rivers. And yet, due to heavy construction of dams, an ever-increasing industrial and chemical pollution and loss of water in lower areas due to holding of water in upstream dams for irrigation, and miles of streams chewed apart by bulldozers and displaced by road beds, the fishing areas have narrowed and become depleted, and two of the state's outstanding attractions— anadromous salmon and steelhead— are facing serious danger of total extinction.

At the present time, however, many species of fish are available to the angler. Among them are: salmon (which includes chinook, kokanee and coho); and trout (including steelhead, rainbow, kamloops, cutthroat, brown, brook, Dolly Varden and mackinaw). Warmwater species are also available in much of the state, with good fishing for both smallmouth and largemouth bass, perch, crappie, sunfish, bullhead and channel catfish.

Idaho has approximately 16,000 miles of fishing streams and some 2,000 lakes. As a large portion of the state is public domain, most waters are available for public fishing. Most large lakes and reservoirs have facilities for boats and other accomodations.

Main highways and Forest Service roads offer ready access to most of the main rivers and streams throughout the state. Many camping areas are available in forested regions.

For those interested in high mountain and back country, Idaho's mountain lakes offer unsurpassed fishing and scenic beauty. Most of these lakes may be reached only by hiking or by packstring. The Selkirk Mountains, the Powell Area, the Burnt Knob area in the Nez Perce National Forest, the Sawtooth Wilderness Area—all these offer lakes of varying degrees of excellence but alike in their unbelievable alpine scenery and refreshing isolation.

The Idaho general fishing season is open from the Saturday nearest June 1 until November 30 each year. There are many waters open the year around for all species, and the large lakes of the 5 northern counties open a month before the general trout season. There are other local exceptions where regulations have been established to protect spawning populations or to aid in the harvest of fish.

Many streams are high and roily in the early part of the season and some sort of bait, such as angleworms or salmon eggs, is recommended. For this reason, usually the numerous reservoirs and small streams are considered best for trout fishing in the early part of the season. As water clears, fishing improves in all waters throughout the state. Fishermen than start using spinning tackle, wet and dry flies and other types of artificial lures.

Some species of trout are caught from practically all the waters of the state. Rainbow trout are predominant, however. Kamloops, mackinaw and Dolly Varden are favorites with many fishermen because of the relatively large size they attain in some lakes.

Starting from northern Idaho and swinging south and to the east, some of the better trout waters are listed here. There are also numerous side streams and lakes that will prove rewarding to trout fishermen.

The Moyie River, between Bonner's Ferry and the Canadian line, is good for dry fly fishing late summer and fall. Priest Lake in the panhandle near the Washington border has good cutthroat, Dolly Varden and kokanee fishing, but is most famous for it's large mackinaw trout. Big Lake Pend Oreille, southeast of Priest Lake, is famed for its large kamloops rainbow trout

These tough battlers are every flycasters dream. Browns of this size, four to five pounds, don't come to net without a terrific fight. These are the kind that can take all your fly line plus several yards of backing in a flash. They come this big in some of the rivers in Arkansas and Missouri.

(world's record 37 pounds) and Dolly Varden (world's record 32 pounds). The most action for catching these big fish is had in May, October and November.

Moving south, there are Spirit, Twin, Hauser and Hayden Lakes which all provide both trout and bass fishing. Coeur d'Alene Lake offers cutthroat and kokanee fishing, and Coeur d'Alene River is good for rainbow and cutthroat, especially in summer and fall. The St. Joe River, flowing out of the mountains east of St. Maries, is an excellent trout stream.

Famous for its steelhead fishing is the Clearwater River. This river system drains an enormous mountain region and offers excellent rainbow, cutthroat and Dolly Varden fishing throughout and smallmouth bass fishing in its lower reaches. The headwaters of the Clearwater include the famous North Fork, Lochsa River and Selway River.

Reaching into the southern part of the state is the Salmon River, another large drainage. The Salmon is Idaho's most famous river because of its wild, beautiful country and the fine salmon, steelhead and trout fishing it offers. The main river and its tributaries provide rainbow, cutthroat, Dolly Varden and brook trout fishing. Some of the most appealing portions of the Salmon River drainage are within primitive areas and are accessible only by pack outfit, boat or airplane. The rugged Middle Fork of the Salmon is floated by hundreds of sightseeing and fishing parties each summer, and the headwaters of the main river drain the spectacularly scenic Sawtooth Mountains, a Mecca for summer visitors.

The Payette River south and west of the Salmon River drainage, drains a large mountain area which contains much excellent trout fishing. Branching into 3 main tributaries, the North, Middle and South Forks, the Payette drains Payette and Upper Payette Lakes, and Cascade and Deadwood Reservoirs—all good trout fishing waters. Payette Lake and Cascade Reservoir contain rainbow trout and coho and kokanee salmon. Payette also has mackinaw trout.

Southeast of the Payette is the Boise River, another drainage with prominent North, Middle and South Forks. The Boise and its tributaries are also good producers of rainbows and cutthroats. The drainage contains 3 large water impoundments—Lucky Peak, Arrowrock and Anderson Ranch Reservoirs. All 3 provide good fishing during the summer and other parts of the year for rainbows, kokanee and coho.

To the east in south central Idaho is the Wood River and the Big Lost River. Both are rather fertile waters that produce fine rainbow trout fishing. Magic Reservoir is located on the Big Wood River and is a favorite producer of rainbows. Silver Creek, below Hailey, is famous everywhere for its large, fighting rainbows, and the exceptionally good fly fishing. Mackay Reservoir is located on the Big Lost River and is another good producer of rainbow trout.

The Snake River flows from eastern Idaho in a broad arc, across the southern part of the state and turns north through Hells Canyon. Good trout fishing spots along the Snake include American Falls and Blackfoot Reservoirs and Blackfoot River in eastern Idaho, all for quality rainbow trout. Trout fishing is best on the Upper Snake in what is known as the Island Park Area. Henry's Lake and Island Park Reservoir are both famous rainbow waters. The north and south forks of the Snake River are both excellent trout waters, producing large rainbows for both bait and artificial lure fishermen. Those streams contain some outstanding dry fly waters. Palisades Reservoir on the Snake River where it enters Idaho is a good producer of large cutthroat and brown trout. Brown trout are occasionally caught from the Snake River drainage in eastern Idaho.

In the southeastern corner of the state, Bear River provides good trout fishing after mid-summer, and Bear Lake is good for cutthroat and fair for mackinaw trout.

Many hundreds of high mountain lakes are to be found in mountainous areas of Idaho. Most of them contain either rainbow or cutthroat trout, but a few have brook trout. Some lake areas are close to roads while others are far even from established trails.

Chinook salmon and steelhead trout—these fish migrate into Idaho from the Pacific Ocean. Their main travelways to the spawning beds are the Snake, Clearwater and Salmon rivers.

Steelhead trout move into the lower drainages in September or October. Best fishing is usually in October and November, or March and April. They stop moving upriver when water turns cold during the winter, and start moving again during warming spring weather. During periods of high runoff in the spring, fishing activity comes to a halt when the waters muddy up.

Three groups of chinook salmon enter Idaho—spring-run, summer-run and fall-run chinook. Nearly all of the sport fishing activity is on the spring and summer chinook runs, beginning in June and extending through July. Fishermen use clusters of salmon eggs or flashing lures.

Salmon probably average about 15 pounds, although many small, immature males are caught early in the season. A few adult females

Fly fishing on the south fork of the Clearwater river in Idaho is excellent. In the fast waters shown you can come up with a brookie or rainbow with the same wet fly. There are browns in the larger pools in quieter water.

weighing up to 45 pounds have been recorded.

To protect spawners many fishing closures go into effect throughout the salmon season. Regulations should be closely checked regarding these rules.

Warm water fish—bass, crappie, perch, sunfish and catfish fishing is not widespread in Idaho. There are many good places, however, numerous lakes in the extreme north from the Idaho-Canadian border, south to Lewiston are excellent for this type of fishing. Southern Idaho sloughs and ponds along the lower Boise, Payette and Weiser rivers, and a number of reservoirs across southern Idaho support bass, crappie and perch fishing.

The Snake River from C. J. Strike Reservoir downstream to Lewiston contains some of the top smallmouth bass waters in the west. The Hells Canyon stretch of the river, with limited access, provides real thrills for the bass fisherman during the spring and summer months.

Float fishing in Idaho really came into it's own when World War II introduced the reliable rubber raft to replace the wooden scows, about 32 feet long, guided by two men using long sweeps which had formerly been used. The dependability, flexibility and buoyance of the ugly black rubber boats brought floating within the reach of everyone. And it is a thrilling and enjoyable type of a trip for the fisherman in Idaho, if

reasonable caution and careful planning are used.

The middle fork of the Salmon River is the favorite of most "river rats". It has everything to offer with it's beautiful crystal clear water and excellent fishing for salmon, steelhead and trout. This is one float trip never to be forgotten. The main floating area of the middle fork is 125 miles long.

There are turns, rapids, boulders and chutes that require skill and experience. Alternating between the swift currents and white dovetail rapids are placid pools of blue tinted water. These tranquil spots give one time to look up from the battle of the river and scan the towering cliffs that reach the sky to form the Middle Fork Gorge. Copper-toned suntans and loss of weight around the mid-section come free with the trip.

There are white sand bars with cold streams that make good

One of the many kinds of bream is taken on a fly rod in this scene on a Georgia farm pond. Though small, bream are fairly scrappy and provide action when taken on a sensitive rod. They are plentiful and good eating.

camping spots. Some of the better ones are Marble Creek, Thomas Creek, Cougar Creek, Whitey Cox's Bar, Loon Creek, Hospital Bar, Tappan Cabin, Mormon Ranch, Wilson Creek, Elk Bar and Stoddard Creek.

The floater should select the periods of "good water". The turbulent Middle Fork is a place to avoid during extreme high water, and caution is the by-word when running rapids during low water. During extreme high water, the raft moves so fast, trees along the side resemble a fine tooth comb. In low water, sharp, jagged rocks, outcroppings, and shallow sand bars become trouble spots. The choice season for floating is from July to October with July the prime month. August and September are also good, but from mid-August, lowwater rapids can be treacherous.

A floater should be cautious on any river for the first few miles until he gets the "feel" of the raft and the river. He should watch ahead for "bad water". One type is when the river ahead seems to fall out of sight and white spray can be seen flying above the river. Dangerous rapids should be checked out before being run to see where the rough water and boulders are. The raft should be portaged or "lined" over especially dangerous rapids. Loss of time is better than loss of equipment. Bad rapids encountered are Marble Creek, Tappan Falls, Haystacks, Redside, Scoup and Hancock.

In April, steelhead fishing is great although the trip can be cold, wet, and miserable. From June to September, the native cutthroat trout fishing is out of this world. Because fish are difficult to keep in hot weather, most of the fishing is done to get a mess for eating, or to catch and release for sport.

If time is not available for the ten-day trip, one can still float part of the Middle Fork. The float distance can

be reduced by flying into one of the small landing fields along the river. Bush pilots with many hours of mountain flying time are available to land the floater and gear along the river.

Fly fishing is at its best in these waters. There are some quiet pools so be sure to bring dry flies as well as streamers and bucktails.

Kansas

Fly fishing opportunities in Kansas are limited due to the fact that there are no trout waters in the state. However, there is considerable interest in fly fishing for members of the sunfish family wherever the water is clear enough for such activity.

As far as stream fishing is concerned, many of the small springfed creeks in the Flint Hills and Chautauqua Hills areas produce well for the fly fish man who is in pursuit of bluegill, green sunfish and bass. Both largemouth and spotted bass are taken on medium sized or large streamers or bucktails. Black and yellow seems to be a popular color. Popping bugs are also a favorite with some anglers with green and yellow being popular colors.

Smaller lakes and ponds produce the best for fly fishermen; generally there is little activity with this tackle at the larger lakes and reservoirs. Some of the better public lakes for fly fishing are Bourbon County State Lake. Chase County State Lake, Elm Creek Lake and Pottawatomie County State Lake #2. Cowley County State Lake is also productive.

May, June and October are probably the best months for Kansas fly fishing.

Maine

From the earliest days of the nineteen hundreds, when the "True Sportsman" arrived with his touring car packed to the flapping canvas windows with heavy, cumbersome equipment, the state of Maine has held an unequalled place as the Mecca of fly-fishermen. From his dandy regulation Army brown duck hat to his high cut laced leather boots (complete with pocket knife) his expensive gear reflected a winter of thought and planning.

Yet today the dedicated angler—with his light weight, much more reasonably priced clothing and equipment is able to travel faster and in a much shorter length of time amass his limits of trout, salmon and bass. The enthusiasm and enjoyment are the same—these never change in the true fisherman, no matter the generation into which he is born.

The vast expanses of forest lands and waterways within the boundaries of the state of Maine are regarded by many sportsmen as one of the last frontiers remaining on the American continent.

Despite the gradual encroachment of civilization upon her woods and waters, Maine, through a carefully planned conservation and stocking program, has worked with nature to maintain a favorable balance, assuring an abundance of game fish for any and all who wish a peaceful vacation amidst the surroundings of nature's own greenery.

Due to the unpredictables that make the sport what it is, big fish catches vary from year to year, but Maine fish are either at, or near the top in national honors every year. In past years Maine fish have captured nation-wide "firsts" for four different species: landlocked salmon, eastern brook trout, white perch and Atlantic salmon.

Variety is but one of the rare pleasures Maine has in store for all fishermen. Whether it's the silvery, lightning-like acrobatics of a landlocked salmon "tailwalking" at the end of your line, the powerful, deep-fighting surge of a heavy squaretail or the explosive smashing tactics of a fighting black bass—it's all there—and more.

There are brown trout in many waters, big rainbows in the Kennebec River, and white perch to spare. From the Atlantic salmon in Maine's eastern coastal rivers to the wary brook trout in thousands of rushing streams and wilderness ponds, or the hungry pickerel waiting under lily pads at the water's edge—there's action to please every taste in fresh-water fishing.

Maine's landlocked salmon are ready for action the minute the ice leaves lakes and ponds in the spring. This ice breakup usually occurs between the first of April and the middle of May each year, depending upon weather conditions.

In the early part of the fishing season, millions of fresh-water smelt, a food of the landlocked salmon, move toward the mouths of tributary streams and over shallow sand bars in their annual spring spawning run. At this time the salmon crowd in close to shore to feed on these silvery little fish. During this period streamer flies or almost any small lure that resembles a smelt will produce results.

Fly-fishing with wet flies of the conventional type as well as many patterns of streamer fly design also work well at this time. Later, as the season progresses and temperatures rise, the salmon move back, seeking cooler areas in the deep water. Cooler surface temperatures during September again bring these silver-sided battlers near the surface and once more fly-fishing close to the mouths of streams is at it's best, with both wet and dry flies productive as the salmon congregate for their own spawning run.

This is the east outlet of the Moosehead River in Maine. It is cool, clear water that produces some fine catches of brook trout and salmon. Water is at ideal fishing level.

Eastern brook trout fishing in Maine is a special sort of fun all by itself. These speckled beauties can be found in small, clear, cold water brooks in every section of the state as well as in most of Maine's deeper springfed lakes and ponds, where water temperatures remain low even during the hottest of summer weather. From the eight and nine-inch "pan size" to the five and six pound "lunkers" there are thrills galore for the trout fisherman.

Smallmouth black bass fishing, Maine style, is a thrill never to be forgotten. These northern bronze-backs, frequenting more than 300 of the Pine Tree State's clear, cool waters, rise to almost any bait or fly. They're ready and spoiling for battle at the slightest provocation.

From June 1 to June 21 bass may be taken on any single-hooked artificial lure. During this period the

Colonel Fuller, White Miller or any fly predominating in the colors of red and white will keep you busy. Better be sure to include a landing net in your equipment if you are of a mind to try Maine's black bass. They're never down until they're out, and out means right in the frying pan, alongside strips of crisp brown bacon.

Lovers of true lake trout fishing have been enchanted for years by the top notch togue fishing enjoyed in many of Maine's deeper lakes and ponds. One of the heaviest of these rugged battlers, netted recently, weighed 31-1/2 pounds with a great many others taken that ran between ten pounds and this mark. Average catches go from 2-1/2 and 3 pounds up to 6 to 8 pounds. These deep-fighting togue can be taken with almost equal success all during the entire open season in Maine.

Early in the season, togue are near the surface and frequently fall prey to streamer flies, much as both landlocked salmon and squaretails do.

For the past few years, Maine's Inland Fish and Game Department has been gradually introducing brown trout in waters of the state particularly adapted to these sporty gamefish. Recently, one of these stubborn fighters weighing 19 pounds 7 ounces came to the net of a very surprised angler.

The average weight of brown trout taken in Maine, however, usually runs between 1-1/2 and 7 or 8 pounds, with some specimens much larger. They frequent many of the so-called warmer waters and more shallow ponds and rivers. They are particularly susceptible to flies in both the wet and dry types.

White perch, cousin of the black bass, is one of the easiest of all Maine's fish to catch. Rated as one of the very best panfish, these snappy little dark-colored hustlers are found in great numbers and furnish plenty of action. Don't underestimate white perch when it comes to fly-fishing. They are an "all season fish" but afford the best fishing of all during the warmer days of mid-summer.

Maine's Penobscot County, boasting the famed Bangor Salmon Pool, Lincoln County's Sheepscot River and Washington County with its Narraguagus, Dennys, Pleasant, Machias and East Machias Rivers are now the major spots in the United States where sport-fishermen can take that king of all gamefish, the Atlantic salmon.

The Narraguagus, Dennys, and the other rivers mentioned above are increasing their yield each year under the careful supervision of the Atlantic Sea Run Salmon Commission. Atlantic salmon in these rivers vary from 8 to nearly 30 pounds in weight.

Probably the fishing is the "hottest" as Maine natives say, between May 15 and the end of June. FLY FISHING ONLY is the order of the day with these king-size fish. The Dennys, the most easterly river, at Dennysville, is the smallest of the popular salmon fishing rivers. The first fish are taken about mid-May, and fishing reaches a peak over Memorial Day and the first two weeks in June, and from mid-June the runs decrease. Fishing is done from the banks, as a rule, but the canoe trip from Meddybemps to Dennysville can be expected to produce both trout and Atlantic salmon fishing early in the season.

The East Machias River, 5 miles east of Machias, is productive during the same period as the Dennys. Depending on how the water flows in the Machias River, angling on the East Machias may be a week or 2 longer than on the Dennys.

The Machias River, largest and latest running of all, comes into production during the latter part of June and first 2 weeks of July. New fish come into the Machias and anglers fish throughout the summer. The first 2 weeks in September, with normally cooler weather, can provide a fall fishery not known on the other rivers.

The Narraguagus River at Cherryfield produces the earliest catches, with the peak of fishing before mid-June.

The Sheepscot River in Lincoln County provides a small but attractive fishery for Atlantic salmon from early July through the remainder of the fishing season. Fishing areas are mostly in the lower reaches of the river at the tidal falls and a few pools farther upstream.

On all but the upper reaches of these rivers, the angling is limited to the use of artificial flies. Even in areas not restricted to fly-fishing, fish are taken most readily on flies rather than on other types of lures. It is advisable to purchase flies on the rivers being fished. While Atlantic salmon flies used anywhere in the world may take Atlantics, the locally tied patterns are, more often than not, the ones that take fish locally.

In fishing for landlocked salmon, some of the better known and most productive areas are listed below by county: *Aroostook, Eagle Lake outlet; Penobscot, Matagamon Lake outlet; Piscataquis, West Branch Penobscot River [below Ripogenus]; Washington, Grand Lake Stream; Washington, Saint Croix River at East Grand Lake; Oxford, Kennebago River; Oxford, Rapid River below Middle Dam; Oxford, Upper Dam Pool—Richardson Lake; Cumberland, Crooked River.*

For better casting and lower visibility, a leader should be tapered and from 8 to 12 feet long, depending on water clarity. The breaking strength should be around 8 pounds (1X size). Streamers and bucktails

Fly fishing is also highly effective in salt water as this photo shows. The striper above is being taken out of the surf from the shoreline of Rhode Island. The surf fly fisherman can choose Rhode Island terrain ranging from ledges and rocky cliffs to sandy beaches to fish for striped bass, bluefish and tautog.

are popular for land locked salmon on many waters and are especially effective in large pools, at the mouths of streams, or in high, cloudy water where a large fly is needed for higher visibility to the fish. Some fishermen use these flies to the exclusion of all others. The Grey Ghost, Black Ghost, Nine-Three, Mickey Finn, and Muddler Minnow. No. 4 or 6 long shank hooks are about right for size.

Just 2 of the many excellent lakes in Maine are Kennebago and Sourdnahunk lakes. Kennebago (in Franklin County) has an area of 1,700 acres and is 5 miles long. Its maximum depth is 116 feet, and surface temperature is 70 degrees (F.), 107 feet—46 degrees (F.). Salmon, brook trout (squaretail), brown trout, smelt, minnows, lake chub and blacknose dace are found in its depths, but it is famous for its salmon and trout fishing.

Water analysis shows satisfactory temperatures from surface to bottom and high oxygen concentration at all depths. Kennebago Lake provides a good example of water quality encountered in ideal salmon and trout lakes. This lake is open to fly fishing only, and contains several excellent pools, fishable from the shore.

Sourdnahunk Lake, in Piscataquis County, boasts of brook trout (squaretail), minnows, blacknose dace and freshwater sculpin. It has an area of 1,394 acres, with a maximum depth of 46 feet, and surface temperature of 62 degrees (F.) 46 feet—61 degrees (F.).

The lake is managed exclusively for brook trout. This is one of the few large lakes where there are practically no competing species and where other conditions are very favorable for brook trout production. Excellent fishing is enjoyed throughout the season and undoubtedly will continue as long as competitory fishes are not introduced.

The outlet produces all the young trout needed to keep the lake well stocked. The fishway is properly maintained to allow the trout to migrate up and down. The small inlets and shore spawning also contribute brook trout to the fishery.

Stocking hatchery fish in this lake is not necessary under present conditions and fishing pressure. Sourdnahunk Lake is sometimes called the "most natural trout factory" in Maine.

Maryland

Three species of the trout family comprise the cold water fishery in Maryland. Trout require lower temperatures found chiefly in the mountain streams in the western counties of the state.

Of the 3 species of trout stocked in the state, only the Eastern brook trout is native to Maryland. The brown trout, a native of Europe, and the rainbow trout from the western United States are the other species stocked.

With the intensive agricultural practices, lumbering and synthetic manufacture, most of the state's cold fast running streams have decreased in volume and water quality to such an extent that natural reproduction of trout is almost non-existent. Due to the physical, chemical and biological changes in the Appalachian and Piedmont trout streams and increased fishing pressure, it is necessary to produce the majority of the trout caught, by artificial hatchery methods. The Maryland Trout Hatchery Program and Cooperative agreement with Federal hatcheries brings the present annual production to approximately 150,000 for stocking, prior to and during the trout season.

Certain Maryland waters are designated as trout streams by the Fish and Wildlife Administration. The list of designated streams remains fairly constant but may change annually depending on fishing pressure and water quality. In Garrett County, these are: Youghiogheny River, Mill Run, Bear Creek, Puzzley Run, Piney Run, Buffalo Run, Salt Block, Muddy Creek, Glade Run, Savage River and Little Youghiogheny.

In Allegany County, Jennings Run, Mill Run, Laurel Run, Staub Run, Winebrenner Run, Mathew Run, Evitts Creek and Flintstone Creek. In Washington County, Sidling Hill, Little Tonoloway Creek, Little Conococheague, St. James Run, Marsh Run, Beaver Creek and Little Antietam.

In Frederick and Carroll Counties, Middle Creek, Friends Creek, Owens Creek, Hunting Creek, Little Hunting Creek and Fishing Creek in Frederick. And in Carroll, Piney Branch and Beaver Run. In Montgomery County, Little Seneca Creek, Rock Creek and the Patuxent River.

In Baltimore County, Beetree Run, Little Gunpowder Falls, Big Gunpowder Falls and Jones Falls. In Harford County, Deer Creek. In Cecil County, Basin Run and Principio Creek.

In addition, there is a special fishing area in the Savage River, Garrett County which is a catch-and-return trout area from Merrill Bridge to the mouth of Poplar Lick for use of artificial flies, barbless hooks (spinners prohibited). All trout must be returned to the waters except that 1 trout per day of over 14 inches in total length may be kept. On Hunting Creek in Frederick County an area of approximately 1 mile from Camp Peniel Bridge to the eastern boundary of the National Park

Trout fishing is rapidly coming into its own in many southern states. This scene is a beautiful trout river in Georgia. There are many good producing waters in this state.

Service now designated by wire boundary line is also a special catch-and-return trout area with the same regulations.

Brown trout [*Salmo trutta*] are native to Europe from the Mediterranean basin and Black Sea, north to the British Isles and the Arctic of Norway and Siberia. In the late 1880's, brown trout eggs from Germany and Scotland were shipped to North America and the resulting fry reared to adults to provide the original brood stock for the browns fishermen catch today. The popular names "German brown" and "Loch Leven" trout reflect the place of origin of the first introductions. Since then brown trout have been introduced wherever suitable trout water exists.

They are very closely related to our rainbow trout and at first glance look much like the rainbow. They have dark spots imposed on a lighter background, but the spots are much larger and do not extend to the head. The tail has only a few spots or the spots are lacking. A few red or orange spots are found along the side of the trout. As the name suggests, the upper surface of the trout is a dark, golden brown blending into a dusky yellow or creamy-white on the belly.

Brown trout are cold water fish, native to meandering, lowland streams and rivers and tend to be inhabitants of the pools and undercut banks. Brown trout can adapt to warmer water temperatures, up to 80 degrees F. and do well in streams that have temperatures up to 77 degrees. Their ability to withstand warmer temperature is related to size. Trout eggs and fry need cold, well-oxygenated water below 50 degrees. Fingerling brown trout grow best in water that is below 68 degrees, but the larger browns can withstand much warmer water temperatures.

Brown trout spawn in the fall and early winter, October to December, in gravel areas with adequate flows of oxygenated water. The female usually releases 600 to 2,000 eggs, depending on her size. Fertilized eggs develop for approximately 30 days before hatching and the larval trout remain in the gravel living off the yolk sac for an additional 14 days before they come to the surface of the gravel and start feeding.

Growth of brown trout is dependent on the food available and trout size. The smaller browns feed on insects, snails, and other small invertebrates in the stream. They grow approximately four inches per year for the first three years of life and by the end of the third year will weigh one to two pounds. As the trout gets larger, the diet changes to crayfish and minnows, and growth increases accordingly. The majority

This beautiful scene is the famous Madison River, one of the better known Blue Ribbon streams of Montana. It has given up some of the finest specimens of rainbow, brown and cutthroat trout ever to be caught anywhere. One of the better stretches of this stream is located near the town of Ennis, Montana.

of the brown trout in streams live two years or less, but in every population a few individuals learn to stay away from hooks and can live 10 or more years. Weights of 8, 10 or 15 pounds are not uncommon.

Hatchery propagation of brown trout is much the same as for rainbows. Brown trout in the hatchery are slower growing than rainbows so the cost per fish raised to release size is higher. The higher initial cost is offset by the fact that brown trout are harder to catch and survival after release to become trophy-sized fish is greater. Restocking every year is generally not necessary.

When you have caught one of the lunker browns you know you have a well earned trophy. The world record brown is a 39-pound, 8 ounce monster caught in Lock Awe, Scotland. At least one brown trout over 14 pounds has been caught in Missouri.

Fly fishing with dry or wet flies is still one of the most popular and enjoyable ways of fishing for browns, but spinning gear with spinners, small lures, and live bait is rapidly gaining in popularity. Live bait—minnows, crayfish or night-crawlers—fished in the evening or early morning usually produces the largest browns.

A light flyrod, a handful of flies, and the perserverance to entice a wary brown from his hiding place will add many hours of enjoyment to an afternoon, but don't forget the frying pan. Freshly caught brown trout cooked on a stream bank rates as a culinary delight fit for a king and a fisherman.

Massachusetts

Massachusetts has primarily put and take fishing with streams and lakes being stocked in spring beginning March 1 up to June 1.

There are very few waters of suitable quality for fly fishing, but these are:

1. Squannacook River located near three towns—Groton, Shirley and Townsend.
2. Nissitissit River—located near the town of Pepperell.
3. Swift River—below Quabbin Reservoir.
4. Green River near Greenfield.
5. Deerfield River—west of Greenfield—best early in the year.
6. Farmington River—best in spring Otis and New Boston.

In the Berkshires may be found some good trout fishing. There are many good rivers and streams that are fishable. Three are: The Green River, near Greenfield, the Westfield River (with three branches) and the Farmington. These three rivers will give a good cross section of Berkshire waters. The Green River is fast, cold and gin-clear, whereas the Westfield River is bigger, slightly darker and covers a full spectrum of water conditions. The Farmington is the smallest of the three, with the darkest water. All three rivers have some of the best trout fishing offered in the Berkshires.

The Green River has its start in the foothills of the Green Mountains of Vermont. It flows due south through the town of Leyden to empty into the Connecticut just below Greenfield. Once in Greenfield, a quick stop for directions will put you on the road to Green River. This road will soon turn into dirt a short way outside of Greenfield. Green River Road follows the river all the way up into Vermont.

Notice, in fishing the Green, how clear the water is. This will mean long leaders, small flies and a careful approach. Some of the best pools on this river are in the lower section. Most of them are found from a point where the dirt road first meets the river, downstream to the dam. These pools are six or so feet deep, crystal clear and ledge-lined. Some of the

nicest brookies in the state have come from the Green River.

The Westfield River is a large watershed which drains most of the east-central portion of the Berkshires. Fishing from the town of Norwich Bridge upstream will bring you to the best water. There are some big trout in the Westfield, and some nice brooks that enter the west branch offer good fishing for small brookies.

Now, the Farmington River. This was one of the rivers that were set aside for flyfishing only a number of years back, but has now been returned to open fishing. It starts around the town of North Otis and follows Route 8 south all the way into Connecticut. The river has both brook and brown trout in it, with some better than average fish in the lower reaches. Flies work well on this water, with the muddler minnow top choice.

In central Massachusetts, try the Quabbin Reservoir for big trout. The size of fish that this water has produced in the past should be enough to make every fishermen want to go. Also any tributary that enters Quabbin should be a hot spot.

The Swift River and the Squannacook River in Townsend are both good. The Squannacook has a good deal of natural cover with lots of fallen trees, old stumps and undercut banks. The fishing gets pretty tough, but has turned up nice brown trout.

There is good fly fishing below Nickerson at Goose pond, Chatham, where the water is very clear and the fish spooky. Early morning and late evening are best here, with long leaders, small flies and a good share of luck. There are some scrappy rainbows there.

For a change of pace, look up Long Pond, Brewster-Harwich. It's a large lake, featuring smallmouth bass and trout. Other good bets in the general area are Baker Pond, Crystal Lake in Orleans, both with trout.

Outside the park, Long Pond, Brewster-Harwich has good fishing for trout and smallmouth bass.

Just below Nickerson, in Chatham, you'll find good fly fishing at Goose Pond. There are some nice rainbows in there and they put up one whale of a fight.

Missouri

The main fly fishing in Missouri is done in the trout parks. However, as you might imagine, some people will fly fish in any body of water from farm ponds to the Missouri River. For instance, the pole and line record for flathead catfish is 61 pounds; taken on a flyrod. However, for the purist, the rainbow trout, Salmo gairdneri, is the species commonly found in Missouri. It is hatchery raised, the fry being placed in hatchery troughs until they are big enough to be transferred to rearing ponds.

About 14 days after hatching the young fish begin to feed. They are fed on a special diet of commercial feed. The composition and size of the food pellets are varied as the fish grow larger. After the transfer to rearing ponds the feeding continues. Trout from the Commission's hatcheries on the average measure ten inches on their first birthday. Then they are considered large enough to plant in streams.

None of the salmon family is native to Missouri. They all are known as cold-water fishes, meaning that they cannot live long in water which gets warmer than about 75 degrees. Except for numerous isolated springs and spring branches, there are few natural waters in Missouri which meet this requirement. However, the demand of trout fishermen for the op-

portunity to practice their sport has resulted in numerous attempts to establish various species of trout in the state.

At the present the Commission maintains four trout fishing areas located in Montauk, Bennett Spring, Roaring River and Maramec parks where catchable-size trout are planted daily. Fishermen in these areas must buy a special tag each day for the privilege of fishing the trout water. The receipts from the sale of these trout tags help to defray the relatively high cost of this "put and take" type of stocking.

The waters of Lake Taneycomo became suitable for trout when the cold outflow from Table Rock Dam started to enter. The lake is stocked regularly with trout and the fame of its fishery has spread. In addition, several cold streams and spring branches receive periodic stockings of rainbows.

Fishermen who catch trout in these areas are required to have a special trout license, the revenue from which helps to pay the cost of stocking. This specialized type of fishing can be justified only when those participating in the sport are willing to bear part of the cost of the program.

The rainbow was selected for stocking in Missouri waters for its game quality, because it is the most adaptable of all the trouts to waters of this state and because it is more susceptible to domestic culture. All trout stocked in the parks and most of those freed in other areas are at least ten inches long. The world record rainbow trout caught on fly fishing tackle in 1960, a monster weighing 13 pounds, 12 ounces, was caught at Bennett Spring by H. N. Branson.

In Missouri the fly rod seems to be the favorite type of trout fishing gear, although spinning tackle is gaining

in favor. Casting rods and the bamboo pole are seldom seen on trout waters but occasionally the operator of one or the other will have a nice string of fish. Flies, both wet and dry, are highly favored.

Brown trout are one of the most sought after, talked about, cussed and discussed, and loved of the trouts. This is the trout Izaak Walton wrote about in his book, *Compleat Angler,* in 1653. The brown trout does not put on the aerial acrobatics of the rainbow trout, but is a head-shaking tackle-buster that knows every root, tree limb and rock in his underwater home. Trout anglers consider him a trophy that takes skill, cunning, and just a bit of luck to capture.

The brown trout is a new species introduced by the Department of Conservation into some of Missouri's trout waters. They have been introduced as a supplement to the rainbow trout fishery. Browns are generally warier and harder to catch than rainbows, and utilize portions of the streams where rainbows usually are not found.

These two fine brook trout were taken from cold, fast water. They are about ten to twelve inches long, good size for most streams today. Although the worm like markings on their backs is hard to see, the white stripe on their fins identifies them.

This is Johnson Lake in the Deerlodge National Forest, Montana. The lake contains rainbows and cutthroats and is located at a rather high altitude in the Anaconda-Pintlar Wilderness area.

Montana

Big Sky Country is Big Trout Country as well. Montana is a state very large in area, and even though only the western part of it is considered to have top-notch trout fishing, that part is as large as the total area of most other states.

Montana's vast and beautiful outdoors provides fishing in abundance, not only in quality but also in variety of fish. Following are brief descriptions of the major watersheds of the state and of the species of fish which are likely to be found therein.

Montana is traversed by 4 major streams—the Yellowstone, Missouri, Kootenai and Clark's Fork of the Columbia. These streams with their many tributaries and hundreds of connected lakes, offer to the angling enthusiast a diversity of fishing that can be found in few other places in the United States.

Yellowstone River

The Yellowstone River watershed offers such a variety of fishing that it would take many pages to describe all of its waters in detail. The headwaters of this river are in Yellowstone National Park and it flows through Montana in a northeasterly course until it crosses the boundary line between Montana's Richland County and North Dakota. It joins the Missouri River a few miles after crossing into North Dakota. In many of its headwater streams, especially those originating in Yellowstone Park and the Beartooth Mountains, the fisherman will find splendid cutthroat trout fishing.

As the Yellowstone flows down into Park, Sweetgrass and Stillwater Counties, the rainbow and brown trout reign supreme and a number of prize specimens of these species have been taken from this stretch of the river. It might also be mentioned here that he who prefers the art of white-fishing will have no trouble in indulging in this sport to his heart's content, as long as he remains in any of the waters within the 3 counties mentioned above.

By the time the Yellowstone River has reached Yellowstone County, it is biologically a much different stream than it was when it left Yellowstone Park. Improvements in water quality are gradually extending the brown trout fishery downstream so that catches are becoming more numerous in the river as far downstream as the mouth of the Big

Horn River. During the summer months, prevailing temperatures of the lower Yellowstone are relatively high and this area provides good warm water fishing. Chief among these are the sauger, walleye pike, channel catfish, fresh water drum and ling. Paddlefishing near Glendive offers a unique sport during spring months.

The tributaries of the Yellowstone will also provide the angler with good to excellent fishing. Some of the more important tributary rivers and streams are the Stillwater River, Sweetgrass River, Shields River, Boulder River, Hellroaring Creek, Slough Creek and many others. Cutthroat trout can be found in the headwaters of these and rainbow and Brown trout in the lower stretches. The Big Horn River below the Yellowtail Afterbay Dam has developed into an excellent rainbow and brown trout fishery as far downstream as the Two Leggins Dam. Yellowtail Reservoir and the Afterbay Dam are providing good fishing for rainbow and brown trout and also for walleye.

Missouri River

This watershed embraces the largest part of Montana and drains all the remainder of the state lying east of the Continental Divide which is not drained by the Yellowstone.

In this watershed can undoubtedly be found the greatest diversity of fishing that exists anywhere in the United States. In its headwaters can be found grayling, cutthroat, rainbow, brook and brown trout while the lower stretches offer every advantage for warm water fishing ranging from sturgeon, sauger, walleye and northern pike to sunfish, crappies, catfish, yellow perch, paddlefish and freshwater drum.

It might be well to start at the Montana-Dakota line on this great drainage system and work upstream to develop a picture of the transition from warm water to trout fishing.

There are fine sauger and walleye fishing in the Main Missouri from the North Dakota line to the Fort Peck Dam, especially during the spring migration of these species. Fresh water drum, channel catfish, ling and various rough species such as carp, suckers, goldeye and many others, are commonly caught in this section of the river.

Immediately below the Fort Peck Dam there is good sauger and walleye fishing.

Some of the more important tributaries of the Missouri River are described in the following paragraphs.

Milk River

The Milk River has its confluence with the Missouri a few miles below the Fort Peck Dam. Good walleye and sauger fishing is found in this river, particularly in the spring.

The creation of Fresno Dam has added another fishing area to the northern part of Montana. Northern pike, and walleye are the principal inhabitants of this impoundment.

The headwaters of the Milk River which originates in Glacier County and Canada afford some mighty fine rainbow trout fishing.

Fort Peck Lake

Fort Peck Lake, being such a large body of water in a sparsely populated area, has hardly been touched so far as fishing is concerned. The available fishing facilities are limited to the Fort Peck Dam area, the areas below and above the dam, the Rock Creek area which is approached from Glendive, Montana, and the Hell Creek area on the south side of the lake which is approached through Miles City and Jordan.

Incidentally, this latter area is approached through the Badlands of Montana and the Missouri River breaks, famous in the history of the West. Many fossils have been found along this very scenic approach to Fort Peck Dam.

Musselshell River

As we progress upstream, we come to the junction of the Musselshell which drains a vast territory in Meagher, Wheatland, Golden Valley, Musselshell and Petroleum Counties.

The headwaters of this stream contain brook, brown trout and rainbow, as do several of the large reservoirs such as Martinsdale, Deadman's Basin, Harris and Sutherland.

The Musselshell River from Ryegate to its headwaters affords some of the best brown trout fishing in Montana and ranks as a very highly productive stream. The trout fisherman might well consider this stream one of the most important in Montana for brown trout fishing. Catfishing is good in the lower river area.

Judith River

The Judith River which converges with the Missouri quite some distance upstream from the Musselshell is also worthy of special mention as many of its tributaries are quite famous for the large specimens of brown trout, brook and rainbow trout.

One of the Judith's tributaries, Spring Creek, near Lewistown, is a good fishing stream and is also accessible to the angling public, an important feature of this stretch of water.

Marias River

The Marias River was named by Lewis and Clark who thought it might be the main stem of the Missouri. The headwaters of this stream on the eastern slope of the Rockies afford good trout fishing.

One of the creeks which flows into the Marias heads on Three Waters Peak in Glacier Park, from which water flows into the Atlantic

This wide, shallow river is fine for fishing dry flies as the current is not very fast and gives the flycaster a chance to work the fly over choice spots using his own technique. Lots of overhanging brush provides excellent cover and shade for fish lies.

(through the Marias), into the Pacific and into Hudson Bay. This example shows how Montana's Rockies stand at the peak of the continent.

Beginning with the Two Medicine River in Glacier Park, Cut Bank Creek, Birch Creek, Willow Creek and the main Marias River all afford rainbow trout fishing in the area adjacent to and east of Glacier Park. The Tiber impoundment has rainbow. Good trout fishing is offered in the Marias River below the dam.

Main Missouri River

From Great Falls upstream, the main Missouri River becomes a trout stream worthy of special mention and from its waters are made many fine catches of rainbow, brown trout and whitefish.

Continuing upstream, the impoundments created by Holter Lake, Hauser Lake and Canyon Ferry Lake provide excellent boat fishing. Here catches of brown trout and rainbow are making these impoundments more important to lake fishermen who desire this type of fishing. The river proper is also very good fishing.

Further upstream near Three Forks, is where fishing history is really made, for it is at this point that 3 major watersheds—the Jefferson, the Madison and the Gallatin Rivers converge to form the Missouri River. River.

Gallatin River

The Gallatin River, with its tributaries draining Gallatin, Park and Madison Counties and also a portion of Yellowstone National Park, offers a diversity of fishing for brown, rainbow, cutthroat, brook trout, and whitefish.

Madison River

The Madison River, rising in Yellowstone National Park and draining much of Madison and Gallatin Counties, offers good fishing and attracts anglers from all parts of the country.

The headwaters of the Madison rise in Yellowstone National Park and carry a wealth of minerals from the Hot Springs area. Rainbow and brown trout are supreme and the river is a paradise for the fly fisherman. Hebgen and Meadow Lakes, artificial impoundments of the main Madison River, are famous for the sport they offer the fisherman who trolls and even to the ardent fly fisherman.

Near the headwaters of the Madison River are located Cliff, Wade and Hidden Lakes that provide excellent trout fishing, either by trolling or fly casting.

In the headwaters of both the Gallatin and Madison drainages, there are lakes that afford rainbow, cutthroat, golden trout and grayling fishing, important to the backwoods

This fisherman will find scrappy rainbows and cutthroats in this high country river. It is the beautiful Stillwater above Big Park in the Custer National Forest. The fish don't run much over twelve inches, but there are plenty of them and they are easy to catch on flies.

packer and outdoor enthusiast wishing to explore Montana's high mountain lakes.

SUN RIVER: Entering the Missouri at Great Falls, the Sun originates in the high mountain country of the Bob Marshall Wilderness Area to the West. Exciting pack-in fishing for rainbow and cutthroat trout is provided by the upper forks of the Sun above Gibson Dam.

The lower reaches of the Sun, down to the town of Vaughn, provides excellent brown trout and rainbow fishing.

THE BIG HOLE RIVER: The Big Hole River in southwestern Montana is very famous for its brown trout and rainbow trout fishing, and its upper watersheds afford grayling and brook trout fishing. People from many states travel to the Big Hole each year to participate in this outdoor recreation.

It may be said that the Beaverhead and the Big Hole Rivers will meet the expectations of any trout fisherman, fishing with either Spinning Equipment or dry fly gear.

In this drainage there are many high mountain lakes that may be explored for their fishing and camping by those who wish to go into some of the back country.

CLARK FORK OF THE COLUMBIA RIVER: So far only the waters on the eastern slope of the Rockies have been covered. Let's cross the Divide and drop down into the headwaters of the Clark Fork of the Columbia River which has its origin in Silver Bow, Powell and Granite Counties.

Practically all of its tributaries in these counties afford very good brook trout and cutthroat fishing, while rainbow may be found further down stream. Brown trout are also to be found on the western slope. The Little Blackfoot which flows through Powell County is an outstanding example of a brown trout stream.

GEORGETOWN LAKE: Of all the headwaters of the Clark Fork drainage, Georgetown Lake, which was created many years ago by impoundment, may be considered the best lake fishing that is accessible by motor traffic.

The Fish and Game Department has maintained a good supply of rainbow trout by stocking and regulating this species throughout the years. Many large catches and limits of fish are taken annually by trolling and fly fishing. The lake itself is in a very beautiful setting of mountains and timberland and is an ideal location for fishing and outings.

FLINT CREEK-ROCK CREEK: Flint Creek, the outlet of Georgetown Lake, is a part of the headwaters of the Clark Fork River.

Rock Creek, which is almost entirely within Granite County and which flows into the Clark Fork a few miles below Bonita, is one of the finest trout streams on the western slope. It is mainly a rainbow and cutthroat stream. Rainbow and brown trout are found in the lower stretches and cutthroat in its headwaters.

BIG BLACKFOOT RIVER: As the Clark Fork passes through the town of Bonner, it is joined by the Big Blackfoot River which drains much of Powell, Lewis and Clark and Missoula Counties with its headwaters in the famous Clearwater Lakes region.

The Big Blackfoot, like many of the streams on the western slope, is not drained by a large number of irrigation diversions and is one of the outstanding trout streams in that region. This stream, like Rock Creek, produces principally rainbow, cutthroat trout and brown trout.

Near Missoula, the Big Blackfoot River joins the Clark Fork of the Columbia and drains a large area east and north on the west side of the Continental Divide. This drainage area affords rainbow, cutthroat and Brown trout fishing in the entire area.

Joining the Big Blackfoot River is the Clearwater River which drains the Clearwater chain of lakes. The headwater lakes (Clearwater, Summit, Rainy, Alva and Inez) have cutthroat trout.

Sockeye salmon have been introduced into several of the Clearwater Lakes and these introductions further supplement the fishing enjoyment of this region.

In addition to the brook trout, these lakes also have another member of the char family—the Dolly Varden which is sometimes called bull trout. The area is most scenic and is well worthwhile for the traveling angler to explore and enjoy.

The Blackfoot River from Lincoln to Bonner is a valuable recreational area which affords excellent float trips. Float trip maps are available for the Clark Fork, the Big Blackfoot and Bitterroot Rivers at the Fish and Game Headquarters in Missoula, Montana.

The Clearwater chain of lakes and all of the area of the Clearwater drainage north and south of the Blackfoot River running east and west comprises a huge area of recreational possibilities with key passes through and into the upper South Fork of the Flathead and the Bob Marshall Wilderness area. Dude ranches and guides are available in this area at all times of the year.

BITTERROOT RIVER: A few miles below the city of Missoula, the Bitterroot River contributes its water to the Clark Fork of the Columbia. Fishing possibilities in this area are almost unlimited. Practically all of Ravalli County lies in the Bitterroot

This is the North Fork of the Snake River in Idaho. Almost every type of fishing is being done in this one stretch of the river. There are three men fishing from a rubber boat, two men are wading and flycasting, two men are spincasting from shore, one man is flycasting from shore and another is just watching. These are good waters for rainbows and cutthroat.

This is a part of the Stillwater River about two miles from where it comes down out of the mountains. This stretch has good sized rainbows up to three pounds and fine brown trout, some as big as six pounds. They are not easy to get in this area, but a knowledgeable fly fisherman can score. Location is in the south central part of Montana.

drainage, and at its headwaters may be found many beautiful sub-Alpine lakes which provide predominately cutthroat trout fishing.

Rainbow, brook and brown trout are the principal trout inhabitants of the Bitterroot River. During the winter months, whitefishing is a very popular sport.

LOWER FLATHEAD RIVER:

Not far from the town of Paradise, the Clark Fork of the Columbia is joined by the Flathead River. The Flathead River below Flathead Lake is a large meandering stream and catches of cutthroat, Dolly Varden, brown trout and rainbow trout can be made in this area. It, too, is a stream well suited for boat trips.

FLATHEAD LAKE: From Flathead Lake upward, including all of the tributaries and connected lakes of this vast drainage system, the utmost in fishing, recreation and pleasure may be expected.

At the present time, Flathead Lake is open to fishing the year around for all species of fish in open waters and through the ice. Cutthroat, Dolly Varden, mackinaw and kokanee are the most sought game fish found in this lake.

However, bass fishing enthusiasts may find a number of protected bays and side sloughs where specimens ranging up to 5 and 6 pounds are not at all uncommon.

Perch fishing is popular in Polson Bay during the late summer months and through the winter. While some specimens are not as large as those caught in the warmer waters in the eastern part of the state, the meat is of a very high quality.

Within the waters of Flathead Lake are found the Rocky Mountain and Lake Superior whitefish with many of these specimens averaging 2 to 3 pounds.

One of the highlights of the Flathead Lake fishing comes during the fall of the year when the inland water sockeye salmon (also called kokanee), having completed their 4 year cycle of growth, reach maturity and congregate on the gravel-rimmed shores of the lake to spawn. It is at this point that hundreds of fishermen break out snagging equipment.

Upper Flathead River

Flathead River above Flathead Lake is divided into three main tributaries—the North Fork, the Middle Fork and the South Fork. The fishing in all of these is indeed worthy of special mention and consists principally of cutthroat, Dolly Varden, and Mountain whitefish. During the fall, large concentrations of kokanee ascend the river and are available to snaggers.

In this river system are many remote and primitive areas including the famous Bob Marshall Wilderness area, accessible only by trail. To those who wish to sacrifice the comfort and ease of riding on the main highways and hit the back trails on foot or horseback will come the rich reward of hard-fighting trout.

Over half of the Glacier Park area is drained by tributaries of the Flathead. In this area are many lakes which afford fine cutthroat, rainbow and kokanee fishing.

Swan River

The Swan River drains into Flathead Lake from Swan Lake. The Swan River drainage is about 60 miles long and is comprised of many miles of excellent cutthroat, rainbow, brook trout, and Dolly Varden fishing in the main river and its tributaries. The headwaters of the Swan River are Holland and Lindberg Lakes. There is a through highway system from Big Fork, Montana, at the confluence of the Swan River, and Flathead Lake, south through the valley between the Swan Range and the Mission Range, through the Clearwater drainage to the Big Blackfoot River. This makes an excellent large fishing area comprised of both lake and stream fishing.

Lower Clark Fork River

From the mouth of the Flathead River, the Clark Fork River winds down through canyons and forms Noxon and Cabinet Gorge Reservoirs on the boundary between Montana and Idaho.

These reservoirs can be reached handily and access is available from the highway for boat fishing. The lakes contain rainbow trout and cutthroat trout.

Kootenai River

The Kootenai River, situated in the very northwest corner of Montana entirely within Lincoln County, rises in Canada. It flows into Montana and through Idaho, then back into Canada, through the Kootenai Lakes and thence into the Columbia River.

This region possesses a number of outstanding streams such as the Fisher River, Tobacco River, Yaak River and many smaller tributaries in addition to a large number of mountain lakes. All of these abound with trout of either cutthroat, brook or rainbow variety.

The main Kootenai River offers very good cutthroat and Dolly Varden angling, and the only sturgeon fishing in northwestern Montana. Winter fishing on this river provides the largest mountain whitefish in the state, and abundant ling.

Lake Fishing in Eastern Montana

In the development of the west, everyone considers the raising of cattle as a primary industry. Coupled with the livestock industry in later years was a program geared to increased production. With this came the necessity for water.

Through different governmental and state agencies, stock water reservoirs and lakes ranging in size from 5 to 500 acres were created as catching basins for snow and rain water runoff. On the prairies of eastern Montana, throughout both the Missouri and Yellowstone River drainage, are many of these reservoirs.

Many isolated waters of the prairie lands provide excellent rainbow fishing while others offer bass, blue gills, crappie, walleye and northern pike.

Anyone wishing to roam over the historic prairie lands where the buffalo and antelope formerly were the only inhabitants will come upon small lakes with fishing for both warm and cold water species.

Nebraska

This "where the west begins" state is laced with streams and dotted with lakes, most of them underfished. From giant reservoirs to rushing streams, any fisherman can find his heart's desire, whether he be canepoler or an expert with the fly rod. With 11,000 miles of streams and more than 3,300 lakes, there's ample room to wet a line.

Starting in far western Nebraska—the Panhandle is the spot for trout. And, anglers can take their choice of rainbow, brown or brookies from streams in three drainages—the North Platte Valley, the Pine Ridge, and the Niobrara Valley. While trout are not confined to this region, it is here that most of the strictly coldwater enthusiasts come. For those who prefer warm water species, there are lakes like Box Butte, Minatare, Whitney and Walgren. U.S. Government stocked ponds around Crawford add a plus for those with a yen for bass and bluegill. Crescent Lake National Wildlife Refuge offers some excellent angling for northern pike, bass and bluegill at two natural Sand Hill lakes, Island and Crane. From the rolling cattle lands of the Sand Hills to the majestic high country of the Pine Ridge and Wildcat Hills, this scenic and history-rich area has a special appeal to the entire family.

Here are some of the better areas:

Fishing aplenty exists in northeast Nebraska—for the fisherman who knows where to find it. Gigantic Lewis and Clark Lake, with 31,000 surface acres and over 100 miles of shoreline, tops the angling scene. Numerous streams, including the mighty Missouri, offer their wares.

Fine strings of smallmouth bass like these can be taken with poppers on fly rods. It's easy casting from a boat because casts can be short.

SPECIES, BEST TIME, AREA, METHOD, AND BAIT

Lewis and Clarke Lake	Crappie, inlets, May, June, September, October, still fishing, casting, minnows, jigs. White bass, along dam, rocks, bays, spring and fall, trolling, casting. Minnows and jigs. Walleye, same areas as white bass, spring and fall, trolling, casting, minnows and jigs. Sauger, same as walleye. Channel catfish, deeper water, May to October. Still fishing, bait casting. Minnows, worms, crayfish, prepared baits. Drum, entire lake, summer, still fishing, worms, minnows, crayfish. Carp, entire lake, summer, still fishing, corn, worms, prepared baits, wet flies.
Decatur Lake	Walleye, entire lake, winter and spring, trolling, ice fishing, minnows. Crappie, around pilings, spring, still fishing, minnows. Carp, entire lake, spring, still fishing, corn, worms, wet flies, streamers.
Niobrara River	Channel catfish, below Spencer Dam, May to October, bait casting, setlines. Live baits.
East Branch of Verdigre Creek	Rainbow, brown trout above Grove Lake at Royal. All year. Fly fishing, spinning, artificials, worms, minnows.
M. Branch of Verdigre Creek	Brown trout, upper five miles, N.E. of Page. All year. Fly fishing, spinning, artificials, worms, minnows.
Steel Creek	Brown trout, upper eight miles, N.E. of O'Neill. All year. Spinning, fly fishing, artificials, minnows, worms.
Big Springs Creek	Brown trout, upper two miles, north of Orchard. All year. Fly fishing, spinning, artificials, minnows, worms.

NAME	SPECIES, BEST TIME, AREA, METHOD, AND BAIT
Monroe Creek	Brook, year around, upper 2 miles, work pools.
Sowbelly Creek	Brown, brook, year around, upper 5 miles, work pools.
Hat Creek	Brown, rainbow, year around, both branches to forks, work pools.
Soldiers Creek	Brown, rainbow, year around, middle branch, work pools.
White River	Brown, rainbow, year around, upper 15 miles, bait and fly fishing.
Deadhorse Creek	Brook, year around, upper 3 miles, bait fishing, pools.
Chadron Creek	Brown, rainbow, year around, upper 9 miles, bait fishing, pools.
Bordeaux Creek	Brown, rainbow, year around, upper few miles, bait fishing, pools.
Beaver Creek	Brown, year around, upper few miles, bait fishing, pools.
White Clay Creek	Brown, rainbow, year around, upper 8 miles, bait fishing, pools.
Niobrara River	Brown, rainbow, year around, state line. Box Butte, bait and fly fishing.
Pine Creek	Brown, year around, upper 10 miles, bait and fly fishing.
Deer Creek	Brown, year around, entire stream, bait and fly fishing.
Sheep Creek	Brown, rainbow, winter, spring, early summer, upper 10 miles, bait and fly fishing.
Spotted Tail Creek	Brown, rainbow, winter, spring, early summer, upper 5 miles, bait and fly fishing.
Tub Springs	Brown, rainbow, winter, spring, early summer, upper 5 miles, bait and fly fishing.
Winter Creek	Brown, rainbow, winter, spring, early summer, upper 4 miles, bait and fly fishing.
Nine Mile Creek	Brown, rainbow, winter, spring, early summer, 10 miles, bait and fly fishing.
Wildhorse Creek	Brown, rainbow, winter, spring, early summer, both branches 16 miles, bait and fly fishing.
Red Willow Creek	Brown, rainbow, winter, spring, early summer, 9 miles, bait and fly fishing.
Greenwood Creek	Brown, rainbow, winter, spring, early summer, upper few miles, bait, fly fishing.
Lodgepole Creek	Brown, winter, spring, early summer, upper few miles, bait, fly fishing.
North Platte River	White bass, channel catfish, rainbow, winter, spring, early summer. Rainbow, October to March. White bass, walleye, channel catfish, spring, early summer. Garden County, set lines, casting.
Stuckenhole Creek	Brown, rainbow, winter, spring, early summer, upper end, bait casting.

NAME	SPECIES, BEST TIME, AREA, METHOD, AND BAIT
Long Pine Creek	Rainbows, browns, all year, above Bone Creek. Casting, still fishing. Minnows, flies, worms, spinners.
Plum Creek	Browns, all year, north of Highway 20. Casting, still fishing. Worms, flies.
Schlagel Creek	Browns, all year, lower six miles. Casting, still fishing. Flies, minnows, worms, spinners.
Snake River	Browns, all year, south of Gordon to south of Merriman. Casting, still fishing. Flies, minnows, worms, spinners. Access poor.
N. Loup River	Browns, all year, north of Whitman to north of Mullen. Casting, still fishing. Worms, minnows, spinners, and flies.
Coon Creek	Browns, all year, entire creek. Casting, still fishing. Flies, minnows, worms, and spinners.
Gracie Creek	Rainbows, Browns, all year, entire creek. Casting, floating bait. Flies, minnows, worms, and spinners.
Niobrara River	Channel catfish, May to October, near power dams at Valentine to Spencer Dam. Still fishing. Catfish baits, crayfish, worms. Sauger in the spring. Streamer flies.
Calamus River	Northern pike, spring, west of Highway 7. Still fishing plugs and spoons. Channel catfish, May to October. Burwell west to Highway 183. Minnows, frogs, bucktail flies.
N. Loup River	Channel catfish, May to October. Cushing west to Brewster. Minnows, frogs, prepared baits. Still fishing, set lines.
M. Loup River	Channel catfish, May to October. Boelus west to Thedford and below Milburn Dam. Still fishing, set lines. Minnows, frogs, prepared baits.
Dismal River	Browns, all year, west of Highway 97. Casting, still fishing, float bait. Spinners, flies, worms. Channel catfish, May to October. Usual baits.
Hofelt Lake	Bullhead, late spring, summer, early fall. Still fishing, worms.
Long Lake	Renovated in 1966. Bullhead fishing in 1967. Bass, bluegill, northern pike, yellow perch.
Clear Lake	Bullhead, bluegill, entire lake, spring and fall, worms. Largemouth bass, spring or fall. Casting. Spoons and plugs, flies.
Swan Lake	Bluegill, west end of lake, spring and fall, flies and worms. Northern pike, entire lake, spring and winter, spoons, minnows. Bullhead, May to September, entire lake, worms.
Merritt Reservoir	Smallmouth, largemouth bass, Boardman Bay, spring and fall, plugs, spoons, minnows. Bullhead, shallow bays, summer, still fishing, worms. Trout, winter, early spring, entire lake, artificials, trout eggs, worms, wet and dry flies.

Nebraska continued:

Southwest Nebraska is the state's land of big-water fishing, with 10 major reservoirs, 5 smaller empoundments, and 4 state lakes scattered over this sprawling land of prairie and rugged canyons. Fishing the big reservoirs proves most productive for rainbow, walleye, black bass, white bass and northerns. Lake McConaughy is the king of fishing in Nebraska.

It has given up state records of a 27 pound, 8 ounce northern, an 11 pound, 4 ounce brown trout, and a 12 pound, 8 ounce rainbow. Streams and lakes flowing into Lake McConaughy yield lunker rainbows in late winter and early spring, and brown trout the year around. Other angling opportunities await fishermen in the canals that lace parts of the Platte Valley. Rainbow trout, walleye and white bass are common on stringers along the banks of the canals.

In the southeast, perhaps the most popular area is Two Rivers State Recreation Area and it's put-and-take trout lake. Many thousands of anglers jam the shore each year to go after their limits. While Two Rivers may lack the peace and solitude of a Panhandle trout stream, it does offer opportunity for rainbow fishing on a close-to-home basis.

New Jersey

The freshwater gamefish of New Jersey include brown, brook and rainbow trout, largemouth and smallmouth bass, pickerel and walleye. Stocking by the Division of Fish, Game and Shell Fisheries of the state of about 500,000 trout annually supplies most of the trout in the state, although there are also some native browns and brook trout.

The Ken Lockwood Gorge Areas of the south branch of the Raritan River and the "fly" stretches on the Big Flat Brook and the Musconetcong River ("no-kill" regulations here) are generally considered as the top fly fishing waters in the state primarily because of the "fly fishing only," restrictions imposed. Browns are the chief target and the late May — June period sees the peak activity. This is probably due to the ready availability of newly-stocked trout at this time.

Fishing in these waters is almost entirely by wading. Boating and bank fishing is almost impossible due to the terrain.

The use of popping bugs for bass and sunfish is very popular throughout much of the state in any of the lakes containing these species.

New Mexico

The streams and lakes that offer some of the better fly fishing in New Mexico would include the Latir Lakes Chain, Stone Lake of the Jicarilla Apache Indian Reservation, Bluewater Lake, the gorge portion of the Rio Grande River, from Pilar north to the Colorado state line, San Juan River below Navajo Dam, Cimarron River and the Pecos River.

In addition, there are a number of small trout streams and high mountain lakes in the Sangre de Cristo Mountains that stretch south into New Mexico for about 100 miles. Most of these can be reached only on foot or by horseback, but all offer some excellent fly fishing. Also there is some good stream fly fishing in the Gila Wilderness in southwestern New Mexico.

The New Mexico State Game Commission in May, 1965 obtained a ten-year lease from the Rio Costilla Cooperative Livestock Association for a vast stretch of high mountain land, dotted with lakes and laced with streams for the express purpose of permitting the Commission to plant, propagate and protect game animals, game birds and game fish therein and to make hunting and fishing available to the public.

The 97,000-acre property at altitudes ranging up to 12,700 feet, contains 10 jewel-like lakes and miles of icy streams: the nine Latir Lakes and Little Blue Lake with a total of 25 surface acres; and the Costilla River, Latir Creek and Ute Creek comprising 15 miles. Located in north central New Mexico, the area is bounded on the north by the Colorado line; east by Vermejo Park; south by the Carson National Forest; southwest by the Cater and Anderson ranches; and on the northwest by State Road #3.

The Latir Lakes in the above described area have both rainbows and natives as does Stone Lake. Bluewater has mostly rainbow trout. Rainbows and browns up to 10 pounds are caught from both the Rio Grande Gorge and from the San Juan. Most of the fishing in the Cimarron and Pecos Rivers also is for rainbows and browns. In the high mountain streams and lakes, the fishing is for rainbows and cutthroats, with some browns in the lower reaches of the streams. In the Gila, there is some extremely good brown trout fishing and also some good rainbow fishing.

As for the best fishing months, it depends on the particular water. Latir Lakes usually aren't accessible until some time in June. Fishing usually is excellent for the first few weeks that the lakes can be reached and remain good until the season closes November 30.

Stone Lake is open year-round but the fly fisherman's best bet is early fall, with early spring next. The same applies for Bluewater. The Rio Grande Gorge is open year-around but the best fly fishing months would be late September, October and November.

The San Juan is open year-around and it would be hard to pick a time of year on it, as the quality of the fishing is often dictated by the

This is the West Rosebud Lake, high in the Beartooth Primitive area. It is accessible only by walking in or by horseback. There are rainbows and brook trout in this lake in Montana. They take flies readily.

amount of water being released from Navajo Dam. Probable late July through the end of the season in November would be best on the Pecos and Cimarron and the same for the high country and the Gila waters.

Almost all of the stream fishing is done by wading. Most of the fishing in the Latirs is done from the shore, but a few take rubber rafts to these lakes. On the larger lakes, Stone and Bluewater, there is quite a bit of fly fishing done from boats, with some wading and from shore.

The following waters are restricted to angling by artificial lures or flies:

San Juan River
Rio Chiquito Creek
Pot Creek (Rio De LaOlla)
Little Rio Grande and tributaries.

The Jicarilla Apache Indian Reservation, located in north central New Mexico, is comprised of approximately 750,000 acres. The reservation extends south from the New Mexico and Colorado State line for a distance of 63 air miles and averages 25 miles in width.

The northern half of the reservation is mountainous with deep canyons and broad valleys and is timbered with spruce, fir and pine. It is in this area that can be found lakes which provide excellent trout fishing. Stone Lake has already been mentioned, but Mundo, Dulce,

Buford and Embom Lakes are all superior fly fishing streams.

The Navajo River also affords very fine stream fishing. A special tribal fishing permit must be obtained at Dulce, the headquarters for the Jicarilla Apache Tribe. There is a modern motel, cafe, lounge, supermarket and other facilities at Dulce. Guide services are available, and camping is permitted in posted areas.

Snow Lake is on Snow Creek in Catron County. At an elevation of about 7,400 feet the lake is situated on a high plateau in a short-grass basin and is surrounded by ponderosa and pinon pines and juniper.

Rainbow trout are regularly stocked in the lake and provide some nice catches. Trout planted in Snow Lake have shown a rapid growth rate and numerous large trout are caught. A dam and reservoir on Snow Creek in the Gila National Forest were constructed and maintained by the Department of Game and Fish. The reservoir is approximately 42 miles southeast of Reserve and northeast of Glenwood, N.M.

The San Gregorio Reservoir, in Rio Arriba County, lies at an elevation of 9,400 feet and is within the San Pedro Parks Wild Area. The area adjacent to the lake is wooded with spruce, pine and aspen, while the shoreline is covered with grasses. There are no recreational sites at the lake but there are sites a short distance south of the lake, just out of the wild area and along NM 126.

San Gregorio is regularly stocked with catchable size rainbow trout in addition to fingerling natives. Numerous good catches of natives and rainbow trout are made with a few large natives being taken.

The San Juan River provides some of the best stream fishing for trout in New Mexico. A major reason for this is that downstream water releases originate in the subsurface area of Navajo Reservoir, making water temperatures in the river favorable for a year-around trout growing season.

Numerous limit catches of rainbow and brown trout are taken on the San Juan, including lunker fish up to 10 pounds. Fishing is open to the public in an area that covers approximately 6 river miles of the San Juan below Navajo Dam in the northwest corner of the state.

The river in the area flows from northeast to southeast and is bordered by high sandstone cliffs on the northwest and rolling hills to high mesas on the southeast. A variety of vegetation occurs along the river bottom. Strands of cottonwood and willow are found with pinon, juniper and sage brush on the adjacent slopes. In many areas the sage brush extends down to the river banks. Elevation of the river in the general area is approximately 5,600 feet.

Because of the year-around growing season on the San Juan, the management program consists of stocking with fingerling trout. Recently, cutthroat trout have been included in the program as well as browns and rainbows.

There are no recreational facilities available on the easement area along the river, but such facilities are available in the nearby dam area.

For a really remarkable example of New Mexico wilderness fishing, try the Pecos Wilderness Area in the Santa Fe National Forest. 165,000 acres of rugged timberline, alpine forests and peaks and high mountain lakes accessible only by foot or horseback.

Lakes in the Pecos Wilderness are stocked each year with cutthroat trout fry by the Department of Game and Fish. The small fish now are dropped into the lakes from the Department helicopter. Streams in the wilderness are also stocked, but fish for them are packed in by mule.

When the temperatures begin to soar on waters at New Mexico's lower elevations, and they become crowded with summer recreationists, the Pecos Wilderness high country is the place to go for cool comfort—it is sometimes downright cold even in July—and for good trout fishing. July, August and early September are the best times to make a fishing trip into the wilderness. But be sure to take a poncho or slicker. It rains almost every day.

Go in from the east side of the Pecos Wilderness and fish Middle Fork, North Fork and Santiago. Or go in from Cowles and try Spirit Lake, Lake Katherine and Stewart Lake. Go in from Trampas Canyon and try some of the streams and lakes in that area, or go in from any of the numerous entry points into the Pecos Wilderness.

New York

The tendancy to discount New York from the list of fishing states arbitrarily is a natural error—one is inclined to think immediately in terms of population saturation. But this state has a wealth of water resources—70,000 miles of streams and rivers; more than 3-1/2 million acres of ponds and lakes; 600 miles of coastal marine waters.

The renowned run of great trout in the Finger Lake region of central New York; the world famous stream trout fishing in the Adirondacks and Catskills, and the muskie and bass grounds of Chautauqua Lake, Lake Ontario and the St. Lawrence River are but a few of the delights held out to the game fisherman.

Many of the best trout water in the state are on privately owned lands. Recognizing this, the Conservation Department, way back in 1935, undertook a pioneering program to acquire permanent fishing rights easements to top quality trout streams in private ownership.

Today, thanks to this far-sighted program, New York sportsmen have access and fishing rights on nearly 1,000 miles of first class trout streams all across the state.

For wilderness fishing, try some of these remote Adirondack trout ponds which are stocked by airplane. These ponds have been completely cleaned of all trash fish and restocked with trout:

Essex County:
  Bass Lake
  Big Cherrypatch Pond
  Goose Pond
  Moose Mt. Pond
  Grizzle Ocean
  Hatch Pond
  Little Rock Pond
  Rock Pond

Franklin County:
 Big Fish Pond
 Horseshoe Pond
 Little Polliwog Pond
 Mud Pond
 So. Otter Pond
Fulton County:
 Fourth Lake
 Nine Corner Lake
 Stewart Pond
Hamilton County:
 Bennett Lake
 Bullhead Pond

 Clear Pond
 Lower Sargent Pond
St. Lawrence County:
 Curtis Pond
Washington County:
 Fishbrook Pond
 The choice of New York's top trout streams, based on estimated amount of good trout water and poundage of trout available, and those outstanding for fly fishing, are listed below with counties in which they are located.

Battenkill (Washington).
Beaverkill (Del. 85 per cent, Sull., 14 per cent, Ulster).
Salmon River (Clinton).
West Canada Creek (Herkimer 60 per cent, Oneida).
Willowemoc Creek (Sullivan).

Four fine brown trout this size could make a trip anywhere, worthwhile. These are two and three pounders.

The best fishing months are May, June and September. Fly fishing on streams is mainly for brown trout, some for brook trout and rainbows; on lakes, mainly for brook and rainbow trout.

In the following waters to promote quality trout fishing, trout caught must be returned to waters: In the Beaverkill River in Delaware County from Sullivan County downstream 2 miles; in Genegantslet Creek in Chenango County from the first Route 220 bridge north of Smithville Flats upstream, approximately 1 mile to the mouth of Five Streams; in Oquaga Creek in Broome County from old Route 17 bridge east of McClure downstream approximately 3 miles to new Route 17 bridge west of Deposit; and in Willowemoc Creek in Sullivan County from mouth of Hazel Brook upstream to mouth of Bascom Brook.

Artificial lures only: west branch of the Ausable River in Essex County from Monument Falls downstream about 2.2 miles; in the north branch of the Saranac River in Clinton County from mouth of Alder Brook downstream to mouth of Cold Brook (also only one trout per person per day).

Only artificial lures allowed in the Spectacle Ponds in St. Lawrence Count; in Wiscoy Creek, in Oatka Creek in Monroe County, in the Cohocton River in Steuben County.

The state conservation department carries on an extensive fish propagation program. Nearly 3,000,000 trout are stocked in some 1,100 streams totaling 4,400 miles in length and over 2,000,000 trout in 700 lakes and ponds totaling 250,000 acres. Eighteen State fish hatcheries produce a variety of fish species including 4 varieties of trout (brook, brown, rainbow, lake) salmon, pikeperch (walleye), black bass, and muskellunge to stock thousands of miles of streams, lakes and ponds throughout New York. The output of

these hatcheries can be conservatively averaged at close to four hundred million fish, weighing in excess of one-half million pounds each year. One fish hatchery (Rome) supports a complete fisheries research laboratory.

Some of the New York rivers which are, and have been for years, famous for fine trout are the Kinderhook in Rensselaer-Columbia Counties, the Mettawee in the Granville area, the Battenkill in the Cambridge area, the Saranac in Clinton County and the West Branch Ausable near Lake Placid.

North Carolina

In the west the state is bounded by the running ridges of the tallest mountains in eastern America. This is a heavily forested region etched with fast-flowing, clear and cold streams. Water conditions in these southern highlands approximate those found in the northeastern United States and southern Canada. They support species within the range of the brook trout and the smallmouth bass.

The Piedmont section runs in a descending roll from the shoulders of the Blue Ridge east to the fall line of the rivers. This region also is laced with streams, many of them large, and its hilly nature lends itself to impoundments that run from thousands of small farm ponds on up to some 19 power reservoirs. Water conditions of the Piedmont are similar to those found in many sections of the mid-west. Smallmouth bass abound on the high western edges of the Piedmont while in the east warm water species like the bream and largemouth bass predominate.

Approximately 1/5 of the entire population of the United States lives within 500 miles of North Carolina trout waters, and the problem posed is just how to make some 2,000 miles

of trout water, open to public fishing, meet the recreational demand—along with supplying some fish to all comers.

About 1500 miles of the waters are kept open to public fishing through agreement with the landowners, and these waters are regularly stocked throughout the open trout season with yearling fish to protect the natural trout population against over-exploitation. Another 300 miles of waters on lands owned by the Federal Government, or under long-term lease by the State, plus 200 miles within the Wildlife Management Areas, are similarly managed.

Also, within the carefully controlled Wildlife Management Areas are some 140 miles of water subject to special Native Trout, and 14 miles of water subject to Trophy Trout, fishing regulations. The latter regulations are predicated upon a "high-catch but low-kill" philosophy which at this time appears the ultimate answer that trout management can provide to satisfy the ever-mounting pressures for trout fishing being applied to the very limited waters capable of supporting it.

These regulations form a compromise between the prohibitively expensive "put and take" stocking, and the purely "fishing for fun" concept that holds the interest of only the more dedicated fishermen. All streams under Native Trout and Trophy Trout management were annually subjected to biological evaluation to determine if the existing year-class recruitment was adequate to support acceptable levels of recreational fishing along with sufficient harvest to maintain angler interest.

Where a deficiency in either appeared likely, and the natural food supply could support additional fish, the population void was filled by stocking young-of-the-year trout.

Fresh water fishing from the Tidewater region to the upper Piedmont is much like the fishing found in other Southern states. It is a transitional step to the mountain fishing lands—different, challenging and rewarding. The variety of the fresh-water fishery is a result of the long runs of mountains, the highest in Eastern America, which border the western section of the state from Virginia to Georgia.

These mountains—the Blue Ridge on the east, the Great Smokies and Unakas on the west and transverse ranges like the lofty Blacks creating a step-ladder effect in between— offer a wide range of water conditions.

In the lower mountain valleys, 2,000 to 2,500 feet above sea level there are big streams and lakes rich in largemouth and smallmouth bass, bream, crappie, walleye, and white bass.

As you follow the stream to higher elevations the largemouth give way to the trimmer smallmouth and the bass give way to the trout; brown trout and rainbow trout farther down and, in the pools high up the mountain ridges, the cold water native brook or "speckled" trout.

No one ever has measured the mileage of North Carolina's trout waters. But in the 25 mountain counties there literally are thousands of miles of clear, cold waters which produce trout ranging in size from 12-inch brookies on up to 10-pound browns and, in the lakes, even larger rainbows.

Probably no more than 2,000 miles of this water is stocked regularly from the state and federal hatcheries. The rest, the smaller and less accessible back country streams, are not stocked because natural reproduction keeps these waters near their carrying capacity.

Many of these streams, like Forney,

Eagle, Hazel and Noland creeks in the Great Smokies, are accessible only to anglers crossing Fontana lake by boat. They stretch back through the roadless forest towards the spine of the Smokies.

Transylvania County streams like Horsepasture, Whitewater and Toxaway are lightly fished because their rugged, deep gorges discourage all but the truly ardent. The same is true of the wilderness areas threaded by the white runs of the handsome Linville river. Great brown trout streams like Slick Rock, which feeds into Calderwood Lake, are visited only by the relatively few willing to make the effort...and there are few enough willing to walk perhaps six miles of mountain ridges to reach this water.

On the Wildlife Management areas in western North Carolina — areas jointly managed by the Wildlife Resources Commission and U.S. Forest Service — there are hundreds of miles of great trout streams. On streams designated "Native Trout Waters," the daily creel limit for trout is 4 and the minimum size limits are 10 inches for rainbow and brown trout and 6 inches for brook trout. On these streams bait other than artificial lures having a single hook is prohibited. On certain of these streams, only artificial flies may be used.

One of the astonishing facts about North Carolina trout fishing is that it is located within easy reach of the great population centers of the east and mid-west—and is located in an area where cool mountain weather attracts people from those areas in large numbers—and, yet include long runs of water that are seldom fished as often as once a year.

Another equally curious fact is that many trout streams have headwaters up near mountain ridges 6,000 and more feet high which contain staircased pools that are both deep

and a reasonably long cast in length. That's where a man can watch five or six brook trout flash up as his fly begins its float.

North Carolina requires a special trout permit in addition to the regular fishing license. On the wildlife management areas an additional season or daily permit is required.

Trout is the only fresh-water species in North Carolina on which there is a closed season. The trout season ordinarily runs from the first Saturday in April thru Labor Day plus an extended season thru October in which only trophy fish may be kept. With local exceptions, there is no size limit on trout. The creel limit is seven. Fishing in the refuges is limited to specified days, usually Saturday, Sunday and Wednesday, but this should be checked—as all other regulations—through the Wildlife Resources Commission, Box 2919, Raleigh, North Carolina 27602. There are special regulations regarding fishing in the Great Smoky Mountaiins National Park. These may be obtained from the Superintendent, Great Smoky Mountains National Park, Gatlinburg, Tennessee 37738.

Farther down, in the river valleys, there are some top-quality smallmouth bass streams. The New river, including both the north and the south forks, of Ashe and Alleghany counties is one of the best. So is the Watauga in Watauga County, the Upper Yadkin, Elk Creek, the Johns River, lower Wilson's Creek and a number of others. While these streams don't produce big fish—anything over 5 pounds requires a celebration—they do produce as scrappy smallmouths as you are likely to find anywhere.

But the best of the bass and pan fishing is found in the mountain lakes—some 75 all told—that are strung like long beads along many of

A nice sized brown, typical of those caught in North Carolina's streams. Though most of the streams in the state are stocked with rainbows every year, the browns reproduce well and don't have to be planted as often.

the Western rivers. Many of these lakes are linked into the TVA system and control the heavy annual rainfall of these rain-rich mountains.

Fontana Lake is particularly well-known for its white bass fishing and its walleye fishing in the spring.

North Carolina anglers would also include Lake Chatuge, a 7,150 acre lake which offers particularly good crappie, largemouth and small-mouth bass fishing, on that list. Lake Lure, in Polk county, Glenville (Thorpe) Lake, Nantahala Lake, and Cheoah (a trout lake directly below Fontana), and Lake Calderwood, below Cheoah, can be just as good.

This lake fishing is best in the spring—May and June—and again in September and October when the leaves turn. At those times big bass—10 and 12 pound fish—work the shallows to the delight of anglers who cast the shore-line.

During cold weather hardy anglers fish these lakes near the mouths of major trout streams—the mouths of Hazel and Forney creeks on Fontana Lake, for example—for trout preparing for their annual spawning run.

There also are a number of small trout lakes scattered through the mountains. Price's Lake off the Blue Ridge Parkway near Blowing Rock, Bee Tree Reservoir near Asheville, Tater Hill near Boone, the Sparta Reservoir in Alleghany county and the rainbow trout lakes located on the headwaters of the East fork of the Tuckaseigee river are examples. Unlike the big reservoirs, where trout can be taken the year around, these small lakes are open to fishermen only during the trout season. However, Bear Creek, Wolf Creek and Tennessee Creek lakes are open all year.

Species introduced in recent years—white bass and, particularly, walleye—have thrived in some of the mountain lakes.

Accommodations of all sorts—swank resorts to modest rooming houses and motels—are available throughout western North Carolina. Rough camping facilities are provided at most of the wildlife management areas. The wildest of the wilderness fishing—and it can be wild and rugged in Rocky Mountain terms, rarely is located more than an easy drive—and a reasonable to stiff walk—from a comfortable bed and well-suppled table. Those who prefer it otherwise can pack their gear right to streamside.

The larger mountain lakes have accommodations and facilities where boats can be launched or rented. In 1969 the State operated over 90 areas providing public access to major fishing waters. More are being built.

As you move up the streams into trout water, brown and rainbow first and then the brook trout—"speckled trout" to the mountaineer—in the highest and coldest headwaters, your tackle should be more refined.

Lighter, shorter rods—down to six feet but with seven foot rods being more nearly the usual choice—are in order, as are longer leaders and lighter tippets. Here, as elsewhere, far-and-fine is the rule for the trout fisherman working a North Carolina stream in times of low, incredibly clear water.

On these streams your approach to the water you intend to fish should be as stealthy as a stalking cat. This and the care and delicacy with which you present your fly are more important than your fly size or pattern.

Fish slowly and fish with short casts that you progressively lengthen as you carefully work over the water ahead of you that is within delicate presentation range. Don't let the promise of great pools blind you to the productivity of riffles, runs and hard to reach pockets.

North Carolina trout fishermen tend to use standard patterns in the standard (10 to 16 ordinarily) hook sizes. A list of the favorite dry flies would include the Wulff Royal, Lady Beaverkill, Irresitible, Cahill (light and dark), Hendrickson, Mosquito and the like. The Deer Hopper frequently is a good late summer choice.

The favored nymphs and terrestials include the Tellicoe, black ant and a variety of stone fly, caddis and May fly nymph imitations.

Some very productive native anglers tie on a bushy dry—a heavily tied Wulff Royal, for example—and then tie a 12 to 16 inch tippet to that fly and put a sinking pattern—often a black ant—on it.

The dry fly serves as a bobber signaling a strike and will take fish as well. While the technique is far from easy, nymphs are most effective when fished in the upstream cast—downstream float manner of dryflies.

Don't let a sharp shower with accompanying rising, dingy water send you scampering for home. On the good trout water of this state the water clears rapidly and some of the very finest trout fishing occurs as the water begins to fall and clear.

At this time large nymphs and streamers are most effective. The Muddler Minnow, Mickey Finn, Black Nosed Dace and Gray Ghost all are good bets as streamers.

Now, let's turn to the lake fishing to be found in western North Carolina.

There are no natural lakes in the area. There are, however, a rather large number of man made impoundments. These range from great power reservoirs like Fontana (10,670 acres) on down to trout ponds only a few acres in size.

The reservoirs ordinarily are fished from boats. They are water filled mountain valleys and, as such, offer very little shelf for the wader to work.

The species found in lakes like Fontana, Nantahala, Santeetlah, Cheoah, Calderwood and the like include large and smallmouth bass, walleye pike, white bass, crappie, a number of the sunfish, rainbow and brown trout as well as cats and some other rough fish. (Not all species are found in all the lakes named.)

Tackle used on these species is the same as used elsewhere with a few local exceptions in tools and techniques. On Nantahala, for example, a silver and brass spoon trolled deep is favored for summer trout fishing.

On Cheoah some of the best anglers stalk fish in canoes. Once they spot a cruising trout they guess his probable course and place a small dry fly out ahead of him.

Fishing in the reservoirs is best in May and June and from mid-September on to cold weather, ordinarily early in November. During hot weather, fishing is slow for all anglers except the most experienced local men who know intimately the water depths, oxygen distribution and spring holes of the reservoirs.

Lacking that, fish very early and very late and keep your eye peeled for a native who is willing to share his accumulated know-how with you on either a fun or fee basis.

In the spring and fall work the shoreline and the shallows. Popping bugs and lures are a good choice in this fishing. In mid-summer, except at dawn and dusk, hunt your fish in deep water with deep running lures. Fish the points carefully bumping the bottom on your retrieve. This last is done best with plastic worms with weedless hooks or with plugs that retrieve on a nose down, tail up manner.

Dedicated winter anglers have surprisingly good luck on North Carolina's mountain lakes. Some work the deep water of the points of land with plastic worms for bass and walleyes. Others fish the mouths of streams for trout entering on or returning from spawning runs.

Small, slow moving river that holds smallmouth and largemouth bass that will take poppers and dry flies on their morning and evening feeding sprees. Angler here is waiting for backcast to straighten out.

(Trout fishing in the reservoirs is permitted year around. This is not true on the streams).

Salmon eggs (often encased in a bit of sheer nylon stocking) are productive in Winter trout fishing on the lakes. For the strictly artificial man a small spinner is probably the most popular lure.

There are boat launching areas on all the lakes. Boats can be rented on all the major lakes although on some—Nantahala in particular—the choice is limited.

Whatever your choice, lake or stream, fly, spinning, bait, rods or cane pole, North Carolina has a variety of choice to offer you.

You might bear a few points in mind:

1. May and June are the best months, both on the lakes and on the streams. September and October are best in terms of weather. For stream trout fishing the best of the state's stocked water remains open until the last of October. But September and

October trout fishing is limited to trophy fish. In these color rich months there is a creel limit of one fish, of a specified minimum size, each day.

2. The best trout fishing is found on the most remote sections of wilderness streams. These include Smoky Mountain National Park streams like Hazel, Forney and Eagle Creeks and the harder to reach sections on streams located in wildlife management areas (Areas operated jointly by the U.S. Forest Service and the N.C. Wildlife Commission). Among the latter, Slick Rock Creek, the Upper South Mills River above the Turkey Pen Check Station, Harpers and Lost Cove Creeks all are good choices.

3. To reach the best water on these and other streams be prepared to walk (some six miles to hit Slick Rock) trails which are well marked but often are goat killers.

4. If you are less athletically inclined you might bear in mind that

North Carolina stocks some 2,000 miles of public trout waters most of which are easily accessible. These waters are open to fishing seven days a week from the first week in April through the Labor Day weekend and, on a Trophy Trout basis, through October. (Management area streams are open over the same period but only on weekends, Wednesdays and on a few holidays like the Fourth of July and Labor Day.) There is no fall Trophy Trout season on the management area streams.

5. Even in mid-summer come prepared to experience weather a good deal cooler than you would expect in the land of grits and you-alls.

The thousands of acres of U.S. Forest Service land within the Nantahala National Forest include some of the best-managed and best-protected watersheds in the eastern United States. In a valley in the heart of this extreme western North Carolina national forest, receiving water from several of its watersheds, is Lake Nantahala.

This lake was impounded on the Nantahala River in Macon and Clay counties in the early 1940's by the Nantahala Power and Light Company. Also known as Aquone Lake, the hydroelectric impoundment comprises 1,610 surface acres and is the largest single body of water designated as public mountain trout water in North Carolina. The elevation of the lake at high water level is 2,890 feet. There are several tributaries but the Nantahala River is the most important water supply.

The headwaters of the Nantahala River originate at altitudes up to 5,500 feet and lie within the boundaries of Standing Indian Wildlife Management Area, managed by the Wildlife Resources Commission in cooperation with the U.S. Forest Service. The river and tributaries inside the refuge offer some of the finest brook, rainbow, and brown trout fishing in the State. The river flows for approximately eighteen miles from its headwaters to the lake. The smaller tributaries also originate on Forest Service property and all the water entering the lake is crystal clear and low in temperature.

The rugged terrain and extreme fluctuations in water level has made boat launching in Nantahala Lake somewhat of a problem in the past. This problem has been lessened to a great extent by the Wildlife Commission's purchase and development of two boating access areas on the lake. One of these areas is located on the Big Choga Creek arm of the lake and can be reached from Andrews, N.C. A second area, offering a better launching ramp, was later developed just off the Wayah Bald Road approximately 19 miles west of Franklin.

There are few overnight accomodations on Nantahala Lake. Most fishermen staying overnight camp along the shore where the Nantahala River enters the lake, or next to Wayah Road where Jarrett Creek enters the lake.

Nantahala is like "a lake on top of a lake." It is located in the extreme southern range of the Appalachians and a large part of its surface is exposed to the sun. Although the lake is nearly 3,000 feet in elevation, the hot summer sun tends to warm the surface. The warm surface temperature and the cold-water trout streams entering the lake result in two distinct types of game fisheries. These two types of fisheries seem to be for the most part independent of one another. The warm-water species include smallmouth bass, largemouth bass, walleye, bluegill, robin, crappie, and northern rock bass. Separated from this warm-water group of fish and inhabiting deeper water with colder temperatures are the large, lake-run rainbow trout and kokanee salmon.

Because of the very large population of rainbow trout in Nantahala Lake, a program of stocking kokanee salmon into the lake once a year for four years was initiated in February, 1960. The kokanee salmon is very similar in appearance to the well-known sockeye. The smaller kokanee, however, is land-locked and its average length is seldom over 15 inches. The purpose in stocking the little salmon into Nantahala is to provide the lake-run rainbow trout with additional forage.

Arrangements for this four-year stocking of kokanee were made with the U.S. Fish and Wildlife Service. Each year kokanee eggs were received at the Federal Hatchery at Davidson River and in early spring, several weeks after hatching, the little salmon were stocked in the lake.

Natural spawning was attempted by these fish for the first time in 1963. The adults observed surpassed the average size figure for this fish elsewhere, and several over 18 inches were found. Sport fishing for the kokanee should continue to improve as natural spawning is successful.

The Nantahala River and other tributaries and the Nantahala Lake form a relationship that provides almost ideal environmental conditions for a good population of rainbow trout. Rainbows, being migratory by nature, characteristically move down into big water where they live and grow and then, in late winter and very early spring, move back up the streams to spawn. The trout spawn very successfully in the Nantahala River.

The trout which live in the deep cold waters of the lake all year—except for their annual journey up one of the tributaries—are usually

Fisherman is working a muddler minnow in fast water. It is being taken under water and into a trough. A minute or so after this photo was taken a brown trout took the muddler.

very large. In the lake they may grow as much as 8 inches in just one year. Many of them 18 or 20 inches long are not any older than some of the much smaller rainbows found in streams.

At the beginning of their journey up the stream, and upon their return, the big rainbows seem to congregate near the mouths of the tributaries, and it is here that most of the trout fishing is done.

Quite a bit of variety is used in methods of fishing for these rainbows, but the most popular method is to fish with worms on the bottom of the stream channel a hundred yards or so from where the stream enters the lake.

Many of the trout fishermen anchor their boats just off to the side of the channel of the Nantahala River and cast "globs" of worms out over the channel, letting them sink to the bottom. A large part of the trout fishing is also done from the bank.

As winter sets in, spin-fishermen catch good rainbows on small spinners and spoons, and on some of the cold dark winter days, good rainbows are taken on wet flies. The trout are usually anywhere from 13 to 24 inches long. Regardless of which method is used, catching one of these big rainbows can be the thrill of a lifetime, if the fisherman has a "true love" for trout.

It takes a rugged individualist to fish for trout in Nantahala Lake during the cold winter months. The wind blowing across the lake is piercing cold and the boat fisherman must take a chilling boat ride before he can reach an area where the trout might be congregated.

The bank fisherman planning to fish in the backwaters of the Nantahala River must either go bouncing in a jeep down the trail which leads from the road near Rainbow Springs, or he must climb down the mountain side—almost straight down—from

the Forest Service road above the lake.

Why all this fishing activity during the coldest part of the year? It's all because a trout is a different kind of fish, and a trout fisherman a different kind of fisherman. No sudden rain storm or cold snap is going to chase the trout fisherman away from the shore of the lake.

To the man who has not yet cultivated a "true love" for trout, the whole activity of fishing for them, especially during cold weather, may be something he just doesn't understand. The man on the shore of the lake, patiently waiting for a bite, does understand it, and even though he's probably shivering with the cold, he's at peace with the world.

Beyond the shadow of a doubt, he will find himself back again at the same spot on a day when the trout just aren't hitting. On such a day he may not catch any trout at all, or he may hook just one trout and then lose it.

But when he is back home by the warmth of his own fireplace, he will certainly still remember the big purple and silvery rainbow thrashing on the end of his line in the clear cold water. The memory alone is more than enough to make him always want to go back to Nantahala Lake.

Oregon

Fishing in the coastal area of Oregon offers variety difficult to match elsewhere in the state. Stream, lake, bay, rock, surf, and deep sea fishing are all available; the choice is yours. Stream angling is enjoyed in at least fifteen major rivers and hundreds of miles of smaller streams.

Principal game fish taken in coastal streams are chinook salmon, silver salmon, steelhead, cutthroat trout, striped bass and shad. There are both spring and fall runs of chinook salmon. Spring runs in the coastal area are not of sufficient size to offer much attraction. Fall

This is the famous middle fork of the Willamette River in Oregon. Fine fishing for rainbows and especially for steelhead that run up to 20 pounds and seem to spawn in every month in the year.

chinook and silver salmon are taken from late August to mid-November with the peak usually in October. Many are taken by fly casting.

Steelhead, the sea-run form of the rainbow trout, enter coastal streams after the fall rains commence, and fishing is at its peak from December through February. Boat and bank angling are equally popular.

Trout angling is most popular in late spring and early fall, with the midsummer period less productive. Sea-run cutthroat are taken on their downstream migrations in late May. These fish return to fresh water commencing in July and the peak of cutthroat fishing occurs in September and October. Sea-run cutthroats are know locally as "harvest trout" and "bluebacks".

Cutthroat trout are available in most of the coastal lakes.

Shad move into Coos Bay and the lower Coos and Coquille Rivers and provide a spectacular fishery during June and July. Small spinners and flies are used in taking shad. Bank and boat angling are equally popular.

In the Willamette Basin, the principal streams are the Willamette and its tributaries and the Sandy and Hood Rivers. The Willamette is the most important stream system in the state, with some of its major tributaries, the Clackamas, Molalla, McKenzie, Santiam, and Middle Fork of the Willamette, included among the better fishing streams flowing from the Cascade Range and such streams as the Tualatin,

Yamhill and the Luckiamute flowing from the east slopes of the coast range.

Salmon, steelhead and rainbow and cutthroat trout, plus several species of warmwater game fish are among the more important fish in the area.

Spring chinook are taken from March through June with the later fishery occuring in upstream areas. Fall chinook enter from August through October. Winter steelhead begin to appear in January with the run extending into May and June in up-stream tributaries.

Both cutthroat and rainbow trout are taken from most of the streams. Cutthroat are most common in the tributaries of the Willamette River entering from the west and in the upper waters of other major streams. Some of the better rainbow waters include the Clackamas River,

McKenzie River and middle fork of the Willamette River. Streams in the Mount Hood area contain both rainbow and cutthroat.

Lake fishing for trout is confined primarily to mountain lakes within the Mount Hood and Willamette National Forests. More popular areas are the Olallie Lake basin, Marion Lake basin, and the Taylor Burn. These lakes contain either eastern brook or rainbow trout, and in many cases both species. Brown trout are also found in a few of the high lakes.

Although some of the high lakes can be reached by road, many are accessible only by trail. Because of snow conditions, these high lakes ordinarily cannot be reached until late June or early July. Many of the mountain lakes lying on the west slopes of the Cascades are most easily approached from the east side of the mountains. Campgrounds are available throughout the Cascades.

The Umpqua Basin includes the Umpqua River drainage, one of two major stream systems heading in the Cascades and cutting through the coast range mountains to the Pacific Ocean. The river branches near Roseburg into the North and South Forks. Approximately 5,500 square miles are included in the drainage and the distance from the mouth at Winchester Bay to the headwaters is nearly 250 miles.

The upper portion of the system lies within the Umpqua National Forest. The North Umpqua is the larger stream, and, along with its tributaries, provides better angling than the South Fork. Smith River flows into the Umpqua at Reedsport and is one of the important tributaries of the system.

Chinook and silver salmon, summer and winter-run steelhead, resident rainbow, resident and sea-run cutthroat, and brown trout are all available to the angler. Eastern brook, German brown, and rainbow trout occur in lakes in the drainage. Striped bass and shad may also be taken from the Umpqua River on sporting tackle. Paved or gravel roads enable one to reach nearly any section of the stream system.

Excellent salmon fishing is had at Winchester Bay from June through August. The fish are taken by trolling various types of plugs or bait fish. Charter boats are available in the area. Spring chinook are taken from the river in April and May with spinners or cluster eggs the usual lures.

Fall chinook angling is best in the months of September and October from the bay to the forks using similar equipment. Best months for summer steelhead are July and August on the North Umpqua. Summer regulations provide that flies must be used on that stream from Rock Creek up to Soda Springs Dam site. Winter steelhead are caught from November through February.

Sea-run cutthroat trout are taken in the main river below the forks and in lower river tributaries primarily from August through October. Flies or spinners produce most of the catches. Resident forms of rainbow and cutthroat may be had throughout the summer months on all types of lures, with best fishing occuring from May to July. The north and south forks and their tributaries provide the best angling for these forms.

The Rogue River system, in southwestern Oregon is the other major drainage heading in the Cascades and flowing to the ocean. Principal fisheries are for chinook salmon, silver salmon, steelhead, resident rainbow and cutthroat trout. Brown trout are available in limited numbers also.

Chinook salmon fishing is the best at the mouth of the Rogue in April and May for the spring run, and September and October for the fall run.

Steelhead are taken in the Gold Beach area from late August through February. Spinning, casting, and fly fishing are preferred methods. Guides and boats are available for trips up the river.

In the Grants Pass area, the best steelhead fishing is from September through November with a peak in October. Water conditions permitting, good catches continue through February from Grants Pass through to Gold Beach.

Rainbow trout and eastern brook are taken in the North and South Forks and their tributaries in the upper reaches in June and July. The best month for fishing the upper portion of the main river is June on dry flies. Good catches continue to be made through July, August, and September. The upper river is closed to boat fishing after June 30. Resorts and campgrounds are available.

Squaw lake at the head of the Applegate River near Medford produces good cutthroat and rainbow fishing during the summer with the best catches made in May. Fish Lake near Mount McLoughlin has good rainbow and eastern brook fishing with June, July and October the most productive. Howard prairie reservoir is an excellent producer of rainbow trout through the entire season. Willow Creek Reservoir near Butte Falls has good early and late season fishing for rainbow and kokanee.

The Deschutes River area is comprised mainly of the Deschutes River which heads in southern Deschutes County in the Cascade Mountains and runs northward to the Columbia River just east of the Dalles. Principal tributaries are the Little Deschutes, Crooked, Metolius, Warm Springs and White Rivers. The basin contains about 10,500 square miles and represents one of the most important recreational and fishing areas of the state.

Principal species of game fish are spring chinook salmon, summer steelhead, rainbow trout, eastern brook trout, German brown trout, kokanee (landlocked sockeye salmon), and lake trout.

The Deschutes River can be fished either from boats or from the bank above Bend, but angling is not permitted from boats in the river below Bend.

Steelhead fishing is best in July through September. Most of this fishery takes place from the mouth of the river upstream to Maupin. Steelhead are taken on flies or spinning or casting lures.

Rainbow, eastern brook, and brown trout are taken in the upper Deschutes. Brown trout have extended their range downstream into the lower river, but the catch from Redmond to the mouth is mostly rainbows.

The Metolius River, a full-fledged stream when it issues from giant springs at the base of Black Butte near Sisters, is the most important angling tributary of the Deschutes. The main fishery is for rainbow trout, but browns and some large Dolly Varden are taken. A portion of the upper Metolius is reserved for fly fishermen.

White River, draining the east slopes of Mount Hood, empties into the Deschutes near Tygh Valley. The river is discolored when snow runoff occurs in early summer, but at times provides excellent rainbow trout angling. Best fishing occurs from July through September.

At higher elevations, the back country lakes lying in profusion on both sides of the Cascade crest are approached mainly from the Deschutes side. Excellent trails and camp sites available throughout the lake basin areas. The mountain lakes contain either rainbow or eastern

brook trout, and in some cases both species.

Trophy fish for the discriminating angler are the golden trout available in a number of lakes in the Chambers Lake Basin in the Three Sisters Primitive Area and the streamlined Atlantic salmon in Hosmer Lake near Elk Lake.

The Wallowa area is bounded on the west by the Blue Mountains, on the east by the Sanke River forming the boundary between Oregon and Idaho, and includes the picturesque Wallowa Mountains.

Major stream systems include; the Grande Ronde with its most important tributaries the Minam, Wenaha, Lostine, and Wallowa; the Imnaha River at the far eastern edge of the state; the Powder River; and the Burnt River at the southern end of the area.

Pine and Eagle Creeks are two important fishing streams in Baker County at the southern end of the Whitman National Forest. All these streams flow into the Snake River, also an important fishing center.

Chinook salmon, steelhead, rainbow, eastern brook, kokanee, and cutthroat are the most important species. Dolly Varden, lake trout, golden trout and whitefish are also present. As in most eastern Oregon streams, the chinook run is not of sufficient magnitude to be attractive to tourists. Substantial numbers are taken, however, in the Snake, Imnaha, and Grande Ronde Rivers.

Steelhead are taken in the Snake and Grande Ronde Rivers in late fall and early spring. These great game fish are also taken in the Imnaha and Wallowa Rivers and in Pine Creek. Baits include flashing lures and

This high country lake is easily fished because of the rocky shore that provides good footing. Lake has rainbows, kokanee and some cutthroat. Angler is fudging because, though he is using flies, his rod is a spinning type and he has the fly attached to a glass bubble that furnished needed weight for casting. Lake is in Oregon.

cluster eggs, but anglers also have good success on drifted night crawlers and crawfish tails.

Trout season usually extends from May to early October. There are numerous streams in which to fish for rainbow and the upper reaches of some produce good eastern brook angling. A few major streams are readily accessible by road but many of the better ones, particularly the Wenaha, Minam, and the upper Imnaha are reached only by trail.

Of major interest to tourists is the Wallowa Mountain area, with the center of attraction Wallowa Lake near the town of Joseph. The lake contains rainbow, lake trout, and kokanee with the latter fishery in the early part of the season. There is a resort at the lake and an excellent state park with overnight camping facilities.

Trails from the lake and from trail access points on the Imnaha and Lostine Rivers and Hurricane Creek lead into the high mountains where there are many lakes containing eastern brook, rainbow, and cutthroat.

A few lakes at extreme elevations have been stocked with the colorful golden trout. Most of the lakes at high elevations are not readily accessible until the first of July because of snow. Additional trail access points to the high Wallowa Lake country may be reached via Catherine or Eagle Creeks on the south side of the mountains.

In many of the high Wallowa lakes, eastern brook have over-populated to the point where the average size is small. A liberal bag limit of 30 eastern brook trout per day and 60 in possession is allowed in these lakes.

These mountains are precipitous and the trails, though well maintained, are steep in places. Guides and horses are available at Wallowa Lake and several other points. There

are undeveloped but adequate camp sites throughout the Wallowa Mountains.

Warm-water game fish may be taken from the sloughs and borrow pits adjacent to the Grande Ronde River in the La Grande area. Good rainbow fishing is obtainable in the upper waters of the Burnt and Powder Rivers in Baker County.

Brownlee Reservoir on the Snake has become a popular warm-water game fish center for bass, crappie, and bullhead catfish. Channel catfish, some going to 20 pounds, are also available in the Snake River and upper portions of Brownlee pool.

Smallmouth black bass have increased in numbers in the Brownlee pool and Snake River areas and provide exciting fishing. Sturgeon are also present in good numbers south of the Burnt River.

The Snake River from the Oregon border south to Johnson bar offers the best smallmouth bass, channel catfish and sturgeon angling in eastern Oregon. Access to this isolated area is mainly by boat from the mouth of the Grande Ronde River or from Lewiston, Idaho. River experience is needed to negotiate the many Snake River rapids. Traveling and fishing in this Hells Canyon of the Snake River is an experience never forgotten.

Fish Lake, in Baker County near Halfway, provides excellent fly fishing for eastern brook trout. A good campground is located at the lake.

The Columbia River zone encompasses the main stem of the Columbia River forming the boundary between the state of Washington and the state of Oregon and is one of the most important salmon and steelhead fishing centers of the state. In addition, sturgeon, cutthroat trout, rainbow trout and several species of warm-water game fish are included among the more

important game fish of the streams.

Spring chinook are taken from mid-February through the summer months and fall chinook from July through October. A sizeable run of silver salmon enters the lower Columbia in October.

Fall chinook enters the river from August through September. An extensive offshore fishery exists at the mouth of the river for both chinook and silver salmon from late June through September.

Jack salmon are taken both in the fall and spring in the Columbia. A favorite method of angling is casting.

Summer steelhead are taken in June and July in the lower river and into late fall at upriver points. Here again, bank angling provides a favorite pastime for many anglers.

Pennsylvania

Pennsylvania is blessed with hundreds of miles of trout streams and vast acres of deep water trout lakes. The propagation facilities of the State Fish Commission provide thousands and thousands of trout to be stocked in these waters each year. This stocking, combined with the natural reproduction that occurs in many streams, adds up to a fantastic number of scrappy game fish available for the fisherman to harvest.

There are three main species of trout found in Pennsylvania waters - brook, brown and rainbow. Generally, the brook is found in the cold, smaller headwater streams; the brown trout, in the larger streams; the rainbow trout in lakes and other impoundments. Many waters will contain all three species.

The opening day of trout season occurs around the middle of April. Early spring weather and water conditions can have a tremendous effect on how you fish for trout this time of year.

Early in the spring the water is likely to be high, cloudy, and fairly

The Province of Quebec is a fly fisherman's paradise as it has hundreds of rivers and lakes filled with the scrapping speckled trout, Atlantic salmon and smallmouth bass. The angler shown netting a good sized speckled trout is fishing a river in the 4,000 square mile Laurentides Park. The whitewater rock spills in the central background are choice spots for using streamer flies to take speckled trout.

low in temperature. Trout are usually a bit sluggish and tend to lie in the deeper pools feeding near the bottom. It is most important, when these conditions exist, to add weight to your line to get your fly or nymph down to where the fish are feeding. The general rule is to fish slow and deep.

Early fishing can be productive if you use many of the natural trout baits. You will consistently take trout in the early spring on weighted artificial nymphs. At this time of the year, Big Fishing Creek near Lamar, in Clinton County, which is a limestone stream, has a large number of big brown trout. Around Memorial Day the large Mayfly hatch comes off, and fly fishermen can have some of the best fishing of the year.

As the water clears and warms, trout become more active. Fly fishing begins to pick up as some of the early hatches begin to emerge. This is the time of the year trout fishing is at it's best in Pennsylvania. Early morning and late evening are generally the best times for trout.

Many excellent catches of rainbow trout come out of the dams and lakes where the fishermen have been on the water at the crack of dawn. Late evening fishing on a good brown trout stream such as the Allegheny River in Potter County will result in a well filled creel.

Late season fishing for trout demands some special skills. The water is usually low and crystal clear. Trout are spooky at this time and will often shy away from many of the larger flies. The general rule is to fish with small terminal equipment and take care not to scare feeding fish with noisy wading or sloppy casting. A good dry fly fisherman with the right fly pattern can catch a lot of trout in Pennsylvania at this time of year.

Boots or waders are helpful when fishing the larger streams but are not an absolute necessity.

The Pocono Region, which annually attracts thousands of vacationers from the large eastern cities and is located in the northeastern section of the state, offers some excellent streams for fly fishing. They contain brook trout, rainbows and browns. The Lackawaxen River, Equinunk Creek, Pocono Creek, Tobyhanna Creek and the upper Delaware River are good examples.

In the north central region, a mountainous and wooded area offers some of the prime trout fishing in the state. Kettle Creek, Hammersley Fork Creek, Sinnemahoning Creek and Loyalsock Creek are heavy in both browns and brookies. In the early spring, Clearfield, Cameron, McKean and Potter Counties offer great native brook trout fishing.

In southeastern Pennsylvania, which is quite heavily populated and industrialized, try Koon Lake for big rainbows, and Honey Creek near Reedsville for brook trout and browns.

Some of the Fish Commission Lakes and Access areas which have good to excellent trout fishing are:

County	Property	General Location
Sullivan	Hunters Lake	2 miles north of Muncy Valley
Susquehanna	Quaker Lake Access	Montrose, Rt. 29
Tioga	Roaring Branch Creek	1-1/2 mile west of Roaring Branch
Washington	Canonsburg Lake	3 miles east of Canonsburg on Rt. 19
Washington	Dutch Fork Lake	4 miles west of Claysville off Rt. 40
Wayne	Alder Marsh Creek	3 miles west of Rileyville, Rt. 371
Wayne	Duck Harbor Pond Access	3 miles SW of Hilltown
Wayne	Dyberry Creek, EB	3 miles east of Rileyville
Wayne	Equinunk Creek	4 miles SE of Lake Como
Wayne	Lake Lorraine Access	2 miles east of Orson
Wayne	Long Pond	5 miles north of Bethany
Wayne	Upper Woods Pond	2-1/2 miles north of Cold Spring
Wayne	Lackawaxen Creek, WB	Pleasant Mount
Wyoming	Bowman's Creek	3 miles south of Tunkhannock
Wyoming	Meshoppen Creek	5 miles east of Meshoppen
York	Fishing Creek	Lower Windsor and Chance Ford Twps.

Pennsylvania has set aside many areas on which only fly fishing is permitted. Some of them are listed below:

NAME OF STREAM	COUNTY	MILEAGE	LOCATION OF FLY—FISHING AREA
Conewago Creek	Adams	2	From bridge at Rt. 34 upstream to bridge at Zeigler's Mill.
Coves Creek	Bedford	1	Downstream from Shaffer Dam on Percy Smith property to the boundary of the Sam Deal and James Shoemaker properties.
Potter Creek	Bedford	1	From a concrete bridge on the property line of Ulery and Steele downstream to the vicinity of Twp. Rt. No. 594.
Yellow Creek	Bedford	1	From mouth of Maple (Jacks) Run upstream to Red Bank Hill.
Tulpehocken Creek	Berks	1.4	From line fence .2 mile below Route 06024 bridge upstream to 486 yards above Scharff's Bridge on Route 498.
Mud Run	Carbon	2.6	In Hickory Run State Park.
French Creek	Chester	1	From the Dam Breast at Camp Sleepy Hollow downstream to the Robert's Food Locker.
Trout Run	Clearfield	3	From L.R. 17126 near Shawville to one-half mile above Kurtz Camp.
Young Woman's Creek (Right Branch)	Clinton	6	From confluence with the Left Branch up to Beechwood Trail.
Green Spring	Cumberland	1	In the lower portion of the stream on the C. F. Beckner property.
Clarks Creek	Dauphin	2	Rt. 225 crossing downstream to O'Brien's Dam, a distance of 2 miles.
Ridley Creek	Delaware	1	From the falls in Ridley Creek State Park, downstream to the mouth of Dismal Run.
Mill Creek	Elk	1	From Nagle Bridge to headwaters of Norton Reservoir Dam.
Dunbar Creek and tributary	Fayette	14	From stone quarry to headwaters including tributaries.
Falling Springs Creek	Franklin	2.25	From the concrete bridge between the Adin L. Frey and Earl Stull property downstream to a wire fence crossing the Robert E. Gabler farm.
Little Mahoning Creek	Indiana	4	From the bridge at Rochester Mills upstream to Cesna Run.
Donegal Creek	Lancaster	2	Beginning at the upper boundary of the John Heir Farm below Rt. 141 downstream to a bridge on Rt. T. 334 near the confluence with Chickies Creek.
Little Lehigh	Lehigh	1	From Laudenslager's Mill Dam upstream to Twp. Road No. 508.
Slate Run	Lycoming	6.5	Lycoming County, Brown Township; Tioga County, Elk Township
Loyalsock Creek	Lycoming	3	From Lycoming County line downstream to Sandy Bottom.
Gray's Run	Lycoming	2.5	From Gray's Run Hunting Club property line downstream to concrete bridge at the old C.C.C. camp.
Penns Creek	Mifflin & Union	3.5	From a wire below the railroad tunnel downstream to the upper property line of A. T. Soper, including that portion of Cherry Run lying south of L.R. 59001.
Big Bushkill Creek	Monroe	6	On the Ressica Falls Scout Reservation property except 200 yds. on each side of the falls.
McMichael's Creek	Monroe	2	From Rt. 80 bridge upstream to west end of Glenbrook Country Club property.
Upper Tobyhanna Creek	Monroe	1.25	Between Tobyhanna Lakes No. 1 and No. 2.
Cross Fork Creek	Potter	3.2	From lower end of the Weed property upstream to the upper State Forest line.
Lyman Run	Potter	4	Lyman Run Lake to Splash Dam Hollow.
Clear Shade Creek	Somerset	1	Upstream from cable located across stream above Windber Water Dam.
Francis Branch, tributary to Slate Run	Tioga	2	Elk Township, from mouth upstream to Francis Leetonia Road.
White Deer Creek	Union	2.5	From Cooper Mill Road bridge which crosses White Deer Creek upstream to Union-Centre County line.
Little Sandy Creek	Venango	2.5	From L.R. 60073 bridge at Polk upstream to old bridge at Polk State School pump house.
Brokenstraw Creek	Warren	1	From 500 yds. below Rt. 27 bridge downstream to 100 yds. above the L.R. 61010 bridge.
Caldwell Creek	Warren	1.2	From Selkirk highway bridge downstream to Dotyville bridge.
Butternut Creek	Wayne	2.5	From bridge on L.R. 63004 downstream to the mouth.
Dyberry Creek	Wayne	1	From the Widmer property line about one mile below Tanner's Falls downstream to Mary Wilcox Bridge.
Bowmans Creek	Wyoming	1	Bridge on Rt. 292 to Marsh Creek Bridge.
Muddy Creek	York	2	From Bruce to Bridgeton.

South Carolina

Trout fishing opportunities in this state are confined, with a few exceptions, to the mountainous areas of the western counties—Oconee, Pickens and Greenville. Within this three-county area are located many small communities and cities offering lodging, commercial services and supplies. Three state parks, a national forest and some private concerns have camping facilities. The region is well served by good primary and secondary roads. Trout require cold, clear-running streams or rivers with gravel bottoms. Rainbow and particularly brown trout are the least exacting in their habitat preferences, and are stocked regularly in most South Carolina streams suitable for their survival. Also, they are stocked in the cold-running tailrace water below Hartwell and Murray dams. Our truly native trout, the speckled or brook trout, is strictly limited to the more remote small-streams with very cold-clear water. Because of their limited range they are not often stocked.

Although all stocking operations are carried out on a prescribed schedule, stocking times and sites are unannounced, thus increasing the sport in catching these gamely fighters. Stocked areas generally are easily reached, but larger fish and better fishing is to be found in the more remote areas having limited access and less fishing pressure. In these areas, native or two and three-year-old survivors of previous stocks (resident fish) provide the best sport to those who seek them out.

Trout fishing in South Carolina is good all year, but May is considered the best month. September and October are also highly recommended.

Many baits are used with success. Wet and dry flies are classically the bait preferred by ardent trout fishermen, but for those who lack the skill or inclination, small spinners, spoons and Shysters are all popular and produce good catches.

UPPER CHATTOOGA RIVER: This river and its tributaries provide good trout fishing. Among the better tributaries, the east fork of the Chattooga River and Whetstone Creek have excellent native and stocked populations of rainbow and brown trout. The Chattooga River itself offers good native trout fishing down to Russell's Bridge on state highway 28. From Earl's Ford to Fall Creek the river is only marginally suitable for trout. There is no stocking below state highway 28, but many trout are caught in this section along with excellent catches of redeye (coosae) bass. (The redeye or coosae and smallmouth bass are very close relatives, so close, a controversy exists as to whether they differ enough to be classed as separate species.)

The redeye bass prefers marginal trout-water and cannot survive in either cold trout-water or warmer water preferred by other species of bass. This fish is found on the Chattooga River from south of state highway 28 down to Tugaloo Lake.

In addition to its excellent trout fishing, the Chattooga River is a challenge for the white-water canoeist.

CHAUGA RIVER: This stream is somewhat of a marginal stream for trout, and rainbow don't survive well in it. However, it is an excellent brown trout and redeye bass river.

WHITEWATER RIVER: Above the falls to the North Carolina line this is a remote stream with good resident populations of rainbow and brown trout.

BIG EASTATOE: The headwater of this river is cold and clear, suitable for rainbow. A few brown are also found. This river is stocked regularly, and on the lower end, brown trout and redeye bass are found in abundance. Spring and early summer are the best times to fish this river.

SOUTH SALUDA: From Table Rock Reservoir down, this river offers marginal but good trout fishing, February through June. Fishing opportunity diminishes the remainder of the summer due to the heat. Blythe Shoals is a popular fishing site on this river. The river is also good for canoeing.

MIDDLE SALUDA RIVER: The head-water of this river, above U.S. 276 offers excellent rainbow fishing and some brown trout. Oil Camp Creek, a feeder stream, has a good population of native fish. Farther down the Saluda there is good green-water canoeing.

NORTH SALUDA RIVER: A very favorable river for rainbow because of the cold water running into it from the North Saluda Reservoir. Trout fishing extends from the reservoir. Trout fishing extends from the reservoir down to U.S. 25.

SOUTH PACOLET RIVER: Down to the Greenville-Spartanburg County line, good stocked-trout fishing, late winter through June. Some resident fish may be found.

OTHER TROUT STREAMS: Many other streams (see map) afford good trout fishing opportunities, such as Laurel Fork, Cane and Matthews Creeks, to name a few. The challenge is finding the less frequented streams with sizable populations of resident fish. Fishermen who accept this challenge won't be disappointed.

If you like fishing you will like South Carolina. Its abundance of public fishing waters range from trout in the lower end of the Appalachian Range to numerous reservoirs, streams, natural lakes and ponds in the central and lower half of the state and to pier, surf and deep sea fishing off the coast. These waters, plus an ideal climate, allow the fisherman to pursue his hobby throughout the year.

Some 250 miles of public trout fishing streams are in the northwest corner of the state. Brook, rainbow and brown trout reproduce naturally and thousands of catchable size fish are also stocked each year. A 13 pound 4 ounce brown trout established the state record in 1961.

Eight major reservoirs comprising a total of 400,000 acres provide ample freshwater angling opportunities from the Piedmont to the coastal plain. Lodging, food, boats, guides and all accommodations are available on the reservoirs.

The trout season in South Carolina never closes. Neither are there any size limits so it is unnecessary to take along your ruler.

The trout are confined to the mountain sections of Oconee, Pickens and Greenville counties and most of the fishing waters are easily accessible from good highways. For the hardened anglers who can rough it, native trout can be caught in some of the remote, hard-to-reach mountain streams.

Annually over 170,000 rainbow, brown and brook trout, of catchable size, are stocked. These fish are stocked at intervals to meet the fishing pressure. Although South Carolina has only a limited amount of trout water, the fisherman will be well rewarded for his efforts.

Hartwell Reservoir, the newest of the state's reservoirs is located on the upper Savannah River between South Carolina and Georgia and extends in two branches up the Tugaloo and Seneca Rivers. The 61,350 acre reservoir has a shoreline of 962 miles. The dam is situated about 305 miles above the mouth of the Savannah, 98 miles above

Augusta, Georgia and 67 miles above Clark Hill Dam.

Rainbow and brown trout are stocked annually below the dam and afford fishing on approximately 15 miles of stream. This stocking has been very successful with a large percentage of the released fish being caught.

In order to provide the public with free access the Corps of Engineers has constructed numerous launching ramps, camping and picnic facilities.

Utah

The best fishing months in Utah vary according to the water. Some streams remain high and roilly until the end of July. Reservoirs subject to drawdown often become unproductive during hot summer months, but they generally pick up in the fall.

Most stream fishing in Utah is done by wading or from the banks as almost all of the streams are small. The exception is the Green River which is fished from shore or by boat. Reservoirs may be fished from shore, with waders or tube floats or by boat.

Some waters which are managed as quality fishing areas, i.e., wild fish and artificial flies only are:
Cache County:
Blacksmith Fork River from its source to its confluence with Rock Creek.
Duchesne County:
Strawberry River from Willow Creek downstream to its confluence with Red Creek.
Summit County:
Weber River from the stone gate cattleguard which marks the boundary of the Thousand Peaks Ranch property, 6.2 miles upstream to the Holiday Park Corporation gate.
Wasatch County:
Strawberry River from Willow Creek

downstream to its confluence with Red Creek.

Utah game fish include rainbow, cutthroat, German brown, Eastern brook, golden and lake trout, kokanee salmon, grayling, Bonneville cisco, crappie, largemouth and white bass, walleye, whitefish, and channel catfish.

Fly fishing begins with the first insect hatches and continues through November. Patterns that generally produce well in Utah waters are the Captain, Renegade, Rio Grande King, Coachman, Royal Coachman, Grey-hackle Yellow, Mormon Girl, Adams, Ginger Quill, Mosquito, and Red Ant.

Some of the best areas for fly fishing are the Logan River—rainbow, brown, brook, and cutthroat trout; Rocky Mountain whitefish. Logan Canyon and U.S. 89. Forest Service campgrounds throughout the canyon; also, motels and cafe.

Weber River—rainbow, brown, brook, and cutthroat trout; Rocky Mountain whitefish. Campgrounds, picnic areas, motels, and cafes in nearly every community.

Provo River—rainbow, brown, cutthroat, and brook trout; Rocky Mountain whitefish, kokanee salmon, walleye pike, and bass. Flows through Utah, Wasatch, and Summit Counties.

Strawberry Reservoir—rainbow and cutthroat trout; brook trout. Elevation 7,557 feet. U.S. 40 east out of Heber City. Camping grounds, cabins, boats, equipment, bait, cafes, and fishing licenses available.

Strawberry River—rainbow, brown, cutthroat, and brook trout.

Green River—rainbow, brown and cutthroat trout downstream from Flaming Gorge Dam to Colorado border. From Dinosaur National Monument downstream principally channel cat.

This river is in the famous and great fishing area in the Uinta Mountains in Utah. These waters contain rainbow and cutthroat in quantity.

Fish Lake—lake trout, cutthroat, rainbow, brown and brook trout; kokanee salmon. Richfield via U.S. 89, U-24-25. Lodge, cafe, cabins, Forest Service campgrounds, picnic areas, boats, tackle, bait groceries. Fishing licenses available.

Fremont River—brown and rainbow. Garfield and Wayne Counties. High Uinta Lakes—cutthroat, brook, rainbow and golden trout; grayling. Most of the area is inaccessible because of snow until around July. Duchesne, Uintah, Summit, Daggett Counties. Elevations 9,000-11,500 feet. Most lakes and streams support good populations of fish. No mechanized form of transportation is allowed to enter the primitive area. No campgrounds inside the primitive area. The primitive area itself contains a quarter of a million acres of lofty mountain peaks ranging up to 12,000-14,000 feet, virgin forest, and

hundreds of lakes and streams flowing through deep canyons. The high Uinta Mountains generally trend east and west; they are about 150 miles in length. Horses and pack-in guide services are available from several points. Improved campgrounds are located at nearly every lake accessible by automobile. Kolob Reservoir—rainbow, cutthroat trout. Private land around reservoir. Some camping nearby. North from town of Virgin.

Virginia

The Virginia game, inland fish and dog code defines this state's game fish as brook, rainbow and brown trout, all of the sunfish family including largemouth bass, smallmouth bass, rock bass, bluegill and crappie, and walleyed pike and

white bass.

All three trout species found in Virginia waters are highly sought-after game fishes. Only the brook trout is native to Virginia. Rainbow trout were originally found in Rocky Mountain streams and brown trout were imported from Europe.

Trout require a constant supply of cold, clear, well aerated water for the establishment of self-sustaining, thriving populations. All prefer summer water temperatures below 65 degrees and can seldom survive temperatures greater than 75 degrees for more than brief periods.

The native brook trout is by far the most widely distributed species in Virginia and is apparently well adapted to the soft, moderately acid waters which characterize most of Virginia's trout range. The introduced rainbow shows some preference for limestone streams but is often found in the same waters with brook trout. Brown trout have been introduced only recently, but experience elsewhere indicates it can be expected to thrive in the same waters as brook and rainbow trout. While all 3 species can tolerate more adverse environmental conditions when stocked as adults for put-and-take stocking programs, there is some indication that brown trout will thrive better than the other species in the lower and more turbid reaches of trout streams.

Native brook trout reach 18 inches in length occasionally, but a 9-inch brookie (6 ounces) is considered better than average in Virginia waters. 6 to 10-pound rainbow trout have been creeled occasionally in Virginia, and it is hoped that recent plantings of brown trout will provide more larger trout in future years.

Only the headwater sections of mountain streams meet the exacting habitat requirements for spawning and establishment of self-sustaining trout populations. Since the vast majority of these streams are small, averaging less than 20 feet in width, the potential production of natural trout is not sufficient to meet the demands of the angling public. Watershed and stream improvement practices offer some promise of increasing the carrying capacity of existing native trout streams. To further augment the supply of naturally produced fish, the Game Commission annually stocks catchable size trout in the better public trout waters. The number and size of trout produced is limited by revenues generated by trout license sales. These stocked fish are readily caught, and management measures to date have been directed toward refining stocking techniques to extend the fishing season and provide more sport from the number of fish available. Such measures which have proven successful include in-season stocking and establishment of artificial lure-only streams and "fish for fun" areas.

Over 160 public streams in 40 counties are stocked annually by the Commission of Game and Inland Fisheries and the U.S. Fish and Wildlife Service. In addition, there are many native trout streams on the Shenandoah National Park and Blue Ridge Parkway which are not stocked but provide public fishing.

Some of the larger and more important trout streams include the Rapidan River (fish-for-fun only) in Madison County, Bullpasture River in Highland County, Jackson River in Bath and Alleghany Counties, Tye River in Nelson County, Smith River in Henry County, Dan River in Patrick County, Big Stony Creek in Giles County, South Fork Holston River in Smyth County and White Top Laurel River in Washington County.

Another new plan is Pay-as-You-Go Trout Fishing on the Clinch Mountain Wildlife Management Area. The concept being tried out in this area is a new approach to the old problem of trying to provide good trout fishing throughout the season. The trout stocked generally stocked throughout the state are produced mainly from trout license revenue—not sufficient to stock in greater quantity or more frequent intervals than is now done. The pay-as-you-go stream is financed solely from the sale of daily permits. Thus, you pay for the fish you catch and they are replaced in the stream for the next angler. By this process the stream is kept stocked with catchable size fish throughout the summer months.

"Fish for fun" means just that: Catch the fish on an artificial lure with a barbless hook and immediately release it unharmed to bite again another day. The headwaters of the Rapidan River in Madison County are operated in this manner. The Rapidan River watershed en- compasses the Rapidan River from its source above Hoover's Camp to the lower boundary of the Shenandoah National Park and all its tributaries including the Stauton River (also known as Wilson Run) and its tributaries. The Commission has stocked large rainbow trout in the three-mile section of the Rapidan River that flows through the Ward-Rue management area. These stocked fish will measure from 12 to 16 inches and will be fin-clipped for later studies.

Many people enjoy fishing a trout stream but not just to fill the creel. Children are thrilled with the quick strike of a trout—mother and dad are too! For these and the many others who take fish home but give them away for various reasons, "fish for fun" streams are a possible answer.

When to Go. Fly fishermen made good catches of 6"-10" brook and 18" rainbow trout during the last half of April in the Rapidan and Staunton Rivers Fish-for-Fun section. May and June creels were fair. Bullpasture brown and rainbow trout, averaging 10" in length, were being taken in fair numbers in mid-April. May, July and August reports rated Bullpasture trout fishing excellent.

Hidden Valley Lake—stocked with rainbow trout. Most April, May and June fishing was good, declining through July and August.

Famous for its big rainbows, Philpott Reservoir anglers found July trout fishing good. Excellent trout catches were reported from the Dan and Smith Rivers in mid-May (following closure for stocking) and mid-August. Good to fair fishing other weeks lasted through early September. Philpott Reservoir, on the Smith River, and Carvins Cove, a 640 acre water supply reservoir on Carvins Creek near Roanoke, share top honors as hot spots for lunker trout. Rainbows and brown trout stocked have reached the 5 to 10-pound class in recent years. Lake trout introduced into Philpott show promise, with several over 5 pounds reported caught.

Hidden Valley Lake, located on Game Commission property in Washington County, is another unusual small impoundment. In this 66-acre mountain lake stocked with trout, anglers are restricted to barbless hooks and may keep only those trout that are over 10 inches long.

Washington

Trout are the major interest of the Washington angler, whether the fisherman is a season-long die-hard or an opening-day vacationer. From remote high mountain lakes to the mighty Columbia, Washington has an outstanding variety of fishing conditions and fish.

This state's trout include the rainbow, cutthroat, golden and brown. Species which belong to a separate group known as "char" include the brook, Dolly Varden and lake trout. Two species of salmon—normally a saltwater fish—are commonly found landlocked in certain Washington lakes; these are the kokanee (freshwater sockeye salmon), and the silver (freshwater silver salmon). All trouts, chars and salmon belong to the scientific family *Salmonidae*, which also includes the whitefish and grayling.

These fish are know as "soft-rayed"; as contrasted with bass, perch and the like, commonly referred to as "spinyrays," and have hard spines in the dorsal fin. The *Salmonidae* all possess an adipose fin, have rather fine scales and small mouths. With few exceptions, the salmonids migrate upstream to spawn. All spend part of their lives in freshwater, and some migrate between fresh and saltwater. As a general rule, salmonids prefer and

tolerate colder temperatures than do spinyrays or minnows. The salmonids tend to be plankton and insect feeders and—with some exceptions—are not predaceous as are members of the sunfish family (which includes the bass). Most of the salmonids require cool, clear water, gravel spawning beds, and water with high oxygen content. Some are able to thrive at great depths in very cold water. Outstanding as food fish, the salmonids are an indispensable ingredient in the sporting diet of Washington's anglers.

The things that decide the success of a fish population are not entirely understood by biologists even today. Sometimes physical features such as mountain ranges limit fish distribution. Other factors are chemical and physiological in nature.

It is generally true that trout must have a minimum of five parts per million of dissolved oxygen in the water to thrive. Browns are generally able to survive at lower oxygen levels and higher water temperatures than other salmonids. The brookie requires high oxygen levels and cold water temperatures, while the rainbow has requirements between the brown and brook. The rainbow, however, has a far greater range of tolerance. Many claim rainbow are more active during the warm summer months than other trout.

The rainbow is also generally thought of as fighting harder than the brook and characteristically clears the water in fighting the hook. The cutthroat is also a known "jumper," while the char tend to be sub-surface fighters.

Rainbow are thought to stand up better to competitive species than do either brook or cutthroat. On the other hand, brookies typically out-compete cutthroat when both occur in the same stream system. Browns can out-compete brooks in the

stream environment, while goldens are thought to stand little pressure from other trout.

Rainbow are said to be best able to utilize the limited productivity of small, relatively infertile ponds. Brookies placed in a similar situation successfully reproduce, but characteristically develop a "stunted" population. In waters of limited fertility the rainbow tends less to stunt, but reproduces more slowly than the brook. This characteristic of the rainbow is also of significance when this trout is placed in competition with members of the sunfish family. The common pumpkinseed sunfish often develops a "stunted" population—maturing at far under desirable catch size. As the more adaptive sunfish increase and approach the carrying capacity of the lakes's food supply, rainbow production slows and the trout population goes downhill.

The rainbow is normally among the fastest growing of the trout and does best in hard, alkaline waters rich in minerals—but this is modified by many other factors. In its native east coast environment, the brook tends to prefer waters on the acid side.

Cutthroat and goldens are spring spawning fish and the brook, lake trout and brown are fall spawners. Resident rainbow show a wide variance in spawning time, but most naturally spawn in the spring.

As sport fish, many anglers consider the rainbow easier to catch than the brown, but more difficult than the brook. Cutthroat seem close to the rainbow in difficulty to catch, while goldens seem relatively easy for the anglers to crop.

Trout feeding habits vary greatly. The brown and Dolly Varden are generally predatory in nature. Characteristically, the rainbow is a plankton feeder, whereas the cutthroat prefers an insect diet. The cutthroat also has a more narrow

Here is fine fly fishing water. Plenty of white oxygenated riffles, some pools and lots of shallows for easy wading. Also much open space for long, free casting.

habitat tolerance than does the rainbow. A cold lake of relatively low productivity might make a fine cutthroat water, but a warmer lake, with greater plankton productivity, best hosts the rainbow.

Rainbow range and feed throughout the entire body of a lake (where sufficient oxygen exists) and thus utilize a lake more efficiently than many other trout. The rainbow is also able to utilize a wider range of food organisms than any other species, thriving on zooplankton, insects, snails and other fish. These factors can result in natural annual production per surface acre of up to 400 pounds of fish—unheard of with other species.

Cutthroat are found in Washington as native to coastal and peninsula streams which flow to saltwater. They are also well established in northeast Washington.

Brookies seem to do best—not on the coast—but in the foothills of the Cascades and in northeast Washington.

Rainbow occur statewide, while brown trout habitat is largely limited to the warmer and slower portions of certain streams in eastern Washington.

Comparing the desirability of one trout to another is, in the end, a matter for the angler, not the biologist.

Rainbow Trout. The most valuable freshwater game fish in Washington is undoubtedly the rainbow, both in its non-migratory status as a "rainbow," or the larger "steelhead" in the sea-run variety. The rainbow grows well in both stream and lake environment, and its fine table and sporting qualities make this species the most sought after game fish in Washington.

Native in those waters flowing into the Pacific Ocean from Alaska to northern Mexico, rainbow thrive in a habitat where optimum water temperatures do not rise higher than

65 degrees to 68 degrees. Rainbow are widely stocked in Washington waters; about 17 million are annually reared and released from Game Department hatcheries. Although they thrive within a wide tolerance of habitat conditions, larger rainbow occur more often in the feed-rich lakes of eastern Washington. Rainbow less than one pound primarily subsist on such invertebrates as zooplankton and small insects. Larger rainbow are more piscivorous—that is they feed more on other fish. Rainbow, however, more than any other species of true trout, feed on plankton.

The rainbow derives its name from a prominent red or pink streak, running down both sides from just behind the gill covers to the tail. The streak is most pronounced during the spawning season and may be indistinct or absent in the young. In typical coloration, sides are olive to greenish-blue above and silvery below. Small, easily seen black or brown spots on the body are scattered and irregular in size, becoming more evenly distributed on the sides and tail. As is also true of cutthroat, rainbow show a great variation in color pattern depending on where found and genetic strain. Although this game fish is released in both fingerling and legal sizes, the trophy trout angler should seek those lakes and streams where insect and plant growth is especially good. It is here that rainbow averaging 12-16 inches will be found.

Steelhead Trout. The trophy fish of Washington is the steelhead. It has all the appeal to attract the angler—size, fighting ability, and a little bit of mystery involved in the catching. The steelhead is a rainbow that migrates to sea where it finds a plentiful supply of food needed to attain large size. Occurring in both "winter-run" and "summer-run" races, they can be caught somewhere in Washington during every month

of the year. Steelhead are a stream fish, being caught largely on their upstream migration to spawn.

Steelhead runs occur in most Washington streams and rivers which empty directly into either Puget Sound or the Pacific Ocean. It is in these waters that winter fishing is most productive. It is in the Columbia, Grande Ronde and Snake rivers that an outstanding summer fishery for steelhead exists. Many smaller, Washington rivers also provide excellent summer-run angling. The Kalama, Lewis and Klickitat have a reputation for providing top sport during the summer.

Winter-run fish move upstream from November to June and spawn in the spring. Summer runs may travel upstream as early as April or May, but usually during the period June to September. Summer runs lay over in deep pools until the following spring before spawning. Seaward migrants of both races move downstream from February through June. Runs usually peak around the first of May in western Washington and about a month later east of the Cascade mountain range.

Immediately upon entering a stream or river from the ocean, steelhead are a bright silver color. Typical black spots of the rainbow still show, but whereas the resident rainbow is greenish-blue to olive on the back and tail, a fresh steelhead is blue-black to very green-black on the back and tail. As spawning time approaches, the darker color and prominent red streak of the typical, resident rainbow begins to show. Size is the most distinctive steelhead feature. While you may catch a 6 pound resident rainbow in a lake, it's not likely you will catch a resident, stream rainbow of this size. Steelhead caught average 8 pounds, but numerous 20 pounders are taken each season. The Washington record is over 33 pounds.

Wild-reared steelhead spend two years in the stream after hatching, then migrate to fertile ocean pastures. There, most spend two years and return as fish of 7 to 9 pounds. Steelhead of hatchery and rearing pond origin are now grown to the 7-10" migrant size one year after hatching, spending two years at sea prior to returning to spawn. First-return fish constitute over 90% of all steelhead caught. The bigger fish caught are those that stay out longer—spending three or more years in saltwater. Re-spawning fish only gain 2-3 pounds, as it takes considerable energy to recover from first-time spawning efforts.

Steelhead tackle consists of bait casting, fly and spinning outfits—heavier than those used for resident trout, but slightly lighter, longer, and more sensitive than conventional salmon tackle. Various flies, often used with a sinker or other weight, comprise the terminal gear.

The increasing steelhead catch has been due to an increase of anglers as well as the increasing number of hatchery-reared and released fish. Released as out-going migrants, they are responsible for the greater numbers of returning fish caught. Through selective breeding, use of semi-natural rearing ponds, and other refinements, the Game Department, within limits, can produce a fish which will return to spawn in a desired area at a desired time.

Cutthroat Trout. As its name implies the cutthroat is often a relatively easy fish to identify. A slash mark, either deep orange or red in adults, is usually visible under each side of the lower jaw. Juveniles and fresh, sea-run adults often do not contain the naming characteristic. Back and sides are frequently steel gray to bluish and covered with spots, larger and more regular in shape than those found on the rainbow. While the rainbow's spots are fairly evenly distributed, the native cutthroat's are concentrated toward the tail. The tail itself is slightly forked, while the tips of the dorsal, pelvic and anal fins be light cream, brownish-rose or red in color. The anal fin of the coastal cutthroat is often spotted.

Of all the northwest trout, the rainbow and cutthroat are most abundant and widely distributed. Although the rainbow and cutthroat generally differ from one another in color and body markings, both species show considerable variation in marking patterns. For the angler who sometimes has trouble telling a cutthroat from a rainbow, whether found in freshwater or salt—the best single characteristic is the presence of small teeth on the back of the tongue, occurring only on the cut-throat.

Cutthroat occur in the widest assortment of color patterns of any trout species. Washington varieties include the coastal cutthroat of westside counties that is found in streams as both resident and sea-run. The cutthroat of eastern Washington and many high altitude waters is a somewhat different strain. This type is often called the "native" and is similar to the Montana Black-spotted cutthroat. Resident cut-throat prefer the colder sections of streams and thrive best in cold lakes, some to 10,000 feet elevation.

Common in many lakes, resident cutthroat may weigh to 10 pounds. In larger bodies of water this trout prefers rocky areas, sandy shorelines and deep waters. Riffles, and deep pools under logs or overhanging brush, are preferred habitat in fast water. Because the cutthroat also does well in high altitude lakes of clear, cold water once barren of fish life, the Game Department utilizes this fish extensively in its aerial stocking program. Not to be overlooked by the angler are many

beaver ponds throughout the state which also provides outstanding cutthroat fishing.

As resident cutthroat mature, they feed on large invertebrates such as insects, as well as small fish fry. These adults are often carnivorous, subsisting entirely upon a fish diet.

The Puget Sound region is centered within the sea-runs' native range of northern California to southeastern Alaska. The sea-run variety of cutthroat migrates upstream to feed and spawn. Young sea-runs migrate to sea, from the stream of their births, with spring high water. Adult sea-runs frequently enter the tidal influence areas of streams in the spring to feed on seaward migrations of young salmon. After these forages, they may return to saltwater—and in fall and winter re-enter in spawning migrations. Sea-runs are nomads, however, and may be found in the streams at nearly any time of the year. The sea-run may wander about in schools not far distant from their parent stream outlet.

Size and age composition of saltwater cutthroat schools may vary considerably. Wild, resident cut-throat mature in 3 to 4 years when reaching 8 to 12 inches long. Most sea runs caught average 12-18 inches in length and weigh more than the average resident cutthroat. Sea runs to 4 pounds are taken, although an average of 1-2 pounds is more common. This large size is attained predominantly on a saltwater diet of small fish and crustaceans.

Cutthroat can be caught on a variety of natural and artificial baits. This trout seems to favor almost any type of lure with touches of yellow and red. Since these fish tend to hybridize with other strains of trout, fisheries management directs their establishment in waters where pure strains can be perpetuated.

Brown trout. One of Washington's several introduced fish species is the

brown trout, originally imported to the United States from Europe. The brown is presently established in a few scattered eastern Washington lakes and streams. It produces an incidental fishery for those angling for other species. Mature browns are generally considered to be very difficult to catch.

Browns prefer cool lakes and streams, although they have a better ability to withstand warm waters than do many other trout species. Fishermen find that large browns are most active during the early morning and evening hours, when they feed heavily on other fish. Smaller browns consume mostly invertebrate food consisting of earthworms, crayfish and insects such as mayflies, caddis flies and stoneflies. As browns mature they become very piscivorous in their feeding habits.

Browns are distinguished by rather large, dark spots appearing on the back and sides, together with reddish spots surrounded by pale borders which are scattered over upper portions of the body. The back is olive to greenish-brown, while the lower portions of the body are yellow, fading to gray or white near the undersides.

Although fish over twenty pounds have been taken from Washington waters, any brown exceeding 5 pounds is considered large in this state. Browns spawn in the fall from October to January, preferring to ascend cold, clear tributaries of the parent body of water.

Flies and artificial baits resembling smaller fish or any of the larger crustaceans and invertebrates are excellent lures for tempting this fine game fish.

Golden Trout. Established in a few remote mountain lakes of Washington, this beautiful trout was originally introduced from wild stock of the northern California high country. Goldens are charac-teristically adapted to waters of cold, high altitude lakes, and differ from rainbow chiefly in brilliant, distinctive coloring at certain times of the year. Most brilliant coloration occurs during the spawning season, anytime from June to late August, depending upon time of ice-out on the lakes. Spawning habits are similar to its close relative, the rainbow. The fish spawn when water temperatures approach 50°, and eggs may hatch in 20 days with favorable temperatures of 58°. The influence of habitat limitations in high altitude waters is illustrated by those goldens which may mature at 6 inches and spawn 300 eggs. Under more favorable conditions of growth, a mature golden of 12-13 inches may spawn 12,000 eggs.

Because it subsists largely on plankton, the golden is best adapted to high, rock-bound lakes which contain this nutrient. Goldens are primarily insectivorous, if given the opportunity, and prefer caddis fly larvae and midges, but also thrive on a microcrustacea diet of straight plankton.

Physically, the golden is similar to the rainbow, but has smaller scales. Distinctive parr markings, of adult fish, deep orange color of fins and belly, and reddish gill covers are its most distinguishing features. A bright red band runs along the side, with the upper parts of the body yellowish-olive, and sides below the lateral line of golden yellow. The dorsal, anal and pelvic fins often have distinct white tips offset by a black bar. Parr marks, red coloring, size and distribution of spots may vary greatly from water to water.

Average size of mature females is around 9 inches. Goldens can reproduce efficiently in high, cold mountain lakes, but must have stream spawning grounds to produce a population large enough to withstand moderate fishing pressure. This game fish is considered large at 12 inches and a fish of 2 pounds or

more is unusual.

Being relatively easy to catch—taking flies and small lures readily—goldens in Washington are presently placed in high Cascade lakes where fishing pressure is limited. In addition, the golden readily interbreeds with other trout, and may become eliminated as a distinct species when placed in waters containing other types of trout.

Brook trout. A favorite with many anglers, the brookie is one of Washington's introduced species. Now common in the northeastern and some mountainous portions of the state, the brook trout does reproduce naturally in many waters.

Originally, this trout's native habitat extended east of the Saskatchewan river to the headwaters of various rivers in the Carolinas and the interior upper Mississippi River.

In Washington, the brook is now common in cool, clear headwater ponds and spring-fed streams, and in larger lakes having cool, well-oxygenated lower layers of water. Optimum water temperatures have been experimentally determined to be near 59°. Many small lakes and ponds throughout the timbered hills and lower mountainous areas contain brook trout populations.

Brookies are undoubtedly the most colorful of trout. Streamlined, with a compressed body, their coloration ranges from olive, blue-gray, or black on the back to white on the belly. Worm-shaped tracks called vermiculations, occurring along the back and upper portions of the body, are characteristic of this species. Red spots, with or without bluish rings around them, are evident on the sides. Other distinguishing marks are the white and black stripes along the leading edge of the lower fins.

Under optimum growing con-

ditions, brookies grow rapidly and may be well over legal length their first year. Best growth is in lakes and lengths of 18 inches may be achieved in 4 years.

Brookies take a fly readily as their dominant diet consists of caddis flies, insect larvae and stonefly nymphs. Although brook trout eat worms, crustaceans and other fish, the angler's best bet is to fish a large, wet fly or feathered spinner.

In suitable waters, Washington brook trout may reach a size of over 5 pounds, but in an unbalanced environment brook trout populations may become excessive and stunt the growth of other trout in the same body of water.

Lake Trout. Like the Dolly Varden and eastern brook trout, the lake trout is a char. They have been successfully established in Cle Elum, Bonaparte, Loon and Deer Lakes. Two other waters, both mountain lakes—Eightmile in Chelan County and Isabel in Snohomish County—contain this large, deep-water trout. Both these lakes require a hike to reach, and offer good fishing during the early part of the season. Normally, lakers are found in colder parts of the lake, but will move inshore to feed during the spring, before temperatures rise above 60°. Of the salmonids, lakers are more tolerant to extremes of low water temperature and low oxygen content.

The laker has a background color of gray, overlaid with light spots occurring on the back, sides and fins. On the upper portion of the body these spots become fused into vermiculations, similar to the pattern of the brook trout. Large size and forked tail also help to identify this outstanding food fish.

Unlike other trout, lakers require a rocky shelf upon which to spawn. Located in 6 to 20 feet of water, the eggs are spawned haphazardly in rock rubble. Young lakers feed almost entirely upon crustaceans and

This is a beautiful specimen of Grayling, an inhabitant of fast, clear water.
It is an excellent fish to take on flies and puts up a terrific battle.

insects, and entirely upon other fish when reaching a size of 2 pounds. Adults, however, will resort to forms of plankton and aquatic invertebrates when necessary. This largest of all freshwater salmonids grows slowly and large adults are usually quite old. Lake trout of over 30 pounds have been caught in Washington waters.

Because they prefer the deeper parts of a lake, this trout requires heavier-than-normal trout tackle for successful summer fishing. Most anglers use a leaded line.

Dolly Varden Trout. A native Washington game fish, the Dolly inhabits rivers and lakes on both sides of the Cascades. It often occurs in fast water at the headwaters or outlets of lakes. Many Dollys are taken as an incidental catch when angling for sea-run cutthroat and steelhead in downstream areas.

In waters where saltwater migration is possible, the Dolly takes to the ocean and brackish areas for short feeding forays, migrating back into freshwater for part of its life cycle. Some Dolly Varden exceed 20 pounds, although most caught average 1 to 3 pounds.

This game fish can be distinguished from other trout by its general, overall color of olive-green, becoming white on the belly. Many round, light spots appear on the sides and upper portions of the body. Near the lateral line the spots are usually orange or red and larger than adjacent markings. Significantly, the Dolly lacks the "worm tracks" found on the other two char, the brook and lake trout.

Dollys will hit a variety of flies, lures and baits. Not particularly hard to catch, this hard-fighting game fish offers thrills each summer for Washington anglers.

Grayling. The arctic grayling occurs only in limited numbers in Washington. Preferring clear and very cold waters, these game fish are limited to an area that will limit pressure as well as provide suitable habitat.

There's no mistaking the grayling. It's the only member of the trout family with a spectacular dorsal fin—long, high and brilliantly colored. Its sides are silvery to light purple and the back darkens to a gray or olive-green. Additional markings include a number of small X-shaped spots near the mid-portion of the body.

Grayling spawn in shallow streams. During mid-summer they will take a dry fly readily. Washington grayling average about 12 inches, although in arctic waters they can reach 24 inches. Chief foods for this exotic trout are various forms of terrestrial and aquatic insects.

Silvers. Several bodies of water in Washington have established populations of silvers, such as Goodwin, Blue, Park and Lake Washington. Basically, all these lakes are large, deep and cold. There is no body of fresh water in this state large enough and with attendant spawning streams to permit natural reproduction. Easy identification of young or adult silvers is given by the sweeping, sickle-shaped anal fin.

Silvers in Washington waters average 7-14 inches by maturity, and resemble the kokanee. Approximately half a million fingerlings are released into silver lakes each spring. Two years later they can be caught near the surface in late spring and early summer when they assemble into feeding schools. Silvers are an important sport species in this state, providing fast fishing when conditions are favorable.

"Silvers" are landlocked, fresh-water silver salmon and presently occur in some large lakes where growing conditions prove suitable. Both Kokanee and silvers die after spawning; but unlike kokanee, silvers do not spawn naturally when landlocked. Management of this species, therefore, requires the regular stocking of small silver salmon fry.

Kokanee. The kokanee, often-times called the silver trout, is not to be confused with the "silver"—another landlocked, freshwater salmon species found in Washington waters. The kokanee is a variety of sockeye salmon which completes its whole life history in fresh water.

They reproduce naturally and are capable of over-producing to the extent the populations become stunted. Furthermore, as the kokanee is a true salmon, it dies after spawning. For these reasons, liberal bonus limits are established to harvest kokanee in those waters where spawning success is high.

Kokanee are thought to be native to a few landlocked drainages along the Pacific coast. This salmonid is very responsive to temperature and prefers temperatures close to 50°. Large lakes, with clearly defined thermoclines, generally provide a good environment. Kokanee feed almost exclusively on plankton, and travel in large schools. This is the type of nutrient produced in such established kokanee lakes as Rimrock, American, Whatcom, Chelan and others. In smaller, fingerling sizes kokanee provide excellent forage for large lake trout, cutthroat and rainbow.

Catchable kokanee from Washington waters average about 9-16 inches, depending upon where found. Largest kokanee come from lakes and reservoirs with a low relative density of population. In some waters this game fish has reached 5 pounds, but this is extremely unusual. Maturity is reached anywhere from 2 to 7 years, when they spawn once and die. Although they prefer to spawn in streams, kokanee will spawn in shallow water near lake shores. It is when they utilize lake shorelines for spawning beds that future populations are most likely to be affected. Fluctuations in water levels kill the eggs, thereby reducing potential populations. Artificial spawning channels, have greatly enhanced chances of fry and egg survival.

The distinguishing characteristics of this fish are its deeply forked tail and the length and proportion of the peduncle. The peduncle—or end of the body at the tail—extends further into the rayed portion of the tail on the kokanee, as compared with other salmonids. Like the sockeye, the kokanee is a silvery color on the sides with a blue back. One of the surest identification methods is to count the number of full-length rays contained in the anal fin. On members of the trout family they number no more than 12. On salmon they number 13 or more. During spawning time, the kokanee turns a deep red and the lower jaw of the male develops the characteristic hook common to many species of salmon. Kokanee are well equipped for their diet of minute plankton, and possess an unusual number of fine gill rakers. Abundance of these filter mechanisms is one of the surest methods of identification of this salmonid.

Kokanee are attracted to a variety of lures including flies, spoons and salmon eggs. Care should be exercised in bringing this soft-mouthed fish to the net.

Mountain Whitefish. The mountain whitefish provides an additional fishery for trout anglers in most of the major river drainages on both sides of the Cascades. In Washington, mountain whitefish occur only in streams.

Whitefish resemble a large herring, and in fact are sometimes called "mountain herring". Sides and belly are white and silver, while the back and fins are a light brown. It is closely related to other salmonids, but is easily distinguished from them by its large scales, small mouth, and large adipose fin.

During the summer, mountain whitefish inhabit the deeper pools, ascending upstream a short distance in the fall to spawn. Caddis flies and grubs are an important diet, and when salmon fry come down from tributary streams, they often become an important food item.

No attempt is made to artificially propagate whitefish, as they spawn adequately in those streams where fast water is still available.

In Washington waters mountain whitefish average 11-12 inches and 1/2 to 3/4 of a pound, although they occasionally reach weights of 3 pounds. Whitefish are taken with a variety of lures, mainly flies and long bucktails. Most are caught when the fish are "schooled" in winter months.

Wyoming

Wyoming has over 264,000 acres of lakes, reservoirs and beaver ponds and almost 20,000 miles of streams. More than 5,000 miles of streams and thousands of acres of lakes and reservoirs contain abundant trout populations. Trout caught in Wyoming's icy water, when fried, baked, broiled or barbecued, will probably be the best fish you've ever tasted. Six varieties of trout live in Wyoming's waters—brook, brown, rainbow, golden, mackinaw (lake), and Wyoming's native cutthroat plus hybrids of these species.

The worlds record California golden trout—11 pounds, 4 ounces—was taken in Wyoming at Cook's Lake in northwestern Wyoming in 1948.

Trout fishing in Wyoming, although originally and by nature excellent, has been given a great deal of thought and attentive planning by an energetic and active Game and Fish Commission. Although not yet plagued by large populations and heavy fishing pressure, the Commission realizes that every year the job of finding a place to fish is getting tougher—even in the "wide open spaces" of Wyoming. With this in mind, the Commission is continually acquiring and developing new, prime fishing properties. These areas are being obtained to insure high quality fishing for present and future generations. In addition a continuing program of obtaining easements and fishing permission for the public from private landowners is being carried on.

New fishing areas are constantly being added to the state of Wyoming's roster—as witness the wonderful new opportunities to fish offered by the famous Flaming Gorge Reservoir and the Yellowtail Reservoir—marvelous boat fishing among the scenic wonders of deep canyon walls.

Perhaps the best natural trout fishing in America today comes as a result of Wyoming's location at the headwaters of 3 major river drainages—the Colorado, Columbia and Missouri. Add to this the thousands of sparkling, tumbling streams filled with trout in the mountain areas, some so wild they must be reached by foot or horseback—all this adds up to a veritable fly-fisherman's paradise.

Bridger National Forest and Wilderness Area presents miles of lakes and streams which offer some of the most prolific catches of trout in the entire nation. The area is beautiful and wild, and if a guide is used who is familiar with the area you may be assured of bountiful catches. Rainbow trout fishing in the Green River is outstanding, along with cutthroat and brookies. Soda Lake and Duck Creek provide brook trout in abundance. Also in southwestern Wyoming, Fremont Lake which has 5,000 acres of very deep waters offers perhaps the largest trout in the state, with mackinaw averaging 15-25 inches and rainbow 15 inches. Many mountain lakes in this area contain the rare goldens, and cutthroat and mackinaw are large and plentiful.

The Snake River in northwestern Wyoming has about 65 miles of prime trout fishing waters with large cutthroats predominant. A float trip on these waters is a thrill long remembered.

The North Fork of the Shoshone River is another lunker-producing trout water. Cutthroats, browns and an occasional brook trout are offered.

It is impossible to list the many prime trout waters, but a partial listing is given here of some of the more popular and productive lakes and streams:

Name of lake or stream	Location of nearest town	Variety of trout
Snake River	Jackson	Cutthroat
Jackson Lake	Jackson	Brown, cutthroat, lake
Clark's Fork River	Cody	Rainbow, cutthroat, brook
Buffalo Bill Reservoir	Cody	Brown, rainbow, cutthroat, lake
Shell Creek	Greybull	Rainbow, cutthroat, brook
Little Horn River	Ranchester	Brown, cutthroat, lake, brook
Yellowtail Reservoir	Lovell	Brown, cutthroat, lake
Boysen Reservoir	Shoshoni	Brown, rainbow
Clear Creek	Buffalo	Brown, rainbow, brook
Sand Creek	Sundance	Brown, rainbow
New Fork River	Pinedale	Brown, rainbow
Pyramid Lake [Pack trip required]	Bounder	Golden
Hams Fork River	Kemmerer	Brown, rainbow, brook
North Platte River	Saratoga	Brown, rainbow
Encampment River	Encampment	Brown, rainbow, brook
Lake Hattie	Laramie	Brown, rainbow
Granite Lake	Cheyenne	Rainbow
Alcova Reservoir	Casper	Rainbow
Pathfinder River	Casper	Rainbow

Where and How to Fly Fish the Midwest

Basically, most anglers think of trout, when you mention fly fishing, but in the midwest it can mean anything from bluegills and crappie to Musky and salmon.

I have experimented over the years with the fly rod and the uses it could have on the various species of fish. Not only from the purist attitude, far from it, using it to cast small spinners, spoons, mini-plugs, ultralight bottom-bumping rigs for walleye and weighted jigs.

Of course, I have not neglected dry and wet patterns, nymphs, midges, streamers, ozarks when warranted by occasion and conditions. To a fly fisherman, nothing is more satisfying than having a trout rise to his dry fly offering, but to the novice, the reward is the first fish that supplies a graceful arc to his rod, even at the expense of using "garden hackle" on a number 10 hook.

ROD...REEL...LINE SELECTION

Best for the majority of fishing in the midwest, the use of the 7½ to 8 foot, 4 ounce rod to handle no. 6 or 7 line, with a leader of 9 feet and 3X tippet for handling flies tied on No. 10 to 14 sizes. The reel can be single action weighing about 4 to 5½ ounces with appropriate backing to fill the spool ½ inch below the reel braces. This basic outfit will handle most stream type fishing and lake shoreline angling.

Rule of thumb concerning terminal tackle has been made simple by the new standards set by the American Fishing Tackle Manufacturers Association (AFT-MA) and copies of recommended line sizes, weights and casting distances are available from most sporting outlets.

Selection of floating or sinking lines is determined by the species of fish the angler is after and conditions that designate where the species will be at any given time. For the panfish, such as bluegill, crappie and white bass I suggest floating lines and many times for bass and northerns in the spring of the year when they are in short water. Sinking line is used for walleyes and in deep lakes during summer when the fish are down. When panfish and bass are in 6 to 8 feet of water, use the new WF7FS, only the forward section sinks as the rest floats. This line is excellent for fishing wets and nymphs.

I suggest tapered leaders for the beginners as they cast easier than the level ones. Leader length is governed by the condition of water, that is clear, low or roily and size of area you are fishing.

Tippet selection is governed by the size of the fly being used and most leader charts are mentioned on the back of packets.

Selection of the tippet size is most important as the presentation of the fly will be sloppy with an improper tippet and wear will be excessive and cause failure of the tippet section.

The conventional fly reel does not have a drag, but rather a clicking type rachet which helps prevent overruns. The larger, heavier salmon-steelhead reels do come with adjustable drags.

Reels can be purchased for about $9.00 and this should give you all the quality you need for some time.

LURES...FLIES...WORMS AND WHEN TO USE THEM

Early spring finds the fly rodder out and working his favorite area, stream, brook, channels off large lakes, weedy shore areas on smaller lakes and isolated spring holes found in Wisconsin, Michigan and Minnesota. Matching the hatch and putting on a fly that closely resembles it, has been the accepted way for successful trout fishing on our streams.

Trout as a rule feed twice a day as rises occur on the stream and at this time dig out a dry pattern to match. Between hatches try wet flies. I have enjoyed some of my best fishing the last hour of daylight and especially after dark. For night fishing, it is of paramount importance that the angler know every inch of the water he is fishing.

DRY FLIES

Brown Hackle	Light Cahill
Beaverkill	Parma Belle
Blue Dun	Coachman
White Miller	Black Gnat
Quill Gordon	Yellow May
March Brown	Muddler

WET FLIES

Black Gnat	Erie
Col. Fuller	White Miller
Dark Cahill	Woolly Worm
McGinty	Ibis
Gray Hackle	Silver Doctor
Yellow May	Blue Dun

POPPERS

Frog	Midgepop
Minnepop	Babypop

NYMPHS AND CREEPERS

Brown Drake	Light stone
Light March	Gray Drake
Dark Stone	Ginger Quill
Tellico	Yellow May

STREAMER FLIES

Black Ghost	Silver Doctor
Mickey Finn	Parma Belle
Grizzly King	Silver Minnow
Supervisor	Edison Tiger
White Marabou	Green Ghost
Chamois Tail	Lord Baltimore

SPINNERS

Single spin, size 00 on No. 10 hook

dressed with fly fleck. Colors in gold, brass and silver.

RIVER RIGS

Spawn sacks weighted with small split shot on number 4 hook, drifted. Single No. 8 hook with nightcrawler hooked once thru head, drifted.

BASS BUG

Deer Hair Popper in various sizes.

FLY RODDING BY SPECIES AND STATES

The following lakes and streams offer the fly fisherman the most opportunities to ply his trade:

ILLINOIS

ILLINOIS for the most part offers the fly rodder excellent panfish and bass fishing thruout the state. The Chain O' Lakes area in northeastern Illinois has 11 lakes to test your prowess. Favorites are Marie, Channel, Petite and Catherine. Spring fishing is by far the best and the many channels that connect the lakes together are the early hotspots. Size 12, wet flies such as McGinty, Ibis and White Millers account for most of the crappie and bluegills. As the water is high and roily, I use a 7½ foot leader, tapered, 4X and maximum casts are 15 to 20 feet. Allow the fly to sink and then work it back in a darting manner, allowing it to dip down but keeping all slack out of the line.

When the water sets down and stabilizes the bass move into the same areas and can be taken with short streamers, size 2 and 4, working them much the same way. Bonus fishing includes northern just about the first week in May. In Illinois, this fishing continues until the water warms, generally the middle of June.

Now its time to switch to 1/32 ounce deer hair jigs and start casting over the low water sand bars for white bass which make up 50 per cent of the fish in the Chain.

Longer casts are needed here and I change to 12 foot leaders, WF7S line

helps to get down where the fish are. Vary the retrieve, in quick darting pulls as white bass react better to a fast moving bait. It is not uncommon for anglers to come back with more than 100 of these scrappy, fine eating fish. Dropper flies work well here and "two at a time" white bass is fast fishing once you locate the school.

Nothing is prettier than to see a fly line caught by the setting evening sun, being worked over lily pads, as the angler puts a deer hair popper-bug on the surface. I believe Illinois lakes are ideally suited for this type of fly fishing as the state contains a splendid bass population thruout its length and breadth. Bug fishing is slow, easy tugs, allowing the rings to disappear before giving it another pull. The hit can come as a slurp with the surface water hardly moving or a headfirst leap into the air with your bug looking like a large wart attached to its lips.

Coho and chinook salmon are now a part of Illinois fishing and the most practical way to fish them is by deep trolling and surface trolling well out in the lake. But at times, the smaller salmon, jacks, come well into fly rod distance and will readily take streamers and large wet flies.

Lake Michigan along Chicago's lakefront has a general depth of 16 feet off the built up rock-pile shoreline and the young salmon, combined with rainbow and brown trout come within easy casting for fly fishing.

The productive fishing is accomplished about 3 to 5 feet below the surface and streamers-wet flies in the larger sizes such as No. 1,2,4 including 4 to 6 inch split-wing streamers have taken many fish. The best areas have been Montrose Harbor, 79th Street, 106th St., Foster Ave. beach and Monroe Harbor. Diversey Harbor has been excellent for brown trout.

WADING AREAS

Wading is popular along the northshore area from Evanston to

Winnetka and public beaches afford access in and around warm water discharge areas from Edison Plants. In October, the brown trout will be spawning in 5 feet of water and rainbow-coho will be in the same water raiding the brown spawn.

I suggest using the heavier type salmon-steelhead rod while fishing Lake Michigan as some of these trout-salmon will be in excess of 10 pounds. Select a rod of 8½ to 9 feet, weighing about 5½ ounces, reel should have drag and ample line capacity, line can be WF7F or WF7SF, 12 foot leader with 0x tippet.

Illinois has many excellent smallmouth bass streams that meander thru the state, gaining access to fish them is the problem. A unique law gives landowners ownership of stream beds to centerline and the water above it. Thus you can be charged with trespassing unless you obtain permission from the owner to fish the stream where his land abuts it.

IOWA

Along Iowa's many trout streams nestled in the rugged limestone valleys of northeast Iowa, fishermen from all the midwest come to enjoy the fine trout fishing.

The state's well-stocked streams with excellent numbers of acclimated fish should tempt even the most pessimistic angler. Iowa has over 100 miles of trout waters and the state stocks eating size trout every few weeks starting in early spring.

The streams of Iowa's "Little Switzerland" without a doubt are some of the state's most beautiful and interesting. The narrow valleys wind sharply and are bounded by abrupt, heavily timbered bluffs.

What more could a person ask than to spend a day along one of Iowa's many fine streams? Whether he is on his first trip or has many years experience, the angler will find a challenge in outwitting the cagey brown, brook, or rainbow, while enjoying some of the most spectacular scenery in the midwest.

In trout territory, the Turkey, Upper Iowa, Yellow and Wapsipinicon rivers and their tributaries reward fishermen with fine smallmouth bass fishing. The Mississippi River, adjacent to trout territory, offers some of the best all-around fishing in the country.

One of the best ways to fly fish is to also camp because there are fine timbered camp areas adjacent to the best streams: *French Creek* — 9 miles northwest of Lansing. *Big and Little Paint Creeks* — North of McGregor, off Highway 13. *Grannis Creek* — 6 miles east of Fayette. *Richmond Springs* — In Backbone State Park, near Strawberry Point. *Dalton Lake* — 1-1/2 miles south of Preston. *Cold Water Creek* — 3 miles northwest of Bluffton. *Canoe Creek* — 8 miles northeast of Decorah. *North Bear Creek* — 3 miles east of Highlandville. *South Bear Creek* — In the town of Highlandville.

WISCONSIN

One of the best fly fishing states in the midwest and blessed with many no-pressure type streams and brooks. Most small streams are overlooked by the angler who is looking to fish the "name" waters. Hence, most of the waters that contain native trout are by-passed and remain fished by local anglers only.

A case in point occured some years ago in northern Wisconsin while I was traveling from Lake Superior to Hayward Lakes area for opening of walleye season. I had stopped for gas in Drummond and noticed a beautiful selection of flies in the showcase of the service station. Talking with the owner, he suggested if I had some time I might drift a few flies thru the White River, a small fast moving stream about 2 miles north. I noted some fair sized pool areas and downstream, a fine shelf of ripples.

The water was basically flat and no evidence of rises, so I selected a No. 12 Quill Gordon and laid it out along the opposite bank, which was heavily overhung. It drifted high and upright in a controlled drift and a slight dimple signaled it had been inspected and refused.

"Fussy," I thought and began to suspect a brown trout had been the intruder. I changed to a No. 10 Henderson and repeated the cast. As the current moved the offering close to the bank he engulfed it and a 2 pound brown slid into my creel. An hour later, 4 brown trout had entered the creel on 3 different patterns but all on the No. 10 hook.

Certainly the brown trout is one of the most difficult to take on the fly and he can tax the best angler on any given day. He can be extremely shy and fussy, many times rising slowly to inspect your offering and then sinking back into the depths. If he moves against your cast he is worth taking a little time to work smaller patterns on him.

Native brook trout can be caught in the smallest of streams, ones that can be jumped by the average angler. I like to select spring holes in northern Wisconsin and they can be found along most of the roads, secondary county roads. A lush growth that occurs along a cold, fast, clear moving brook always invites my inspection as the brookie likes cold water and spring holes are his favorite stamping grounds.

He is not impartial to feeding on insects, other fishes, leeches and small mammals. He will take small spinners, spoons and terrestrials such as grasshopper, beetles and leaf hoppers. Nightcrawlers drifted along the bottom have more than caught their share of this delicious table fish.

The list of Wisconsin trout streams is virtually endless with more than 1400 trout streams listed in the Department of Natural Resources

new book, "WISCONSIN TROUT WATERS" and is available from that dept. at Madison, Wisconsir for $3.50 and is worth every penny. Perhaps I should clarify that the brook trout is the only native trout in Wisconsin and every once in a while I classify some waters as native, but should say natural. The classic wet-dry, streamers, nymphs, midges work well in all of these waters.

OTHER GAME FISHES

Wisconsin anglers are generally after walleye and musky, many times neglecting the excellent bass fishing throughout the state. The small glacier type lakes are a fly rodders dream with fine lily pad areas, gentle sloping shores with good weed cover. Popping bugs and streamers produce above average catches here. Lakes such as Nelson, near Hayward, Geneva at Lake Geneva, Cross near Antioch, Shawano at Shawano, Wissota at Chippewa Falls are just a few.

WHITE BASS

The Wolf river, both above and below the town of Fremont, in early spring hosts one of the finest white bass runs in the country and anglers flock in to reap a harvest of these game fish. Fly angling consists of small ⅛ ounce jigs worked on the sand-bars and bends of the river. Door County in the thumb area of Wisconsin, particularly around Gill's Rock affords us some of the best smallmouth bass fishing. Best time is early June and July with streamers and large wet flies doing well.

Later on, lake trout cruise along shore in August and September and anglers limit out using large split-wing streamers and fast sinking lines. Weather conditions, that is, high winds and cold fronts make this area highly unpredictable.

Northern Pike over the years have provided many hours of pleasure for bay-fishing fly rodders. I like the 7½ foot rod, single action reel with 50 yards of backing (10 lb.

braided nylon will do nicely), line is WF7F with 9 foot leader with 2X tippet and the use of streamers almost exclusively. On waters where large northerns are known to roam, its not a bad idea to bring along that steelhead-salmon rig. Mylar bodied flasher flies by Luhr Jensen work well on large northerns and the yellow-white combination is my personal choice.

MINNESOTA

Most trout streams in Minnesota come under one of the following categories,

P, private ownership with written permission needed.

SE, private owned but easement granted to fishermen.

S, state owned lands open to the public.

The last four rivers mentioned in the chart on page 219 are along Minnesota's northshore and empty into Lake Superior. All have falls above the entry point and early spring finds steelhead trout boiling into the rivers from Lake Superior. All these rivers have early openings and you should check local restrictions before fishing.

It is not unusual to pick up small coho salmon in some of these rivers. Above the falls, you will run into some private stretches of these rivers but permission is given by request. The areas above the falls offer excellent rainbow and brook trout fishing with the standard size stream flies.

Walleye fly fishing is tops in Minnesota, as the state has many large, shallow lakes such as Winnebigoshish at Grand Rapids, Mille Lacs at Garrison, Cass at Cass Lake, Upper and Lower Red Lake at Ponemah, Leech Lake at Walker, Detroit Lakes at Detroit Lakes, are some of my favorites.

Presentation with fly rod is fairly easy due to the short water and the first requisite is to get down on the bottom with your fly-bait-lure. Small spinners, mini-plugs, spoons with fly

fleck and small hooks dressed with crawlers worked slow at the bottom are heavy producers of walleyes. Streamer flies worked slow over sand-bars, minnow imitators, seem to take the bigger fish on these shallow lakes.

Gull Lake above Brainerd, 17 miles long with fine bars and rock piles, is another good lake for lunker walleyes. Best time for fly rod is early evening just as the sun goes down and walleyes pile into the beaches looking for minnows, larvae and insect life shaken loose from rocks and stones by earlier swimmers.

Matching the hatch is not necessary on lakes like these as walleyes will strike anything that looks like a minnow, (streamers) a juicy bug (wet flies) or larvae (nymphs) as long as it's close to the bottom. Gull lake is a chain of 3 interconnected lakes; Margaret on the back side is superior for large bass in the evening with poppers in the pads.

Fine concentrations of bluegill and bass are found in the north end of the lake and the channel that goes into Margaret Lake. For the bluegills, size 10-12 poppers in red-yellow and black worked slowly are best. Bluegill size is large for this spring fed lake and one pounders are common. Shoreline fishing around the lily pads on the east side of the channel is the best.

GRAVEL BOTTOMS

Wilson's Bay at the south end of the lake is weedy, shallow water over a sand and gravel bottom, with an occasional rock "crib" that makes it perfect for crappies and smallmouth bass. Small 1/32 ounce jigs in white deer hair with a No. 12 White miller as a dropper are deadly for giant crappies up to two pounds.

Broad daylight didn't seem to make much difference to the "smallies" as they hit well on top-water bugs and poppers. Early May and into June is by far the best time

for all species on Gull Lake. Many other fine lakes dot the area and the Nisswa Bait shop at Nisswa is fishing headquarters for the area.

Northern Minnesota with its fine glacier lakes such as Rainy, Basswood, Snowbank, Pine, Seagull, Trout, and Pike offer lake trout fishing, small and largemouth bass, walleye, whitefish, northern and jumbo pan fish for the fly rodder. I would have to classify Basswood as one of the best smallmouth lakes in the north American continent.

In late June the smallies start to rub up against the shorelines and streamers, wets, dries, nymphs all pay off with this high jumping acrobat. Points of land that tumble rocks into the water edge are fine playgrounds for both fish and anglers. Narrows of islands, where the speed of water picks up are natural areas for "smallies". Many feeder streams to these lakes offer excellent river-type bass fishing in the early spring as the bass move in to spawn, using streamers and flies.

The Mississippi River, where it broadens to form Lake Pepin on the eastern edge of Minnesota at the town of Wabasha, has some of the best jump fishing for huge white bass in the midwest. In mid-August, the shad minnows move into the lake and the hungry white bass drive them to the surface in a feeding frenzy, turning the water into a foaming cauldron.

Don't bother to use fancy tackle here, 8 foot rod, the cheaper level line, leader is straight 6 pound test mono, mini 3-way swivel with short dropper and long dropper with a red-headed, white deer hair jig on each end. Not the perfect way to use the fly rod, but what action when the "stripers" hit two at a time. Best method is to glass the lake surface until you see the boiling baitfish on top, run the boat up to the edge on the leeward side and start casting. Short casts of 10 feet are the norm, allow the jigs to settle a few feet and start a moderate retrieve.

Solid hits will peel line from the reel and as the fish makes his run, another is going to sock the other jig as it dances along. These fish average close to two pounds with lunkers approaching 3 pounds. Its not so much the four pounds of fish that are on the line as it is the fact that they're both going in opposite directions at the same time. The six pound mono allows you to pick them up by the swivel and pop them into the boat without the use of a net. Two white bass in the same net is pure murder to untangle.

Suddenly, the school leaves the area and again its time to start looking for surface action elsewhere. On windy days when the shad stay below the surface watch the gulls for the tip-off where the fish are feeding as they penetrate the water in steep dives. Feeding gulls always mean white bass on Lake Pepin.

MICHIGAN

Trout fishing is by far the most popular type of fishing in Michigan and the fly rod takes its place at the top, when it comes to lake run steelhead, browns, brook, lake trout and splake. Both coho and Chinook salmon have also been introduced to the fly fisher's tackle and in some cases left it a little worse for wear.

As this case in point, when I was bank fishing the Manistee and in this particular stretch there were only small areas to wade and some anglers across from me were doing just that. One of them had a slashing strike and the battle was begun, even tho it was short lived, the salmon took off with two wild leaps and made a downstream run that left the angler with the rod over his head and every inch of backing tearing down the river. He had no chance to move with the fish and pick up line.

If you can stop the first run, you have a fifty-fifty chance of at least seeing your fish.

The streams that run into the

Great lakes have early spring and late fall runs for lake run rainbows and most banks are lined with anglers soaking spawn-sacks, nightcrawlers, drifting streamers and flies and most anything else that they think will earn them a trout. Some of these rivers are kept open with a special season for this fishing. Its a good idea to check local restrictions before starting out.

Lake fishing in Michigan is always close at hand with the many glacier waters that dot the entire state. Starting with the south central area: Coldwater Lake at Coldwater, Klinger Lake at White Pidgeon, Sturgeon Lake at Mendon, Devil's Lake at Devils Lake.

Northeast-central contains Maceday west of Pontiac, where splake trout can be taken near shore in early spring and late fall. The lake also contains rainbow and brown trout. Oxbow Lake west of Pontiac has good size rainbows, northerns and panfish. In the north section, Houghton and Higgins Lakes supply action with walleyes, bass, northerns and large panfish.

Northwest area has Torch, Crystal, Charlevoix Lakes for walleye, bass, panfish.

Every year great migrations of lake perch move into the Lake St. Clair area near Metropolitan Beach and anglers using all kinds of tackle have a field day catching these scrappy fish. Sizes range from½ to 2 pounds.

Smallmouth bass fishing is excellent near the mouth of the Detroit River but in the lake proper, around small, rock edged bays on the Michigan side. Artificial crayfish and grasshoppers work well in the fly rod sizes.

INDIANA

The Hoosier state has long been noted for its bass and catfish angling. Many major rivers run thru its length and breadth, although some are polluted in varying degrees, it is not unusual to find good fishing on them.

The major streams get all the pressure in Indiana and I would suggest trying the smaller ones that basically have to be waded or bank-fished. Access to these streams has never been a serious problem in the state and permission is readily granted by owners. It is not unusual to have the entire stream to yourself and most all these small areas have excellent populations of basses, large and smallmouth, catfish, and panfish.

Major lakes include: Lake Shafer, Salamonie Res., Mississinewa Res., Monroe Res., Lake Greenwood and Morse Res., Lake Lemon and Lake Freeman.

Open pit strip mining has also provided anglers with fine areas to fish the basses around the Clinton, Brazil sections on the western border.

Some trout are stocked on streams but it's on a put and take basis and lists of stockings can be obtained from the conservation department.

Although Indiana has only a small section of land bordering Lake Michigan, the spring and summer runs of coho and chinook salmon have provided fine angling from Michigan City to East Chicago. Some of the best areas are: Michigan City, Burns Ditch, Millers Beach and the Dunes. Heavy schools work close to shore during April, May and again later in Sept., Oct. Basic salmon techniques are used here as in Illinois fishing.

There are many good fly fishing spots in the midwest. Some of the more productive areas are shown in the charts on the opposite page.

ILLINOIS FLY FISHING AREAS

NAME	LOCATION	SPECIES
Chain O' Lakes	Northeastern Illinois	Crappie, bass, northerns
Carlyle Resevoir	Vandalia	Crappie and bass
Apple River	Warren	Put and take trout
Kankakee River	Bloomington	Smallmouth and walleyes
Kiswaukee River	Belvidere	Smallmouth bass
Siloan Springs Lake	Sterling	Smallmouth bass
Andalusia Islands	Mississippi River	Topwater bass bugging
Lake Michigan	Waukegan, south to Indiana line	Trout and salmon.

INDIANA FLY FISHING AREAS

NAME	SPECIES	NAME	SPECIES
Tippecanoe R.	Bass, cat, panfish	Kankakee R.	Northern, walleye, bass
Eel River	Smallies, catfish	St. Joseph R.	Smallies, catfish
Salamonie R.	Bass, catfish	Sugar Creek	Basses, catfish
Deer Creek	Basses, panfish	Wabash R.	Basses, catfish

TROUT STREAMS IN MICHIGAN

NAME	TOWN	SPECIES
Au Sable River	Oscoda	Brook, brown, rainbow
Au Gres	Au Gres	Brown, rainbow
Muskegon River	Newaygo	Brown, rainbow
Pere Marquette	Scottville	Lake rainbows, brown
Manistee River	Manistee	Salmon, rainbow, brown
Platte River	Honor	Salmon, rainbow, brown
Betsie River	Beulah	Rainbow, brown
Pigeon River	Afton	Brown, rainbow
Two Heart R.	McMillan	Rainbow, salmon, brown, brook

MINNESOTA TROUT STREAMS

NAME	TOWN	COUNTY	LENGTH	TROUT	Cate.
Trout Run Cr.	Saratoga	Winona	11 mi.	Brown	SE
Whitewater River	Elba	Wabasha	7 mi.	Brown	S,P
Bee Creek	Spring Gr.	Houston	1 mi.	Various	SE
Baptism River	Silver Bay	Lake		Rainbow	
Temperance R.	Schroeder	Lake		Steelhead	
Poplar River	Lutsen	Lake		Steelhead	
Knife River	Knife	Lake		Rainbow	

WISCONSIN FLY FISHING AREAS

NAME	TOWN	COUNTY	LENGTH	SPECIES
Devils Creek	Mellon	Ashland	1.5 mi.	Brook, brown, rainbows
Flag River	Port Wing	Bayfield	5 mi.	Brook, brown, rainbow
White River	Drummond	Bayfield	2 mi.	Brown
L. Sioux	Bayview	Bayfield	6 mi.	Brook, brown, rainbow
Brule	Florence	Florence	11.6 mi.	Brook, brown, rainbow
Elvoy Creek	Brule	Forest	12.3 mi.	Brook, brown
Spencer Creek	Padus	Forest	4.9 mi.	Brook
Beef River	Price	Jackson	3 mi.	Brook, brown
Prairie River	Parrish	Langlade	8.6 mi.	Brook, brown, rainbow
Pine River	Doering	Lincoln	9 mi.	Brook, brown
Plover River	Hogarty	Marathon	10 mi.	Brook, brown, rainbow
Oconto River	Breed	Menominee	19 mi.	Brook, brown, rainbow
Pike River	Goodman	Marinette	30 mi.	Brook, brown, rainbow

Fly Fishing Areas in Canada

Alberta

Trout are the chief game fish in the mountainous western portion of this province. This is the area to head for since the plains region is mainly given over to commercial fishing, which has developed into a huge industry.

The headwaters of the Athabasca River system are noted for native char. Arctic grayling and trout.

Cutthroats are found largely in the southwestern area of the province in such waters as Daisy Creek, Dutch Creek, Racehorse Creek and the Livingstone River.

Rainbows are not only stocked in Alberta, but are native to the Athabasca River. They may be most successfully fished in the Bow River.

Brown trout may be found in the west-central part of the province in such streams as Dogpound Creek, Fallen Timber Creek and the Raven River.

Look for brookies in Elbow Lake, Rat Lake, Lookout Creek and Alford Creek.

Dolly Vardens may be found in waters throughout the entire province of Alberta. Large Specimens have been taken from the Wildhay River, Musked River and Cardinal River.

BRITISH COLUMBIA FISHERIES MANAGEMENT

Modern fisheries management began in British Columbia in 1948 with the appointment of the first trained biologist. Prior to that time fresh-water fisheries were administered with little professional guidance other than in the fields of law enforcement and the operation of hatcheries.

The first task was to make extensive biological surveys of lakes, streams, and fish populations to find out what existed, and to develop some rational basis for angling regulations and the planting of hatchery trout. When the post-war boom of industrial development burst upon the Province, it was quickly necessary to develop means of tackling all the problems and conflicts between recreational fishing and the use of water for industrial and commerical enterprises. It soon became necessary to have Fisheries Biologists stationed in the various regions of the Province as well as a supporting group of specialists at Brach headquarters.

Today, fisheries management, in pursuing its main objectives of protecting and enhancing recreational fishing in the fresh waters of the Province, has six principal functions:

1. Formulation and Enforcement of Regulations.—Fishery regulations are enacted by order in Council of the Federal Government on the recommendations of the Fish and Wildlife Branch. A guiding principle in these recommendations is that restrictions to angling should be as few and as uncomplicated as possible.

2. Fish Culture—Over 400 lakes, which otherwise would produce little or no fishing, are regularly stocked with young trout produced by the branch hatchery system.

3. Habitat Protection—Desirable species of fish can exist and flourish only if suitable natural environment is available to them. A great deal of effort is expended to prevent ex-

This is a typical small, fast water stream that is ideal for fly fishing as it can be easily waded or fished from shore. The rocky bottom would make felt soled waders a necessity for safety. Both brook trout and rainbows would be found in this kind of water. The flycaster is sending his line across the current and rightly so because brookies often face the bank, not upstream.

cessive damage to natural aquatic habitat by dams, irrigation diversions, logging, flood-control works, and pollution of all types.

4. Research—Additional factual knowledge of fish and their environment is being continuously obtained. Some difficult and long-term studies will lead to improved fishing in the future. Other short-term investigations are conducted to solve immediate management problems.

5. Habitat Improvement—Positive improvement of fish habitat is carried out by altering stream channels to provide trout-spawning, by diverting streams to improve lake conditions, by removing obstructions in streams, and by eradicating coarse fish from lakes.

6. Communication with the Public—Since fresh-water fishing is a common property resource, there is a recognized need for close and continuous communication between fisheries management and concerned organizations and members of the public. This inter-change of information and opinion takes place in a variety of ways at all levels of the Fish and Wildlife Branch.

SKEENA WATERSHED

THE SKEENA RIVER, which drains an area of fifteen thousand square miles in the west central portion of the Province, is the second largest river wholly within British Columbia. It provides a large portion of the Province's fishery resource and has become known only recently as a mecca for sport fishermen. Although the main stem of the Skeena is not extensively utilized by sportsmen, most of its many tributaries provide excellent fishing for anadromous species (salmon and trout). Expansion of logging activity in the forests of the Skeena watershed has made these tributaries accessible. Rivers such as the Kispiox and

Kitsumkalum have become world famous as a result of producing the world's record rod-caught chinook salmon and steelhead. Listed below in sequence upstream from the Skeena's mouth are the most important tributaries.

LAKESLE RIVER: A short river draining Lakelse Lake into the Skeena. This river is fairly accessible by road from Terrace. Accomodation in hotels and motels in Terrace is excellent. There is also a Provincial Park site in Lakelse Lake. This river provides good fishing throughout the year, with the exception of a period of high water in the spring. *Steelhead*—October to March. Spinning, bait, and fly. *Cutthroat*—March and April. Spinning or fly casting usually with silver-bodies lures or flies. *Chinook Salmon*—There is a small early run of chinook salmon. These are fished for by spinning and fly fishing. *Coho Salmon*—September and October. Excellent fishing; spinning with crocodiles (spoons) T-spoons, flies. *Dolly Varden*—Good fishing throughout the year, generally with bait, such as salmon eggs and flies.

KITSUMKALUM RIVER: This river is located one mile west of the town of Terrace. Most fishing occurs at the mouth of the Kitsumkalum River where it enters the Skeena. The river is mainly known for its salmon runs, but does produce a few steelhead. *Chinook Salmon*—July and August. Spinning with large wobblers (1 oz.) or bait fishing with salmon roe are the common methods of fishing. *Coho Salmon*—September and October. Spinning with wobblers and T-spoons. *Dolly Varden*—Good throughout the year, using bait, spinning lures and flies.

ZYMORTZ (COPPER) RIVER: This river is located approximately five miles east of Terrace.

It has an excellent coho salmon and steelhead fishery. *Coho*—

September, October. Spinning with wobblers, flies. *Steelhead*—October to May. Spinning lures, bait, and fly.

KITWANGA RIVER: Located approximately 30 miles west of Hazelton on north shore of the Skeena. This is a short river (approximately 12 miles long), draining Kitwanga Lake, and produces excellent coho and steelhead fishing. Nearby accomodation is limited, but is good at Hazelton. *Coho Salmon*—Late August to October. Spinning with wobblers and T-spoons and flies. *Steelhead*—Late August to March. Spinning lures, bait, and fly.

KISPIOX RIVER: This is a fairly large tributary of the Skeena which enters the main river near Hazelton. Accomodation is available at Hazelton and at Wookies' Fishing Camp, 17 miles up the Kispiox Valley. Trailer and tenting space is available at the Indian Reserve near the mouth of the river.

There is a roe ban on the Kispiox River; also, angling from a boat is prohibited. *Chinook Salmon*—June and July. Spinning with large wobblers and flies. *Coho Salmon*—Late August, September and October. Spinning with wobblers and T-spoons and flies. *Steelhead*—Late August to March. Spinning and fly fishing.

BABINE RIVER: This is an excellent stream to fish for rainbow trout, coho, chinook salmon, and steelhead, in the early fall, near its source at the outlet of Babine Lake. Accessibility is limited but there are several fishing lodges located at Smithers Landing (Tukii Lodge) and Nor-lakes Lodge. These lodges may be contacted via Smithers, B. C.

MORICE RIVER: This river is approximately 50 miles long from its source at Morice Lake to its confluence with the Bulkley River near Houston, B. C. The river is accessible by road over most of its length and accomodation can be obtained at Houston or Smithers.

Fishing with roe is prohibited. *Chinook Salmon*—July and August, Spinning with large wobblers and T-spoons, flies. *Coho Salmon*—Late August to October. Spinning with wobblers and T-spoons, flies. *Steelhead*—Late August to March. Spinning and fly fishing. Fly-fishing on this river is particularly good.

BULKEY RIVER: The Bulkey River is one of the main tributaries of the Skeena and below its confluence with the Telkwa River at Telkwa is usually highly coloured with glacial ice. Below this junction, most of the fishing is done at the mouths of creeks entering the Bulkey. The main Bulkey is fished near Barrett Station, approximately 8 miles west of Houston. All anadromous species, plus resident rainbow, cutthroat, and Dolly Varden may be caught in season. Fishing is best with spinning lures, bait, or flies.

NORTHERN DISTRICT-
WESTERN PART

VANDERHOOF

CLUCULZ LAKE: Approximately 12 miles long, 44 miles west of Prince George along Highway No. 16, ice leaves the lake approximately May 15th, freezes up in late November or December. There are three resorts in operation on the lake, housekeeping cabins, boats and motors. Trolling for rainbow and char throughout the season. Char have been taken up to 30 pounds, rainbow up to 2 pounds.

CALDER (HORSESHOE) LAKE: This lake is situated approximately fifty miles north of Fort St. James on the McKenzie Highway. Char are taken up to around five pounds; rainbow trout up to around one pound. These latter fish are not

plentiful. Excellent camping area. No facilities available.

CUNNINGHAM LAKE: Approximately 20 miles long, situated west of Stuart Lake, no roads into this area. This lake can be reached by aircraft—either Northern Mountain Air Lines or Omineca Air Lines, Fort St. James, or by pack trail, no cabins or resorts on this lake. Open in May and freezes up in November. Char up to 20 pounds, rainbow trout around 5 pounds, fly fishing very good at mouths of streams entering the lake during the months of July and August.

ED FISHER LAKE: Approximately 6 miles long, located near the Highway No. 16. Open about May 15th, freezes up in November. Cabins available, no boats or motors. Char fishing very good on breakup and rainbow trout during June, July, August and September. Char upl to 15 pounds and rainbows up to 3 pounds, trolling and some fly fishing. Contact Wilfred Lobley, Vanderhoof, B.C.

FRANCOIS LAKE: Approximately 60 miles long, located along the route of Highway 16 from Burns Lake to Fraser Lake. Two roads on east end of Lake serve this area. Lake is about 6 miles south of the highway, one road goes in from Endako another from Fraser Lake. Cabins and boats are available. Opens up about May 15th and freezes up in November. Char fishing very good during the season, up to 20 libs. Rainbow trout up to 5 pounds, mostly trolling in this area. Very good fly fishing on Stellako River which leaves lake at the Eastern end and empties into Fraser Lake. Fishing best during July, August and September.

FINGER LAKE: This lake is situated two miles north of Tatuk via a good foot trail. Rainbow trout

taken up to one pound. Fair fishing through July, August and September.

FISH LAKE: Is situated approximately fifty-five miles south of Vanderhoof on the Kenney Dam Road opens May 24th. Rainbow trout taken on the troll up to one and one half pounds. No resort facilities available. Fair camp site.

FISH LAKE: Is situated at Mile 32 on the McKenzie Highway. Rainbow trout are taken up to two pounds on the troll, and fly. No facilities available at this lake. However, there is a fair camping ground for tenting.

FRASER LAKE: Situated twenty-five miles west of Vanderhoof on Highway 16. There are excellent facilities available at the Provincial Government Campsite known as Beaumont Park. This is a fair lake for char fishing. Rainbow trout are taken up to one and one half pounds.

GERMANSEN LAKE: Approximately twelve miles long, located near Germansen Landing opens June 15th. Rainbow trout taken up to two pounds. Cabins and boats are available. It might be mentioned that the road into Germansen Lake is not in condition for an automobile. This is strictly a road for a vehicle with plenty of clearance.

INZANA LAKE: Approximately 20 miles long, located west of the McKenzie Highway about 40 miles north of Fort St. James, no auto roads into this lake, trails lead off the highway into the lake, pack horse or by foot; good lake for aircraft, no cabins or boats available. Char and rainbow taken mostly by trolling, char about 10 pounds and trout up to 3 pounds. Opens about May 15th and freezes up end of October or November. For cabins contact

George Fleger, Ft. St. James, B.C., or Northern Mountain Air Lines; 20 minutes via aircraft from Ft. St. James.

NULKI LAKE: Approximately 5 miles long, located about 12 miles south of Vanderhoof on good highway, this road proceeds to the Kenny Dam. Opens about May 15th and freezes up in November or December. Very good rainbow trout fishing up to 3 pounds, cabins and boats available, this lake is also good lake for landing aircraft. Trolling and fly fishing best during July, August and September. Lodge available at lake. Cafe facilities and landing strip for wheel planes as well as float planes.

NATION LAKES: Situated approximately 115 miles north of Fort St. James. Excellent fly fishing at the mouth of the Nation River which flows out of Chuchi Lake. Rainbow are taken up to one pound. Rainbow are taken in Chuchi Lake and all the lakes connecting Chuchi, which is known as the Nation Lakes Chain, up to around four pounds and char are taken on the troll up to seventeen pounds. Excellent facilities are available at Chuchi Lake such as cabins, boats, and motors for hire. There are also fishing guides available at Chuchi Lake for any person wanting to venture through the rivers connecting these lakes.

NALTESBY LAKE: Approximately 10 miles long, located along the Old Telegraph Trail between Vanderhoof and Quesnel, about 30 miles south-east of Vanderhoof. Fishing for rainbow up to 1 pound, mostly trolling, no cabins or boats available, good camping sites. Open from May 15th onwards. Not considered a good fishing lake.

OONA LAKE, ORMOND LAKE, TOP LAKE, & PETA LAKE: Are located by travelling through the Nautley Indian Reservation at the east end of Fraser Lake and are reached via a forestry access road which is in good condition at a distance of approximately eighteen miles from Fraser Lake. These are small lakes about 1 to 2 miles long and located quite close together. These lakes open up about the end of May and freeze up at the end of October. Char and Rainbow.

PINCHI LAKE: Situated thirty miles north of Fort St. James via the McKenzie Hwy. This lake is fair for char fishing and rainbow trout are also taken up to two pounds. Pinchi Creek, flowing out of Pinchi Lake and into Stuart Lake, is excellent for fly fishing during the month of July. Housekeeping facilities are available at this lake, also boats and motors are available for hire.

STUART LAKE: Situated at Fort St. James which is forty-one miles north of Vanderhoof. This lake produces char up to thirty pounds and rainbow trout have been taken up to seventeen pounds on the troll. This lake is approximately sixty miles in length. Boats and motors are available for rent and several modern motels are available together with a modern hotel. This lake is connected with the Tachie River, Trembleur Lake, Middle River, and Takla Lake. There is also excellent fly fishing in the streams flowing into Takla Lake.

TREMBLEUR LAKE: Approximately 25 miles in length, this lake can be reached from Stuart Lake by boat, no roads into this area, this lake is served by camps located on Stuart Lake and take their guests by launch or outboard into the area. Opens about May 15th and freezes up in late October or November. Rainbow trout up to 16 pounds have been taken and Char about 12 pounds. This lake is especially good during July, August and September. There are no cabins as yet on the lake, Trembleur Lake is a good lake for aircraft landing, the waterway connecting Stuart Lake to Trembleur, "Tachie River" should not be navigated unless a person has someone with them with a knowledge of the river as there are several rapids in the river which are quite dangerous if not taken properly. Indian Guides can be hired for the day to take boats up the river and return if necessary at almost any time.

TACHICK LAKE: Five miles south west of Vanderhoof. Opens approximately May 15. Rainbow trout taken up to four pounds. Resort facilities available and also boats and motors for rent.

TAKLA LAKE: Approximately 60 miles long, opens about May 15th and freezes up at the end of October or November. This lake is located north-west of Trembleur Lake and is one of the chain of lakes making the Stuart Lake Waterways. This lake like the others previously mentioned is reached by boat from Ft. St. James on Stuart Lake. This lake is joined to Trembleur Lake by the Middle River approximately 16 miles in length; the water on this lake is quite easily navigated at all times during the season. This lake is excellent for aircraft and there are very good camping grounds on it. Char and rainbow trout are the main fish caught there as elsewhere, fishing is very good during the months of July, August and September. Char taken up to 12 pounds and rainbow up to 15 pounds; trolling is largely done on this lake, fly fishing is very good on the creek outlets into this lake. Fishing camp and cabins at Takla Narrows; Contact Jack Roach. Lodge known as Takla Rainbow Camp.

TATUK LAKE: Situated sixty-two miles south of Vanderhoof and is reached via a forestry access road on the Sinkut Mountain trail. This is an excellent lake for trout fishing and

This brook trout being taken in shallow water located in deep brush and tree cover. It is a small stream, typical of the type water that brook trout favor. Wading is easy, but casting here could be a problem because of the lack of room.

kokanee. No resort facilities available at the east end of the lake. By proceeding ten miles west by boat on the lake, there are facilities available and reservations to use this camp can be made through the Nulki Lake Resort at Vanderhoof.

TEZZERON LAKE: Is situated approximately four miles north of Pinchi Lake. No facilities are available at this lake. Char are taken up to eighteen pounds on the troll.

BURNS LAKE

AUGIER LAKE: Approximately 12 miles long, situated approximately 20 miles northwest of Burns Lake. Good char fishing and trout fishing throughout the summer months. Beautiful lake, 18 miles out of Babine Lake Road and 5 miles north in on a good gravel road. No cabins or boats but good camp sites.

BURNS LAKE: Approximately 30 miles long, docks and wharfs right in the Village. Hotels and auto camps, ice leaves the lake approximately April 15th, freeze up in November. In early spring char fishing very good, all during the summer fair char fishing up to 25 pounds and trout up to 2 or 3 pounds.

DECKER LAKE: Approximately 6 miles long, is about 1 mile west of Burns Lake and is joined onto Burns Lake by the Endako River, fair fly fishing in this slow running slough between the lakes. Char and trout the same as Burns Lake.

DIVISION LAKE: Approximately 1 mile long, situated 9 miles north of Burns Lake on the Babine Road, fish up to 2 pounds (rainbow) fair fly fishing in early mornings and evenings. No cabins or boats, plenty of good camp sites.

KAEGER LAKE: Small trout very plentiful, one mile north of the Village of Burns Lake. Early spring

the road suitable only to jeep travel, in summer any car may travel the road. The rainbow trout average about 9 inches. No cabins or boats.

NADINA LAKE: Situated approximately 75 miles out on Tahtsa Access Road, southwest of Burns Lake. Deep trolling for rainbow trout up to 15 pounds, very little fly fishing for some reasons unknown.

PINKUT LAKE: Situated approximately 15 miles out on the Babine Lake Road northwest of Burns Lake Village, lovely beach and camp site (Parks Branch camp-site). No boats or cabins, fishing for trout and char quite good. The trout are around 1-2 pounds, and char as in all other lakes from small to 30 pounds.

SWEENEY LAKE: Approximately 94 miles out on Tahtsa Access Road, plenty of trout up to 2 pounds. No boats or cabins. Lake is approximately 1 mile long.

TAGETOCHLAIN LAKE: Situated up the Tahtsa Access Road and 1 mile off same on a good solid road, but rough. Lake is approximately 10 miles long, very pretty spot, no cabins or rental of boats, trout up to 3 pounds, char to 25 pounds.

TALTAPIN LAKE: Approximately 12 miles long. Very good lake for deep char fishing. Situated 24 miles north of Burns Lake, 12 miles out on the Baine Road and 12 miles in on a good gravel logging road. Trout also plentiful during July, August and September. No cabins or boats, but good camping grounds.

TCHESINKUT LAKE: Approximately 10 miles south of Burns Lake on the Francois Lake Road. Rainbow trout to 3 pounds, char to 42 pounds, a very pretty lake right on the road. Boats and cabins available

at 3 resorts along the Highway and lake.

TWINKLE LAKE: Approximately 85 miles out of Tahtsa Access Road, lake is approximately 6 miles long, plenty of small rainbow trout up to 2 pounds, no boats or cabins, but good camp site. There is a sign on the road to show drive into lake approximately 250 yards off road.

SOUTH OF FRANCOIS LAKE - ACROSS FERRY:

BINTA LAKE: Very fine char and trout fishing from breakup about May 1st to Nov. 1st. Rough road approximately 3 miles in from Uncha Lake. Moose Horn Lodge have guides who will take guests into this lake too.

OOTSA LAKE: Since the flooding of this area by Alcan, fishing is difficult except along the shore where one can, at times, get fair fishing for trout. To fish the lake and other lakes adjoining it, such as Big Eutsuk and others on the circle trip, guides are recommended, unless a person is well experienced and has good equipment.

TAKYSIE LAKE: Approximately 30 miles south of Burns Lake in the Grassy Plains area. Lake is approximately 6 miles long, rainbow trout up to 3 pounds. Boats available, but no cabins.

UNCHA LAKE: To your left off ferry, 10 miles south Uncha Lake is quite good fishing from break-up until freeze up. Lake is approximately 12 miles long. Rainbow trout to 3 pounds and large char. Moose Lodge has cabins and also a dining room. Boats are available.

SMITHERS

BABINE LAKE: One hundred and ten miles of lake, 45 miles from Smithers by car. Major salmon spawning area of Skeena River system, Cutthroat trout to 2 pounds;

These fine looking fly waters are the swift currents of rapids near Hatchet Lake in Saskatchewan, Canada. The angler is near the end of a battle with a Grayling, the fish with the sail-like dorsal fin. Grayling are scattered throughout the most northern range of Saskatchewan and most areas are accessible only by fly-in bush planes.

Rainbow to 14 pounds; Char to 35 pounds. Fly fishing and trolling for rainbow trout is at its very best during June, July, and August. Cabins and boats available at Topley Landing, Babine and Smithers Landings. Parks Branch Campsite—Topley Landing.

BABINE RIVER: Forty-five miles from Smithers by car and 25 miles by boat to the very best fly fishing for rainbow trout up to 6 pounds throughout the season. Cabins and boats available same as for Babine Lake.

BILL NYE (HELENE) LAKE: Fourteen miles west of Houston, 4 miles from Highway 16. This lake has been stocked with Kamloops trout and produces excellent fly fishing and trolling for same up to 4 pounds. No accomodation but good camping area. Lake approximately 1 mile long.

BULKLEY RIVER (HAGUELGATE): Two miles from Hazelton on Highway No. 16. Bait casting for salmon - steelhead in the fall. Excellent bait fishing for Jack Springs in late May and early June. Hotel accommodation at Hazelton, New Hazelton, and south Hazelton.

BULKLEY RIVER (MORICETOWN): Nineteen miles from Smithers on Highway No. 16. Spring and cohoe fishing through summer; steelhead in the fall; bait casting. Excellent sport fishing is obtained with most conventional types of spinner. Fly fishing for steelhead has met with some success. Hotel and motel accommodation at Smithers.

BULKLEY RIVER (TELKWA): Same as Bulkley River (Moricetown).

BULKLEY (HOUSTON) RIVER: Three miles from Houston at Junction of Bulkley and Morice Rivers, 1 mile from Highway No. 16, steelhead, rainbow and Dolly Varden, steelhead up to 20 pounds.

Use of large plastic steelhead flies has given wonderful sport. Hotel & Motel accommodation at Houston.

CHAPMAN LAKE: Thirty miles from Smithers by road. Rainbow and cutthroat trout up to 2 pounds, char up to 8 pounds, fly fishing and trolling - good camping sites. Lake is 4 miles long.

ELWYN, SWANS AND DAY LAKES: Grouped near Forestdale 75 miles east of Smithers by car. These lakes are not fished to any extent due to their location and lack of accommodation though they produce char and cutthroat which may be caught on a troll.

FISHPAN (GOVERNMENT) LAKE: On Highway No. 16, 30 miles east of Smithers, covers approximately 30 acres. Cutthroat trout up to 1 1/2 pounds, caught on fly throughout the season. An excellent spot for the traveller to spend a few hours or camp overnight when passing through the district. Generally this lake is heavily stocked but periodically is cleaned out by so called "winter kill."

FULTON LAKE: Thirty-five miles from Topley by car. Good fly fishing and trolling for cutthroat and rainbow trout, also some char. No accommodation, but good camping sites.

FULTON RIVER: Twenty-eight miles from Topley by car. "Millionaires" Pool at the base of the falls in the Fulton River is known as such for the fine rainbow trout up to 4 pounds, taken on flies throughout the season. Usually best in July and August. Good cabins available, also Parks Branch campsite.

GUESS (PARADISE) LAKE: Approximately 20 miles from Smithers, can drive to lake but last 5 miles rough. Cutthroat trout up to 3/4 pound, taken on fly. This is a

high altitude lake and is heavily stocked though the fish are small. Good camping.

IRRIGATION (DUNALTEN) LAKE: Nine miles west from Houston on Highway No. 16. About 50 acres of Lake supporting good population of cutthroat and rainbow trout up to 1 1/2 pounds. Trolling throughout season. Good dry fly fishing in June and early July. No accommodation, good camping.

JOHNSON (VALLEE) LAKE: Ten miles west of Houston on Highway No. 16, about 50 acres of lake supporting heavy population of cutthroat and rainbow trout up to 2 pounds. Excellent fly fishing and trolling throughout the season. cabins on lake & good camping sites.

KATHLYN LAKE: Three miles from Smithers on Highway No. 16, cutthroat trout up to 1 1/2 pounds taken on troll. Cabins and boats available.

KISPIOX RIVER: Eight miles from Hazelton, good road. Bait casting and fly fishing for steelhead in the spring and fall, fast clear water. Salmon, rainbow and cutthroat trout and Dolly Varden. Good campsites, steelhead are large. Hotel accommodation at Hazelton, cabins available at Kispiox Village & at 19 mile.

KITSEGUECLA LAKE: Twenty-five miles from Smithers (west by car.) High altitude lake heavily stocked with cutthroat trout up to 1 1/2 pounds. Excellent fly fishing and trolling throughout the season. No accommodation. Hotels, etc., at Smithers, good camping sites.

KITWANGA LAKE: Thirty-five miles west of Hazelton. Supports good rainbow trout to 3 pounds but due to its location and lack of accommodation is not popular.

KITWANGA RIVER: Twenty-five miles from Hazelton (west).

Fisherman above is battling a Grayling in a fish rich Saskatchewan River. Waters of this type are not safe for wading, but there are many spots that are accessible and suitable for fly casting. Most of the Grayling waters in this province can only be reached by float plane or back-packing.

Steelhead up to 26 pounds taken on spinners in spring and fall. No accommodation.

LACROIX (ROUND) LAKE: Fifteen miles east Smithers and 6 miles from Telkwa by car. Cutthroat trout up to 2 pounds and Kamloops trout to 4 pounds mostly trolling. This lake has been stocked with Kamloops trout for a number of years and is now showing results. Hotel accommodation and parks Branch campsite at Telkwa.

McLURE LAKE: One mile from Telkwa. Cutthroat trout up to 2 pounds, rainbow trout to 4 pounds taken on troll. Parks Branch campsites. Hotel accommodation at Telkwa.

MOOSESKIN JOHNNY (HOWSON) LAKE: Thirty-five miles from Telkwa on foot or pack train. Is a headwater of the Telkwa River system and is heavily stocked with cutthroat trout up to 1 1/2 pounds, which may be caught on fly or spinner—no accommodation.

MORICE RIVER: Empties into Bulkley River. Three miles from Houston - approximately 50 miles long. Steelhead up to 25 pounds, rainbow up to 5 pounds, cutthroat up to 2 pounds, also Dolly Varden, coho and spring salmon. Bait casting, plugs and spinners, and fly fishing for steelhead. Good campsites. Hotel and motel accommodation at Houston.

MORICE LAKE: At head of Morice River, 45 minutes by air from Burns Lake or Smithers, or on good gravel road 52 miles from Houston. Rainbow trout to 5 pounds, cutthroat up to 2 pounds, and char up to 12 pounds. This lake is situated on the east side of and at the base of the Cascade Mountains Range, is approximately 25 miles long and is noted for quick and violent storms. Excellent fly fishing in lower end of

lake. No accommodation, good campsites.

MORRISON LAKE: From Smithers 45 miles by car, 15 miles by boat and 5 miles on foot. Supports rainbow trout up to 3 pounds and char up to 12 pounds, both can be taken on flies and troll. No accommodation, good campsites.

NADINA LAKE: Sixty miles from Smithers by air. Rainbow trout up to 4 pounds taken on fly from June to September. No accommodation.

NILKITKWA LAKE: Approximately 70 miles from Smithers by car and boat. This lake is situated on the Babine River 2 miles below Babine Lake and supports the same fishing as Babine River.

SEELEY LAKE: One mile long, 3 miles from South Hazelton on Highway No. 16, some accommodation and good Parks Branch campsites. Fly fishing for cutthroat all season. Hotel accommodation and auto courts at South Hazelton.

WILSON LAKE: Forty miles east from Smithers by car and 3 miles by foot. Excellent fly fishing all season for rainbow up to 2 1/2 pounds. Good campsites.

TERRACE

COPPER RIVER: Seven miles from Terrace on Highway No. 16. Excellent Dolly Varden fishing during annual salmon runs, August, September and October. Tee spoons or salmon eggs used. Very good steelhead fishing from November till March. Access along river via good logging road.

DRAGON LAKE: Approximately 10 miles from Tseax River in Nass River area. Access to lake along good logging road. Excellent rainbow trout fishing with fly or spinning outfit. Average length of fish approximately 12 inches. Good campsites, no accommodation. ANY TRAVELLING IN THE NASS

RIVER -- EXTRA GASOLINE SHOULD BE CARRIED.

EXCHAMSIKS RIVER: 35 miles west of Terrace on Highway No. 16. Coho fishing at mouth of river in September. Government Campsite.

GITNADOUX RIVER: 30 miles west of Terrace along Highway No. 16. Boat required to cross Skeena River to reach river. Excellent cohoe and trout fishing September - October. No accommodation. Government Campsite in vicinity.

KASIKS RIVER: 45 miles west of Terrace on Highway No. 16. Cohoe and trout fishing at mouth of river. No accommodation other than campsite ten miles east.

KITIMAT RIVER: Twenty miles south of Terrace. River follows the Kitimat-Terrace highway approximately 20 miles. Cuthroat and Dolly Varden may be taken all year. Excellent spring and coho salmon fishing in the months of July, August and September. Bait fishing and spinning. Accommodation may be had at Kitimat.

KITSUMKALUM LAKE: Six miles long by 1 mile wide. North of Terrace, 19 miles by good road. Cutthroat and Dolly Varden up to 20 inches. Due to unusual coloring of water, spoons with worms are the best lures. Good fishing from June 1st to end of July, then again in September and October. No accommodation. Good campsites.

KITSUMKALUM RIVER: Three miles west of Terrace on Highway 16. Flows into Skeena River from Kitsumkalum Lake approximately 25 miles. Easy access to any part of the river. Steelhead up to 20 pounds, cutthroat, Dolly Varden, springs and coho. Coho taken in the latter part of August and September. Bait castings and spinning. Accommodation in Terrace.

KITWANGA LAKE AND RIVER: Four miles long and 3/4 mile wide. Sixty miles east of

Terrace. Good road to within walking distance of lake. Rainbow and cutthroat trout up to 14 inches taken in the lake. Steelhead taken in the river during the fall and winter.

LAKELSE LAKE: Six miles long and average of 1 mile wide; 14 miles south of Terrace on good road. Accommodation available. Cutthroat and Dolly Varden plentiful from May till October. Flys and spoons with worm for best results. Cutthroat up to 18 inches.

LAKELSE RIVER: Flowing out of Lakelse Lake to the Skeena River approximately 10 miles long. Access from the lake or road from Terrace to the outlet. Excellent fly fishing for cutthroat. Dolly Varden, steelhead and salmon (Spring and Coho) may be taken. Accommodations at Lakelse Lake or Terrace.

NASS RIVER: Seventy-five miles north of Terrace. Good road (logging) completed. Virgin area to sportsmen as this road is only access to the area other than boat from Prince Rupert. Cutthroat, rainbow, Dolly Varden, steelhead, spring and cohoe salmon, no accommodation.

SKEENA RIVER: Follows highway No. 16, excellent cohoe and spring salmon fishing, months of July, August and September, particularly at the mouths of some of the larger streams which flow into the Skeena. Cutthroat and Dolly Varden may be taken at anytime of the year. Bait fishing and spinning. Good campsites.

TSEAX RIVER: Flows into the Nass River. Distance of approximately 70 miles north of Terrace access along good logging road completed. Excellent coho and spring salmon fishing from August till October. Cutthroat and Dolly Varden may be taken all year. Area know locally as being Spencer Lake is an excellent fishing spot, good camping but no facilities. Spin fishing is largely carried out.

PRINCE RUPERT

BELLA COOLA RIVER: Forty miles long from Bella Coola to Stuie. Two hundred and fifty miles from Vancouver and Prince Rupert. Open all year, steelhead, cutthroat and Dolly Varden. Gravel road follows river bank. Nearest accommodation Bella Coola.

FISHERMAN'S COVE LAKE: Two miles long, 90 miles from Prince Rupert. Cutthroat trout up to 4 pounds, no facilities. Five minutes walk from Beach.

KAHTADA LAKE: Thirty miles from Prince Rupert by chartered aircraft from Prince Rupert. Very good cutthroat fishing up to 6 pounds. No accommodation or boats.

KEMANO RIVER: Ten miles from Kemano Bay, gravel road follows river. Cutthroat up to 5 pounds. Steelhead from December to March. No accommodation.

KITIMAT RIVER: Twelve miles from townsite of Kitimat. Gravel road follows river. Cutthroat trout, steelhead good from December to March. Hotel accommodation is available as well as stores and car rentals.

KLOIYA RIVER: Fifteen miles from Prince Rupert on Highway No. 16, 1-1/2 miles long. Highway follows the river. Very good for steelhead fishing from December to April. Nearest accommodation Prince Rupert or Rainbow Lake Lodge. Good coho fishing first two weeks in September.

LEVERSON LAKE: Sixty miles from Prince Rupert by boat, very good cutthroat fishing. No boats or accommodation available.

LOWE INLET LAKES: Sixty miles from Prince Rupert by boat. Four lakes, Lowe, Gamble, Simpson and Wear. All about 5 miles long, joined by streams. Very good cut-throat fishing. No accommodation, boats or other facilities.

PRUDHOMME LAKE: Fourteen miles from Prince Rupert. Some cutthroat. Five miles from Rainbow Lake Lodge. Good coho fishing during September.

RAINBOW LAKE: Sixteen miles from Prince Rupert. Four miles long, 1/2 mile wide. Cutthroat trout up to 3 pounds, Rainbow Lake Lodge.

DIANA LAKE: 1 1/2 miles from Prudhomme Lake (rough gravel road). Good cutthroat fishing up to 1 1/2 pounds. Accommodation Prince Rupert or Rainbow Lake Lodge. No boats.

For further information please apply to
FISH AND WILDLIFE BRANCH
1600 - 3rd Avenue
PRINCE GEORGE, B.C.

Manitoba

Manitoba is truly a "land of lakes". Thousands of lakes dot the province, but the superior game-fishing waters lie in the northern part of the area in the Pre-Cambrian Shield. Whiteshell Park, with it's two hundred lakes, offers fine lake trout.

Northeastern Manitoba has both lake trout and brook trout in Gods Lake and Gods River. These are native and wild stock, and grow to trophy size and fight like mad.

Really wild country is that north of the 56th parallel, but brook trout and Arctic grayling in abundance will be found in the Limestone and Weir rivers and other streams tributary to the Nelson River.

New Brunswick

Sport fish to be found in this province include Atlantic salmon, spring salmon, trout, landlocked salmon and togue. Generally speaking the Atlantic salmon fishing can be done from shore or from a canoe with the exception of spring (black) salmon fishing which is most often done from a boat.

Stocking of lakes and rivers is carried out by the Federal Department of Fisheries and Forestry, Resource Development Branch. Generally speaking, they stock large numbers of eastern brook trout and Atlantic salmon smolts.

New Brunswick, 28,354 square miles in area, of which 80 per cent is forested land, has long been known as a "Sportmen's Paradise". It has been so called by many of the best known sportsmen of the North American continent and Europe, as well as by thousands of rod and gun enthusiasts who have been the guests of the Province of New Brunswick down through the years. Perhaps the greatest tribute is that those who love the outdoors and who come to fish and hunt, return year after year for their favorite sport.

There are lots of smiles in a New Brunswick fishing trip. Sport angling begins as soon as the ice breaks up in the spring—the first target being Atlantic spring salmon.

The best way to plan a fishing trip to New Brunswick is to write one or more of the guides or outfitters. From them should be procured full details as to accommodation and other desired information, since rates vary according to facilities offered. Many outfitters, particularly those who cater to salmon anglers, have water under lease. All, however, will be able to guide sportsmen to water recognized as suitable for the type of fishing desired and for which they advertise. When fishing for Atlantic salmon from a canoe, boat, or any type of watercraft, each holder of a non-resident angling license is required to employ the services of a licensed guide.

Of New Brunswick's many attractions, undoubtedly the best

known is the recognized "king" of all game fish, the Atlantic silver salmon. To confirmed anglers, catching an Atlantic salmon is the supreme sporting thrill. This magnificient fish is found in many New Brunswick waters. The mighty Main Southwest Miramichi is one of the world's great salmon streams. Its many tributaries such as the Northwest Miramichi, the Cains, Bartholomew, Dungarvon, Renous and Sevogle are all well and favorable known in their own right.

The list of salmon rivers is a long one. It includes the renowned Restigouche; the Kedgwick which is a tributary; the Nepisiguit, the Tabusintac. At certain times of the year Atlantic salmon may be caught in such rivers as the Magaguadavic, Kennebecasis and Nashwaak. Young salmon, ranging in size from 3-1/2 pounds to 5 pounds, are known as grilse and are noteworthy because of their fighting qualities. Generally speaking a salmon rod from 7-1/2 to 9 feet in length and weighing from 5 to 7 ounces is suitable for salmon angling on most rivers. Some sportsmen, however, prefer a larger and heavier rod. The reel should be large enough to handle 300 feet of backing, and 100 feet of casting line. The leader should be a 9 foot tapered one. Most of the standard salmon flies are used although the advice of the guide is helpful in this respect. There is a decided preference for single hooks in the province at the present time with sizes ranging from No. 10 to No. 2.

When planning a salmon angling trip it is suggested that the outfitter or guide who has been engaged be asked for advice since rivers vary as to size of fish taken and in other ways as well.

Salmon Seasons

Spring salmon angling, which annually gains more converts, begins immediately after the ice goes out on

certain rivers. No more than 5 black salmon may be hooked in one day by any angler and not more than 1 salmon per day may be retained by any angler and any other such salmon shall be returned alive and uninjured to the water.

On the Restigouche River the provincial government has reserved a few miles of the best Atlantic salmon waters for anglers who pay a daily rod license. This is known as Crown Reserve Water. Applications to fish these exclusive waters will be received beginning January 1st each year. The Restigouche Reserve water, comprising five and one-half miles of the Main Restigouche River, is limited to eight rods per day from June 5 to August 31. Sundays are excepted in both cases. Licensees will be accommodated at a government approved camp.

Most Atlantic salmon rivers are excellent trout streams as well and many anglers combine both salmon and trout angling on their fishing trips. The speckled or brook trout is the chief species. Trout are plentiful in rivers, streams, brooks and lakes. The season generally is from April 15 to September 15. Several New Brunswick rivers also have runs of sea trout which occur around the end of May and first of June and provide excellent sport.

During a large run of salmon in late September of one year one hundred and thirty-four anglers were counted in the Quarryville pool on the Southwest Miramichi River. To some anglers the quality of salmon fishing is ruined by these crowded conditions often experienced on the Miramichi, Cains and Tabusintac Rivers.

The better known rivers attract most anglers, but there are also several "elbow-room" rivers with good salmon runs that are practically overlooked. These rivers receive relatively light fishing pressure and

This happy angler is wading ashore holding a beautiful Atlantic salmon by the tail. The river, is in New Brunswick where these fine scrappers will attain a weight of up to 25 pounds. They are on their way upstream to spawn after spending about three years in the Atlantic Ocean.

usually from local anglers. If one is to have successful angling in the "Elbow-Room Rivers", however, he must know when the salmon run enter these rivers. A phone call to the local Forest Ranger Station or Fishery Office is one good way to obtain these fishing tips.

Several good producing rivers which have "elbow-room" are Jacquet River, Black River, Tracadie River, Alma River, Baribog River and Hammond River.

The Hammond River has a good run of salmon and grilse which generally begins late in September or early October. This river is located near several large urban centers, but is often overlooked by many anglers "in a hurry" to fish the mouth of Big Salmon River.

The Alma River has late August and late September-early October salmon runs. 207 anglers took 363 salmon (including grilse) on the Alma in 1968 while 1,005 anglers caught only 541 (salmon and grilse) on the Big Salmon River!

The Black River is a small river which flows into Miramichi Bay. Because of its location on the Miramichi watershed, it attracts many more salmon and grilse than a river of this size would elsewhere. Generally, the Black River salmon run enter the river in late September.

The Bartibog River is well known to most N.B. salmon fishermen. However, due to absence of roads or trails many miles of this river are inaccessible to most anglers. The lower 16-mile section of the Bartibog consists of "elbow-room" stretches accessible to those anglers resourceful enough to use a canoe.

The Big Tracadie River has recently (1966) regained its production of good salmon runs as a result of increased protection. Most fish taken on the river have been salmon ten pounds and over. July runs are common in this river but a larger run usually enters the river during the second or third week of October. Good canoeing conditions prevail for those who wish to float the river.

The Jacquet River has been producing good grilse runs during the past few years. Anglers checked by ranger patrols last October had average catches of 0.50 grilse per hour. This river is canoeable only during high water conditions.

"The Best Miramichi Salmon Producers of Them All'

That's what well-known fishing tackle dealer Wallace Doak has to say about the "Engles Butterfly". The butterfly is a fly pattern which was developed by Maurice Engles from the State of Maine. Because this fly was "kept under wraps" for many years by Engles and his angling associates, its outstanding salmon catching ability was not recognized by Miramichi Anglers until 1965. Since that time, the "butterfly" has been responsible for taking more salmon and grilse on Miramichi waters then any other fly pattern. Perhaps a conservative estimate would be that 25 per cent of Miramichi bright salmon and grilse catches have been taken by the butterfly pattern!

The "Conrad", "Cosseboom" and "Squirrel Tail" rank as 2nd, 3rd, and 4th respectively, as wet fly choices of Miramichi anglers. The "Big Bomber" and "Royal Coachman" are the most frequently used dry flies.

Here is the formula for an "Engles Butterfly":

PATTERN: "Engles" Butterfly

HOOK SIZE: No. 6 Sproat

FLY TYPE: Wet

BODY: Peacock Herl

WINGS: White Goat Hair, tied into two upright wings

TAG [optional]: Silver Tinsel

TAIL: Red saddle or neck hackle Fibers.

HACKLE: Natural brown or royal coachman red, sparsely wrapped.

New Brunswick fishermen have little difficulty catching brook trout, togue, or landlocked salmon in the spring (May and early June). These species are hungry after a winter period of little food and roam unrestricted throughout New Brunswick's cold, well-oxygenated lakes in search of food. But what happens to the good trout, landlocked salmon and togue fishing after June? Most Anglers know that lake waters warm up and fishing drops off. But many do not know that at this time, most game fishes move to live in certain deeper, colder areas of the lake.

The information collected by biologists indicates that each of these species has a fairly narrow temperature preference where its body functions are best co-ordinated. Trout, landlocked salmon and togue prefer to live near or very near the "thermocline" temperature layer (zone of rapid temperature drop) which ranges 48-60°F., just as people prefer temperatures of 70-75°F. It is evident that New Brunswick lakes, less than 25' deep, do not adequately meet the temperature requirements of landlocked salmon or togue. Brook trout can survive in these shallower (marginal) lakes, however, as they can seek out spring holes. Finding where spring holes are usually takes a considerable amount of time by the angler, but the results are well worth it. Here are a few tips:

(1) Spring water maintains a constant temperature (about 45° F.) year around. In the fall when a lake begins to freeze over, the spring hole area will be the last to become ice-covered.

(2) Many spring holes have mounds of sand around them. Aerial

views of a lake on a clear day can sometimes show the white sand outline.

(3) Fish-eating birds (loons, mergansers and kingfishers) often haunt spring hole areas.

(4) Underground spring seepages may be present beneath a dried up brook run and enter the lake shore four to eight feet under the surface.

(5) Brook trout in spring hole lakes spend most of their daylight hours around the spring area and then move to nearby shallow areas for early morning or evening feeding. Observations of this initial feeding behavior can often give the angler a good idea of the approximate area of the spring hole.

Newfoundland - Labrador

Salmon fishing is a prime offering of this area of Canada. Labrador, the mainland portion, offers brook trout in it's many streams but accomodations are limited, and most fishermen camp out. Wilderness fishing arrived at by chartered

Here are a few New Brunswick lakes surveyed or well known to Fish and Wildlife Branch biologists which have good healthy fish populations. But, be sure to fish where the fish are!

airplane is rugged and productive.

The Avalon Peninsula offers sea-run trout of sizes up to 25 pounds. This Peninsula also has four excellent Atlantic salmon rivers—the Placentia, Trepassey, Colinet and Salmonier.

Ontario

This province, which is the second largest in Canada, has over 68,000 square miles of water area. In looking for best trout spots, Algonquin Provincial Park, which is located in the Pembroke Forest District, is outstanding for brook trout and lake trout. In this huge park may also be found the following species which have been stocked: Atlantic salmon, brown trout, rainbow trout, splake, alpine char.

The size composition of lake trout catches varies considerably with different lakes. In lakes such as Sanisbay, Louisa, Source and Delano, the average length of each year's catch is 14 to 15 inches, and the average weight, 1 to 1-1/2 pounds.

Brook or speckled trout occur in about half as many lakes in the park as do lake trout. They are confined largely to lakes, as summer temperatures become too high in most streams. Like the lake trout, in summer they migrate to deeper water, where they are more difficult to catch. Most of the speckled trout fishing is in May or June. Dickson, Lavielle, Redrock, Proulx, Big Brow, Welcome, Harry and Stringer Lakes are some of the better brook trout lakes on the south side of Algonquin Park. Fishing quality varies between one or two trout per hour of fishing for many of these lakes with the average length from 12 to 15 inches.

Plantings of trout hybrids of the lake trout and brook trout, called the splake or wendigo, have been made in a number of the park lakes. Among these are Opeongo, Redrock, Sproule, Brewer, Jock, Scott, Found

Species of Game Fish Present					
Lake	County	Type of Lake	Brook Trout	Landlock Salmon	Togue
Antinouri	Restigouche	Spring hole	X		
Baker	Madawaska	Deep	X		X
Chamcook	Charlotte	Deep	X	X	X
Clearwater	Northumberland	Spring hole	X		
Eight-Mile	Restigouche	Spring hole	X		
Caron	Madawaska	Deep	X		
Long Lake	Victoria	Deep	X		X
Maguagdavic	York	Deep	X	X	
Mains	Northumberland	Spring hole	X		
Quisibis	Madawaska	Spring hole	X		
Palfrey	Charlotte	Deep	X	X	
Second Portage	Restigouche	Deep (No oxygen below 45')	X		
States	Restigouche	Deep	X		
Upslaquitch	Restigouche	Deep	X		X
McDougall	Restigouche	Spring hole	X		
Livingston	Albert	Spring hole	X		

and Little Minnow Lakes. These introductions have been particularly successful in smaller, deep waters.

The hybrid trout is an excellent game fish, although here, too, it reveals its split personality. Some fight much more like brook trout, while others fight deep and doggedly like lake trout. The hybrid has a very marked schooling behaviour and this profoundly affects your fishing luck. Anglers may be rewarded by large catches in a short period as a school moves into shallow water to feed and then fishing may be unsuccessful for several hours.

Because of the rapid growth of the trout hybrid and its excellent angling qualities, a program of heavy stocking has undertaken in Lake-of-Two-Rivers, Whitefish, Rock and Galeairy Lakes in 1962. These four lakes are important components of the fishery for campers, and in recent years they have not been too productive. It is hoped that the hybrid's rapid growth, coupled with the heavy stocking, will produce greater success for anglers.

It is clear, however, from plantings made in a wide range of lakes that hybrid trout do best in the deeper, cold, lake-trout lakes. They do not do as well as the brook trout in the shallower, boggy, more marginal waters of Algonquin Park.

Kamloops trout, a close relative of the rainbow, were introduced into Lake of Two Rivers in 1954 and, although catches have been few, appear to have become established.

Alpine char, a northern relative of the brook trout, were planted in Westward Lake in 1955 and some are caught each year.

Rainbow trout are found mainly in the tributary streams of Lake Ontario, Lake Erie, Lake Huron, Georgian Bay and Lake Superior.

BROWN TROUT
[Salmo trutta]

Of all the trouts, this is the most cautious and difficult to catch. Any sudden movements or noise, or a sloppy cast, and you can forget about catching one.

They are found in southern Ontario in habitat ranging from small brooks to large streams. In Ontario, lake fishing for brown trout is negligible. In any lake that does have them, it is generally by accident that one is caught.

In streams and creeks, fish the same spots that you would try for brook trout, but present your lure or bait even more realistically. If you try a good pool in a trout stream and get no action, then suspect that there is a large brown trout there. They are very piscivorous and will feed on any smaller trout which comes within range. It is for this reason that lake stocking of brown trout is almost non-existent in Ontario. Brown trout will attain a large size in the same creek in which brook trout may reach only 8 to 10 inches, but one will occupy a larger area of the stream than would a brook trout.

If it is a known brown trout stream, and you are unable to catch one during the day, then it may be profitable to return after dark. They seem to be much more aggressive and quicker to strike at this time, losing some of their natural caution.

If you are going to fish for brown trout, then patience is an absolute necessity. If you cannot stand being "skunked", then you might be advised to try for other species.

Saskatchewan

Sweeping northward from the Canada-United States border, where Saskatchewan meets Montana and North Dakota, the province stretches almost 800 miles to the wilderness of the Northwest Territories districts. More than 31,000 of the province's 251,000 square miles are sky blue lakes and rumbling rivers, a fisherman's paradise.

Fishing is fabulous in Saskatchewan, particularly in the northern waters. The most popular sport fish are the big northern pike, walleye, lake trout and that "sailfish of the north" the Arctic grayling. Anglers also go after the brook, brown and rainbow trout, splake, white fish and perch.

As modern roads extend deeper into the northland, the area becomes dotted with fishing resorts and campgrounds. But at the end of the roads, regularly scheduled air services and charter float planes take you to the fly-in fishing camps. There are camps of all types, from fully modern establishments, with all inclusive plans, to those with light-housekeeping facilities.

The angling season opens early in May. Southern lakes are already free from ice and as the month progresses the more northern areas open up. Fishing continues almost year-round. The lakes freeze over in November and December and then ice fishing begins.

The species caught on flies in this province include—Artic grayling, whitefish, brook, brown and rainbow trout.

The grayling (sometimes called standard-bearer and flag fish) is one of the most colorful and highly-spirited fish in Saskatchewan. Of all the freshwater fish in this province, only the brook trout compares with it in appearance and fighting qualities.

The grayling's average size is 1 to 2 pounds and 10 to 14 inches long. The back of the grayling is usually dark blue and the sides purplish gray with a golden irridescence. Some 12 to 18 well-spaced bluish-black spots appear on the forward sides both above and below the lateral line. Its small head is blue-bronze, with a bright blue marking on each side of the lower jaw. A huge sail-like dorsal fin is very apparent on this species. This fin is grayish in color, sometimes pale pink on its upper edge, with crossrows of blue spots edged in red. In all graylings, the dorsal fin of the male is always larger than that of the female.

This fish seems to prefer open, fast moving water. It very often congregates in schools in open bodies of water. Like members of the trout family, the grayling is a "scrapper" when caught on a fisherman's lure. It sometimes leaps completely clear of the water and takes a fly on the downward arc. Because of its weak mouth the grayling should be played more carefully than a trout of the same size. The grayling is mainly insectivorous, and in the evening may be seen rising from the water to feed on low-flying caddis flies, mayflies and midges. The swimming larvae of some of these species probably make up a large proportion of its diet and in the winter smaller fish may be important as foods. Many fishermen consider the grayling a real delicacy when caught in the fall of the year. For its size, it can offer a challenging tussle when caught on a fly-rod.

The grayling's range in Saskatchewan is widespread and virtually in wilderness regions. It is found primarily in these locations: east end of Lake Athabasca, Downton Lake (west of La Ronge), Grease River, Cree River, Fond du Lac River, Reindeer River, Black Birch (Virgin) River, Mudjatik River, Clearwater, Cochrane and Otherside Rivers and other numerous cool, fast waters north of the Churchill River system. To fish for this species means a flying trip of 60 miles in the northwest to from 170, upwards of 350 miles north of La Ronge, which is in the middle of the province—approximately. However, the largest grayling recorded in Saskatchewan have come from the Fond du Lac River system near Stony Rapids in the far north. Nineteen of the record fish caught out of 27 have come from the Fond du Lac.

Generally, most fishing for grayling and rainbows is done from boats, except for the smaller creeks in the southern part of the province, where it is done from the banks or by wading. On the Fond du Lac, Clearwater and Black Birch Rivers, there are places where you can cast from the shore as it is impossible to take a boat down into these fishing holes.

Best fishing times: Artic grayling—can be caught all summer, but during the black fly hatch is best—a liberal coating of 6-12 or OFF is required. Rainbows—spotty, but the biggest are caught in the fall. Brooks and Browns—there appears to be no particular best time. Whitefish—generally during a good May fly hatch.

Fly Patterns
Arctic Grayling:
  Grizzly Wulff
  Black Gnat
  May Fly
  Black Nymph
Rainbows:
  Green Streamer Fly
  Minnow Muddler Fly
  Green Carry
  Original Muddler Fly
  Streamer Fly
Whitefish:
  May Fly
  Brown Hackle

Of course, there are even some adventurous souls who go fly fishing for Northern pike in Saskatchewan, and one 25 pound pike has been caught with a big streamer fly.

Brook trout were introduced into Saskatchewan in the 1920's and early 1930's and were originally found from Labrador westward to Manitoba and southward along the Alleghenies to Georgia. Up to date this fish has been stocked by fish culturists in practically all streams of North America where suitable water temperatures are found.

Average weight of this species is a pound or less in Saskatchewan, but a few have been caught here that weigh 3 to 4 pounds. The all-time angling record for this species goes back to 1916, and belongs to Dr. W. S. Cook. He landed a 14-1/2 pounder from the Nipigon River, Ontario. This trout is probably the most publicized and best loved of all fresh-water game fish. The meat of the brook trout has a firmness and delicacy of flavor to delight the most sensitive fancier of food. "Brook trout" listed on restaurant menus are commercially raised, for conservation laws everywhere prohibit the commercial taking of this species from lakes and streams.

In Saskatchewan they can be found in the Fir River, Little Swan River, McDougall Creek, Echo Creek, Nipekanew River, Low and Broad Creek, and Sealey Lake. In the Cypress Hills area, Belanger, Sucker and Fairwell Creeks are their homes.

Rainbow trout, introduced in Saskatchewan in the 1920's is one of the more colorful fish. It gets its name from the vivid red, or reddish purple band which commences immediately behind the eye and extends along the side to the caudal fin. The average size of this species in Saskatchewan is 2 pounds. The world's record for rainbow trout is 37 pounds taken in Idaho in 1947.

The rainbow trout can live in warm water but prefers fresh cool-running streams. It will take various baits, but when hooked on a fly it goes at once into the air and leaps again and again, sometimes literally dancing on its tail all over the surface of a pool. Rainbow trout like to eat small fish, bugs, insects and even small worms if they are moving. Algae and other vegetable matter are occasionally found in the stomach.

Since its introduction into Saskatchewan, the rainbow trout has lured many fishing enthusiasts to the province. It can be caught by amateur and expert alike, and its game qualities will satisfy the most discriminating. Rainbow trout have been stocked in the streams of Cypress Hills, Shirley Lake, Thompson Lake, Sealy Lake, Piprell

Lake, Proter's Dam and in the White Bear Reservoir.

Brown trout—sometimes called European brown trout, Lock Leven trout and German brown trout—occurs in North America as a result of extensive introductions, which commenced in the United States in 1883. It was introduced into Canadian waters in Newfoundland in 1884, then into Quebec in 1890, Ontario in 1913, and New Brunswick and Saskatchewan in the 1920's and 1930's.

The adult brown trout has a somewhat thick or stocky appearance due to the squarish tail. It is easily distinguished from brook and lake trout by its black spotting, and from the rainbow trout by its practically unspotted tail fin. In Saskatchewan this trout usually does not weigh more than 4 or 5 pounds. The record brown trout of all time is said to be a 39-1/2 pounder taken by W. Muir in Loch Awe, Scotland, in 1866. Several American specimens have weighed over 20 pounds each, but these extravagant fish are very rare.

The brown trout has the reputation of being adaptable to the warm, marginal waters between rainbow and smallmouth bass habitat. However it is believed that brown trout require about the same temperature conditions as the rainbow—cool, clear and moving. Hatchery managers are likewise agreed that brown trout culture requires water supply temperatures similar to those required for other trout species. They are cannibalistic and feed heavily on smaller fish species, although aquatic and terrestrial insects are also eaten. They feed usually at sunset and sunrise but will take insects, etc., during the day. This trout offers great "fun" for fishermen who fish with a flyrod. It may be a very challenging sport fish to the really serious fisherman, but may be a source of frustration to the novice angler because it is so hard to catch. It is found chiefly in the Cypress Hills area in such streams as Bone, Swift Current and Frenchman Creek. It generally favors the waters of southern Saskatchewan.

Lake Whitefish is deep-bodied and laterally compressed. It is characterized by the presence of two flaps between the openings of each nostril and by the snout which slightly overhangs the lower jaw. The color of this species varies considerable from one water to another. In its more common color phase it has a dark bronze to greenish back, white belly, and silvery sides. Fins are light colored.

In Saskatchewan under normal conditions, whitefish grow approximately 1/2 pound per year. The usual weight is 2 to 4 pounds. Though this is a delicate species (mature fish frequently die in hatcheries if not accorded the gentlest handling), it is potentially a long-lived fish. Specimens have lived for 10 years in captivity, and in rare cases wild fish estimated to be 18 years old have been caught.

The Lake Whitefish is not noted as a game fish but during recent years anglers in Saskatchewan have had success in flycasting for them. Once on the end of a line, the whitefish puts up a creditable fight, being chunky and well muscled. Since this fish has a sucking mouth rather than jaws equipped for biting, it takes in the fly by "inhaling". Even though whitefish inhabit most deep lakes in Saskatchewan they are classed as a shallow-water form, preferring a depth range of 50 to 150 feet.

This species may be found in nearly all of Saskatchewan's northern lakes and rivers. Many of the larger lakes in the southern portion of the province also contain this fish.

Through the efforts of the Department of Natural Resources brook trout, rainbow trout, brown trout, splake, kokanee salmon, coho salmon and arctic grayling have been planted in various waters throughout the province.

Quebec

The Province of Quebec covers nearly 600,000 square miles and has over one million lakes and streams. Many thousands of these lakes and streams have never been fished, and each year new waters are being discovered that turn out to be "hot spots" for various types of sport fishes.

Some of the Crown lands in the province are leased to private clubs and outfitters. These are bound by law to have guardians protecting the game and fish on their leases. Large sections of land have also been set aside by the Department of Tourism, Fish and Game as parks and reserves where conservation has become a watchword and still allows the public at large to enjoy the popular pastime of dangling a line in the water.

There are also some 900 outfitting establishments licensed throughout the entire province, which offer a variety of services at prices running from one dollar a day for the rental of a boat to a thousand dollar, six-day package deal for an all-inclusive fly-in trip near the Arctic Circle.

Fishing is a sport that may be enjoyed by young and old, and is becoming more popular year by year, as shown by the increased number of angler permits being sold.

SPECKLED CHAR
[*Salvelinus fontinalis*]

Other common names: *Brook char, speckled trout, brook trout, squaretail, red trout, salmon trout.*

The true fisherman's dream is one day to catch a new record speckled trout. The present world's record was established with a 14 pound 8 ounce trout taken from the Nipigon River in 1916. The best known record of this species, taken in the province, is 11 pounds 12 ounces, from the Broadback River, in 1962, although the Indians claim to have taken larger ones in nets in several of the northern waters.

Found in abundance in practically every corner of *la belle province,* this colorful and delectable member of the char family is the most sought after of all the sport fishes.

It is taken in streams, rivers and lakes in more than half of the counties, from native waters, and has been stocked in many other parts.

Speckled char adapt themselves to almost any clean water, grow rapidly and, therefore, can be raised in man-made lakes and ponds very readily to provide sport for the public in general.

Throughout the Eastern Townships and the Gaspe Peninsula, fish are taken up to 2 and 3 pounds quite commonly. This is also found from the western to eastern boundaries of the province, just north of the St. Lawrence River, and throughout the northern part of the province trophy specimens are caught each year.

Trout are temperamental and, regardless of what type of lure is used, at times cannot be coaxed into biting, even though it was proven they were there.

Great success has resulted from using numerous patterns of flies, such as Dark Montreal, McGinty, Black Gnat and a host of others; both dry and wet flies are used with approximately equal success.

SEA TROUT
[*Salvelinus fontinalis*]

The so-called sea run trout is simply normal speckled char which decided to foresake the fresh water and make a voyage into the ocean. When this happens they lose their bright colors and become quite silvery in appearance.

When the spawning run starts in June into the freshwater streams, they may be taken in the lower stretches; for example, in the mouths of the tributaries of the Saguenay River or of the Gulf of St. Lawrence North Shore, as well as in Ungava, Hudson and James bays.

As the summer wears on, they gradually ascend higher and higher up the rivers until, in the month of September, they will only be taken as far up as they can possibly go. Here they spawn and then return to the salt water for the winter.

After they have fed throughout the summer on insects and other small animal life found in the streams, their bright colors return to quite an extent, and at spawning time it is very difficult to distinguish them from their brethren who never undertook a sea voyage.

Flies suggested: Black Scotland and Grasshopper.

QUEBEC RED CHAR
[*Salvelinus alpinus*] [*marstoni*]

Other common names: *Quebec red trout, marstoni, Canadian red trout or char.*

This species is sometimes mistaken for speckled char, as it is very similar in appearance, but to the true fisherman it is quite easily recognized. One noticeable feature is the deeply forked tail instead of the square tail of the speckled char, and the absence of vermiculation on the back. There is also a difference in the markings on the fins and on the body.

The best known record is 3 pounds, and was taken in one of the lakes in *la belle province.*

The distribution of this fish is in Rimouski County, in the Gaspe Peninsula, just north of the St. Lawrence River, and from lakes north of Hull, to the eastern limits of the Province of Quebec.

It is usually found in the same lakes with speckled char, but as a rule will not be taken on exactly the same tackle. As soon as the ice is out of the lakes, this species may be taken on the surface with worms or flies.

Best fly: Roche's May Fly.

ARCTIC CHAR
[*Salvelinus alpinus*]

This very colorful member of the char family is found at the outlets of rivers leading into James Bay, Hudson Bay and Ungava Bay, in the northern part of *la belle province.*

It is a very exciting fish to catch and is one of the most delectable, from a gourmet's point of view, of any of the game fishes.

The Eskimos and Indians net the char throughout the season. In the Arctic, it is fed to the dog teams during the winter.

The average size of char taken is from 5 to 7 pounds, but specimens have been known to run as high as 29 pounds. In some zones, large searun char of over 30 pounds are sometimes taken during the summer.

Royal Coachman and Trout Fin are favored for the Arctic Char.

LAKE CHAR
[*Salvelinus namaycush*]

Other common names: *Lake trout, laker, grey trout, touladi and togue.*

This is the largest of the char family, and specimens have been taken in nets, weighing over 100 pounds. The record taken by rod and reel was established in 1952, with a 63 pounds 2 ounce fish, in northern Manitoba. The record for this province, as far as is known, was taken in Lake Matchimanitou in 1963, and weighed 57 pounds 8 ounces. This species is found practically throughout the entire province.

Fishermen who start early in the spring, just after the ice melts, have a great thrill using flies and spinning equipment, and specimens are regularly taken up to 25 pounds and over in this manner. Later on, when the water becomes warmer, along in

June, one must then troll with a weighted line and several different types of lures which produce good results.

Fly suggested: Supervisor.

OUANANICHE
[Salmo salar ouananiche]

Other common names: Landlocked salmon, sebago.

The story goes that many years ago, when the Wisconsin glacier waters receded, some Atlantic salmon were trapped in Lake St. John and other of the northern lakes in the eastern part of the province and were unable to return to the ocean. These fish were called aonanch by the Lake St. John Montagnais.

This is probably the greatest fighter, pound for pound, of any of the fish taken in the province, with the exception perhaps of the smallmouth black bass.

Ouananiche may be taken in lakes, but anglers are usually more successful and derive a great deal more pleasure and excitement from taking them in fast flowing cold streams which are tributaries of their home lakes.

Throughout the season this fish may be caught on streamer flies and is also susceptible to the lure of various artificial baits used on spinning tackle, but the ardent angler still prefers his flies.

Hatchery-bred Atlantic salmon fingerlings were introduced into several lakes in various parts of the province, and more especially in the Eastern Townships in such lakes as Memphremagog, Massawippi and Megantic. They accepted these waters readily, and at present it is one of the most sought after of sport fishes in this section of the country.

The world's record is 22 pounds 8 ounces, taken in 1907 from the Lake St. John district, and the record of the transplanted salmon in Lake Memphremagog is a fish of 16-1/2

pounds, taken in 1958. Fish of up to 13 and 14 pounds have been taken in these waters, while fish of up to 10 and 11 pounds of the original ouananiche are taken in the waters of Lake St. John and in several waters of the Gulf of St. Lawrence North Shore each year. The average is 4 to 5 pounds.

Each succeeding year brings reports of discovery of new and exciting fishing for ouananiche in the counties of Saguenay and Duplessis. The most recent is the Kaniapiskau River and its various tributaries and adjoining lakes.

Fly: Van Luven.

ATLANTIC SALMON
[Salmo salar salar]

As there is a king of the animal kingdom, there is also a king of our sport fishes, and this must be considered the Atlantic salmon.

Starting about the first of June each year, the mighty salmon begins its annual spawning voyage from the Atlantic Ocean to as far as it can ascend up the rivers of our Gulf of St. Lawrence North Shore, starting at the Saguenay River and extending through to Labrador and to many of the rivers in the Gaspe Peninsula and Anticosti Island. In some of our rivers, there is a second run of salmon that starts in August, so that the angler may have fishing practically throughout the summer.

In late September, upon reaching the gravel bottom of the shallow stretches of the headwaters of the rivers, the eggs of the female salmon are deposited. The fry hatch in early spring, and when 2 or 3 months old, begin to show bright red spots and dark vertical bars. At this stage the young salmon is call a parr and remains a parr 1 to 3 years, after which it descends to the sea and acquires a bright, silvery color, when it is called a smolt. After remaining in salt water for approximately 2

years, it returns to the rivers from whence it originally came, for its first spawning run. Others may return the first year after going to sea and are known as grilse. Some of the spawning salmon of more mature age never manage to return to the ocean, as they are so spent after struggling to attain the upper reaches of the river that they become thin and poor and do not have enough strength left to complete the return voyage, and subsequently die.

In order to protect this fish, many rivers have been leased to either private or commercial clubs which are bound by law to keep strict supervision over the fishing. In various locations through the Gaspe Peninsula, Parks Division controls the fishing, while in other spots it is controlled by private enterprise.

The Atlantic salmon has been known to attain a weight of 83 pounds and commercial fishermen claim that larger ones have torn their nets and escaped. The largest taken by rod and reel, as far as is known, was a 52-1/2 pound specimen from the Margaree River in Nova Scotia, in 1927. In 1960 a 42 pound fish was taken from the Moisie River on the Gulf of St. Lawrence North Shore in Quebec. The average salmon taken in rivers runs about 15 pounds and several thousands are killed each year, in this category.

Angling for salmon is restricted to fly-fishing only, and different rivers seem to require different flies, or so the fishermen believe. Among the favorites in the wet fly category are the following: Silver Doctor, Jock Scott, Black Dose, Dusty Miller, Fiery Brown, Brown Hackle and Silver Ranger, as well as some of the buck tail and squirrel tail patterns. On the dry fly side, preferences are shown for Brown Hackle, Grey Hackle, Cinnamon Sedge, Pink Lady and MacIntosh.

Normally, rods used are from 10 to 12 feet, equipped with a 2-1/2 to 4 inch reel and 40 yards of tapered line spliced to 100 yards of backing. Most salmon anglers use a 9 to 10 foot leader of 12 to 15 pound test, of gut or nylon.

Salmon fishing in bygone years was considered the sport of wealthy men only, but since more and more public waters are being opened in our province, it is now easily a sport that is within the reach of the average citizen. It is probably the most exciting angling of any that might be experienced in the world, for when a good size fish is hooked, a real battle is on. More often than not, the angler turns out to be the "poor fish".

RAINBOW TROUT
[*Salmo gairdneri*]

Other common name: *Steelhead.*

The rainbow trout is not a native of Quebec, but was brought in from California originally where it is abundant in many lakes and streams. In western North America, when this trout comes in from the sea to spawn, it is called *steelhead.*

This is another of the salmon species and is an exciting fish to catch, for immediately after it is hooked it starts an aerial battle similar to all others of the salmon tribe.

This fish was planted in many of the lakes and streams in the Eastern Townships and took readily to the clear cold waters running from the mountain streams and soon became another of the most sought after fish in Lake Memphremagog. Recently biologists have planted rainbows in the Quebec City district, in the Jacques-Cartier, Montmorency and Chaudiere rivers.

Use Woodcock Quill and Red Ibis flies.

The world's record steelhead or rainbow, taken on rod and line weighed 37 pounds and came from British Columbia. The record for the province, to date, is 12 pounds 14

ounces, and came from Lake Memphremagog in 1956. Ardent anglers from this district say that they are sure there are larger ones in the lake. However, to date, they have not proven this. We do know that every year many specimens of from 7 to 10 pounds are hooked.

In early spring, after ice first leaves the lakes, good success is achieved by using spinning tackle and streamer flies of various patterns. Later on, as the water warms, they are taken by trolling or fishing down, although on occasion, in early morning or late evening, some fine fish are taken around the mouths of tributaries, and throughout summer they are regularly caught with flies in these streams.

BROWN TROUT
[*Salmo trutta*]

This fine fighting trout was brought into the province from Europe many years ago and introduced into the North River in Terrebonne county and into Lake Memphremagog. It was also planted into some other spots, for example in headwaters of the Chateauguay River wherefrom survivors migrate downstream yearly into the St. Lawrence system and are hooked thereafter at several spots such as at the foot of the Lachine Rapids, of the Beauharnois electric dam tail race, etc.

The brown trout is taken easily on spinning tackle in the spring, using streamer flies or other artificial lures, and by trolling later in the summer. It is a hard fighter, but very seldom, if ever, breaks water, preferring to fight deep, more in the manner of lake trout.

The world's record brown trout was taken in 1866 and weighed 39-1/2 pounds, whereas the record in this province is a fish taken from Memphremagog in 1959, which weighed 16 pounds 9 ounces. Every year many nice fish of from 8 to 10

pounds are taken in this lake.

When in its spawning colors, the male brown is a deep golden color with orange and yellow spots.

Flies: Royal Coachman and Black Beauty.

SUGGESTED LURES FOR VARIOUS SPECIES OF FISH TO BE TAKEN IN "LA BELLE PROVINCE"

TROUT and CHAR

Wet flies: Size 4 and 6 in regular patterns, bucktails and streamers (long shank) all sizes: Par Belle, Professor, Silver Doctor, Black Gnat, Red Iris, Dark Montreal, Muddler, Mickey Finn, Bucktail (red and white), Gray Ghost, Dusty Miller, Marabou (black, white or gray), Green Ghost, McGinty.

Dry flies: Brown Palmer, Royal Coachman, March Brown, hair wing Royal Coachman, fan wing extended body, Irresistible.

Nymphs: Various patterns.

NOTE: Large hair and feather dry flies used for salmon are effective, especially at the end of July, also during August and September. In the evening, we suggest small dry flies when trout are feeding on the surface.

SALMON: Flies only allowed.

Wet flies: Black Dose, Durham Ranger, Dusty Miller, Jack Scott, Mar Lodge, Night Hawk, Silver Doctor, Silver Gray, Wilkinson, Cosseboom, Lightning & Thunder, Rats (all colors).

Dry flies: Wulff (assorted colors), Palmer (assorted), Royal Coachman, Cosseboom.

The above list is only a suggestion and there are many other lures and flies that give great success. Always consult your guide or local fishermen in the area you are visiting, as to their recommendations. Every ardent angler, of course, has his own special flies or lures, and he should try these on Quebec fish.

Fly Fishing Clothes

and Accessories

The basic outfitting for fly fishermen never remains basic very long and as new ideas and equipment become available, we constantly add to our gear.

Some of these items will be for the better and some merely to put the bite on your pocketbook. Essential items and those doing a specific task will be discussed in the following:

We will range from the nominal to the most expensive type gear, as each individual has to make his own choice regarding expenditures. A general rule of thumb is to select the middle figure when a number of various costs are presented for the same item.

Undergarments
During early spring and late fall (steelhead runs) the long-wading angler is going to have to take precautions against cold water effects on his body. Standard requirements will be thermal-weave bottoms and tops (navy type), I suggest this type to avoid the bulkiness of dacron or down filled outfits. Its going to be hard enough getting into waders with just an added thin layer, unless you purchased them large to begin with and how many of us did that?

As the weather warms, but the streams remain cool, change to the fish-net type to keep the cold sides of waders away from your legs, chest and back. Waffle-knit of olefin, Norwegian string and silk make up the choices available for our sport. Silk by far is the most expensive but least bulky.

Outerwear
For cold water and cold weather fishing, I suggest all wool shipcord slacks or if wool is irritating to you, cordless corduroy should be fine. Cotton whipcord slacks are also available.

In summer, I use the cotton and dacron blend trousers with two 14-inch front cargo pockets, topped with 7 inch deep button-down flap pockets, which are great for storing additional leaders and flat items. Short pants for those that perspire are also available.

Shirts are various in weight, style and blends. I have found a 20 per cent wool and 80 per cent cotton blend that is feather light and warm to be fine for me. This style shirt is available from Orvis Company of Manchester, Vermont. The shirt is launderable and eliminates dry cleaning bills.

All wool shirts like the Pendleton provide virgin wool warmth without bulkiness and are made to last.

This fly fisherman is well and correctly equipped for shallow water fly casting on a warm day. He has on a canvas hat with a band for flies and a sleeveless vest with a variety of small and large pockets. His hip boots are suitable for the shallow river and he is netting a landlocked salmon with a wooden framed, floating landing net. Photo taken on the Crooked River in Maine.

Sock wear can be insulated, wool or cotton depending whether the waders are insulated or plain. Kaufman of Canada also make felt liners for extremely cold water situations.

Australian Merino wool sweaters are silicone treated, shed water like a duck's back and keep you warm and dry when the going's wet. Turtleneck shirts are also available in the same material.

Hats are selected by choice and mine is one that has a large brim to cut down glare, well ventilated, a good band to mount mosquito netting on and water-proof.

Waders
Perhaps we should state here that different type bottoms require special forms of soles on your waders, not only for balance and comfort, but safety. The cleated or lug sole is used in mud or sand bottoms, while the felt sole is used for wading the rocky streams of the west. Select waders that have a drawstring top, belt loops, reinforced seats, crotch and knees, sponge rubber insole, steel shank arch, inside chest pocket, and that are insulated. Use of a belt with chest waders is most important to prevent flooding through loss of footing.

Waders come in many styles and weights, most are chest-type, some are waist length for summer and low water streams, super lightweight for summer, some have boots built on and other are stocking feet waders that require the use of wading shoes in cleats or felt. The advantage here is that one set of waders can be used in two different stream situations by simply changing wading shoes. Far less expensive than 2 sets of waders. If you have the cleated type sole, wading sandals of felt are made to slip over the boot type. The new woven core felt soles have 3 times the life of the pressed sole.

Wader suspenders should have the metal crossover to keep them in place or the H back type. Invest in a good pair as nothing is more frustrating than to have the darn things fail in mid-stream. Rubberized fabric with elastic webbing and buttonholes reinforced should do nicely.

Wader belts of nylon with slip type clasps are generally the angler's pick.

Hip Boots
Essentially, we look for the same type construction as in waders. Other features include; Lightweight, adjustable belt strap, take-up strap at thigh, inside knee harness to keep from losing boot in mud, semi-hard toe to protect against stone bruises and cushioned insole for all day comfort in a stream.

Converse-Hodgman Co. of Malden, Massachusetts, makes a complete line of waders, hip boots, raingear and repair kits for the various type materials used. One for rubber cloth, another for plast-a-ply-horco-tex, and duck-drill surfaces.

Raingear
Look for vulcanized one piece type construction in deep-waist or 3/4 length for the best length for over waders. The jacket should be both lightweight and flexible for easy storage in your fishing vest, and should include a hood with drawstring and nylon zipper.

Fishing Vests
Aside from the rod and reel, the fly fisherman's vest is probably the most important single piece of equipment he has. It supplies him with the following necessities: Pin-on fleece patches for flies, 2 compartments for fly boxes, map pocket, lunch and raingear pocket, cigarette and sunglass pocket, leader wallets, rod holder, net holder strap, inside pockets for fly boxes, pockets for leader spools.

Vests come in 2 styles, regular and wader length with the vest shorter to ride high on the angler. Some of the pockets will be zippered, while others use the velcro type fastening for one hand opening. Over the years I like the velcro for ease of opening and convenience and it has lasted longer than most zippers.

The more expensive vests come with inflatable compartments and can be used with mouth inflation or CO-2 cartridge inflation. If one fails you have a back-up inflation method. This type vest is a must for non-swimmers who will be wading fast water with deep pools and old deep river beds. On fitting the size of the vest, make sure you wear enough clothes so it will not be too tight at streamside.

Orvis' arcti-creel is made to attach to their Tac-l-pac vests and the principal of the desert water bag is used. Soaking the bag's outer cloth shell, will keep the inside cool by evaporation for many hours. It's easy to clean the water-proof vinyl inside by rinsing in water. Many fishermen still prefer their trout on green ferns and in wicker type baskets and I must say I can not blame them.

Nets
Fly fishing nets will vary according to the size of fish we are seeking, but I use one that has a net loop of about 15 inches with wooden frame and a looped elastic cord which allows using the net without detaching it from the vest. After using it snaps back out of the way. Small collapsable nets that require one hand to use are also used but need a pocket that is handy for storage.

Staffs for Wading
Anyone who has fished fast water, deep pools and new waters will confirm that use of a fishing staff is vital for safe fishing. The staff can test bottoms, steady you in fast currents and keep you from taking a cold dunking while in a stream. One even doubles as a rod case and protects the rod while going thru heavy brush. The lanyard allows the floating staff to stay behind as you cast but is within reach if needed.

Accessories for the Vest
As the wading angler must carry everything with him, various hook-on

That's a German Brown trout going into the creel of a South Carolina fly fisherman. Many fly anglers like creels of the old school, made of wicker and reinforced with sewn leather bands and rivets. They have the advantage of being light and providing ventilation, but the disadvantage of bulkiness. To use properly, the bottom of the creel should be lined with wet grass, leaves or ferns. They keep trout in excellent condition until ready for the frying pan or freezer.

"goodies" are offered by manufacturers and they include: Orvis' anglers clipper with nippers, straight edge cutting blade, awl and hook disgorger, fastened to a steel chain that retrieves into a small container that pins to your vest . . . Surgical forceps for removing hooks also lock to serve as a streamside vise for emergency "hatch matches" . . . Fisherman's Micrometer for measuring lines, leaders, and tippets when the fish get particularly fussy . . . A flashlight that clips on your vest pocket or has an elastic band for head mounting . . . Lens light for tying on flies at dusk with magnifying swing-out lens for easy viewing. Cord around neck allows use of both hands . . . Stripping Basket will eliminate the problem of stepped-on lines in boat and line floating away when fishing fast moving water. It is collapsible for easy storage and tied around the waist . . . Fly boxes in shapes and sizes for the different type flies, bugs and streamers are made by many companies but I prefer Perrine or Wheatly boxes best. The Wheatly box comes with individual compartments that snap open and keep the rest of the flies covered. . .

Looking Back

Regarding clothing, good fits are essential to comfort and performance and I suggest trying on all types of gear when possible. If ordering from a catalog make sure you follow the directions given for taking measurements exactly.

Waders may feel perfectly comfortable while standing but happens when you try to sit down and their is not enough room in the seat of the waders? You are going to feel like the first cousin to a stuffed sausage. Make sure about roominess in the crotch and knee areas, and avoid over-sizing on the boots as they will cause blisters.

Its not a bad idea to have a

This flycasting enthusiast is wearing a fine pair of insulated waders in a cold Canadian river. The vest is well designed with many pockets. The large pocket on the front is for a fly box. Though somewhat difficult to see, he has an aluminum frame landing net attached to one side. His sunglasses are a must.

lightweight windbreaker tucked in your vest for those blustery days when the wind seems to go right thru you. I have never been able to wear gloves while fishing but they do make some that have the ends of the fingers cut out for easy manipulation of fly lines. Toss in a stick of chap cream for hands and lips. In snake country, the Cutter Labs make a handy little snake bit kit that you could lose in your pocket.

Some streams are going to be a problem with mosquitoes and

repellant and face-hand coverings will be neccessary. Best idea is my wife's for netting, she stitches an elastic band thru the netting making it 2 inches smaller than my hat size on the outside. I just pull it over the crown and its all set. Again, one of those little button return items that fasten to your vest with leader cleaning material inside is great for cleaning and getting your leader down where the fish are. Just dunk it in water and pass the leader thru and its done.

Fly Fishing Safety

Fly fishing is great fun but it can be dangerous. Take these precautions and keep safe and sound.

Looking back over the years, I can readily bring to mind certain situations that caused me some anxious moments while fly fishing.

While some were humorous, others were serious and could have been fatal. Perhaps to some of you that seems a little strong, but lets look at some random experiences and you be the judge.

All of us have wanted to fish lonely stretches of rivers and streams, dreaming of virgin waters and native trout or to get back into the bush where the whole stream is ours.

Maybe wading fast water is your bag or night fishing a new stream for lunker browns and bass. Sure, its

challenging and very rewarding but there are some pit-falls to observe and keeping a clear head is your best defense.

Lets look at some of the do's and don'ts involved in our sport.

THE FLY ANGLER AND HIS SAFETY NEEDS

Among the various pieces of gear used in fly fishing, we find a host of specialized equipment that have specific and important uses.

Waders are most important and selecting the kind to be used depends upon the water you will be fishing.

I prefer felt sole waders for the granite rock streams of the west as these rock formations will be ex-

tremely slippery. Cleated soles for the sandy, silty areas of the midwest for good gripping qualities. As the water warms, cotton pants and sneakers will do the job quite nicely.

Hip boots also have their place and shallow streams are perfect for their useage without the bulky weight of waders. Also, the hippers can be rolled up or down for added convenience while walking.

Hippers are more easily shed in case you step into a deep hole. Getting out of chest waders is almost impossible as the water presses them against you like a second skin.

When wading streams with deep pools and holes, make sure that you "tie off" above your waist with a snug fitting belt. If you should go in over your head the belt will keep air trapped in your waders and act as a large inner tube, keeping you afloat until you can get the bottom under your feet again. In deep center type rivers, get your feet pointed downstream and use your hands as rudders to steer your way into shore or tree deadfalls.

Slippery shore rocks, ones that have heavy coverings of moss and algae, have given more than one angler a sudden "sitz" bath and bruised rear end. **Wading Staffs** in areas that are new to us are a must. They can search out a bottom, provide balance in fast water, find soft areas (quicksand) and are fine brush deflectors in heavy cover.
Fishing Vests are mostly a matter of preference and many types are offered depending how fancy you want to get. Sufficient pockets for fly boxes, leader material, lunch, compass, waterproof matches, and extra line are your first consideration. Snap rings for net, staff and pole holder, one shoulder strap (added by wife) to hold creel more firmly, and I prefer a nail clipper pinned to the front for trimming knots and leaders.

Oh, yes, you must have that little piece of sheep wool for effect. I also clip two, cigarette size, rescue packs to the vest. All it takes is a squeeze and you have enough bouyancy to support 400 pounds. Select a brimed hat to cut down on glare from the sun.

READING THE WATER

Glass-clear water can be most difficult to read. What appears to be only a few feet deep, can be over your head, so in this type water make sure you enter the stream where the shore tapers down gradually and not at the overhanging bank. **Polaroid glasses** reduce surface glare allowing you to see into the water, can detect fish,

and ease eye strain from sunlight.

On entering the stream, observe the bottom, color can most times tell you the composition of bottoms. The light yellow-beige usually denotes hard sand, safe bottom but not always. Swirling yellow-beige can mean quicksand blow-holes that can suck an angler out of sight in seconds.

Advance one step at a time and keep most of the weight on the back foot until sure of the next step. Dark bottoms can be holes, sudden dropoffs, deep pools or just plain mud and silt. In high, dark or roily water, especially on streams new to the fly angler, slow and easy is the word.

Everything is by touch and using your eyes. Bends in the stream can form deep, natural pools and use of a staff is almost a must in these areas. Another danger spot can be where the stream narrows dramatically into a funnel-type opening. The unknowing fisherman can be swept thru the opening by the increase in current speed and is in real trouble before he realizes it.

Beneath the water rocks can set up the same situation without being visible to the eye, you could probably describe them as natural "wing-dams" such as found on the Mississippi River for creating artificial current.

When approaching sharp bends in rivers and streams watch out for cross currents which can catch an angler leaning in the wrong direction. The deeper the water the more difficult to retain balance against a slight current. As the water moves faster, maintaining balance is a real chore. Whenever you start to feel like you're "floating" along the bottom, you are too deep in the water and should start backing out to more shallow water.

Climbing rocks is the job of mountain climbers and the safe fisherman skirts them whenever possible. Besides tearing holes in the

waders, they can cause a fall, as most are quite slippery, which again makes you a big bobber going down the river.

A prime example, was one time when I was caught between rocks with my feet rapidly opening into a beautiful ballet split, grasping my prized rod tightly, I dipped below the surface but was able to get my feet under me at once, but there, moving along the surface 50 feet away was my hat with the best collection of dry flies I ever owned, disappearing around the bend.

Another pit-fall of the wading angler is very cold water, which can produce various aches and pains, not to mention a numbing effect that can cause the angler to fall. Early spring means wool socks, thermal "drawers" and tops, light wool pants and shirt and a good windbreaker back at the car for rest periods. I like to limit myself to 15 minutes for the first five morning sessions and 20 minutes each in the afternoon. I suggest fishermen with creaky joints wait until the water moderates as bursitis, "rhumy-tism" and old breaks can cause a lot of sleepless nights.

WHAT TO DO IF YOU'RE HURT

If other people are handy, the situation is not too bad, but what if you're alone? A sprained ankle, broken arm or leg, snake bite, and illness are not only serious, but under certain conditions could be fatal.

Under these conditions, a mile or two from the car might as well be a hundred unless you **KNOW WHAT TO DO!**

Broken bones should be immobilized and splinted as they are. If you feel faint, lower your head between your legs or lie down until the sensation passes. Keep clothing zippered or buttoned and maintain your normal body heat.

Avoid adding unnecessary amounts of heat. A broken arm can be inserted inside a half opened vest using it as a makeshift sling. Walk to the car, taking rests often and avoiding over-exertion, drive for help.

A broken leg presents a problem of movement and if possible try to collect enough wood to make a fire without causing more damage. Once the fire is going, throw green grass, weeds, or any wet material on it to produce a smoky fire. Wardens and watchtower guards are always looking for smoke and readily investigate the source.

If you are close to the car, try to get to it and drive for help. Even people with broken legs have accomplished this task, but everyone is not capable of doing it. Exposure can kill on just relatively cool nights unless you are protected by clothing or fire. Loss of body heat can result in severe shock and death follows soon after.

SNAKE BITE

Most snake bites can be avoided by watching where you put your feet and hands. If bitten by one of the four poisonous snakes found in our country, rattlesnake, moccasins (copperhead and cottonmouth) or coral snake, **where** you are bitten is important. With the exception of the coral snake, the others are pit-vipers and absorbtion of the poison takes between one to two hours unless you are bitten directly into the blood stream where the symptoms of general weakness, vomiting, nausea, weak, rapid pulse and dimness of vision occur quickly.

FIRST AID FOR SNAKE BITE

1. Stop all activity
2. Tie a constricting band above the bite to prevent the return of blood to the wound, but not tight enough to restrict the deep-lying vessels. There should be some oozing from the wound.
3. Sterilize a knife blade and make cross-cut incisions at each fang mark, 1/2 inch long.
4. Apply suction, using the mouth or suction cup, for an hour or more.
5. Obtain medical care.

6. First aid can be administered while enroute to a doctor or hospital.

Keep the injured part lowered and pack in cold cloths or ice bags if available.

PRECAUTIONS

Its a good idea to let someone know where you will be going and what time to expect you to return, especially in areas that are out-of-the-way and less populated.

Its a good practice to know how to control bleeding using the direct pressure and pressure point methods.

It is valuable to know proper use of artificial respiration techniques for drowning victims.

I suggest that all back country and sportsmen who will be going into wilderness areas purchase a copy of FIRST AID, the newest edition from the American Red Cross or local bookstore and read it thoroughly several times. Keep it in the glove compartment of your car.

CASUAL HAZARDS IN THE FIELD

How many times have you been smacked in the face by willowly branches let loose by your fishing partner who was walking just ahead of you? Most times its just a stinging slap but if it hits the eye you could be in serious trouble.

Allow him to get four to five yards ahead and that will correct the situation. Watch where you go, particularly in heavy cover along the stream bank. You could run into bee, wasp or hornets nests and be very painfully stung, and try to get away from these fast fliers in waders is a hopeless task. Back out slowly, taking a few stings, and then when you are far from the nest remain standing perfectly still until the insects calm down. Then leave the area. Apply cold water to the sting area and it should help to reduce the swelling and see a doctor.

Avoid leaning and sitting at the base of trees where vines are growing

as they could be poison oak, sumac or ivy and though they will not manifest themselves until later, this author can tell you the discomfort is enough to lay you low for many days. Preventative tablets are now available at local drug stores and should be taken a few days prior to entering the woods.

Learn to identify the leaves. Poison Oak and Ivy have clusters of three leaflets and are glossy. They can grow as vines, shrubs or a small plant. Poison Sumac has 6 to 9 leaves growing off one small branch and it can be a shrub or tree and grows in the eastern third of the U.S.

If exposed, wash the part with soap and water and rinse with alcohol. Follow this with calamine lotion and if not relieved, apply wet compresses using BUROW'S solution diluted 1 part to 25 parts of water, for 20 minute periods.

When introducing a novice to fly-type fishing he can be your biggest hazard and headache. You will have to watch out for him every minute and take care of yourself. A good point to illustrate is the two anglers in the boat, fly fishing a lake and one is a tyro. High casts with the fly/popper riding down low can cause some nasty hook wounds on the arms, head and back, as the cast is whipped forward. Correct this by teaching the advantage of short, accurate casts first.

Side arm casters cause 90% of the hook accidents in boats. Always look behind when casting and make sure the area of backcast is clear.

When wading, low hanging branches can cause eye damage if concentrating on walking and not watching where you are going. Eye injuries are serious and you must seek medical attention at once, do not take a chance especially if the eye tears for more than 10 minutes.

Cuts, scratches and abrasions should be thoroughly washed with soap and a disinfectant applied. Make sure you have had a booster shot for tetanus before going on your trip. These should be renewed every other year.

Certain streams offer the fly fisherman exceptional opportunities to take trout at night. If you think daylight fishing can be a hazard wait until you step into a stream at night in some remote area. Never fish at night by wading unless you have knowledge of the area to be fished.

Hang a large white, or fluorescent colored item from the branch of a convenient tree where you enter the stream. I like to wear a miner's-type, elastic, banded head-lamp that allows me use of both hands. It will automatically light the area that you are looking at. Make sure you carry spare batteries and bulbs. A good rule of thumb is to fish until the new batteries start to become weak and then go back. This will almost guarantee you returning to your entry point with sufficient light to see your marker. Carry a spare flashlight in your wader pocket just in case of failure of your other light. Keep your car parking lights on as a guide to finding your way back. Three or four hours of their use will not affect your battery.

FISHING FROM BOATS

We have mentioned some of the dangers involved on small lakes but what about canoes and fast water? An expert fly angler could be the world's worst canoeist and river reader. Streams that start out slow could rapidly and subtly turn into rock strewn stretches of white water washes.

Things to look for include: Faster moving feeder creeks and streams that will increase current, rocky shore formations that invariably mean underwater rocks in the stream, rips of water that conceal sand-bars and obstructions, smooth areas in rough water could mean rocks, a bar or a deep pool, faster moving water accompanied by a low

roar that gets louder means a fall . . . pull for shore at once!

Maps of most larger streams are available from outfitters and you should take the time to familiarize yourself with the various portages, waterfalls, rock areas and white water stretches before starting out.

If camping out in the northern section of our country, precautions will have to be taken at each campsite for bears. Loose food or food improperly packed could attract this unwelcome visitor to your area.

Fish that were cleaned and the entrails just dumped in the water is another attractor. Ice chests are not smell-proof unless the food is tightly wrapped in plastic bags and sealed. Coming back to a camp that has been visited by bears in your absence will look like a disaster area. If your camp is invaded at night by bears, use the "feet don't fail me now" antidote and jump in the water until they leave.

Holes in canoes can be fixed by using pitch from birch which is very sticky and water proof plus birch bark. This sounds crude, and it is, but it may just get you back to civilization. Heat birch logs until the pitch oozes out the end, smear around the hole and while its still hot, apply a thin covering of birch bark. Repeat smearing the pitch over the patch until it's 1/4 inch thick and allow to cool.

In spring and fall we have to be careful of sudden cold snaps and snow. Unprepared fishermen and hunters have been known to die of exposure just a short distance from their car when caught in the open. Carrying one of the mini-small space blankets, (about the size of a pack of cigarettes) can save your life.

Fishing our southern waters around the Florida Keys with fly rod, can be most exciting, but, if you're alone, make sure you know the signs of changing weather and carry a small radio and listen for radio

reports which are broadcast every 15 minutes. Observe weather warnings and do not go out when small craft flags are flying.

When bonefishing the flats and you leave the boat to wade, do not attach your catch to a stringer fastened to your body. Bleeding fish attract both sharks and barracuda and a white leg looks just as good to them. Put each fish into the boat.

LOST AND WHAT TO DO

It can happen to the best of us, and, in lesser degrees, does not constitute a real danger. Mostly just a much longer walk to find the road or car. Walking away from camp in a wilderness area or in one unfamiliar to us and then trying to take a shortcut back without bearings or a compass is foolhardy.

A compass is not expensive and I use one that retails for about $3.00 and keep it in my fishing vest pocket. They are not hard to use and learning takes about 15 minutes of reading and stepping-off in your backyard for practice. All of the better compasses come with complete directions and should be carried in the case.

Suppose you do not have a compass. Now what? Darkness is coming and the first thing to do is stop walking around in circles and set up a rough camp. Clear an area and start a fire for warmth, light, and as a signal. Cook those nice trout in the creel, and lay in a supply of firewood for all night. Next in line is a makeshift shelter to keep the dew off and provide some protection from the elements.

If you're in a pine forest, pick out a tree and make your bunk on those soft pine needles. The overhanging branches make a dandy shelter from both wind and rain. Come morning make sure you inspect yourself for ticks that might have nestled on you for a nice drink and sleep.

Make a lean-to out of nearby deadfalls and branches in front of the fire so reflected heat will keep you warm during the night.

Cook those fish by inserting a green stick through the mouth and jam it into the meaty section of the tail, after cleaning them. Three to four minutes over the fire on each side should do nicely.

If near a stream, water will not be a problem, but do not leave camp in search of it. One night without will not hurt you.

In the morning, get the fire going good and then add green leaves, damp brush and leaves to make a smoky fire and stay put. A large smudge fire will be investigated by wardens and rangers. If nothing happens by noon, you might have to find your way out.

Try to find your way back to the river and follow it to camp. Mid-afternoon should have you setting up camp again if you are still lost. Food and water will be of paramount importance and if you have ever fished well, now is the time to be the expert. Making camp along a stream or river will provide the water. Continue making signal fires the next morning. Every situation is different and getting out may take quite a while but you will make it if you do not panic. The previous chapter was not written to discourage fly fishermen from pursuit of virgin-type waters or areas but rather to prepare them for emergencies that might arise in these areas, where you are basically "on your own". The main thing to remember is keep your head and reason the situation out.

To the Reader

If you fished all the rivers and lakes of the United States for thirty or forty years, you would learn a lot about fishing, but far from all there is to know.

It is estimated that over 20 million people go fishing every year, yet the average fisherman knows less about fish than any other wild creature.

This is true because most fishermen are interested in catching fish, not in studying them.

With fly fishermen, it's different. They want to catch fish, but are also interested in their habits, the kinds of waters that are most suitable, the food they eat, when they bite best, best seasons for getting a particular species, and perhaps more than anything, they want to know the types of flies that bring the best results.

When a beginning fly fisherman who has acquired some ability with his new rod and line actually starts to fish a river with flies for the first time, he usually has some doubts as to whether he'll catch anything. He may fish for an hour using one fly pattern, change the pattern and cast another fifteen minutes, catch nothing and change flies again and get a nice trout on the first cast. Though the fly that caught the fish may be his favorite at the time, there's a good possibility that he may never in his life catch another fish on the same pattern.

The opposite could also be a possibility. That particular fly could be the best producer he'll ever use.

This has happened to me in two instances. For many years, while I was still just a bait caster, I used many different kinds of lures with varying degrees of success. Some were better than others, but none were really outstanding.

Like most fishermen, even though I had a tackle box crammed full of lures, I was always ready to try out something new or one that I had not previously used. Thus, one day when I was in a tackle shop in a small Wisconsin town I spotted a small, wooden mouse with a black string tail and bought it. It wasn't a new design, but I had never tried one before.

It turned out to be the best lure I have ever had. Not just for bass, for which it was intended, but also for northerns, walleye, rock bass and coho. It took the two biggest fish of their species that I have ever caught. One was a six pound smallmouth, the other, and this was the biggest surprise of all, a 35 pound muskie.

The best fly I have ever had is a streamer that I have not been able to identify. I've had it over a dozen years and remember that it came on a card with several others.

The hook lost the barb long ago, so I've had to tie replacements myself, since there are none to be found in tackle shops.

This fly took some of the best brookies I've ever caught. These were pulled from the rushing fast water rivers in Ontario, Canada. It is a fine producer of browns in turbulent, roiled spring waters and will take rainbows and cutthroats consistently.

The reason I can't identify it, is that I think it was a mistake or perhaps an unfinished fly. It has three long striped feathers tied on at the head, about eight strands of deer hair also tied at the head, a body wrapped with silver tinsel and nothing else. It has no tail which is unusual and this would seem to indicate it is unfinished.

There are many questions about flies and fly fishing that are puzzling and sometimes unanswerable, but many that are not. Fly fishing beginners usually have much to learn and can benefit greatly by asking questions about particular conditions they have experienced.

I would like to invite those, or even experienced flymen, to write me about any aspect of fly fishing that concerns them. In most cases I'll be able to give a direct answer, but if not, I have sources available to get the answers from.

Books on Fly Fishing

The Atlantic Salmon by Lee Wulff
Bonefishing by Stanley Babson
Simplified Fly Fishing by S. R. Slaymaker II
Trout by Ray Bergman
McClane's Fishing Encyclopedia by A. J. McClane
Flies by J. Edson Leonard
Selective Trout by D. Swisher-C. Richards
Guide to Trout Flies by H. J. Noll
Streamside Guide by Art Flick
The Fly and the Fish by John Atherton
This Wonderful World of Trout by C. K. Fox

FREE FLY OFFER - Just Send Coupon

This fly is being sent to you with the hope that it will produce good catches of fish. Also that, if you do get fish in your area, you will write and let me know what kind of fish you caught and where you got them.

Directory of Fly Fishing Tackle

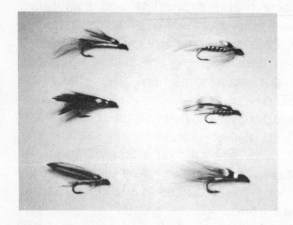

and Fly Tying Material

Manufacturers

Action Sporting Specialties
840 South Fifth Avenue
Wausau, Wisconsin 54401
(Waders, boots and jackets)

Berkley & Company, Inc.
Highways 9 & 71
Spirit Lake, Iowa 51360
(Rods, reels, leaders and
leader making materials)

Betts Tackle Ltd.
Highway 42 W.
Fuquay-Varina, N.C. 27526
(Flies and popping bugs)

Browning Arms Company
P.O. Box 500
Morgan, Utah 84050
(Fly rods and reels)

Cascade Tackle Company
847 West 14th Street
Medford, Oregon 97501
(Fly tying materials)

Challenger Mfg. Corp.
94-28 Merrick Blvd.
Jamaica, N. Y. 11433
(Rod cases and reel cases)

Cortland Line Company
67 E. Court Street
Cortland, N.Y. 13045
(Fly lines, reels, rods,
leaders, and fly tying
materials)

Daisy-Heddon
Division Victor Comptometer Corp.
P.O. Box 220
Rogers, Arkansas 72756
(Rods, reels and lines)

Daiwa Corporation
1526 West 166th Street
Gardena, California 90247
(Importers of quality Japanese
rods, reels, etc.)

Dan Bailey's Fly Shop
209 West Park Street
Livingston, Montana 59047
(Flies and fly tying materials)

DeWitt Plastics
26 Aurelius Avenue
Auburn, N.Y. 13021
(Plastic fly boxes and popping
bugs)

D. H. Thompson Company
335 Walnut Avenue
Elgin, Illinois 60120
(Fly tying vises and other tools)

Dura Pak Corporation
700 East 9th Street
South Sioux City, Nebr. 68776
(Rods, reels, hooks, poppers,
etc.)

Ed. Cumings, Inc.
2305 Branch Road
P.O. Box 6186
Flint, Michigan 48508
(Landing nets, aluminum rod
cases)

E. Hille
P.O. Box 269
Williamsport, Penna. 17701
(Fly tying materials and tools)

Feather River Trading Company
805 W. Tulare Avenue
Visalia, California 93277
(Fly tying materials)

Fenwick-Sevenstrand
14799 Chestnut Street
Westminster, California 92683
(Fly rods and lines)

Feurer Bros. Inc.
"FB" Reel Division
No. 77 Lafayette Avenue
North White Plains, N.Y. 10603
(Fly reels)

Fireside Angler
P.O. Box 823
Melville, N.Y. 11746
(Fly tying materials and tools)

Gapen Tackle Company
Highway 10
Big Lake, Minnesota 55309
(Flies and leaders)

Glen L. Evans, Inc.
P.O. Box 850
Caldwell, Idaho 83605
(Flies and popping bugs)

Gladding Corporation
P.O. Box 260
Syracuse, New York 13201
(Lines, rods and reels)

Gudebrod Bros. Silk Co.
12 S. 12th Street
Philadelphia, Penna. 19107
(Lines and fly tying threads)

Harrington & Richardson, Inc.
320 Park Avenue
Worcester, Mass. 01610
(Importers of Hardy Bros. rods,
reels, lines, flies and
accessories)

Herter's Inc.
R.R. 1
Waseca, Minnesota 56093
(Fly tying materials, tools,
rods, reels, lines, accessories)

Johnson Reels Company
1231 Rhine Street
Mankato, Minnesota 56001
(Fly reels)

Keel Fly Company
1969 S. Airport Road
Traverse City, Michigan 49684
(Unique, virtually snagless,
hooks and completed flies)

Martin Reel Company
30 East Main Street
P.O. Drawer 8
Mohawk, N.Y. 13407
(Rods, reels, lines, flies,
and fly boxes)

Mason Tackle Company
Otisville, Michigan 48463
(Custom fly leaders and hard
nylon for making leaders)

O. Mustad & Son (USA) Inc.
42 Washington Street
Auburn, New York 13021
(Extensive line of high quality
fly tying hooks)

Outdoor Associates, Inc.
1409 Santa Fe Avenue
Los Angeles, California 90021
(Fishing vests, shirts, jackets,
trousers, waders, boots, and
creels)

Perrine
Aladdin Laboratories, Inc.
620 So. 8th Street
Minneapolis, Minnesota 55404
(Automatic fly reels and fly
boxes)

Pflueger Sporting Goods Division
301 Ansin Blvd.
Hallandale, Florida 33009
(Reels, rods, hooks, lines)

Phillipson Rod Company
2705 High Street
Denver, Colorado 80205
(Fly rods and rod kits)

Reed Tackle
Box 390
Caldwell, N.J. 07006
(Fly tying materials and tools)

Scientific Anglers, Inc.
4100 James Savage
Midland, Michigan 48640
(Fly lines, rods and reels)

Shakespeare Company
241 E. Kalamazoo Avenue
Kalamazoo, Michigan 49001
(Rods, reels, lines)

Sunset Line and Twine Co.
Jefferson & Erwin Streets
Petaluma, California 94952
(Fly lines)

Syl-Mark Enterprises
8946 Winnetka Avenue
P.O. Box 806
Northridge (Los Angeles), Calif.
91324
(Fishing pliers and fly tying
scissors)

Tack L Tyers
939 Chicago Avenue
Evanston, Illinois 60202
(Fly tying kits and materials)

The Fly Fisherman's Bookcase
P.O. Box 282
Croton-on-Hudson, N.Y. 10520
(Books on fly fishing and fly tying)

The Fly Tyer's Supply Shop
P.O. Box 153
Downingtown, Penna. 19335
(Fly tying tools and materials)

The Garcia Corporation
329 Alfred Avenue
Teaneck, N.J. 07666
(Rods, reels, lines and flies)

The Orvis Company
2754 River Road
Manchester, Vt. 05254
(Impregnated bamboo fly rods,
glass rods, reels, lines,
flies, and full assortment
of accessories)

T. R. Seidel Company
7645 Vance Drive
Arvada, Colorado 80002
(Leader sink and fly float
chemicals)

The Worth Company
P.O. Box 88
Stevens Point, Wisconsin 54481
(Flies, leaders, fly tying kits)

True Temper Corporation
Cleveland, Ohio 44115
(Rods and reels)

Universal Vise Corporation
22 Main Street
Westfield, Mass. 01085
(Rotating fly tying vise, other
fly tying tools and materials)

Weber Tackle Company
1039 Ellis Street
Stevens Point, Wisconsin 54481
(Fresh and salt water flies)

Woodstream Corporation
P.O. Box 327
Lititz, Penna. 17543
(Rods, reels, cases)

Wright & McGill Company
8720 East Colfax
Denver, Colorado 80220
(Rods, reels, fly tying hooks)

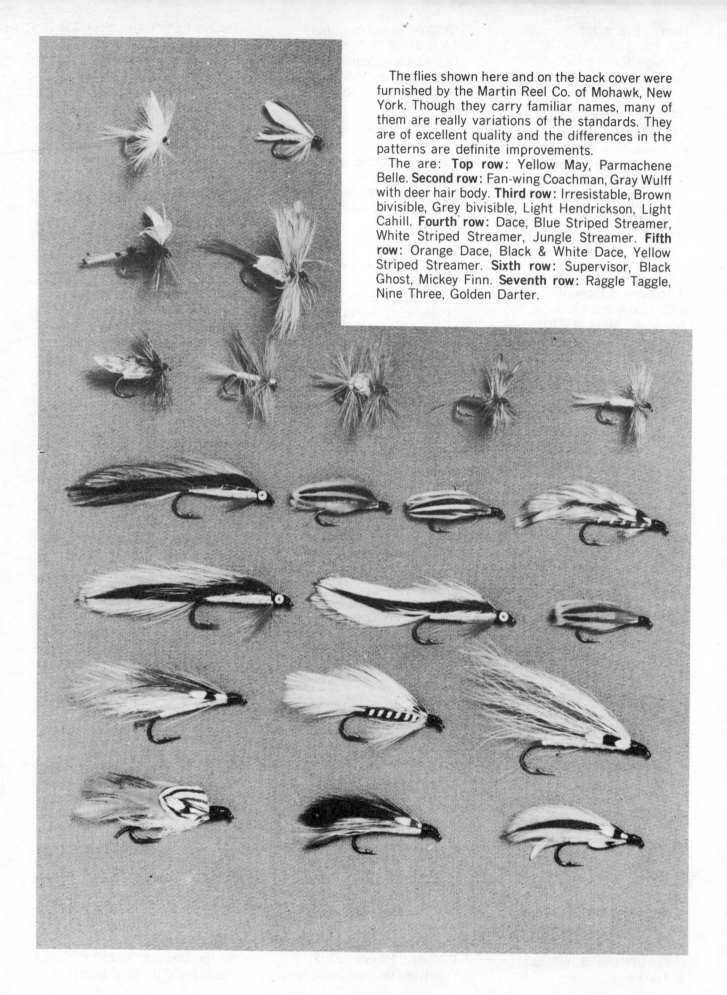

The flies shown here and on the back cover were furnished by the Martin Reel Co. of Mohawk, New York. Though they carry familiar names, many of them are really variations of the standards. They are of excellent quality and the differences in the patterns are definite improvements.

The are: **Top row:** Yellow May, Parmachene Belle. **Second row:** Fan-wing Coachman, Gray Wulff with deer hair body. **Third row:** Irresistable, Brown bivisible, Grey bivisible, Light Hendrickson, Light Cahill. **Fourth row:** Dace, Blue Striped Streamer, White Striped Streamer, Jungle Streamer. **Fifth row:** Orange Dace, Black & White Dace, Yellow Striped Streamer. **Sixth row:** Supervisor, Black Ghost, Mickey Finn. **Seventh row:** Raggle Taggle, Nine Three, Golden Darter.